James Stirling

Colin Rowe

James Stirling
Buildings and Projects

James Stirling Michael Wilford and Associates

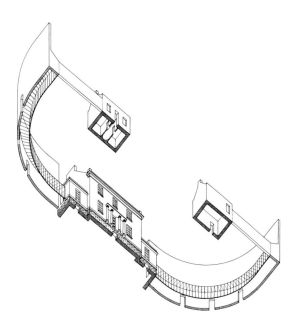

Introduction by
Colin Rowe

Compiled and Edited by
Peter Arnell and Ted Bickford

RIZZOLI
NEW YORK

In compiling this monograph my greatest thanks
go to Colin Rowe for his protracted effort in
recalling our mutual background, a frequently
painful task, I suspect. I also wish to reiterate the
credit due to Michael Wilford for his important
contribution to the projects and thank him for his
continuing support in the partnership. My
gratitude also goes to the Architects who have
worked through the years on the designs and
buildings and who are credited in the project
titles.
JS

The editors would like to extend a special thanks
to Mark Uhlig for his general help and goodwill;
and of course to JS for his unyielding faith and
cooperation.
P.A.   T.B.

Editors:
Peter Arnell
Ted Bickford

Production Coordinators:
Grant Rector
Barbara Weiss

Design:
Arnell/Bickford Associates
Peter Arnell
Ted Bickford
Giovanna Galfione

Published in the United States of America in 1984
by Rizzoli International Publications, Inc.,
712 Fifth Avenue, New York, New York 10019

ISBN: 0–8478–0448–8 Clothbound
ISBN: 0–8478–0449–6 Paperback

Printed and bound by Mandarin Offset , Hong Kong
Set in Simoncini Garamond by Circle Graphics,
Washington, D.C.

Reprinted 1987

Contents

Buildings and Projects

James Stirling: A Highly Personal and Very Disjointed Memoir.
Colin Rowe

Pier Head buildings, Liverpool.

I.

Liverpool, like Glasgow, is one of those unlikely cities of the United Kingdom from which something, sometimes, emerges. It might be a William Ewart Gladstone or it might be an Adam Smith; and, if we descend from this level of publicity to the far more mundane plane of architecture, it might be, from Glasgow, a Charles Rennie Mackintosh or, from Liverpool, a James Stirling.

Liverpool is, or used to be, grim but grand. It was dour, squalid, improbably Piranesian and, characteristically, it was equipped with an apparently endless series of smokily stratified sunsets (light filtered through alternating layers of humidity and dirt) which served, occasionally, to contribute to a highly poignant magnificence. Also it was never a completely provincial nor a merely pragmatic city and, from the late eighteenth century origins of its prosperity, it had typically indulged itself in fantasies which were likely to involve an unmistakably local (and Enlightenment) combination of elegance, information and megalomania.

The acknowledged doyen of Liverpool culture, William Roscoe (1753–1831), illustrates much of the later story. He is self made, an opponent of the slave trade, a Member of Parliament; but, while in the course of his career he becomes a successful banker, he also finds time during the 1790's to become a precociously significant collector of Italian Primitives as well as the author of two internationally acclaimed biographies—those of Lorenzo de Medici and Leo X, of which the first engaged the enthusiasm of the elderly Horace Walpole.

But, if Roscoe (very much the type of Thomas Jefferson?) was an extreme case, he was also almost the distillation of a Liverpool *genius loci*. For, in its grand days—now long vanished—Liverpool was not concerned with anything but the most stylish and with, up to a point, the best. Back in the 1740's it could be no less a person than John Wood of Bath who could be called in to build its town hall; in the 1790's this town hall could only be extended, decorated and furnished by James Wyatt; and, as the city (more abrasive than Bristol, more showy than Glasgow) became increasingly susceptible to the promptings of Neo-Classical largeness, so it was almost inevitable that it should sponsor that often highly regarded conflation of the Madeleine and the Altes Museum, St. George's Hall, which, in its determined parade of know-how and aggressive independence of London models, until recently might still have been the city's most adequate and revealing symbol.

Certainly nineteenth and early twentieth century Liverpool was a triangulation deriving from three important and sophisticated buildings: the town hall, St. George's Hall and the Customs House which, with its somewhat depressive Roman dome, after being bombed and gutted in World War II, was then foolishly and expensively demolished. But, for a full appraisal of this scene, within and around this triangle one then had to supply a texture which could obviously be the substantial drama of the docks—buildings of a brash self-confidence only to be rivalled in Chicago's Loop—or which, alternatively, could comprise an anthology of altogether random and intimate finds—items which might be the set pieces of a somewhat extreme academicism (fastidious beyond need) or which might, just as well, be the differently gratifying evidence of a highly experimental openmindedness.

It was in the Liverpool Cotton Exchange—or so it is usually asserted—that, at least before 1861, the price of Southern cotton was fixed. Apparently for a considerable time Liverpool mediated between Southern agricultural development and Lancashire manufacturing aspiration; and it should, therefore, not be surprising that the complexion of the city, at one time so conscious of its rapports with Savannah and Mobile and always conscious of its relationship to New York, should have become increasingly American.

Memories of nineteenth century Liverpool may often be casually evoked, for instance, in Boston or even as far away as Galveston; but 'American' Liverpool is rather more of an early twentieth than it is a nineteenth century phenomenon. It is evidenced by eclectic office buildings of an abruptness and a grandeur which, in English context, is slightly foreign and, also, by a mildly lunatic concern with the propagation of monuments which, thinking about the United States, might sometimes suggest a less affluent version of Pittsburg—a Pittsburg minus Mellon. But two twentieth century cathedrals! An unbelievably elaborate Anglican episcopal gesture, with an even less credible, bigger, aborted, Catholic and archiepiscopal reply, these performances—both made without reserve—are still merely the registers of an old and absolutely local propensity; and it is into this situation, a situation equipped with the usual bourgeois arcadias and with endless miles of deprivation, that we have now to interject both James Stirling and the Liverpool University School of Architecture.

To deal first with the School of Architecture: one cannot, of course, be concerned with whatever the present condition and direction of this institution might be. Instead, the object must be a discovery of what might have been its public and private postures *circa* 1950. In other words, in the excavation of a pedagogical Pompeii, one must now attempt to distinguish the roles, on the one side, of the academic establishment and, on the other, of the largely student opposition.

The Liverpool academic establishment it might be asserted with some degree of confidence had come into existence *circa* 1910; and one might then suggest that whatever further ideas it had coopted had never seriously disturbed (or even been conceived as likely to disturb) the equanimity of its premises.

It was, at its inception, the product of Professor (later Sir Charles) Reilly, 1874–1948, an engaging and quasi-Irish impresario who seems to have believed that the message had been delivered by McKim, Mead and White and whose Americanism is conceivably of importance.

Reilly was both a pro-American and a *simplificateur*. The McKim message, implicating a Beaux Arts exaltation of the plan, must be an important message but, in a 'progressive' context, it could not possibly be looked upon as ultimate or final; and, therefore, the dictates of Paris received via New York must have been conceived by him as always susceptible to accomodation. A quotation from Lutyens, a concession to Ragnar Östberg, a few excerpts from Dudok, later a casually distant tribute to Erich Mendelsohn—then, if such is the wave of the future, then, so long as the result is conformable to the rules (the 'rules' being irrefutably known), then, just who are *we* to obstruct a rational evolution? Possibly this may be an injustice to Reilly; but it certainly describes the regime of his successor: Liberal and tolerant; but tolerant, perhaps, only of such things as *we* can tolerate.

And so, and maybe obsessively, one builds up a picture which should be reasonably familiar to anyone who is sufficiently old or equipped with sufficient imagination. It is a picture of the gradualistic scene, often still available for inspection on either side of the Atlantic. We (the establishment) proceed incrementally. We have little use for millennialistic fervour. We are concerned with tradition; but, of course, we are also concerned with innovation. We are without prejudice. We are without bias. We are equipped (did you not know it?) with the capacity to make value free and objective judgement. In these, and other ways, we are the heirs of all the ages; and then, as the expositors of 'composition', we are also those who define a situation against which protest will for ever hammer in vain.

Now *can* such a situation ever be a profitable one? Or, to phrase the question differently, might not a somewhat inane, stable and 'liberal' bureaucracy, sometimes, be part of the manure of useful endeavour? There should, one supposes, be no doubt that the history of the academic institution is, more often than not, something totally distinct from the history of the incidence of talent. Which is to notice that the incidence of talent within any specific institution may, occasionally, be related to the availability of independent protest. In which cases the institution must be plausible but not, overwhelmingly, so. Its leading presumptions must be neither excessively stupid nor entirely arcane. They must be sufficiently respectable to furnish the attack of disgusted student intelligence; but, in order to sponsor the articulation of the *enragés*, while stupid, these presumptions and their proponents should never—like a sponge—be totally pervious to attack or totally willing to accept meaningless capitulation.

The type of establishment which one attempts to describe, serenely innocent as to its motivations, may often be a good enemy and therefore, in the end, a stimulating friend; and, if official Liverpool thirty years ago was certainly insipid and uninformed, then what to say about those no less vacuous academic bureaucracies of today—those bureaucracies which have established themselves in terms of systems analysis and which, for their ongoing justification, are about to substitute a semiotic argument? For certainly, the late Beaux-Arts academy, ramshackle, vulgarly impressionist and deplorable in the Liverpool style, because of its patently vulnerable 'truths', its pretentious addiction to 'culture', its visible inadequacy, surely offered a more useful and accessible incitement to protest than anything which is currently available. Indeed today the target is blurred. The Bastille awaiting capture is not evident. For, where everything is 'protest' veneered with 'science', 'concession' veneered with 'participation', 'irony' with a sugar coating of 'populism', the so necessary enraged imagination (the stoic consciousness, the protestant conscience?) can only operate with the most profound—or absurd—difficulty. Imagination may wish to make itself belligerent and 'clean'; but, then, just how can it do so?

However, these remarks only serve to introduce a plaintive parenthesis. Because, in retrospect, however much one may wish to value or to devalue the Liverpool situation of the late 'Forties and early 'Fifties, in England, at that date, perhaps only by the standards of the Architectural Association could Liverpool be considered as having been significantly retarded; and the tradition of the A.A. was always an entirely different one. Always it was more 'English' and William Morrisy, more addicted to small scale and local detail, more tolerant of idiosyncrasy, more distrustful of formal generalisations—whether American *or* French—like London more affiliated to Wren and the seventeenth century than, like Liverpool, to Neo-Classicism and the nineteenth. Which is to say that the tradition of the A.A. was always genial rather than rigorous and which might be enough to intimate that when, *circa* 1938–39, a modern social consciousness began to consume the A.A. (surely the Ruskinian version was always latent), it was enabled to consume it big. For, unlike Liverpool, the A.A. had the minimum of Beaux Arts cultural hangups, and thus, while by the late 1940's, the academic establishment of the A.A. (it would have repudiated any such title) could, just possibly, be considered as illuminated by the important intuitions of the modern movement, was able—perhaps—to conceive of itself as the cutting edge of the future, at Liverpool, where the faculty enjoyed neither such information nor such ambition, simply in default of this input members of the student body (abetted by the occasional deviant critic also rendered slightly scatty by the prevailing imprecision) themselves felt obliged to assume what they certainly thought was a subversive and a revolutionary role.

By the standards of the day these persons were not grossly

misinformed. Among students, the first three volumes of the *Oeuvre Complète* (*not* admitted into the school's library) were an object of connoisseurship; Mies was known through Philip Johnson's publication of 1947 (surely still the best and the least sententious); and Wright was a personage productive of what was often supposed to be aberrant enthusiasm. But then there were also Farkas Molnar and Giuseppe Terragni (known through Mario Labo's little book); there was an awareness of Sartoris, *Gli Elementi dell' Architettura Funzionale*; and, sometimes, an enthusiasm for the works of Connell, Ward and Lucas—greatly admired but not in any way understood as related to Russian Constructivism. However, these same student and deviant faculty circles were equally likely to be excited by the churches of Nicholas Hawksmoor, by a Vanbrughian variety of English and Irish eighteenth century productions, by Soane, by Palladio and by Hardwick Hall. (I)

All of which amounts to no inconsiderable little eclectic collection (Marcel Breuer was admitted, as also Charles Eames, but Walter Gropius was *not* admired); but all of which might permit the observation that, in this little power house, there was an absolute lack of either abstract or concrete political *savoir faire*. These were persons who, enthusiastically, reacted to, talked about and proposed visibles and who, correspondingly, had few ideas—very specific—about realisation. For them, no doubt, modern architecture was to change the world; but then (and this also seems very American), the world transformed was to remain much as the world and particularly England, had always been.

There was, one seems to remember, a cult of Auden at Liverpool. It was the Auden of *Look Stranger* and *New Years Letter* (*Here on the cropped grass I stand, A fathom of life alive in air—The limestone moors which stretch from Brough to Hexham on the Roman wall*). It was a cult of the English rather than the American Auden; and it may have produced a further cult of English topography: a taste for geology, climbing, Shropshire, the Long Mynd, Clitheroe, abandoned mills, derelict mine workings, etc. But, if this was a taste promoted by an overlap of experience, that of Auden and the typical Liverpool student (*As children in Chester look to Moel Fammau—Leaving the furnaces gasping in the impossible air, The flotsam at which Dumbarton gapes and hungers*); and if, perhaps, in this area there was some faint equation to be made of modern architecture with social concern, then it should also be added that, for the most part, the more radical equation with Socialism did not occur. Instead, it should simply be noticed that if, on the one side, there was Auden, on the other there was a profusion of beautiful cult objects of which the two prime might have been Terragni's Casa Giuliano Frigerio at Como and, in Liverpool itself, C.R. Cockerell's building for the Liverpool, London and Globe Insurance Company of 1855.

The Liverpool and London and Globe offices, Liverpool. Professor C.R. Cockerell, R.A., and Frederick Pepys Cockerell, Architects.

Terragni and Cockerell: De Stijl received through the distorting lens of an ingenuous Fascist sensibility and then the work of a Francophile Englishman, acquainted with Ingres and the friend of Hittorff. It would seem that both of these were regarded for reasons of impeccably constructed result; and, if Terragni was available in terms of modern architecture, then the extraordinary Cockerell, playing hyper-Greek, Sanmichele and François Mansart all at once, was always accessible as some kind of local deity.

But the attempted picture is still not complete and, alongside ingredients already listed, there should still be placed two further contributions: officially, the presence of Warsaw and, unofficially, the presence of Thomas Stevens.

The Polish School of Architecture (General Sikorski as the introducer) had come to Liverpool in 1942–43 and its appearance, which deserves to be recorded had constituted an immediate critique of received procedure. There was metropolitan Warsaw and provincial Vilna (two distinct styles); but, for present purposes, this discrimination is redundant. For one speaks primarily of a Polish capacity to condense; while, given this capacity, one must then observe the English passion for elaboration, the English tendency to leave no details alone but, almost, always to articulate, to proliferate and to multiply.

Bernard Berenson somewhere speaks of the English tendency to ooze prettiness (it may, occasionally, be a virtue); but, in Liverpool and at this moment, the endless English drive to particularise, to qualify, and to make cozy, was thrown into relief, was isolated as not quite normative, by the apparent aptitude of the Poles, by an exotic and showy Warsaw, half Corbu inspired and half, reluctantly, Beaux-Arts (Boriseivitch, Czerniowska, Pilsudska, Podwopinski, *et al.*). And, if the Poles may have been rather too prone to a cartoon baroque solution, then their over extended capacity to generalise, their flamboyance, their absolutely different style of attack, still requires to be noticed. The teachers in the Polish School of Architecture (it left Liverpool in 1947) were, if not more enlightened, indisputably more stylish than anything which Liverpool then had to offer; and, if inadvertently, they constituted an establishment, then, by doing so, they unknowingly abetted those Liverpool students who were disaffected. Before the arrival of the Poles Liverpool was addicted to graded washes; but, by the time of their departure, a Letarouillan hard line style had at least come to be tolerated.

However, official, and brilliant, Poland must now be brought into contact with a much more illicit Thomas Stevens; and Stevens is surely here important enough to require a modest excursus. A Germanizer (apple trees, pine trees and the fragrance of the Odenwald); a devotee of Aldous Huxley (the proto-hippy community of non-attachment in California); and, at the same time, an addict of Cistercian architecture (*Existenz minimum*) which was always equatable with Soane (Tyringham) and Mies Van de Rohe (Tugendhat Haus): these—along with heat pumps and plumbing—were the propensities which leap to mind. But Cistercian architecture, related to Soane and Mies (!), was then always no more than an annex to a particular style of religiosity; and Thomas a Kempis, Heinrich Suso, Meister Eckhardt and Zen Buddhism were all contributions to this style which, involving the presence of absence, the cloud of the unknowing, and all of the mystical—and never to be despised—rest, surely produced *something*. Was this untheological something merely Quakerish? Or was it Liverpool's own version of Theosophy and, therefore, along with Blavatsky, Steiner, Itten, Kandinsky, Van Doesburg, Mondrian, Emily Lutyens and all the others of *that* descent, an ultimately valuable lubricant? This is a question not easy to answer. For, with Stevens (apostolic poverty and reflections in the onyx), there always existed Berthold Lubetkin and even a quadripartite house (to be built by Tecton) in Bradfield, Berkshire, where members of the Budapest String Quartet, in impossible rivalry with Glyndebourne, would for ever play the most difficult late Beethoven.

Which is almost to complete a memorial of the Liverpool known to Jim Stirling, to myself and to others whom I highly regard. For *them*, I hope and believe that it will be a recognizable profile, compounded of a love and a hate which I think that they share. Then, to others not on the same track, I have no doubt that it will appear extremely bizarre and not a little mad. However to forget those many 'others' and to concentrate on a personal knowledge of Liverpool in 1950.

In 1950, the term 'brutalism' had not yet surfaced; but apparently the idea of 'brutality' was already around. So one records a conversation between a 'benign' authority and a student charmboat, both of whom will be nameless. The Professor (like the Sun King): *So S . . . what do the initials R.U. mean*; and the stammering Irish reply: *Sir, they mean Residential Unit, sir.* And, then, the further response: *But S . . . I think that there is nothing better than some good, explanatory Roman lettering*; followed by the final defence: *But, sir, I wanted to give a note of b-br-brutality to the board, sir.*

The occasion was evidently a review; and these remarks which I remember were received in London with the derision and amusement which they so obviously should *not* inspire may be allowed to conclude whatever I am able to say about a Liverpool which, in any case, has long since ceased to exist.

II.
With which local criteria established we may now begin to elaborate an approach to Stirling—in the end a highly private and distinctly inscrutable person.

But, at this stage, I find myself obliged to surrender the alibi of critical distance and to confront the need for a change of style. That is: in what has preceeded, assisted by the no doubt spurious perspectives of space and time, I have tried to write as though, personally, I were in no way involved; but now, as I specifically contemplate Stirling, I find myself sinking from the plateau of more or less certainty, however remote, to the swamp of more or less conjecture, however close.

There is a quasi-official Stirling exegesis which was approximately the architect's explanation of himself. We begin with a thesis (not quite routine); we go on to a Honan Competition (externalised structure); we continue with items from Poole (erratic fenestration) and the University of Sheffield (an exceptional urbanistic statement of which the implications are still not yet resumed); and we arrive, 1955–58, at Ham Common, the first significant realization and the initial source of notoriety. Meanwhile we qualify this chronological review with the notice of an emerging typology of buildings which later may become interbred. And then, after Ham Common (Maisons Jaoul with High Gothic Revival overtones), we direct attention to housing at Preston (allegedly rugged and proletarian but, ostensibly, very Dutch), to Churchill College, Cambridge (a type of Escorial with a *parti* which continues to await exploitation), to Selwyn College, Cambridge (a possibly gratuitous Expressionist counter statement); and so, finally, we arrive at the Leicester University Engineering Laboratories of 1959–63 (which, like Honan, can only relate to the Dorman Long project waiting around the corner).

It is by now a well travelled route, entirely familiar; and because the views from this road have become a little dull, in the interests of a change of scenery, it is here proposed to leap frog any immediate analysis of so called early struggles and to place ourselves, without further ado, in front of the Leicester laboratories where the mature Stirling is presumably announced.

On the surface, in-group Liverpool of 1950 had been Corbusoid, Italianate and a little bit late Miesian; but Leicester breaches all of these conventions and cannot, either, easily be written off as a composite of Aalto (in general), Frank Lloyd Wright at Racine, Wisconsin, and the inevitable Melnikov—though influences from all these sources may well have contributed. But Leicester is not quite so easy to decipher. Its derivations are surely not so entirely evident. It is not so glib. It is not the obvious art historical field day which, initially, it may appear.

Certainly it is not quite coordinated—neither plastically or in terms of its supporting fictions. The line of cleavage between the high and the low could be a little too extreme; there are the usual problems of a simulated podium; to any people except the English and the Dutch it would appear a miniature; its Piranesian vibrations are a little demure; its overt toughness a little benign. But, if these may be the defects of its qualities, they may also permit elaboration. For Leicester, after all, belongs to the category of major statements; and, if the building is evidently a breach of institutional decorum; if it is surely improper that the image of an engineering school should preempt the image of a university, then, with so much said, one may still be glad for the breach which was made and one may be abundantly glad for the incomparable manipulation of glass, brick, tile and light.

The advertized images of Leicester are, for the most part, external and technocratic (energetic profile, marine and industrial reference, general protuberance, the crinkle-crankle of patent glazing) and the published observations are further apt to allude to its technicity; but, if these are a substantial part of the reality of the building and have all been heavily interpreted, then it is particularly to light—transforming and validating glass, brick, tile, to light not quite cruel and certainly not gentle—that this observer most wishes to draw attention.

One may think of that ambiguous light—daylight filtered,

neither natural nor artificial, slightly submarine—in the Johnson Wax Building at Racine; but this is not exactly the quality of light which should here be evoked. Instead, a predominant impression of a low glaze terracotta surface—walls, floors and, apparently (though this may be a false impression), ceilings; and then it is, perhaps, the persuasive and uniform tonality induced by light sensations which allows the architect to proceed to the most impeccable and outrageous of interjections. The orchestration of light is magisterial; it is surely far more complete than the integration of form; and, certainly, the pervasiveness of light impressions completely overwhelms the more obvious notices of source and derivation. In other words, hallucination is almost complete; a mood is established; light sets the stage and goes a long way to convince the observer as to any necessity in the action.

But, if the rhetoric is exemplary; if disbelief is almost suspended; if one is almost drowned by the forces of impact; then, as scepticism regains inevitable control, interrogation begins. So *what* is the role of hallucination and is it a characteristic of all superior architectural performance? And what is the status of a *trompe l'oeil* conducted through the agency of light? And how does this differ from the more opaque Corbusian manipulations? And then, a further couple of questions: is *this* a version of Soane's distinctly psychological *lumière mysterieuse*, some extremely augmented commentary upon that Neo-Classical light which is always provocative and often sepulchral? Or are we simply inside some highly idealized Dutch latrine of the period of Berlage—in the presence of the Stock Exchange at Amsterdam—treated simultaneously suave and rough?

These are all questions which might surface; but by what the light permits—a deprivation of gravitational sense, a suspicion that angular and damaging protuberances might lurk around, a feeling that the next director of the institution could well be hanged from a cat head in the course of a forthcoming student riot, a moderately equipped observer may, very well, feel himself transported to the world of Giulio Romano, to a modern Mantua where a multiplicity of images, many of them far from kind, may still act as the indices to notions of history, society and, ultimately, tragedy.

Now judgement as to whether all this is appropriate, as to why an engineering school should engender so great a train of emotions, must be (temporarily?) suspended. For the problems presented by Leicester relate not only to the internal constitution of modern architecture but, even more specifically, to the internal constitution of modern architecture in England; and such general discussion, however necessary, could only destroy the present thread of reminescence. Therefore not to destroy this thread and, rather than any appeal to logic, to seek further assistance from autobiography: My own observations of Leicester are partly self derived, but they also relate to a first, and distinctly Dada, visit in 1964.

One had wished to await the time when the building became uncontroversial history; but the possibility of any such protracted repose had been inhibited by the architect's, supremely, proprietary interest. Accordingly, both he and I were driven up to Leicester in the back seat of some inexplicably English mini-vehicle, arrested and trapped, more or less like Michelangelo slaves and only awaiting the opportunity to lose the *contrapposto* and uncoil. And so, in the building's presence, the uncoiling began. And, since the driver was Thomas Stevens, then it could only be expected that slightly Dada and, sometimes, acute observation would immediately proliferate: But how, *how* little!; But futurism and *Wuthering Heights!* But *you* and Giulio Romano! But it *is* a sado-masochist building! But—like King's College Chapel—its stop, stop, stop, but *do* go on! And out of all this slightly derisive accumulation of jabs—the womb and the winter garden, the cave and the conservatory—there is one, the Castle of Udolpho and the Decimus Burton greenhouse which, as a critical theme, has remained with me on the two subsequent visits which I have made.

However, whatever the respective merits of Gothic monstrosity and the Palm Stove at Kew might be, by all not hopelessly biassed standards, Leicester is an authentic and a beautiful object—beautiful and painful. Indisputably there is a sado-masochist content; one is put through the wringer; like Vasari confronted with the Medici Chapel, one simultaneously admires and registers shock. And, hence, the building is still a politico-cultural challenge. Apparently accurate and astute, while publicly it violates neither the programmes of the welfare state nor the presuppositions of modern architecture, it then, privately, proceeds to escalate all such prescriptions. Apart from a complex play upon the nerves, there is a wide ranging and delicate connoisseurship; and, though the episodes may often seem dangerous, they are never less than ingenious and captivating. Along with a certain obvious hardness, there is a large suggestive softness (Is this building a teddy bear pretending to be a really *big, bad* bear?). For this is a highly introspective and very personal adventurousness. The advertized architect is a Cunard officer of around 1910. He is up there on the bridge, efficient, matter of fact, banal; but the private personality (even though the role of Prince of Denmark might seem unlikely) is, conceivably a species of architectural Hamlet, a vacillating sensibility—tough, refined, informed, abstruse, extravagant.

In any case, such is a possible interpretation which a more recent visit to Olivetti's building at Haslemere—an elegant garden folly or (particularly if carried out in the lime green and violet stripes which were originally intended), a grouping of exotic tents—has only served to reinforce. At Haslemere, as at Leicester, there is an oscillation of ideas—technical,

structural, spatial—as of a barometer telling the weather; and, in both cases, the make of the barometer is aboriginally English *and* nineteenth century. For, De Stijl, Constructivism and 'all that foreign stuff' apart, at Leicester most intimately this architect wished to be someone like a Butterfield (perhaps at Keble), or something like a Woodward (perhaps at the Oxford Museum), and all this with more than a touch of the long vanished Paxton conservatory at Chatsworth. In other words, at the period of Leicester, the Stirling barometer seemed to be a fabrication of, give or take a few years, around 1860; and one may almost imagine it hanging in the entrance hall of some magnificently quirky High Victorian house in north Oxford. Equipped with lots of subdued *terribilità*, while 'pioneering' it is also spiky; and, if the crockets and finials are not overtly on show, then their presence, behind the scenes, is never too far to seek.

However, by the time of Haslemere, the remorseless winds of change have blown; and the barometer now begins to recognize not only the incipience of quite a different climate of ideas but, itself, to be of very different manufacture and chronological *provenance*. So much so, indeed, that with the usual parade of semi-High Tech excluded from observation, the Haslemere barometer is, almost, a product of about 1830, perhaps very tacitly allied to some such extraordinary item as the Brighton Pavilion. For it is scintillating, amusing, astonishingly happy; and, though nothing remotely like it is to be found in the pages of Loudon's *Encyclopaedia of Cottage, Farm and Villa Architecture*, possibly it is, still, ultimately relatable to some arcane category of late Regency pictorialism—'discovered' by the architect but not, as yet, known to the historian.

Nor should such remarks—which, no doubt, will dismay those ever so many who conceive that important architecture can be no more than a matter of fact affair—any longer constitute too private a reading. For it is just about 1967 that Stirling inaugurated his second career as an irrepressible collector of early nineteenth century artifacts and furniture; and it was just about this time that his own house began to assume the dimensions of a battlefield, with the Corbu, the Aalto, the Breuer pieces increasingly driven to the wall and, center stage, an ever proliferating exhibition (it has never been less) of quite other tastes and enthusiasms.

So exactly *when* did Stirling buy his first piece by Thomas Hope, that chair, so satisfying, so grand, so *heavy*, which quickly became so celebrated by the Leon Krier perspective for the Olivetti interior at Milton Keynes? Was it in '69? Or was it in '70? And was it simply an accident of the auction room? In any case, though the taste preexisted the purchase, this was surely a watershed; and, perhaps, the observation and the recording of this beautiful chair has been a continuing directive not only for Stirling but, also and quite differently, for Krier. Because, though something sometimes may begin as a private joke—in this case with the implication that, like Ozenfant and Jeanneret fifty years earlier, Thomas Hope, himself, was the proponent of important *objects types* (Isn't it fun to substitute Thomas Hope for Le C.?)—the private joke may then, occasionally, supersede its origins, may—acquiring substance and seriousness—become an active sponsor of such widely diverse programmes as those of Stirling and Krier at the present day.

However not to dilate upon so potentially embarrassing a topic and simply to argue what, to me, is apparent: that, for rather more than ten years, Stirling's activities as a collector have exercised quite a bit of influence upon his behavior as an architect. Also not a restrictive influence. For the grandest English furniture of 1800–1830 is loaded with the inferences of an exotically complicated world. It is the reverse of anything uptight; and, comparably, whatever Stirling's Neo-Classical propensities may be, they remain the opposites of anything hermetic.

Which could, yet again, lead to an emphasis upon Thomas Hope (the original violet at Haslemere is particularly T.H.); and this time to the Hadrianic order and assumed disarray of his country house, the Deepdene. For, thanks to David Watkin (2), the world is now aware of what was there attempted and realized. And, as we contemplate William Atkinson's contemporary illustrations of the conservatories, the 'amphitheatres', "the glades and the galleries" (3), the controlled glitter and permeability to landscape of this now pathetically mutilated and abandoned villa, then, with the foyer of the almost adjacent Olivetti, Haslemere in mind, we might begin to recognise how, with Stirling, a feeling for a particular furniture style might, by elective affinity, become a sympathy for a general, and casual, Regency coalition of strategies which, in the ignorance or the prejudice of the Fifties (surely the most hopelessly benighted of all twentieth century decades), could only be implicitly known to him.

III.
However, with these remarks, anticipation has proceeded too far; and, if one now may be very well aware of a magpie architect-*bricoleur*, obsessed with the monumentally small, the reflective, the lacquered and the shiny, with French polish and Georges Jacob, with Paris porcelain, Louis Comfort Tiffany, René Lalique, Waterford and Baccarat, with Romantically picturesque Neo-Classicism, Puginian Gothic *and* Art Nouveau, this information should, probably, still be subservient to a further examination of the Stirling of 1949, a student at the beginning of his fifth year, just returned from New York and, almost certainly, over abundantly equipped with American impressions. (4)

Largeness of scale, Fifth Avenue along Central Park, Eldorado Towers, the Palisades from Riverside Drive, the George Washington Bridge, even—surprising at this date—the Chrysler Building, but *not* Aalto at MIT, were, one seems to remember, among the prevailing images which were advertized; and, undoubtedly, they contributed exuberance. Indeed, in its way, all this was a casual, and from the gut, latter day recall of Liverpool's earlier American affiliations. It involved lots of exuberance and panache; and, of course, it occurred at a particularly opportune moment.

For, around 1949–51, while an old guard still clung to anti-modern architecture propositions, while a middle guard was able to devote itself to the propagation of allegedly far out performance, there was coming to exist, embryonically, a species of vanguard, increasingly concerned with the vacuity of content which modern architecture was beginning to reveal. Simply to notice that, until this time, two surely irreconcilable fantasies had survived uncriticized. These were: the notion of the architect as allied with mechanization, production and power (dear to the Deutsche Werkbund) and the contrary idea of the architect as alienated personality, critic of society, agent of 'revolution' and 'life', as—therefore—a precursor, as—like Shelley's idea of the poet—the ultimate legislator of mankind.

To repeat: the two fantasies are irreconcilable; but, if this, nowadays, is clearly visible, it could only have become apparent after modern architecture had become established and institutionalized; and, in both England and the United States, the years around 1950 were crucial to this process which was signalized, in New York by the United Nations and Lever House, in London by the Festival of Britain. For, on both sides of the Atlantic, the alliance of modern architecture with power (whether the power of liberal sentiment, Madison Avenue, or governmental bureaucracy) was now an evident *fait accompli*; and, with this message so abundantly demonstrated, how could the alternative idea of the architect (a person who in the interests of survival/integrity was always working to 'make it strange') be enabled to persist? It was *some* kind of a problem; but if, in America where rationalization could seem to have become complete, it was far from easy to question the 'triumph' of modern architecture, in England the Festival of Britain presented no such issues. As a centennial celebration of 1851, the Festival of Britain certainly offered no Crystal Palace; and, while 1851, under the auspices of Prince Albert, proposed cosmopolitan and international issues, both the substance and the ambition of 1951 were local, chauvinist and intolerably restricted. But, apart from all this, the Festival of Britain unabashedly proclaimed the Picturesque.

One recalls how painful all this was to a particular student in Liverpool. It seemed to be the grossest rip-off. It was a betrayal of all principle (at about the same time Alison and Peter Smithson were reaching comparable conclusions); but, all the same, if a loss of innocence was suddenly apprehended, this was surely to attribute it to symptoms rather than to cause. For the utopian dream of modern architecture could never, in any case, have survived modern architecture's public reception; and, today, hindsight knows this only too well. But, since the Olympian overview of hindsight completely fails to explain the crucial and intimate reactions which make for change, a continued contemplation of the saccharine of 1951 may still be permissible.

It is not easy. It would be too simple to take over Louis Sullivan's belated arguments with reference to Chicago 1893. For, while Chicago 1893 often must have persuaded, London 1951 frequently outraged. The Imperial lion, however irrational his former behaviour might have been, was here transformed into little more than a highly ingratiating pussy cat. The essence of England was 'gently' disclosed to be little more than charm—less than clever and more than supercilious; and, though the advertisement may now seem to have been ambiguously prophetic (it was surely an index to empire lost or about to be lost), at least one result was a widespread disgust.

An increasingly intense disgust which became rapidly focussed, no explanation of English architecture in the Fifties is possible if this reaction of disgust is considered dismissable. Initially, maybe only a disgust with the policies which had launched 1951, ultimately it became a disgust with an entire society: disgust with stylish radicals (professing Marxism and perfectly ready to build American bases), disgust with the promptings of good taste and good manners, sometimes disgust with the trappings of monarchy and the ensuing journalistic soap opera; but, while it was, for the most part, a patriotic and local disgust, it was not without a certain centrality. For, in an interesting way, it recapitulated that much more cosmopolitan disgust which, thirty to forty years earlier, had been productive of what Peter Smithson has called modern architecture's heroic period; and, in a still more interesting way, it might seem to have been a prevision of that more concentrated and massive (but shortlived) disgust which in the mid Sixties began to grip the U.S. of A.

To ascribe so much to the Festival of Britain is, of course, to exaggerate (large social reactions are rarely motivated by architecture alone) and the sudden distortion of the English psyche which occurred between twenty and thirty years ago, without doubt, has multiple origins; but, when the history of general disgust, from Dada to Pop, comes to be written, the contribution of English architects will certainly not appear to have been a minor one. And, for explanation of their would be violence, their *fauve* trappings, their anxiety to damage, for all of the dissident paraphernalia of New Brutalism, as a beginning, one may, quite plausibly, feel obliged to cite the presence of *The Architectural Review* and the activities of Nikolaus Pevsner.

Sir Nikolaus Pevsner, approximately forty five years ago and shortly after the time that Walter Gropius had arrived in England, set out to produce an *English* background for the Bauhaus. It was done in all good faith; it combined regard for German pedagogics with a taste for English idiosyncrasy; and the result was *Pioneers...from William Morris to Walter Gropius* (1937). It was an instructive performance; it is still a text book; and, if English idiosyncrasy and German pedagogics were not necessarily the best of bed fellows, this was something veiled by the future and inaccessible to contemporary scrutiny.

But, if such was Pevsner's English *debut* (the *English* descent of Gropius and what was then conceived of as rationalism), its initial impact rapidly became confused. Very shortly Gropius left London for Cambridge, Mass. (where Sigfried Giedion was soon to produce all the tokens of his *American* descent); and, with the absence of the master, the message became muddy. For while *The Architectural Review* was abundantly interested in England (and after the events of 1940—collapse of a restraining Paris—could only become more so), Pevsner was apparently interested in everything—not only 'good design', but also South German Baroque, the Picturesque, the Perpendicular, Mannerism, and so on and on.

All the same, coming in the early Thirties from Leipzig to London, it is comparatively easy to conceive of the stimulus which Pevsner must have enjoyed. He was an explorer in *terra incognita* where the natives, ignorant, were not exactly savages; and he had a debt of hospitality and gratitude to repay. Also, in the face of Nazi-Fascist enormity, he was surely concerned with the survival of the liberal tradition; and, hence, he became an almost programmed personality. There was something to be said and something to be saved; there was an obligation very properly understood; and thus, first to England and then to the world, Pevsner made extensively public the largely unknown sophistications of German art history. It was a popularization; but it was an extraordinary undertaking and its results have been commensurate. However, if, and by himself, Pevsner was able to do a far more spectacular job in England than ever the Warburg Institute has been able to accomplish, his Anglophilia and his pro-Bauhaus position had, quite rapidly and before 1950, begun to assemble themselves as one of the more bizarre of symbioses.

Of course, *circa* 1950, Gropius was still a name to be conjured with. The Pan-Am Building, the Playboy Club, the project for a university at Baghdad, all the details of the dreary *degringolade*, were still far away in the future; and, if neither Six Moon Hill nor the Harvard Graduate Center were any great revelation, there was still in the background the august and the sanctified mystique of the Weimar Republic. *Circa* 1950 the first anti-Gropius murmurings were not yet. Privately oneself first became aware of them around New

Canaan/New Haven in 1952 and perhaps, publicly, they first erupted in Bruno Zevi's *Poetica dell' Architettura Neo-Plastica* of 1953; but, meanwhile, there was Pevsner, the apostle of Gropius and, simultaneously, the exponent of what he was later to call "Englishness".

The young and the concerned found the apparent double allegiance (abetted by *The Architectural Review*) immensely perturbing. For, if Gropius was the paragon of rationalism and rationalism was the order of the day, then *why* "Englishness"? If, for Pevsner, Gropius was a Moses figure, rigorous and emphatic, delivering the tablets of the law, then how could the law become so easily evadable—by *the English*? How might it be that, at once, there should be both the *law* and *England*—the implacable *law* coexistent with occasionally amusing, seductive, frivolous, not quite scrutable, usually the reverse of intellectual, sometimes intelligent *England*? The two positions, if in any way they could be associated, seemed to be stuck together with scotch tape. It was not clear how a taste for street furniture, poignant vignettes and what was, already, beginning to be called townscape could, in any way, be related to what were still imagined to be the ideal severities of Bauhaus programmatics.

Nor, given the general bias of Liverpool, at that time perhaps still American and French (the Frenchness mostly coming from Ireland, *i.e.* from Robert Maxwell whose impossible ideal involved, I think, a fusion of Cézanne, Le Corbusier *and* François Mansart), was there any desperate student anxiety to seek a *via media* between the polar extremes which it seemed that Pevsner and *The Architectural Review* were, so unknowingly, abetting. Simply, the Pevsner idea (it may also have been the idea of J.M. Richards) appeared to be eighteenth century and, more or less, hopelessly so. It was a case of the Palladian house and the folly in the park, with the proviso that the rational edifice (now the product of Gropius) might and should permit the existence of a distant *chinoiserie*, idiosyncratic and, presumably, 'English to the core'.

Undoubtedly the prescription was enticing—to many; and it was also unacceptable—to a few. It was, evidently, crudely viable; but with his cult of 'England' (so very different from that of Auden), Pevsner had also unleashed a species of demon of which, maybe, he remained unaware. For the Pevsner/*Architectural Review* prescription, criss-crossed with the shreddings of Marxism, was about to become the gospel which the first generation of welfare state architects was excessively eager to receive. 'Building' was to become 'rational' (no more direct or careful historical reminiscence and lots of jerkiness, syncopation, high staccato); but, also, 'building'/architecture was to be 'attractive', popular and a little bit daring. The essential formula had been delivered. Could it be described as Gropius with a sugar coating of blue and white awnings, boats and pubs? Maybe. But, in any case, as the result of a very curious amalgam—the welfare state, the

Bauhaus and *The Architectural Review*—around 1950, in many quarters it must have been felt that both a 'modern' public amenity and an equivalent conception of social justice were, for ever, to be established.

But, alas, for the hopes of at least some; and, perhaps, thank God for the doubts of some others. For, in the rougher freedom of the provinces (I think of Liverpool and I think of the Smithsons) where bureaucratic programs of such slickness were not to be appreciated, where an adulterated polemic was only to be despised, there could be nothing other than dissent. And then what to do?

"More matter with less art": the Queen of Denmark's exasperated cry to Polonius was a possible solution. Its idealistic inverse: *"More art with less matter"* was the other. But, though one seems to remember that both of these solutions were embryonically present, one is also compelled to recognize that, in reality, the two responses are almost one and the same. That, for practical purposes, their results are not all that very likely to be highly distinguishable. For, while the one will clamor for a crude directness and the other for an involuted cerebrality, the expressions which result from either will, almost certainly, be liable to display an identical minimalist look.

So it is into this situation that one now wishes to insert Stirling's undergraduate thesis—a community center for an English new town: Newton Ayncliffe, County Durham; and, about this exhumation, what excuses can now be pleaded?

On my part because it, then, constituted an event in my life—though now I can't see why; and, also, because back in '69, I wrote of this production in a private letter to John Jacobus which, in the extensive quotations which he extracted from it, he then made unexpectedly public. And, therefore, to quote from Jacobus quoting me: "My own tendency in any synthetic activity is towards the making of small aphoristic statements, followed then by a struggle in tying these statements together. One acquires an attachment to small and rather sharp episodes and the relinquishing of this attachment becomes a matter of tremendous difficulty. O.K.: well, I simultaneously dealt with two theses, one of which was by a personality of my own mental bias and the other of which was Jim's. And the situation was also ironical because both problems which involved entirely different requirements could have been solved by the same *parti* and my aphoristic person did not arrive at the (abundantly simple) *parti* which Jim did". Which, with much else that I no longer remember, is what I said to Jacobus; and I wrote this because Stirling, in 1950, seemed to point a way beyond the useless sophistication which, I suspect, habitually engages my attention. He was, as I thought, *The Noble Savage*. He had learned a gratifying simplicity in the United States; and, accordingly, it was to the United States that I increasingly addressed myself.

But to look at these two projects (my 'aphoristic' person is, of course, Robert Maxwell) thirty years later is to annotate a local curiosity in the history of style. Because, though one remembers the passion and the anguish with which they were conducted, though one concedes—in both cases—the intelligence, one is also entertained by their apparent quaintness. And, if Maxwell's Corbusian erudition is a little bit Tectonized, not exactly the dialectical performance which, surely, he would have preferred, nor is Stirling's building quite the belligerently Corbusian endeavor which once, no doubt, it appeared.

For, if Stirling infers a Corbusian affiliation (roof episodes, pilotis, ramp), then and after this much, just *where* is the 'free plan'? Obvious concessions to the 'free plan' are made (the somewhat violent independence of pilotis and ultra-solid, highly directional walls); but, with all this said, there should still be no doubt that we are here presented with an asymmetrical rendition of the unbuilt Library and Administration Building at I.I.T., raised upon a dubious transfer slab which then supports a volume owing as much to Charles Eames (at Pacific Palisades) as it does to Le Corbusier. Ostensibly this community center is a type of distended Poissy, a disturbed memory of the Villa Savoye, but only so at top and bottom; and, fundamentally, its curious middle is apt to betray rather more Los Angeles (of a certain date) than France. Indeed, this project with its un-Corbusian plateau could, if its silhouette and its Eamesian quotations were less vivacious, be perfectly well understood to be the corporate headquarters of an oil outfit, erected *circa* 1965–1970 in the outer suburbs of Houston. Le Corbusier and Charles Eames could then be stripped away and we should be left with no more than the 'successful' banalities of the 'reliable' commercial office.

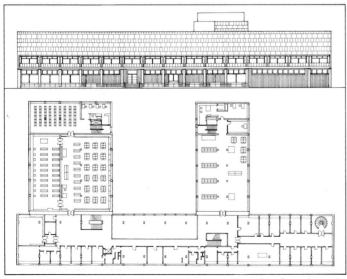

Robert Maxwell, thesis project: Liverpool University, 1949, first floor plan and southwest elevation.

Now to have produced so much, fifteen to twenty years before the appalling reality, might, ambiguously, be considered an achievement; but this particular performance should also be placed within the tradition of English quasi-Corbusiana—mostly of Russian and Jewish origin. And one alludes to the brilliant realizations of Berthold Lubetkin (a topic on his own) who, surely more than anyone else established Le Corbusier as an English taste.

Would it be too much to say that Lubetkin's Corbu (with his background of Moscow and Paris) was primarily the rococo and Surrealist personality of the De Beistegui penthouse. And then would it be too much to add that rococo Corbu was altogether too abundantly presented in Denys Lasdun's Newton Road in Paddington of 1938?

Anglo-Corbu could go two ways: the one in terms of super-articulation (as, surprisingly, Maxwell), the other in terms of *prisme pur* (as, surprisingly, Stirling). But, in Newton Road, Lasdun presented Anglo-Corbu as a miscegenation of Maison Cook and Garches, and, here, the English relation to Corbu was approximate to earlier English relations to Palladio. Everything became flat—and flat without the implications of a third dimension; while the house combining Garches and Maison Cook, successfully missed the animating volumetric idea of either. Like Stirling, top and bottom are one thing; and, also like Stirling, the in between is very much something else.

However the difference of twelve years which separates Lasdun's house from these two Liverpool theses may encourage one further comment. Like Lasdun in 1938, Maxwell in 1950 stays firmly within the stylistic orbit and profile of Lubetkin, whereas Stirling begins to display a new abundance. According to Jacobus: "Since his thesis, Stirling has avoided cubic compression, his designs usually exhibiting a free assemblage of varying accommodations". And it is in the agitated roof incident at Newton Ayncliffe, far more aggressive (and even Russian) than Lubetkin would have countenanced, that premonitions of future development are to be deciphered.

IV.
Apart from the quotations from Jacobus the foregoing was written quickly, with conviction, with amusement, and at the insistence of the architect in August 1973; and then it was that I encountered a road block which, after a lapse of eight or nine years (and at the further insistence of the architect), I must now attempt either to overcome or detour. Meanwhile, as to what this road block might have been, whether a massive inhibition or merely a very minor one, I am now compelled to wonder.

Did I, for instance, experience some theoretical reservation about Stirling which I was unable to articulate? If I did, then

House in Newton Road, Paddington, Denys Lasdun.

appearance *circa* 1954 and who, maybe but not certainly, had bowed himself out of the scene about ten years later (the act here was surely Corbu enlivened by excerpts from Butterfield). But, apart from these, there was—even in 1973—yet another Stirling, an alternative to the so often applauded *Plucky Jim* (5) who ought to have been apparent. And I refer to his pre-cast concrete, pre-fabricated plastic performance, initiated at St. Andrews in 1964, and leading through to Olivetti, Haslemere and to the public housing at Runcorn (1967–76).

So it seems to me that, back in '73, I had caught at least something of this third theatrical protagonist. The previous year I had been taken to Haslemere—by the architect; and, needless to say, it was almost a repeat of the earlier visit to Leicester. J.F.S. was proprietorial—and incredibly so. Here and there, gently and affectionately, he would pat the building and stroke it a bit. So the occasion was highly possessive. However, as I now think about it, it was quite distinct from the inspection of Leicester. For, at Leicester, Jim was the *cicerone,* amused and slightly patronising; but, at Haslemere, he was the intimate lover and, presumably, I was the slightly embarrassed *voyeur.* Or, if this is to exaggerate, then at least the building was an over size circus elephant and the architect was its adoring trainer, encouraging it to show off its tricks. In any case, it was all an occasion of overflowing empathy and, to a certain degree, private mischief. The building was much more than merely the 'friend' of a friend; and, accordingly, it was in terms of intimacy glimpsed that eight or nine years ago I attempted to evaluate Olivetti as a sort of constructive discord between the rat-a-tat of the typewriter and the calm of the Regency *umbrello* or the sleepiness of the Edwardian garden party marquee. But, though I had made, I still think, a partially correct evaluation (semi-High Tech plus Thomas Hope) all the same the road block remained; and it is while writing this that I now begin to recognize why.

It was partly a case of just how many other ghostly Stirlings there might not be around who were only awaiting entrance cues or who were still unable quite to assemble their performance. Very much more than this, it was also a case of critical misdirection. I had been encouraged to see Haslemere in terms of a Regency 'event,' presumably as some sort of prelude to the more explicit Palladianism of the St. Andrews Arts Centre project of 1971; and, though this misdirection was profitable and not without prophetic dimensions, it did mean that my attention was diverted elsewhere when, absolutely, it should have rivetted not upon the Arts Centre but upon the St. Andrews student dormitories of 1964–68.

I have seldom been to Scotland; but I wish now that I *had* visited St. Andrews—a *long* way in the *wrong* direction but evidently *worth* it. For these dormitory buildings at St. Andrews, overlooking that unimaginable northern sea, must,

I doubt whether this problem has entirely disappeared; and I also doubt whether my capacity to spell out such reservation has, in any way developed. So, as I resume this introduction, rather than continue to wriggle like a fish trying to get off the hook, it now seems to me most opportune to suggest that around 1973 was not a very propitious moment for making a critical approach to Stirling. Simply, the appropriate perspectives were not there. For, in 1973, just *how many* Stirling's were there which were visible and competing to attract attention?

Preeminently, of course, the exponent of glass and tile skin, the architect of Leicester (1959), Cambridge (1964), and Oxford (1966) decisively occupied center stage and the role here was mostly High Victorian with, perhaps, a little bit of Old Russia. Then, prominent but subsidiary to this strenuous individual, there was, evidently, the aggressive red brick personality who seems to have made his first public certainly, be the first appearance of Stirling being nothing other than 'agreeable'. They are not pretentious; they are highly 'matter of fact'; they are almost devoid of 'problems'; they are pleasingly vivacious; they are also very relaxed. And might it be suggested that this relaxation must surely be the real preface of later happenings?

Certainly the St. Andrews dormitories are almost the complete opposite of what was going to be Stirling's somewhat frenetic operation at Queen's College, Oxford (the Florey Building) some two years later. For the Queen's building is surely little more than a repetition, just a bit more of the pseudo-aggressive same of Leicester and Cambridge (Jacobus also seems to share this opinion); but, after Queen's, there were going to be no more other quirky little interjections. Simply, apart from the inhibitions promoted by Oxford (and one may also discern just what Oxford wanted. Oxford wanted to be 'with it', wanted something like what had already been delivered at Cambridge), it is apparent that, by 1964, Stirling had surrendered himself to a very simple ambition. And could this have been equivalent to Cezanne's project of doing Poussin over again on nature?

For, by 1964, it was surely obvious to all discerning persons that the social programs of modern architecture were now entirely defunct and that social protest itself—even when highly contorted—had become little more than an alibi for absence of talent and absence of mind. And, with the idea of fighting society more or less drained of meaning, with the asbestos fire curtain run down on the repetition of even Brutalist gestures, then, with the threatening dilemma of either *détente* or kitsch (and these are both versions of '*If you can't lick 'em, join 'em*'), it may be significant that Stirling resisted kitsch (the approximate route which Venturi was to blaze a few years later) and chose *détente*. Perhaps, in the end, no *very* great choice; but, in any case, Stirling *did* relax. And so the St. Andrews dormitory complex, from certain points of view, is apt to look like something which one might expect to find in a propaganda book of the 1930's—accepted into the collection because it must surely 'belong'; but accepted with possible editorial doubts.

In other words, I am proposing that, in '64 (with a lot of passion spent), Stirling collected—or recollected—himself in terms of old time modern architecture—not the content but the form. Technologically, the style was very polished; but, formally, it was quite deliberately incompetent and, for these reasons not to become a fixation. That is: the 'modern architecture' content at St. Andrews in 1964 was not, in any way, to approximate the literal obsessions which, very shortly, were to grip the so called New York Five. Instead, St. Andrews was both a moment, lightly touched upon, and something of a genial rehearsal. For St. Andrews is a highly casual, slightly ingenuous initiation of themes (pre-fab themes and exploitation of site and volume themes) which were to

become more explicit at Haslemere; and then, of course, the themes of Haslemere itself (those Regency inferences to which, in '73, I devoted far too much attention) comprised something which became completely overt in that abrupt appropriation of the Villa Badoer which is the St. Andrews Arts Centre project of 1971.

So now to focus attention upon St. Andrews 1971 with a bleak eighteenth century fragment of Scottish Palladio at its centre. To me, at least, this is a manifesto piece. It is neglected and, of unbuilt Stirling, surely the piece most to be regretted. For had the St. Andrews Arts Centre, with its abundant traces of Haslemere and the 'platitude' of its Palladian *parti*, been built, much in the later Stirling which now appears to be eccentric, unpredictable, bizarre, wilful, haphazard, would be immediately easy to apprehend. Indeed, one is prepared to argue that what Leicester was in 1959 so might St. Andrews have been in 1971.

With this I am thinking about the 'casually' orchestrated Jim of the Wissenschaftszentrum project for Berlin of 1979; and I am listening to what, so far, I have heard about it—in Berlin and elsewhere. So, in many quarters, it is *not* acceptable. It is Wagnerian; it is Wilhelminian; it is Ludwig II; it is Neuschwanstein; it is Hechingen; it is an easy way out. Which, since all this is intended as dispraise, may serve to reiterate the precursive role of the St. Andrews Arts Centre.

At St. Andrews, faced with a respectable—if lugubrious—piece of Calvinist Palladio, Stirling displayed great resource. He placed Calvinist Palladio within italics. He made of it a quotation. And, deriving from Haslemere (also, certainly, Derby) the *barchesse* of this North British villa became the ultimate qualifying items. In other words, the house was given a value, both contextual (6) and contradictory, which otherwise it could not possibly possess; and, meanwhile, in Berlin on the Landwehrkanal, Stirling has intimated something comparable but different.

So the result, no longer a Palladian villa, is now a romantically conceived *schloss* equipped, in characteristic nineteenth century fashion, with a history in reverse. For the existing building (also italicised) is now supported by additions which, conceptually, can only seem to predate it. So the existing building is *circa* 1900 (by the architect of the totally bomb proof Reichstag?) and then Stirling has provided it with an 'antecedent' fantasy apparatus which can only infer that this existing building is not the origin but rather the 'degenerate' Baroque result. For this projected mini-*schloss* on the Landwehrkanal has now, suddenly, become, fictionally, so antique that it possesses even Greek beginnings—the stoa and the theatric piece suggest as much. And then the mediaeval career of this *schloss* is also made evident. The library tower and the 'church', which is probably a reminiscence of

Memorial Hall at Harvard, assist the idea. And so the solution—which is surely both functionally and formally brilliant—becomes predicated by an entirely spurious and eclectic argument.

Deplorable all of this hybridness? By the impoverished standards of modern architecture, post-Modernism, and *architettura razionale* certainly. But by the standards of Karl Friedrich Schinkel who, in Berlin, might well have played an equivalent fantasy game? And, *just what* about this? In any case these questions are only presented as the indications of a strategy. For an opportune and intelligent eclecticism can, sometimes, make its own rules, the private rules of virtuosity; and, in these terms, its process is only to be judged in relationship to its success. So, with a 'disgraceful' and almost ruthless amalgam of pieces, from a complex assignment and a miniature site, Stirling has been able to educe a positive, a picturesque, a reasonably authentic, and a highly Germanic courtyard; and, before the *a priori* theoretician rushes in to condemn such heterogeneity, this well known person (with his well known prejudices) would be well advised to look at the solution which the so reputable Mario Botta presented for the same problem and the same site.

Of course, comparisons are always invidious; but, if judgement can only depend upon comparison, then merely to observe. For Botta is 'basic' and 'sincere'; and, as an obvious result, he is clumsy. His protracted Loosian façade to the Landwehrkanal, apart from producing problems of floor level, could only diminish the impact of the neo-Baroque, Wilhelminian original; while, to the contrary, the evasiveness of Stirling, his conjuror's trickiness, has made possible a solution of indelible directness and economy. Botta's courtyard is strictly a passive and a painful residue (it belongs to the 'Emperor has no clothes' story); while Stirling's courtyard is, almost inexcusably, facile, laconic and elegant.

So what did Germany do for Jim? Did the Germanic lands release a hitherto suppressed vein of invention? For recent German Stirling is invariably a pleasure; and, if one can only regret the unbuilt Dusseldorf museum, then the extensions to the Landesmuseum at Stuttgart should be ample compensation. For Stuttgart must be the most convincing and magnificent Stirling performance to date. The excessive object fixation of Leicester is now quite gone away and, instead, the still unfinished building has become a very highly rewarding sequence of quietly monumental interiors. An Altes Museum without a façade, with a circular courtyard rather than a dome, it is equipped with an extensive series of episodes—entry sequence, ramp, stairs from courtyard to upper terrace—all of which obliterate disbelief. Also, about Stuttgart, the architect is no longer possessive. He seems to accept it without the need (as at Haslemere) to mystify the visitor.

Science Center, Berlin, Mario Botta, 1980, Facade to the Landwehrkanal.

All the same, about Stuttgart, there may still be reservations. For the building remains an Altes Museum without a façade. And might not its principal exposure be, just a little, too sporadic and dispersed? Having been taken around the building by the architect in late July, I produce this suggestion with great diffidence. For the penetration and entrance arrangements are ingenious and captivating—suggesting, maybe, some aspects of Olbrich's Freiekunsthaus on the Mathildenhoe at Darmstadt. But, this appreciated, could there not be something slightly crumbly about the absence of façade? And might not the building's great and indisputable presence be insufficiently, or too casually, disclosed?

Which is to obtrude perhaps too personal an issue. I imagine Stirling's *chateau idéal* as an Empire villa to which a large *art nouveau* conservatory has been appended; and, quite correctly, he imagines my comparable establishment as a very rustic and small sixteenth century *palazzo* to which has been added a not entirely modest Neo-Classical library. So there is a taste shared and then there is a divergence. There is a community of interest in a variety of early nineteenth century phenomena; but then, while I 'back track' towards Serlio, he moves in 'the other direction'. And this, as I now see it, is to frame my problem and my road block of nine years ago.

Myself is addicted to walls—and the *thicker* the *better*. I do not dispute that doctrine of the Ecole des Beaux Arts which was so curiously propagated by Le Corbusier that *'the plan is the generator'*. I merely qualify it (as did Le Corbusier in his practice) by insisting that the *vertical* surface can only *remain* the threshold of understanding. For while the plan, as a document addressed to the mind, will always be the primary concept, the vertical surface, as a presentation addressed to the eye, will always be the primary percept, will never be other than the beginning of comprehension.

Very obvious all this? Though I never hear it talked about I certainly suppose so; and, accordingly, it is the density and opacity of 'constructed' wall, its conduct and its musculature, which is my own prevalent interest. And so my private heroes continue to be certain central Italians of the sixteenth century, then Borromini, then occasionally Hawksmoor (as at Christ Church, Spitalfields), then always H.H. Richardson, then sometimes (as at Villa Schwob and Garches) Le Corbusier.

According to my reading, these were all masters of the

vertical surface; and, clearly, it must have been the relative absence of this concern in Stirling which arrested my writing in 1973 and which remains my reservation about Stuttgart. For, in spite of its admirable merits (and they are extraordinary), Stuttgart is a building with *no* face. And it is not a question that no face could be seen—because of a screen of trees. Instead, it is just the issue that, when considering intercourse with a building, its *face*—however veiled—must always be a desirable and a provocative item.

Now a great building incites the criticism which it deserves (about so many buildings, much applauded, why should *anything* be written *whatsoever*?); and it is because Stuttgart is *almost* so very great that I separate myself from any idea of a Stirling eulogium to produce this not entirely minor qualification. *Face*, except for Le Corbusier from time to time, was never a preoccupation of modern architecture. Nor was *face,* as the metaphorical plane of intersection between the eyes of the observer and what one may dare to call the *soul* of the building (its condition of 'internal' animation) a notable component of eighteenth century understanding. Nor, today, in spite of all protestations to the contrary, does the exhibition of a prime *face*, of a *face* both opaque and revealing, appear to be among the propensities of the various attitudes which, fashionably, may be considered Post-Modern or, alternatively, be ascribable to *la tendenza.* And so, perhaps, I judge both Stirling and Stuttgart by impossibly private and too fastidious standards?

All the same I think not; and, to make my point a little more clear, I will only add that, personally, I would like still further to enrich the entrance arrangements of Stuttgart by projecting upon them something of the abrupt frontality of Le Corbusier's Mill Owners façade at Ahmedabad. An intolerable ambition no doubt; but, to me, an ambition which belongs to unfinished business (and I mean the unfinished business of Stirling). For the results of axonometric projection, which will often disclose the inner workings of a structure but which will, never, yield a prime face, must surely always be revised in terms of a one point perspective, which will rarely disclose internalities but which will always premiate a specific vertical surface and distinguish it from all others. And this is the sole argument of my qualification, that—so far as I know—Stirling has never used one point perspective—that 'poverty stricken' method which can, sometimes, animate the flattest of walls by charging it with the most abundant intimations of rotundity and recession.

But, apart from façade, which I can only think of as the existential interface between eye and idea, it seems to me that Stuttgart has almost everything. It is quiet; it is magnificent; it makes no protest.

V.
In this little essay upon Jim I have deliberately chosen to

violate a strict chronological sequence. Instead I have chosen to hop around like one of those slightly mad squirrels which I constantly observe from my windows. The squirrels, of course, look around for what they might *eat;* and, to the contrary, I have been looking around for what I might *see.* But, perhaps, the permanent predicament of the squirrels and my own temporary behavior are not altogether all that different. For memory, and therefore a situation which involves autobiography, is a strange eruptive thing, and can never possess a rational profile. Nor is intimacy the best guide to judgement. And now, after this protracted tight-rope performance between truth, taste and tact, to proceed to a long overdue cadenza.

In what I have written I have been at effort *not* to see the buildings and projects by Stirling which I *know* that I would *not* like to see. I allude to a variety of 'early struggles' and to Runcorn. Then, among projects, I allude to Dorman Long and Siemens A.G.; and, in all honesty, I have to consider particularly these two both dull and over excited. Then I also allude to what myself considers to be an over frequent and entirely too English hyperarticulation. But, after making these concessions to my own point of view, I find myself still so trapped by the persuasions of Stirling's gaiety and grandeur that I can only proceed to amplify these gratifications.

When Stuttgart is completed and adequately published, general satisfaction and occasional reservation, I think, will not be entirely unlike my own. But, since Stuttgart will not be completed until after the appearance of this book, it can scarcely here be appropriated as convincing evidence of Stirling's peculiar combination of the awe inspiring and the light hearted which, increasingly, seems to present itself as a gift to the world. For this is a 'happy' architecture which is also equipped with the gauntest and most tragic dimensions; and, in default of Stuttgart, how to present its qualities.

I have not seen the extensions to the Architecture Building at Rice University and I could scarcely bear the grief of a trip down to Houston just to take a look. But one knows, of course, the original story of the Rice campus. Ralph Adams Cram had been invited down there to produce what was to be expected from *him.* The trustees were inflamed by the idea of Gothic—and *wasn't* this Mr. Cram's specialty? But, when Cram arrived in that sub-tropical sweat box and was overcome by heat prostration, he rapidly abandoned his *Ile de France* fantasies and enjoyed a change of heart. Mentally he became transported some place else. Quickly he transposed what was then a rain forest in the outer suburbs of Houston into an Italian *pineta* not too far from the shores of the Adriatic. Looking at the site, it was about Ravenna—a Ravenna without disfiguring oil refineries—that he began to think; and it was in terms of an imaginary Byzantine triangle—Ravenna, Ferrara and the Abbazia di Pomposa—that he evolved his buildings. So the Rice campus, with Julian Huxley as an assistant professor, became a monastic fantasy outfit, a quasi-*Liberty* performance, simultaneously located both in Texas and the former Exarchate of Ravenna.

But, intrinsically, was it any the worse for that? From the 1930s onwards, as the social consciousness and attendant *Zeitgeist* obsessions became activated, certainly a lot of people thought so; but if, so far as the fabric of Rice is concerned, it is not abundantly clear that their contributions were other than destructive, then it is to the credit of Stirling's modesty to have respected and even 'restored' the idea of Cram's 'Byzantine' conversion. For one of the most liberating illusions to be experienced in the older parts of Rice still remains the fantasy that the observer is not too *very* far from Ravenna (in spite of recent additions the Faculty Club may still suggest the cottage of Petrarch at Arquá); and there remain traces of the illusion that, not too far beyond the trees, there is to be found a long and pristine sand beach.

A short lived illusion no doubt; but, for that reason, all the more important that it be reinforced; and, particularly so, when in such a *laissez faire, laisser aller* city as Houston, what Cram achieved at Rice is almost the only precinct of order to be discovered. For, while from high up, with towers seen above trees, Houston may occasionally look like a romantic fragment of the *ville radieuse* (7), as one descends to earth, apart from the Rice campus and certain adjacencies, there is little but visual misery to be experienced. So much which was highly adequate and even good has gone away—in the interests of a cheap brashness; and, therefore, Stirling's role at Rice assumes a further significance. He has respected Cram and his City Beautiful strategies. Which means that he has respected an idea of Houston still prevalent thirty years ago. Which also means (just possibly though not very likely) that Stirling's great discretion at Rice *might* produce a minimum of urbanistic reflection—in Houston. For without the preponderant idea of a local whole, what—other than mindless aggregations of a mess—are individual works of architecture however brilliant they might happen to be? Without the *city,* whether New York, New Orleans, Amsterdam, Siena, Paris, London, Rome (which all display their own theaters of discourse), then just *why* the building *anyway?* And, in Houston, a city which has lost its Southern and Texas identity, which is nowadays a boring version of Los Angeles without a topography, since this problem is particularly crucial, it is for this reason that one must salute what has been done at Rice and those persons (not only Stirling and Wilford) who are responsible.

All the same Rice remains a very minor item to use as a theme from which to build a cadenza; and, if it is still premature (for me at least) to speak about extensions to the Tate Gallery in London and the Fogg Museum at Harvard, then, in the absence of recently completed major building,

just how to proceed?

I have already exposed comparisons of Stirling with Robert Maxwell, Denys Lasdun and Mario Botta; and now to introduce a couple more—two Sheffield University projects of 1953: that of Stirling (with Alan Cordingley) and that of the Smithsons which may scarcely seem to belong to the same site.

About the Smithsons Sheffield project, Kenneth Frampton is disposed to write extensively. Apparently this is not simply "Constructivist" in its "restrained structural rhetoric" but it "seems in retrospect to have been of Japanese rather than Russian persuasion," and its not being built "was a loss to English architectural culture" (8). So I look, I am compelled to wonder, and I *just* don't see it. Particularly I look at that infinitely protracted tube *(lasciate ogni speranza voi che entrate),* no doubt so highly endearing to Frampton but, to me, suggestive of one of the worst airport nightmares which I have ever known.

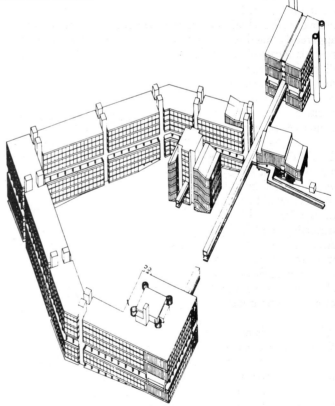

Sheffield University extension, Alison and Peter Smithson, 1953.

Almost certainly, I suppose, I see the Smithsons at Sheffield through the lenses of prejudice (the activities of Team X have always eluded my admiration); and, to the contrary, the Stirling-Cordingley project I have always admired. I have always enjoyed the decisiveness which its authors displayed in their confrontation of the new with the existing. Also, I have always been amused by the consideration of *who* did *what,* what was Stirling and what was Cordingley; and, never attempting to decipher these contributions until now, I am inclined to believe that the attenuated *Zeilenbau* piece just might be Cordingley and that its vertical surface (quasi-Russian agitation in a Corbusian format) is almost certainly Jim.

However, Sheffield requires attention for other reasons. In an overview of Stirling's work it is the initiatory monument in a largely neglected series which might include, not only Sheffield, but also Churchill College, Derby and the projected *Wissenschaftzentrum* for Berlin. So, like most initiatory monuments in a series, Sheffield is not wholly a success. It was an important gesture in the urbanistic darkness of thirty years ago; but, all the same, its authors seem to have been afflicted by almost the same problems which, today, are experienced by Robert Krier. Preoccupied by the idea of Piazza San Marco, they were not too well equipped to distinguish front from back. That is: in place of the Procuratie Nuove (or Vecchie?) they made their *Zeilenbau* piece, but apparently failed to notice that, because of its nature, such a piece is incapable of enclosing space. Meaning that they just didn't notice that a *Zeilenbau* piece is inherently insular and that, for this reason, it can never serve to discriminate spatial realms of different value, positive internal space and less positive external, realms of public order and complementary realms of private idiosyncrasy.

This is close to a problem not present at Churchill but which still persists at Derby, where the primacy of the *galleria,* which almost excludes its communication with the *piazza* outside, would surely have rendered this space without occupation; and it is related to the strategy of an axis traversing the length of a building (also the idea of Siemens A.G.). For should not an axis almost always move the other way? Ideally, should not an axis penetrate or attack the extended surfaces of a building? And, in this context, I think about the Villa Aldobrandini at Frascati—surely the ideal type of a very long building receiving an axis?

All of which is no more than a preface for the *Wissenschaftzentrum* where these slightly tedious problems are no longer an issue, where they are triumphantly solved in a minuscule project which may serve as the culmination of a sequence and as illustration (much better than Runcorn or Lima) of Stirling's mature urbanistic potential.

After this overlong digression on an unconsidered topic, I am now happy to proceed to my second comparison which is related to that taste of circa 1960 for octagonalized buildings—again a taste which myself has never understood. But, thinking about this taste, it seems almost inevitable that, *en route* to the Leicester Engineering Building, one should also visit Paul Rudolph's Prudential Building in Boston and the Smithsons Economist Building in London. For, though all of them are octagons, it is not obvious that they are all members of the same architectural family. Thus, while Rudolph is lacy and quasi-Yamasakian and the Smithsons are urbanely bland and elegant, to me at least Stirling's diagonal corner at Leicester is an altogether different category of event. So, no doubt the three buildings are of radically different volume. The Prudential and the Economist are relatively squat; and the much smaller (but not very high) Leicester is essentially a vertical item—a baby skyscraper. Which, maybe, is ready to infer something about the usefulness, the limitations and the virtues of an octagonal *parti.*

But, this aside, at Leicester the diagonal corner is an extremely active participant in the stereometry of the building. It is one in a series of eight highly emphatic planes; while, at the Economist and the Prudential the diagonal is never much more than the anomalous hiatus in a highly advertized rectilinear grid. Indeed, at the Economist and the Prudential, one might feel that these corners could have been better presented as a *pregnant bulge,* meaning with some late nineteenth century version of a *François Premier* or Scottish Baronial *tourelle.*

Prudential Building, Boston, Paul Rudolph.

Economist Building, London, Alison and Peter Smithson.

So, for me, the Prudential and the Economist continue to be an embarrassment. They are too dumpy for a *parti* which belongs either to a pavilion or a tower; but, if this is to interpret a situation which seems to have rendered the Smithsons unduly genteel and Rudolph excessively garrulous, then now to contemplate the physically invigorating quality of the Leicester corner which is clearly predicated upon the direct antagonism of octagon and square.

For lower Leicester is square and rectilinear and upper Leicester (which provides no intimations of structure) is quite brazenly something else; and the mediation between these two arguments is then exhibited by that incredibly austere and abrupt support which, because it invades the geometry of the tower and because it presents a prominent diagonal on the vertical surface, is then enabled to collaborate with the diagonals of the plan.

To iterate: an immensely absorbing and provocative corner which is altogether the best of Stirling episodes until Stuttgart is appropriately unveiled. For this corner of Leicester will reward a long, very long, regard. It belongs to Viollet-le-Duc. It also belongs to the best English and American nineteenth century traditions. It is both difficult and great. It is

rough-tough and delicately gentle. It carries the memories of both William Butterfield and Frank Furness. Though scarcely to be analysed (do the words exist?), almost acrobatically, it is alert and intelligent.

So, my appraisal of the Sheffield-Berlin sequence and of the Leicester corner is intended to illustrate certain aspects of a repertory which are still without employment. As a potential urbanist Stirling patently deserves more than the repetitiveness of social housing—as at Runcorn or Lima. Then, it can only be surprising that Leicester (as visibly a small skyscraper as the *Wissenschaftzentrum* is a small town) has never resulted in the full scale tower which, logically, ought to have ensued. Also, it is even more of a calamity that Stirling, a very important connoisseur of furniture, has never been asked to design a house, or even an installation of furniture, at the ample scale to which he relates. And, no doubt, such are the misfortunes of being type cast, mostly as an architect of university buildings, museums and research institutes.

But, though one might enormously wish to see the little Stirling town, the big Stirling tower and the comprehensive Stirling house, one must now abandon fantasy for conclusion. Stirling is both a stubborn puritan and an eclectic hedonist; and though there should be no problem about this combination (historically it is highly Calvinist-Presbyterian and belongs to Holland, Scotland, New England), on the whole, the myopic vision of modern architecture invariably refused to imagine any such amalgam of austerity of principle and licentiousness of imagination. These two—I think very natural propensities—were thought never to be compatible; and so, except for very rare occasions, austerity of principle (morality?) is apt to come on like a wilted lettuce and licentiousness of imagination (aesthetics?) like a rampant weed.

Such might describe what threatens to become the architectural condition of the later twentieth century. The puritans will remain naively puritan (and easily corruptible?); while many of the rest will become the absurd debauchees of pleasure (the destiny assembled for them by Charles Jencks and Paolo Portoghesi?). And therefore, if one looks for an architecture of dialectic, an architecture related to the descent: Michelangelo, Vignola, Borromini, Corbu, Terragni, the present condition is *not* auspicious.

However, though the Gadarene Swine may be determined to charge, there will remain, of course, a *remnant*, to borrow from Stendhal there will remain *"the happy few."* These will be those who have always thought that modern architecture was an important and never a simplistic affair, those who are willing to concede both the vulgarization of a dazzlingly new approach to building and the absurdity inherent in the pretensions which belonged to this approach. So, perhaps, a painfully small remnant this will be; and in no way will its mere existence be acceptable to the determinist technophiles, the populists and the proponents of neovernacular. These persons will find their satisfactions far away from any proclaimed doctrine of "*the happy few.*" *Elitists* themselves, they will insist—as ever—that any doctrine of "*the happy few*" must be inexcusable and arrogant.

Because of these highly predictable persons who will always, at the drop of a hat, scream *mandarin,* I shall not attempt a list of those who seem to belong to this Stendhalian elect, that *remnant* to which Stirling is also to be assigned. And this is for the further reason that, unlike many of the self-imagined elect, Stirling has never professed to be anything more than an architect preoccupied with 'the job.' Stirling has declined to assume any public role as either theorist or critic. He is careful to avoid involuted verbal *formulae.* He never talks about infrastructure, superstructure, syntactical structure, semantics or semiotics. He has no desire to utter extravagant pronouncements. He does not exhaust himself in pretentious manifestoes against the Positivist establishment. Instead, very privately—and to think about Voltaire's *Candide*—he has chosen to cultivate his own garden. Unlike the majority of architects, he is a cultural conservative, concerned with the concrete, rather than a would-be innovator, concerned with the abstract. A *Red Tory* rather than a *Blue Liberal,* he has never seemed quite to belong to the architectural politics of London. Notions of *avant garde* solidarity and participation have never much impinged upon his consciousness. He has never (so far as I know) felt 'alienated'. He prefers specific things to general ideas—though always with the understanding that specific things ("Hey, just take a look at *this* chair. It's almost Piranesian") may provide the illumination for general ideas. Which all belongs—maybe—to Edmund Burke's "*art of the possible,*" as it is certainly related to Candide's resolve only to cultivate a small and intimate property. But, of course, concerned with *the possible,* Stirling's private involvement with his Voltairean garden has been pursued with such intensity that, out of this little plot of land, he has elicited such extraordinary growths that, of necessity, they have rendered the whole enterprise notorious, acclaimed and public.

So, hence this book and hence this introduction. But, as I conclude my own part of this enterprise, in which I have correctly stressed Stirling's inherent privacy, I continue to think about those never to be forgotten and ambiguous lines of Auden, that:

> "Private faces in public places
> Are wiser and nicer
> Than public faces
> In private places"

C.R. : Ithaca, 1973; Roma, 1980; Venezia, 1982.

NOTES

1. The mention of Hardwick at so early a date, in present day terms, may seem to be almost unduly fashionable; but several people at Liverpool (including both Stirling and myself) had, by a combination of accidents, been obliged to spend several weeks in the vicinity of this great house which Sacheverell Sitwell has properly called the English Caprarola. '*Hardwick Hall more glass than wall*': Hardwick was witnessed by these persons mostly from below the escarpment—in the morning with the light shining through it; and, in the evening, with the light shining on it, when it then operates as a great, blazoned, reflective surface. But, for people who have spent 'time', almost like convicts, in the vicinity of this brilliant structure, who have been obliged endlessly to run around in the park and who have, thus, been enabled to collect from it an interminable anthology of ideas, Hardwick will always remain an indelible and a primary presence.
2. David Watkin, *Thomas Hope and the Neo-Classical Idea,* 1968. It was Stirling who first directed my attention to this book (as he later gave me Watkin's later piece, *Morality and Architecture,* 1977, which I then read avidly, and almost with approval, on a plane trip from Boston to New York). Myself believes that Watkin's Thomas Hope book may, quite possibly, have influenced something to do with Olivetti, Haslemere; but I also know that Stirling's and my own taste for Thomas Hope predated the appearance of this book by something like ten years.
3. "the glades and the galleries of the DEEPDENE" comes from Benjamin Disraeli's dedication of *Coningsby,* 1844. But the words he uses give something of the shimmer of an 1830's taste which may be relevant to Olivetti.
4. Preceeding 1949, I retain only two very vivid recollections of Stirling. In the first case, he is the sweeper up of the floor at Queen's Barracks, Perth, where the floor to be swept was infinitely long and the work almost approximated a labor of Hercules. The space (it could scarcely be called a room) was more than seven hundred feet in length; and, quite well, might have been erected to illustrate both the curvature of the earth and the implacable laws of perspective. It was enormous, a very big weaving shed; and it seemed to be a Kafka-like career, an inexplicable destiny to which Stirling had been consigned. Indeed, so protracted was the job, that he never seemed to approach us (we being Bill Kidd, Denis Owtram and myself) until the late afternoon which was about the time for, occasional escape to the Station Hotel, its Gothic corridors lined with *vitrines* enclosing the amassed displays of Queen Victoria's breakfast services.
Retrospectively, it is all a bit like an inferior version of Proust's account of the life of St. Loup at Doncières; and, even the hotel itself, a traditional stop for Victoria *en route* from Windsor to Balmoral, seemed to belong to a quasi-Proustian category. It was December (Oh, it's nothing now sir; but you should see in the summer, sir) and, at least that year, the Scottish winter light was brilliant and exhilarating.
So, after this, my second version of Stirling is of some kind of military Christmas tree or trophy. The encounter was in Mount Pleasant, Liverpool and himself was arranged *en parachutiste Ecossais.* Was it Black Watch or was it Argyll and Sutherland? And how to recall the profusion and the jingle-jangle? Epaulettes and red beret, sporran, kilt, dirk, skian dhu? In any case, it was an extreme exhibition of the whole anthology of military costume jewellery with which I was presented; and the spectacle was sparing of neither private expense nor public sentiment.
5. *Plucky Jim* I seem to remember is the title of an article about Stirling by Reyner Banham. It was published, I believe, in *The Architectural Review;* and, presumably, it is derived from the title of the Kingsley Amies novel *Lucky Jim* which was at one time considered to be *very* way-out.
6. The word 'contextual' and, even more, the word 'contextualist' are now grossly over employed. In their origin I think that they were Cornell studio words, useful about 1966. Were they Tom Schumacher's words or Stuart Cohen's? In any case, their present usage derives from the hyper-abundance of talk which these two have always engendered.
7. For instance, looking toward the Texas Medical Center from the upper floors of the Warwick Hotel.
8. Kenneth Frampton, *Modern Architecture: A Critical History,* London 1980, p. 264.

1950
Thesis: Liverpool University
School of Architecture
Community Centre and Town Centre Plan
for Newton Aycliffe

James Stirling

"Digging through the archives at the Stirling office, I came upon the original copy of his 1950 student thesis—a community center. Stylistically, it falls somewhere between the Royal Festival Hall and Le Corbusier's Marseilles Block. Both had set powerful directions for European architecture at that time. But, he doesn't let it go at that. There are peculiar, pointed exceptions to the prototypes.

"Like Marseilles, Stirling's thesis includes a roof-garden with mechanical equipment designed to function as roof furniture. But he rips off the sculptural disguise adopted by Le Corbusier, and fantasizes about the dynamic qualities of the exhaust stack, positioning his by now characteristic wind vane atop the building and strutting out the whole affair with guy wires like the equipment it is, rather than treating it as an abstract sculptural form.

"The building is also on *pilotis*, like Marseilles, but the planning reasserts connections to the ground in a manner Le Corbusier strenuously avoided, by the creation of a lounge-coffeeshop at the interface.

"Finally, like the Festival Hall, there is a sense of veneer, of the building as a thin container. But where Festival Hall's formal composition is gratuitous and ingratiating, the community center

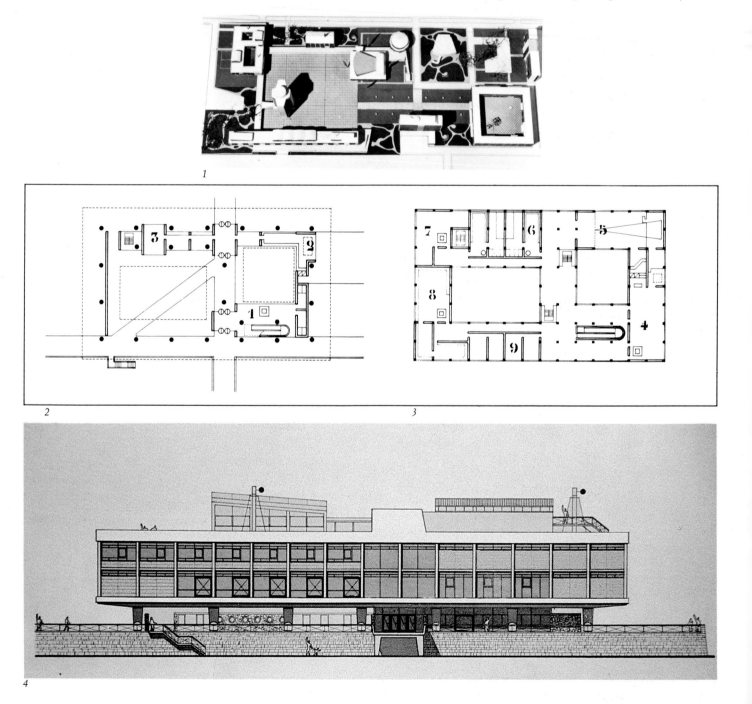

1

2   3

4

becomes airplane-like, with cross-braced wires and modular panels emphasizing the structural rigor of the design. No concessions whatever are made to the paunchy conventions of 'civilized' postwar Britain. It is, over all, an abrupt, rhetorical reply to the signal prototypes after the war. It says, 'I'm not having any,' without so much as a thank you."
C. Hodgetts, *Design Quarterly 100*

1. *Model of the new Town Centre.*
2. *Entrance level.*
3. *Main floor.*
4. *Plaza elevation.*
5. *Rear elevation.*

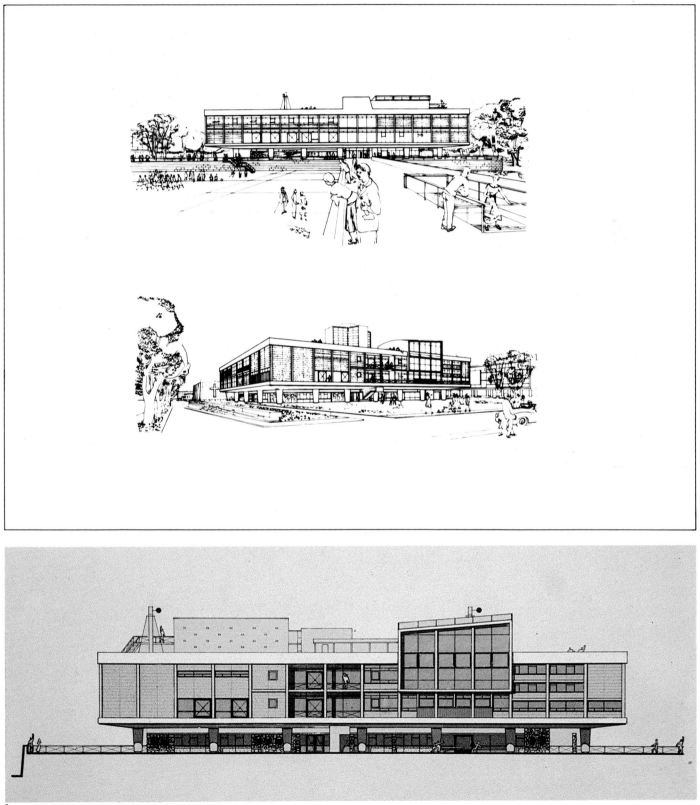

5

Thesis: Liverpool University School of Architecture, 1950

1950
Honan Competition
(local competition)

James Stirling

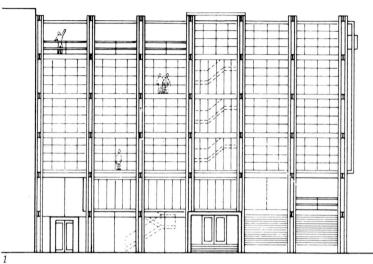

1

This project combines a Film Institute (auditorium and clubrooms) and floor space for professional offices with a separate street entrance. The glass covered foyers of the Film Institute are two stories high and club facilities are approached via a suspended gallery. The steel structure of the office building is positioned outside the facade, leaving the entire floor area free for partition changes and internal subdivision. The caretaker's flat at roof level has an adjoining garden terrace.

"As he himself observed, the Honan project was a reaction to and a rejection of his thesis. The two main parts are separated, even having distinctive entrances, and the six-storey steel-framed office block is a vertical exclamation mark adjacent to the lower film institute. The structural frame, which in his thesis was internal though expressed by the external bays, is externalized in the Honan office block—anticipating the much later Dorman Long project. The glass wall of the Honan block, with its small interval between mullions, anticipated the industrial glazing of later works from the Leicester University Engineering

Laboratories (1959-63) onwards, where small-scaled glazing emphasizes the skin/mesh quality of the exterior surface."
J. Jacobus, "James Stirling, Buildings and Projects, 1950-1974," *Hatje-Verlag,* 1975

1. *Entrance elevation.*
2. *Ground floor.*
3. *Second floor.*
4. *Typical office floor.*
5. *End elevation.*
6. *Section through auditorium, gallery, and offices.*

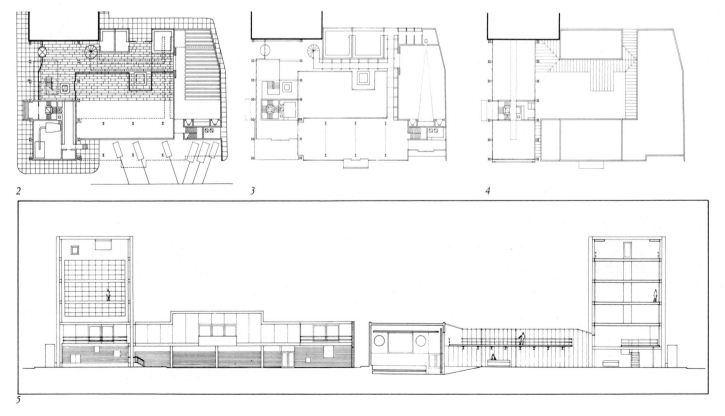

2

3

4

5

1951
ICA Furniture

James Stirling

This table was made by Stirling before he left Liverpool, and was used in his bed-sitting room in London; it was exhibited at the Institute of Contemporary Arts in 1951. Designed as a prototype coffee table, it could be packed and transported in a flat box, and assembled by the

purchaser without tools (an early example of knock-down furniture).

1. Plan.
2. Structural details.
3. Isometric.

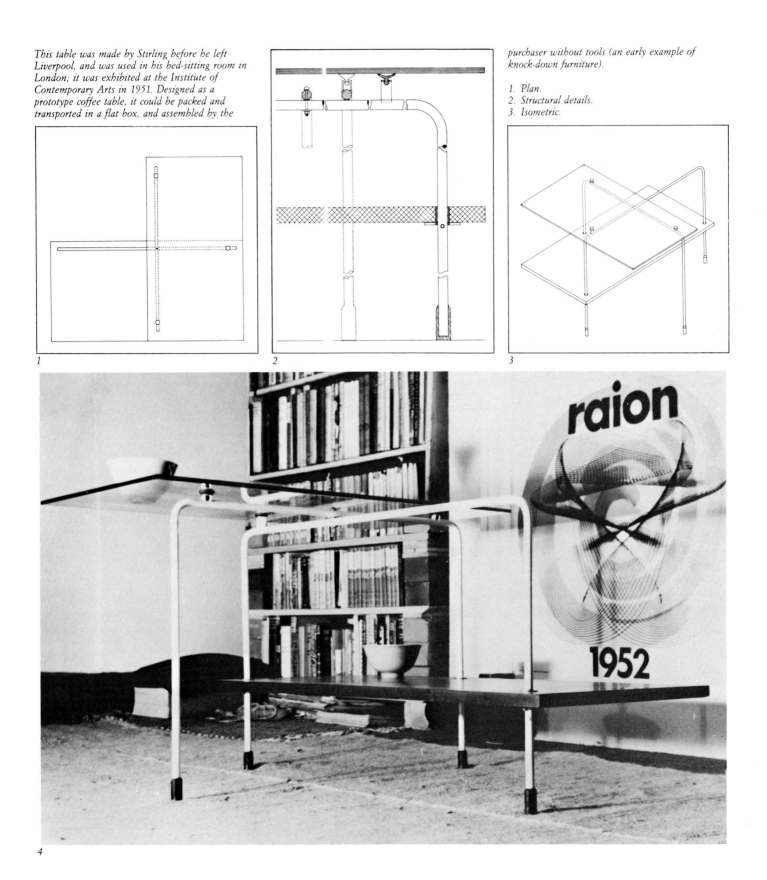

1

2

3

4

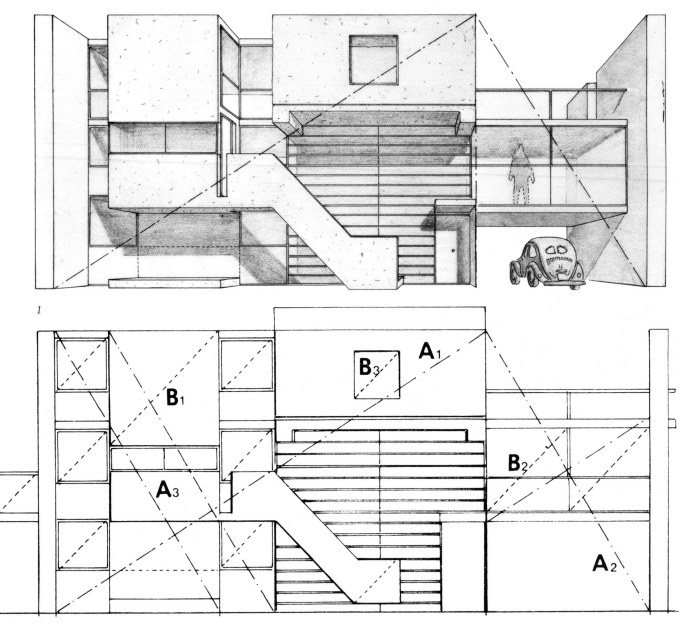

1

2

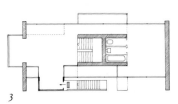

3

The boundary walls and central core were of structural brickwork. Kitchen-dining was at ground level. The middle floor was a large living space. Bedrooms were on the top floor. Contrary to the then current obsession with narrow crosswall planning, this house was arranged on a wide frontage.

"This scheme from the early 50s was for a single family house and was unashamedly and totally 'abstract'—there was no reference to anything earlier than the 20th century; in those days one believed that contemporary design could do it all."

JS, Lecture 81

1. *Perspective*
2. *Proportional study*
3. *Middle floor plan*

1951
Stiff dom-ino housing

James Stirling

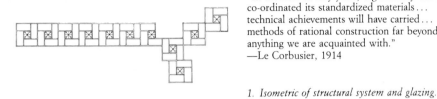

"In the next twenty years, big industry will have
co-ordinated its standardized materials...
technical achievements will have carried...
methods of rational construction far beyond
anything we are acquainted with."
—Le Corbusier, 1914

1. Isometric of structural system and glazing.

1

1952
Poole Technical College
(national competition)

James Stirling

"In the project for Poole Technical College I was beginning to react to my thesis and schooling in the principles of 'Towards a New Architecture,' although I still felt the last significant architecture was the white masterpieces of the 20s and 30s. The problem now, however, was to move to the next stage, which I saw as extending the range and the clientele of modern architecture; beyond luxury villas and apartments to public buildings of low cost (particularly relevant here, as, unlike other European countries, our rich seemed notoriously ill-disposed towards modernism).

"In this situation of expediency a principle of the new architecture which had to be changed was the excessive circulation and compromised room usage that is inherent in the free plan. Materials also had to change; the white rendering of Villa Garche or Tugendhat was never structurally relevant or even appropriate, as an external finish in this country. Brick is our traditional low cost material and, in the design for Poole, it was used as the external veneer to the high block; window openings being located according to the type of room and their size and shape determined by the room usage. However, the r.c. frame showed through indicating that the external surface was not structural. The high block accommodated staff rooms and offices over a canteen and social rooms, and the lower block was an assembly hall over three gymnasiums. There was the necessity to rethink the role of circulation (corridors, lifts, staircases, etc.) and to restate it as the dynamic and motivating element of the building. It was essential to create not merely corridors in the institutional sense but to construct something of fundamental organizational significance, like an armature or skeleton on to which rooms fastened, allowing them to become again private spaces, separate from circulation and movement."
JS, *RIBA Journal,* May 1965

"Brick has been used as the facing material for the building. It has not been expressed as 'infilling' to a frame structure, nor has it been expressed as

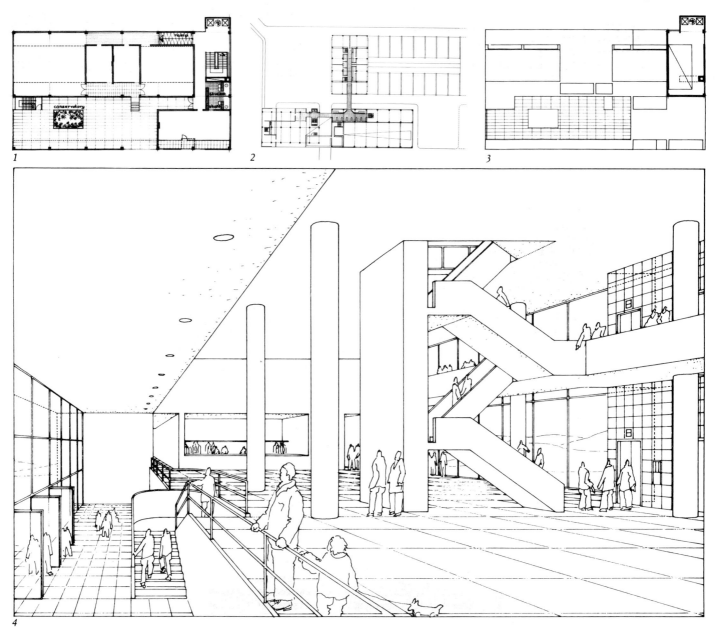

1   2   3

4

structural wall, but rather as a 'skin' clothing the facade. We have become accustomed to the expression of the Georgian facade, and tend to forget that this pattern is only logical where the wall is structural (the spaces between the windows being, in fact, piers). To continue this tradition on a frame building would be illogical.... Now that

the facade is free from the dominating pattern of the frame, window sizes can be varied according to the amount of light required by the internal accommodation."

JS, (from the competition report)

1. *Top floor of tower.*
2. *Second floor of complex.*
3. *Roof terrace.*
4. *Section.*
5. *Section.*
6. *Elevation towards Poole harbor.*
7, 8. *First and second stages of complex.*

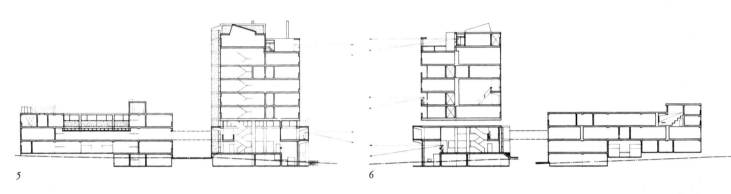

5   6

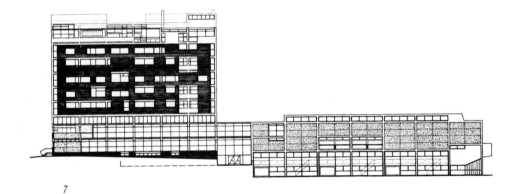

7

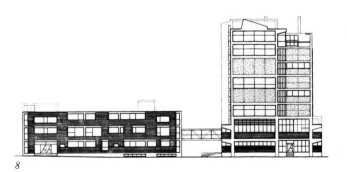

8

1953
Sheffield University
(national competition)

James Stirling, Alan Cordingley

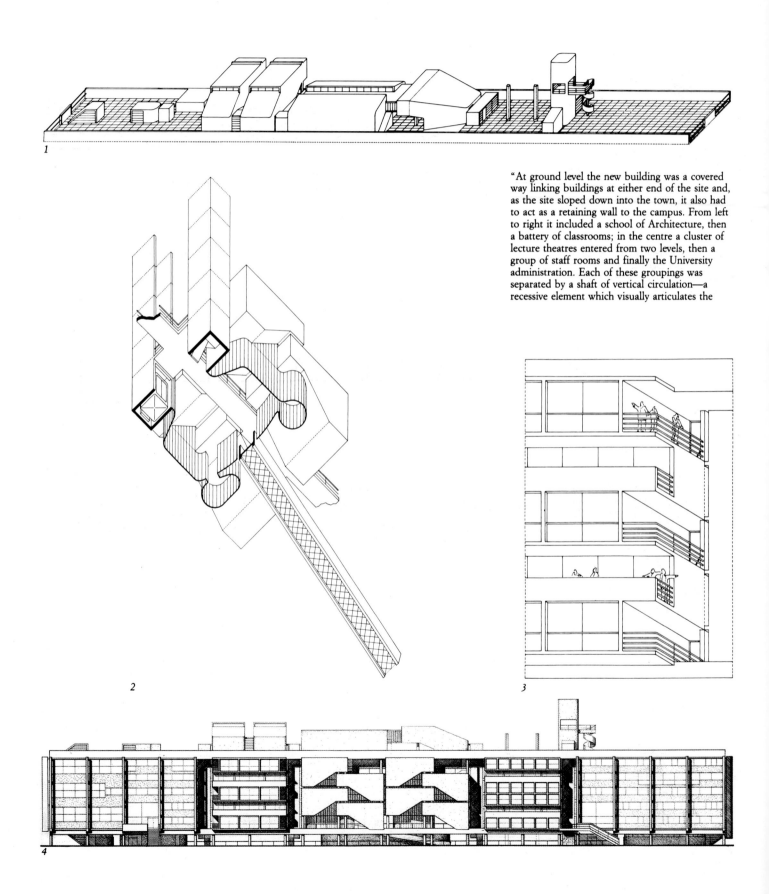

1

"At ground level the new building was a covered way linking buildings at either end of the site and, as the site sloped down into the town, it also had to act as a retaining wall to the campus. From left to right it included a school of Architecture, then a battery of classrooms; in the centre a cluster of lecture theatres entered from two levels, then a group of staff rooms and finally the University administration. Each of these groupings was separated by a shaft of vertical circulation—a recessive element which visually articulates the

2

3

4

5

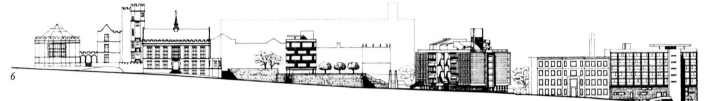

6

different types of accommodation. The horizontal circulation was regarded as a spine or driving axle on to which rooms were connected, like a mechanised assembly. The planning of spaces and rooms was secondary to the creation of a circulatory system."

"Several of the elements which appear in the scheme are put together in differing ways in projects which came after—for instance the circulation armature, i.e. vertical shafts (lifts and staircases) and the corridors as galleries. The approach ramp to entrance lobbies and the sloping undercut to lecture theatres also re-appear in later projects; as does the free-form glazing wall, which in this instance wraps around the space of the principal receiving area."
JS, *RIBA Journal,* May 1965

1. *Roof terrace with lecture theater.*
2. *Axonometric up view of entrance hall.*
3. *Perspective of seminar rooms.*
4. *Elevation towards campus and existing buildings.*
5. *Site plan.*
6. *View from road with existing and new buildings.*
7. *Entrance level.*
8–12. *End elevation and cross sections.*

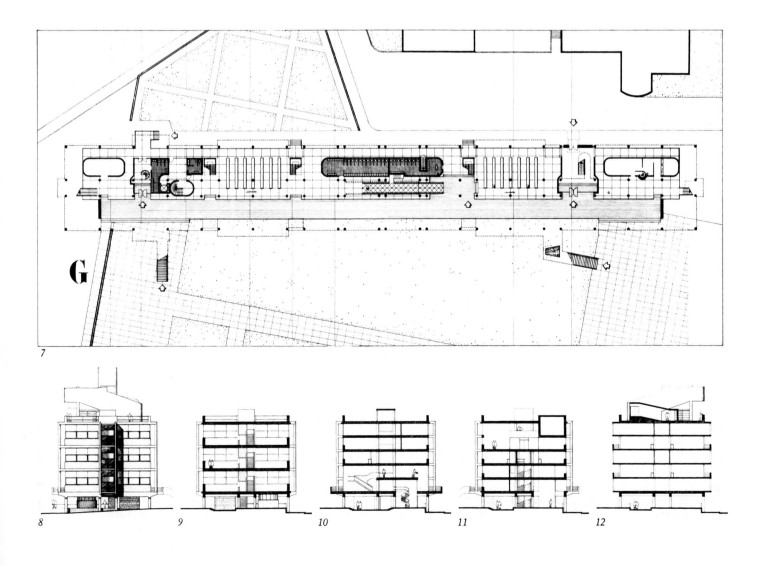

G

7

8   9   10   11   12

1. *Elevation of lecture halls.*
2. *Second floor.*
3. *Third floor.*
4. *Fifth floor.*
5. *Roof plan.*
6–10. *Sections and end elevation.*

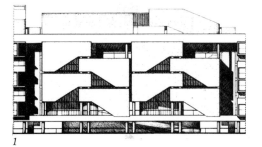

1

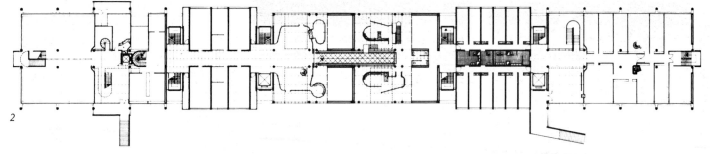

2

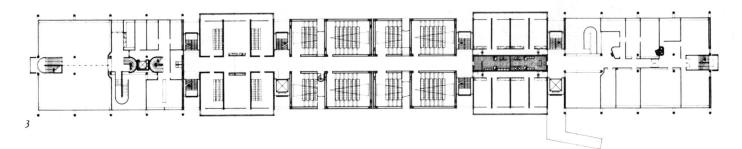

3

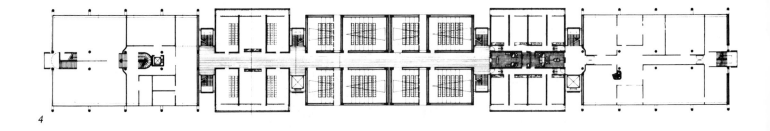

4

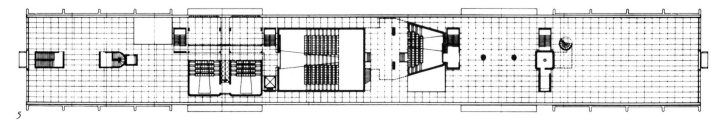

5

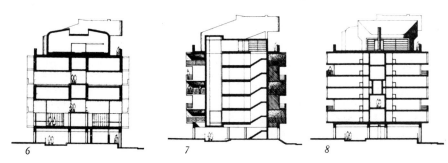

6

7

8

9

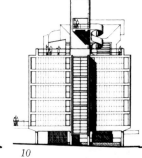

10

Sheffield University, 1953

1953
House in North London

James Stirling

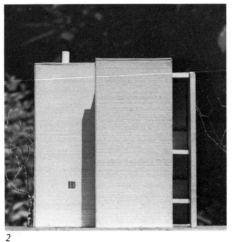

2

3

The plan, two squares offset from each other with the stair at the area of overlap, allowed glazing the full height of the house within the notches of the offset forms. Brick walls were to support timber joists and rafters. The internal faces of the brick walls were to be painted white, as were the plaster

partitions. The project was developed further as a unit for terraced housing.

1–3. Street, side and garden views of model.
4. Axonometric of main floor.

"The site was a left-over corner plot surrounded by acres of suburbia, entirely inter-war, jerry-built, semi-detached ribbon development. The application was rejected by the local authority as not being in keeping with the area!

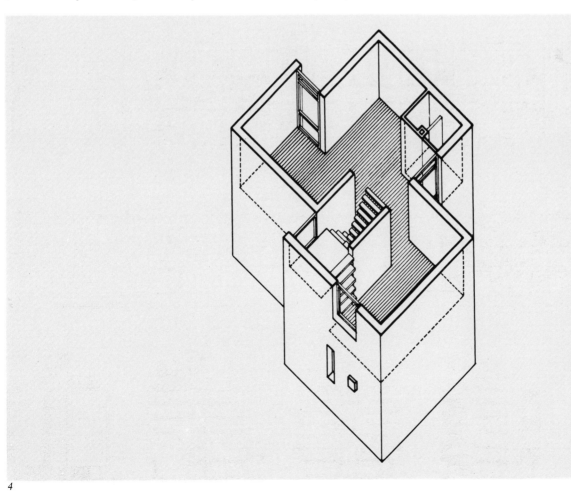

4

"The entire first floor is a single habitable area, and the ground floor, with the exception of the garage, is considered as one space. A 4-foot high counter unit divides the kitchen from the dining area. On the top floor are three bedrooms. The principal sources of daylight (three vertical windows the full height of the building) give an unequal distribution of light to the interior. The diagonal range of internal vision is 34 feet across the living room floor."

JS, *The Architect and Building News*, 7 January 1959

1. *Ground floor.*
2. *Main floor.*
3. *Bedroom floor.*
4. *Section.*
5. *Site plan.*

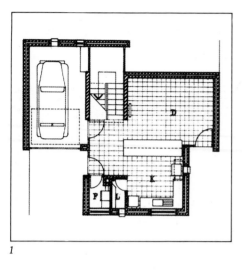

1

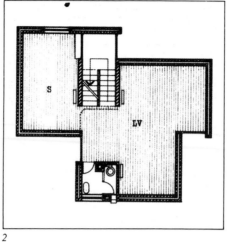

2

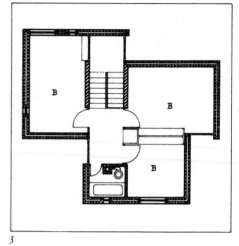

3

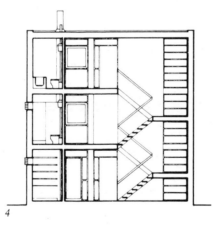

4

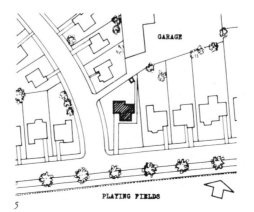

5

House in North London, 1953

1954
Woolton House

James Stirling

This house was to be sited on sloping ground overlooking the south Lancashire plain. Three linear walls form two bays of different sizes (which will accommodate all minimum requirements in a house)—a wider dimension for the living, dining and kitchen areas, and narrower for the bedrooms. Library shelving is off the gallery in the upper height of the living area and this gallery provides access to a guest/study room.

The contractor started the foundations, got down two feet, and found six feet solid of compressed tin cans. So much for rural England! The building had to be abandoned.

1. *Section, ground and first floor plans.*
2. *Model, entrance side.*
3. *Model, view of roofs.*
4. *Perspective of living room and gallery.*

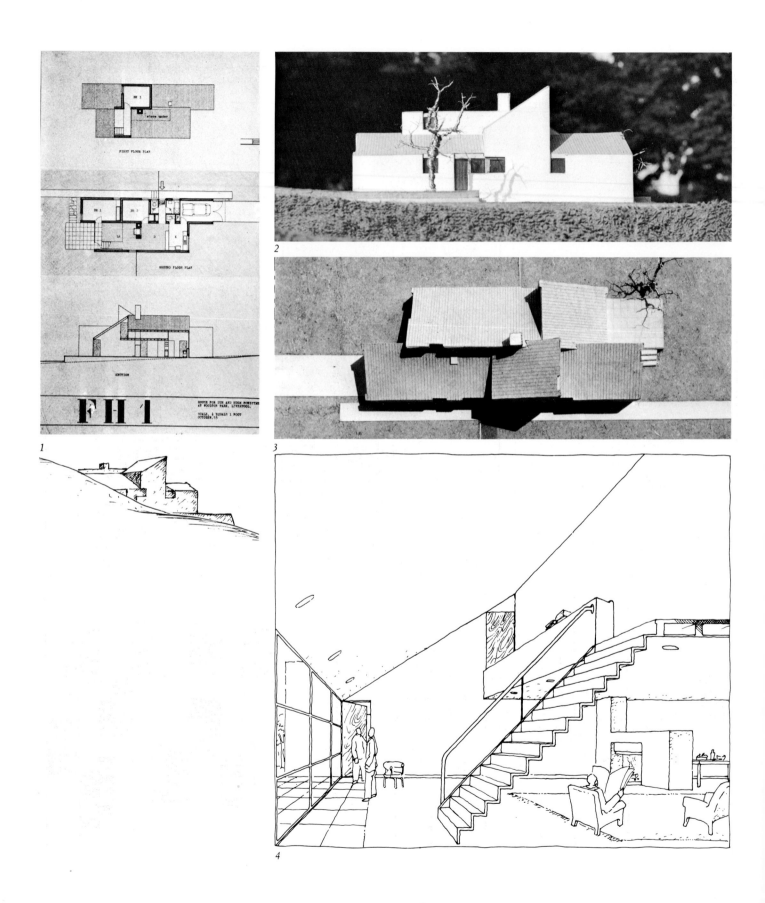

1

2

3

4

1955
Village Project
(a proposal for Team X CIAM)

James Stirling

A method for extending existing villages with unskilled labor. Structural walls could be of any load-bearing material, i.e., brick, stone, compacted earth, etc. Roofs could be of tile, thatch, slate, asbestos, corrugated iron. Rafters and floor joists were to be timber.

These extensions continue the linear form of English villages and would not be visually disruptive since the method of building and materials used would be similar to existing. It would also be possible to extend in depth behind the village street by making footways to groups of houses.

In principle the method comprises a strip of three structural walls making two internal bays of different widths. From the outer walls span lean-to-roofs. Plans could be adapted to sloping ground; half levels and upper floors could be accommodated. Dwellings could vary from small cottages to houses of above average size.

"This project was a theoretical study in how to extend the typical English Village. It was 'representational,' that is traditional, vernacular, and not dissimilar in appearance to High Street villages as they have existed since medieval times.

There is perhaps more 'system' though the building forms and their clustering are quite traditional, even folksy."
JS, Lecture, 81

1. Structural diagram.
2. Development in depth with pedestrian alleys.
3. Ground and second floor plans.

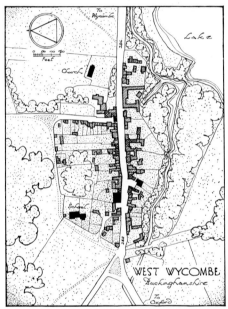

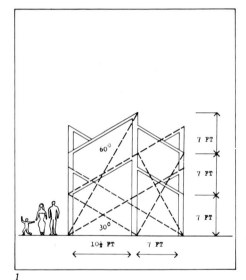

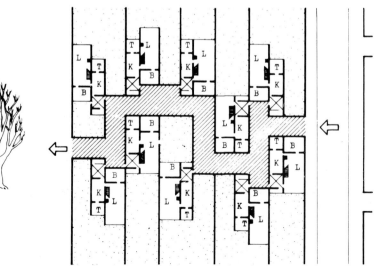

WEST WYCOMBE, Buckinghamshire (pop. 500). A roadside village of the simplest form. Buildings of irregular heights and irregular frontages facing straight on to the road with no gardens intervening. Slight bend about the middle of the street contains the views inwards; while the forking of the roads to the west, and the curving of the road to the east, contain the views outwards. Brick, half-timber, weather-boarding, plaster, colour wash; tiled roofs.

1

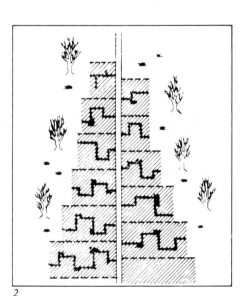

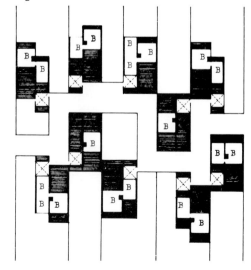

2

3

1. *Linear extension on level ground.*
2. *Linear extension-ground floor.*
3. *Second floor.*
4. *Linear extension on sloping ground.*
5. *Roof plans.*
6. *Typical village.*

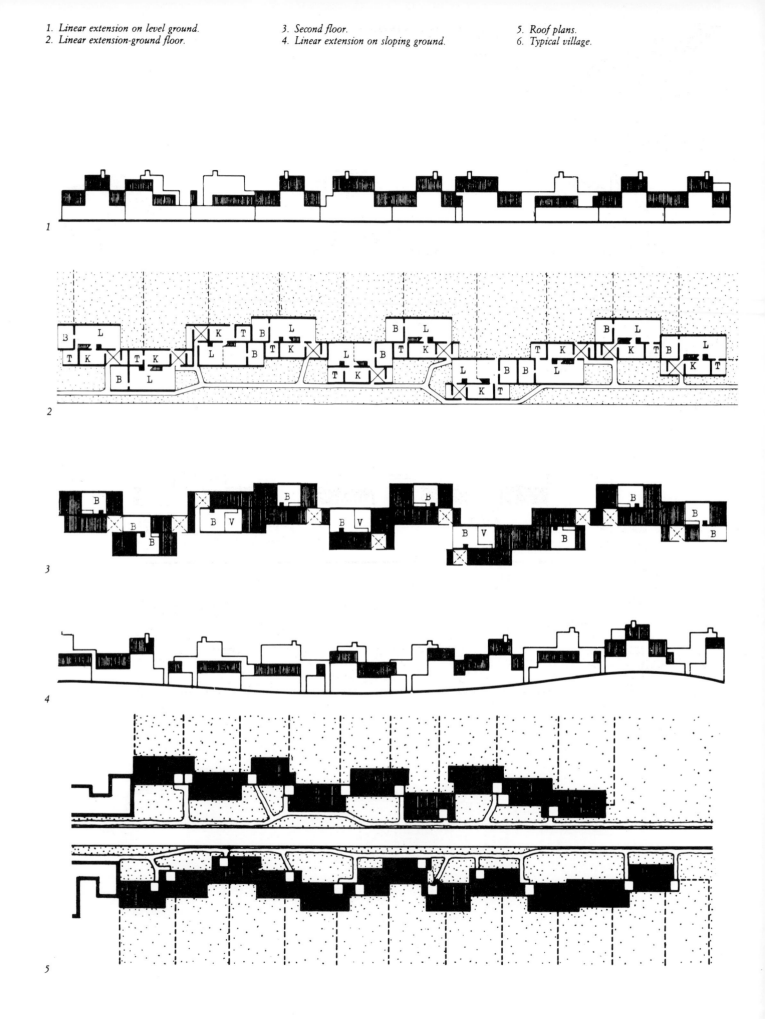

Village Project, 1955

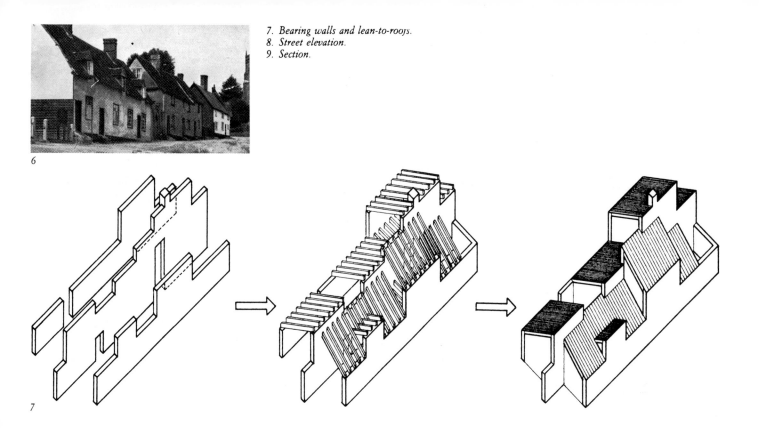

7. *Bearing walls and lean-to-roofs.*
8. *Street elevation.*
9. *Section.*

6

7

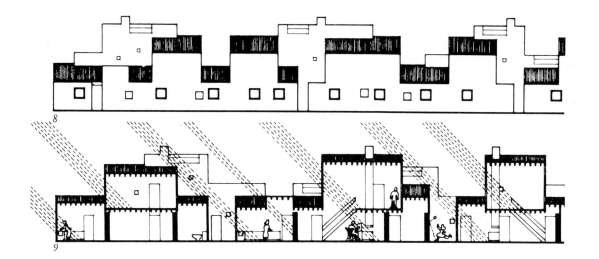

8

9

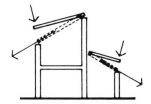

1. *Sections through level and sloping ground.*
2. *Ground plan (larger house).*
3. *Second floor (larger house).*
4. *Cottage plans—ground level.*
5. *Cottage plans—upper level.*

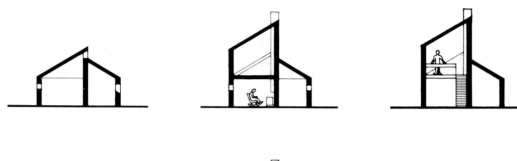

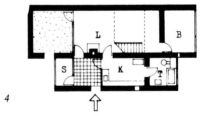

1

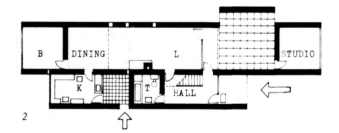

2

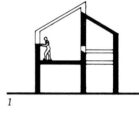

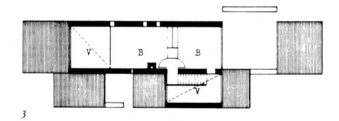

3

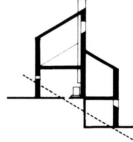

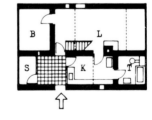

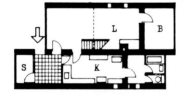

4

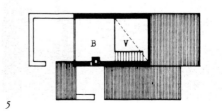

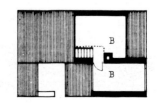

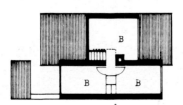

5

1956
House in the Chilterns

James Stirling, James Gowan

1. *Entrance level.*
2. *Main level.*
3. *Top level.*

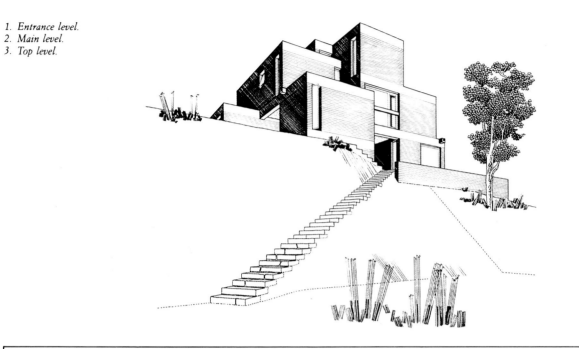

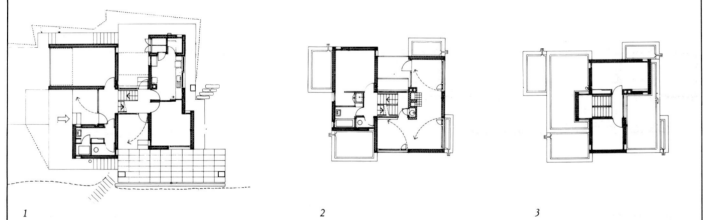

1   2   3

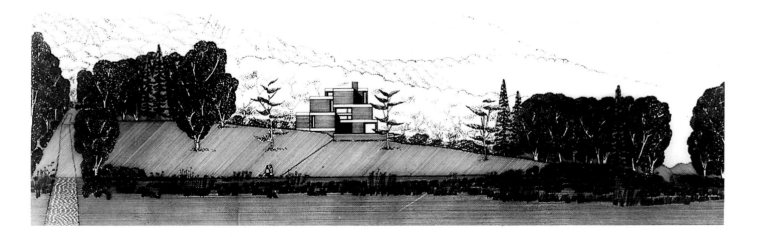

The three acre site was on the side of a steep and wooded hill at the edge of the Chilterns. The design was rejected as being "not suitable for the area." It was not considered appropriate for a rural setting, but, in fact, the modelling and appearance of the house was conditioned by ground sloping in two directions situated on the edge of a steep natural bank which runs across the site.

The pyramidal massing and disrupted periphery occurs as a result of split level planning on falling ground, and also by the client's request that maximum accommodation should be at ground level and only guest bedrooms on the top floor.

1–4. Elevations and sections.
5. Second proposal (flat site).

In the second proposal structural walls are peripheral with concrete beams spanning across free planned internal space to support the timber floor.

The structural wall is of red engineering bricks, with marking courses and other elements of various colors of ceramic bricks.

1

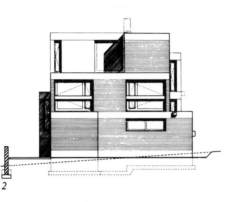

2

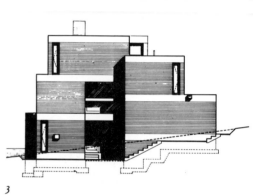

3

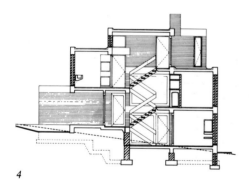

4

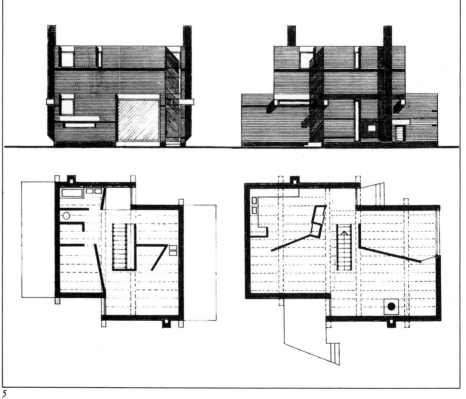

5

1956
House Studies

James Stirling, James Gowan

These were a series of academic exercises undertaken when the partnership was first formed in order to establish a working method. It was considered desirable to express separately the existence of each functioning space within the terms of the main discipline: results tended to be cluster assemblies. We decided that a more spontaneous, less intellectual use of materials, which directly solved each problem as it occurred, was likely to result in greater vitality. Thus the fabric might be an amalgam of different materials each chosen for a specific purpose.

1. Elevation and plans: House A.
2. Elevation and plans: House B.

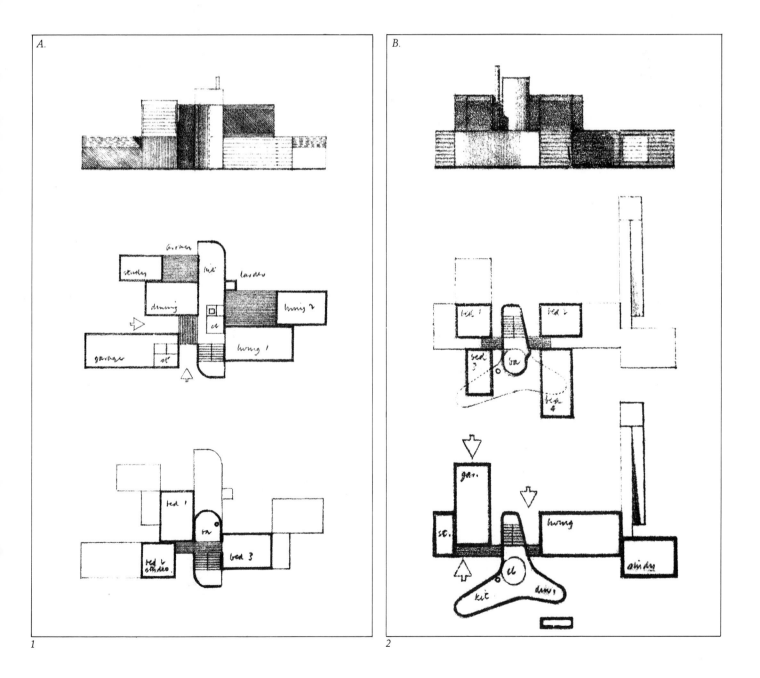

A.

B.

1

2

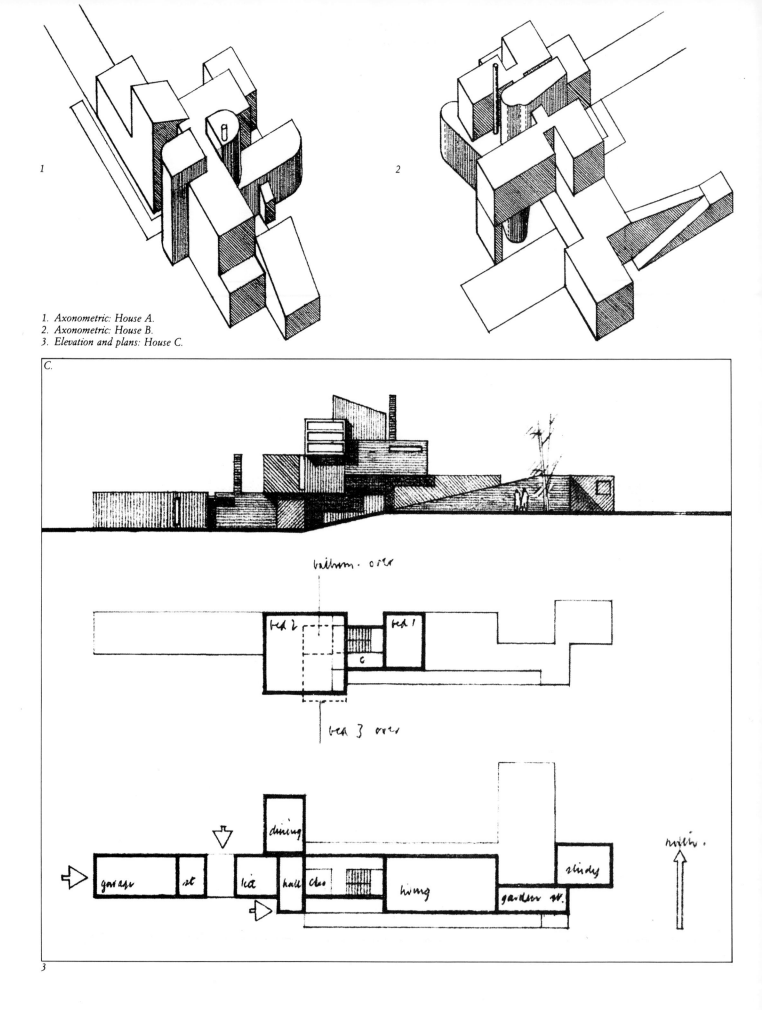

1. Axonometric: House A.
2. Axonometric: House B.
3. Elevation and plans: House C.

House Studies, 1956

1955/58
Ham Common Flats
(Near Richmond, Surrey)

James Stirling, James Gowan
David Walsby

The site was the garden of a Georgian house facing Ham Common, and its long narrow shape determined the layout. From both ends there was restricted road access and the grounds were laid out as communal lawns. The three-story terrace (18 flats) has an east-west orientation, the plans of individual flats being staggered on either side of a spine wall; this has the effect of projecting the living spaces towards the landscape and withdrawing the bedrooms into a recess. The flats (12) in the two-story pavillions (in the narrower part of the site) are approached through an entrance hall which has a suspended access gallery at first-floor level.

"If one is looking for a name to attach to him or stream to put him in, certainly the very last I would like to use is that which tended to be used when I first started becoming aware of his buildings, and that was brutalist. I remember reading a reference, I think by Ian Nairn, in the *Buildings of England,* Surrey Volume, referring to his Ham Common flats saying, rather ambivalently, but saying *it would be nice to see a bloodyminded style in England again*, and these Ham Common flats *were something that was on the way to this new bloodyminded style.*

"There was a feeling in the air that here was this big man somehow producing aggressive, extraordinary buildings that were sort of revolutionary; deliberately different and reacting and protesting and giving you terrific aesthetic shock that could be described by the word brutalist. Then I went out to Ham Common and was absolutely amazed. There I saw, what seemed to me, these exquisite, reticent, beautifully scaled, delicate, totally inoffensive, (in the nasty sense of the word), buildings which really were a pleasure and a delight to look at."
M. Girouard. © *Architectural Design Magazine,* London. AD 7/8 1980 'Stirling Gold'.

1. Section through 3 story apartments.
2. Site plan.

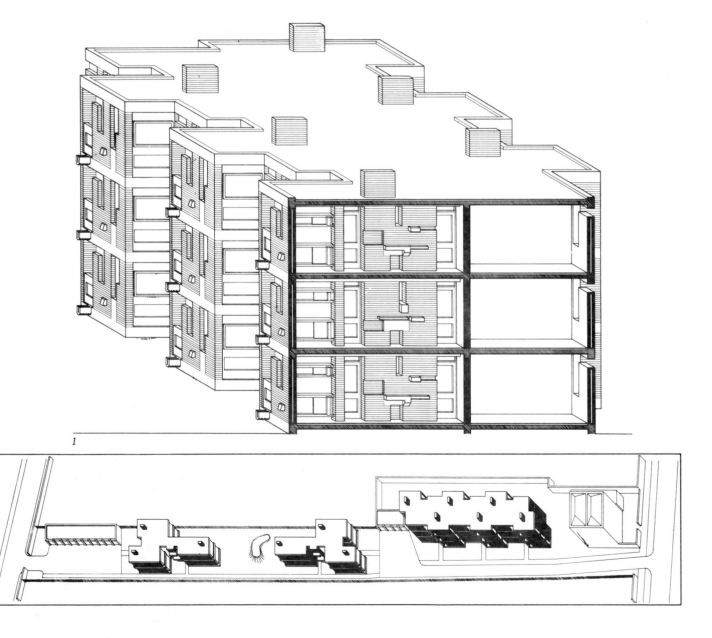

1

2

"In a somewhat obvious way Corbusier's *volte-face* with Jaoul provided Stirling with a source of empirical freedom. It legitimated the flats at Ham Common and the subsequent explorations of a brick vernacular. It was the mastery of brickwork which permitted the greater adventurousness of the later university buildings. The modernity which was sought within the tough discipline of brick cross-walls was then released when larger commissions permitted a freer approach, including the vital element of technological innovation. But what was learned during those largely preparatory years was more than a constructional understanding of brickwork. It was rather a matter of how to extract from a recalcitrant material the immaterial and abstract qualities of a weightless architecture, of an architecture formed in the mind. Form, and its manipulation, becomes the source of infinite possibilities."

R. Maxwell. © *Architectural Design* Special Profile, London. 'James Stirling', 1982.

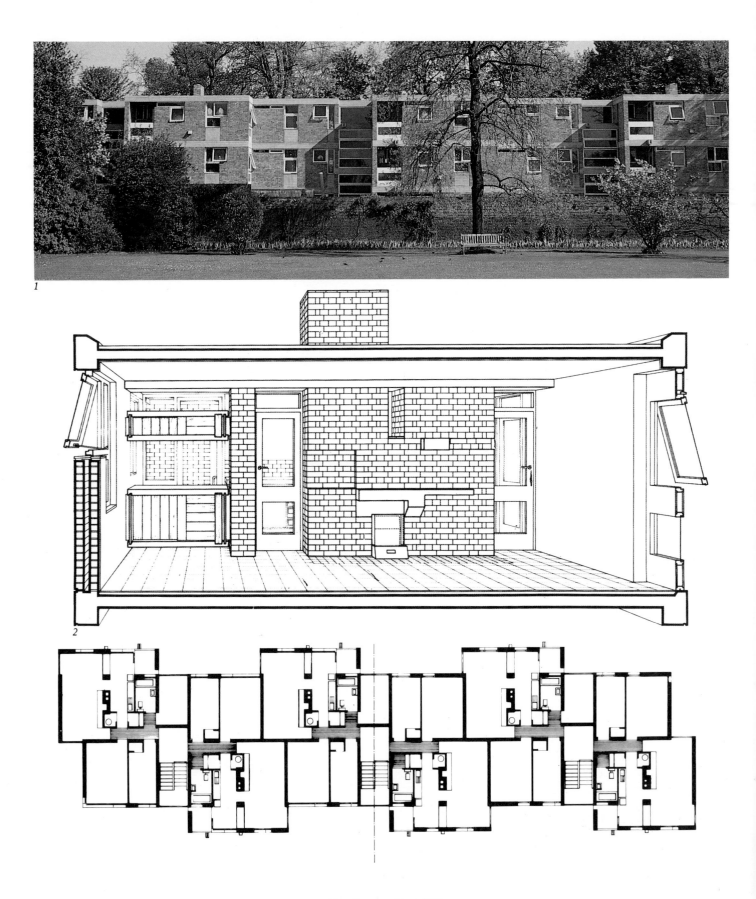

1

2

Ham Common Flats, 1955

1. *View of apartments from adjoining garden.*
2. *Living room in 3 story apartments.*
3. *Second and third floor plans.*
4. *Entrance hall in 2 story apartments.*
5. *Fireplace.*
6. *View down site.*

4

5

6

Ham Common Flats, 1955

"Langham House Close is like an encounter with some Kline paintings or Hecht-Hill-Lancaster films—a smart blow on the head with a carefully shaped blunt instrument. Though a pile of science and subtlety went into the design, the visual image it creates is cheerfully free of suavity."
R. Banham, *New Statesman*, 19 July 1958

1–3. External details.
4. Unbuilt proposal of further extension.
This proposal to extend the development comprised 18 maisonettes staggered about staircase cores. Crosswalls were of brick and east-west elevations were mainly of glass.

1

2

3

4

1956/58
Isle of Wight House (East Cowes)

James Stirling, James Gowan

The site had narrow frontage to the west, a near neighbor to the south, a tree line to the north and a golf course to the east. The design passed the planning authority after a "chilly reception," with the stipulation that the specified red brick be changed to a white sand-lime brick.

The plan has a service court and an atrium. The wings are occupied by living areas and bedrooms; the center by kitchen, bathroom, etc. The fireplace and boiler flues are carried on insitu r.c. beams. The outer lining is constructed of standard concrete drain pipes and the inner of precast refractory concrete units. The interspace is filled insitu with lime mortar.

1

"There is no distinction between indoor and outdoor finishes. And this is emphasized by the cross-views created everywhere by the schematic nature of the plan. Standing, for example, in one of the bedrooms, you look across the courtyard into the living-room through the window that corresponds exactly to your own, and beyond it into the garden through the far window; and standing in the living-room you do the same."
J.M. Richards, *Architects Journal*, 24 July 1958

1. *View into courtyard.*
2. *Entrance elevation.*

2

1. Boiler flue.
2. Plan in perspective.
3. Fireplace flue.
4. Section through courtyard.
5. Living room.
6. Site plan.
7. View through house.

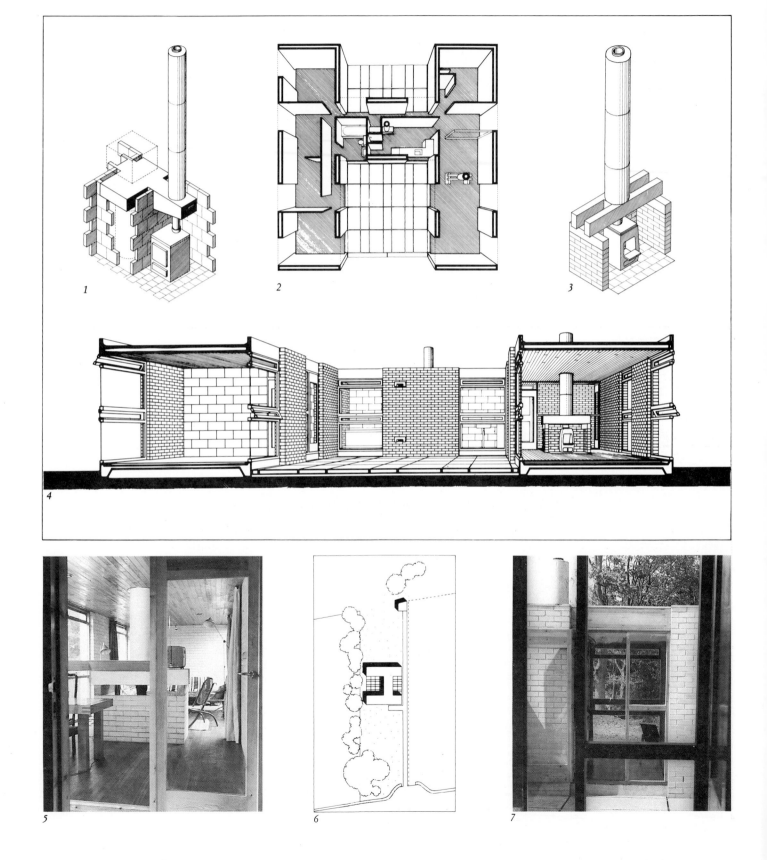

1

2

3

4

5

6

7

Isle of Wight House, 1956

1957/59
House Conversion
Kensington

James Stirling, James Gowan
David Gray

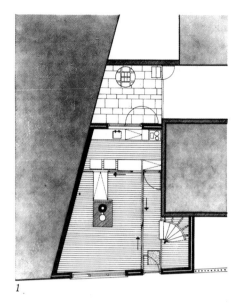

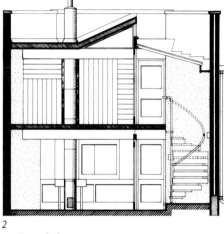

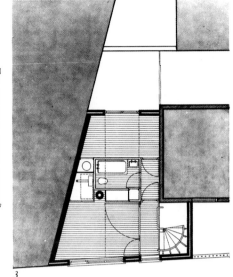

2
1. *Ground plan.*
2. *Section.*
3. *Bedroom plan.*
4. *Axonometric.*

1

3

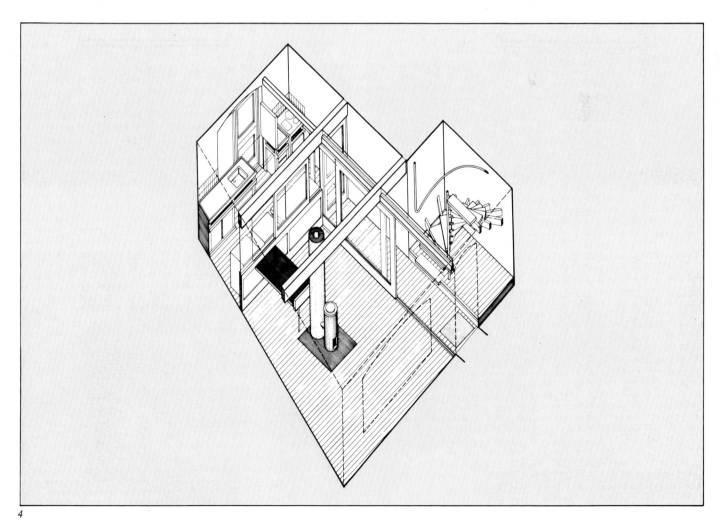

4

The planning of the internal spaces and moving partitions is intended to give two distinct living arrangements. When all the sliding screens and hinged flaps are in a closed position, the internal space is subdivided into a series of small rooms; but on certain occasions, such as when entertaining, the movable elements can be shifted into an open position and a completely 'free' plan results.

"I have found a house which makes more use of space than anything I know of, apart from a sputnik. It is a tiny home, covering under 700 sq. ft., which has been built in the backyard of a tall old house in Kensington. Because there was so little space available the architects were obliged to create it."
Alice Hope's Home Column,
The Daily Telegraph, 19 January 1960

1. *Stair at entry.*
2. *Stair at bedroom level.*
3. *Street elevation.*

1

2

3

House Conversion, 1957

1957
Expandable house

James Stirling, James Gowan

The house which grows with the family has often been attempted, usually by adding rooms and wings to an existing house. Historically the problem did not arise; houses were simply built to the anticipated maximum requirements. Today, because building is expensive, and servants almost unobtainable, dwellings are much smaller. These minimum houses, however, do not allow for the growth and change which form the pattern of family life.

The problem, then, is to build a house which can be added to in stages, which will appear an architectural entity at each step, and which is capable all its life of 100% efficiency, with no overcrowded or empty rooms.

For a single person or newly-married couple (A): there is a multi-purpose room with a service core. A spiral staircase leads to a room for storage, sleeping or study. All load-bearing walls are built

and form a walled garden.

When the children grow up and begin to leave home, the unused space becomes a self-contained room for sub-letting with kitchen and bathroom in the core (as in the first stage) and its own entrance.

1. First stage of building
2. Completed stage.

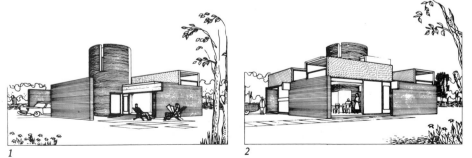

1   2

For a married couple with or without children (B): the second quarter has been developed as a bedroom and garage. The service equipment in the core comprises, as before (moving clockwise from the living-room door), w.c., boiler, linen-cupboard, cooker, sink, shower, and store.

As the needs of the original owners become less, more of the house can be sub-let and the new family can take over the process of expansion so that the house becomes a pair of semi-detached dwellings. The first floor remains with the original family and the garage can be used by either.

For family occupation (C): the kitchen in the core becomes a utility room—a washing machine replacing the cooker. There is a new kitchen separated from the dining-room by a counter unit, and a back door has been added. The first floor has been expanded.

All the children have left home and the parents' needs in retirement are again very simple. The growing new family takes over the first floor and another quarter of the ground floor. The fourth conversion comes when the house reverts to one-family occupation as in the fourth stage.

For the family at its largest (D): the house reaches its limit of expansion. The sitting-room increases in size and there are two large bedrooms on the ground floor. At each stage partition walls are simply used again in new positions.

At the third stage the spare room (for storage, sleeping or study) of the first stage is turned into a bathroom and clothes cupboard, and two small bedrooms for children are added. This upper floor remains with the original family until the third conversion.

1. Interior of completed house.

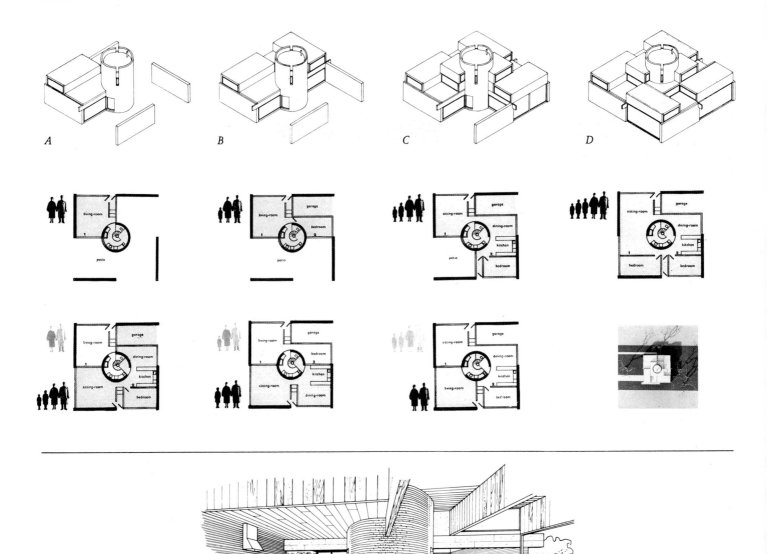

1

1957/59
Preston infill housing
(tender cost competition)

James Stirling, James Gowan
David Walsby

The character of a society is formed to a great extent by the buildings it inhabits, and we have tried to maintain the spirit of the alley, yard, street terraces that the new development is replacing and from which its occupiers have recently moved.

The monuments of worktown are the cotton mills, and from these we acquired the idiom of functional brick detailing; bull-nosed cills, splayed set backs, and brick on edge copings, and by using the local red Accrington engineering bricks we have tried to reiterate the brittle surface quality of the outsides of the mills.

"All are built, basically, of a yelping red Accrington brick, with white painted woodwork, and they come in three basic types. Down one side of the site is a terraced block of four-story flats, which strikes the eye as being rather perverse—particularly in the way in which changes of ground-level combine with windows set at different heights above the floors to give a switchback up-and-down rhythm that looks—repeat, *looks*—slackly wilful, whatever inner logic may underlie it.

"Then, on two of the other sides of the site, and helping to frame the inner play-court, are two terraces of three-storey, maisonettes-over–flats accommodation, with a small street-deck at first-floor level for access to the doors of the

1

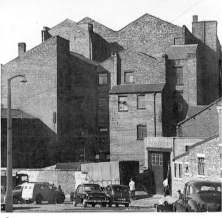

2

maisonettes. The deck is carried on the projecting kitchens of the flats below, and each kitchen structure is carried up, outside the deck, to form a coal-hole and dust-bin niche facing the door of the maisonette above. An analogous relationship of house to outhouse is fairly common in Victorian developments in this part of Lancashire, and these two terraces have the air of a vernacular tradition craftily re-assessed in terms of a society in transition.

"The third type of housing in the scheme is a cluster of almost cubic, two-story cottages (some, in fact, are flats) standing apart from the main rectangle of the site. They share the same hard-faced scarlet bricks and white woodwork as the rest of the development, but they add bands of dark blue engineering brick at floor and roof-slab levels, and precast lintels over the windows and doors. The colour-scheme is High Victorian, and—a few details aside—the whole effect is so Victorian that they could almost be re-named Bessemer Cottages and dropped down beside the railway anywhere in the North, and no one would notice."
R. Banham, *New Statesman*, 9 February 1962

1–2. Preston and typical warehouses.
3. Site plan.

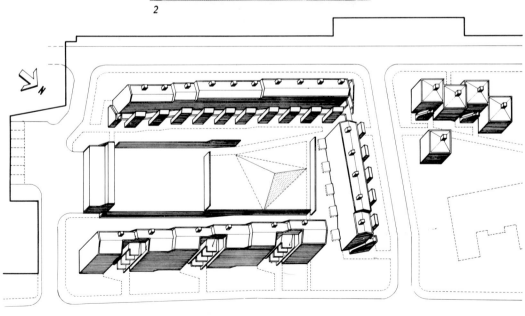

3

1. *Old people's housing.*
2. *Ramp access to terrace housing.*
3. *4-story apartment from courtyard.*
4. *Terraced housing.*
5. *4-story apartments—plan.*

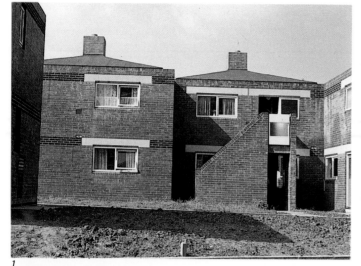

1

2

3

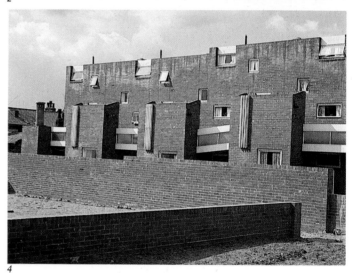

4

Preston infill housing, 1957

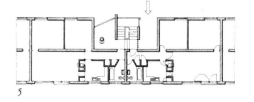

5

Preston infill housing, 1957

1. Access ramp.
2. 3-story terrace housing.

3. Section through ground floor apartment and maisonette above.

4. Elevated foot path.
5. Foot path and outhouses.

1

2

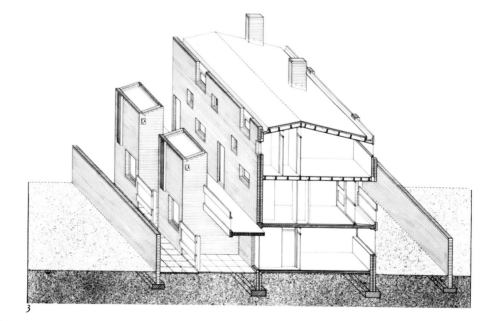

3

Preston infill housing, 1957

6. *Ground floor (1 bedroom apartment).*
7. *Second floor (entrance level of 2 bedroom maisonette).*

8. *Third floor.*

4

5

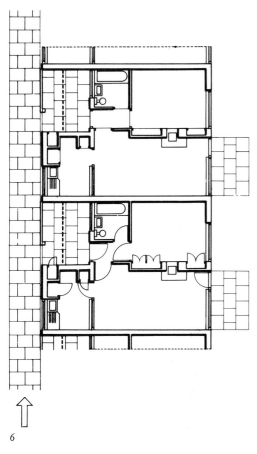

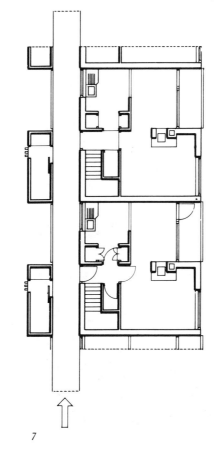

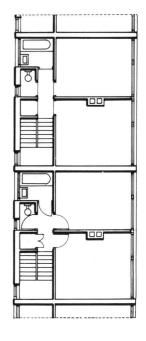

6

7

8

1. *Old people's housing from above.*
2. *Terraces from above. Existing and new housing.*
3. *Old people's housing—second floor.*

1

2

3

Preston infill housing, 1957

1958
Steel-mill cladding

James Stirling, James Gowan

A system of sheet-steel cladding panels to cover an already planned steel mill, the layout for the production line having been determined by the specialist engineers.

1. Part elevation of production plant.

1

1957
Three houses for B. Mavrolean
South Kensington (limited competition)

James Stirling, James Gowan

These three houses were for Basil Mavrolean (the Greek shipping magnate), his two sons and their families. The site opposite the town house of Sir Winston Churchill was flanked on either side by seven-story Victorian terraces.

The client required the houses to be independent but grouped privately with combined access to the street. They were not to exceed three stories in height. The accommodation required by each family was slightly different, but common to each was the

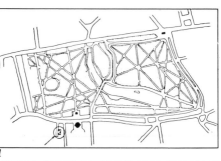

central top-lighted entrance hall which rises vertically through the house, also the servants' quarters which were situated in the roof.

External walls were veneered in white marble slabs, with exposed floor slabs of rough concrete. Windows were bronze and roofs of copper, treated chemically to prevent verdigris. Ultimately the L.C.C. decided that this type of development was of too low a density for the area.

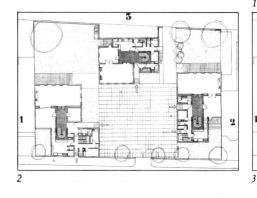

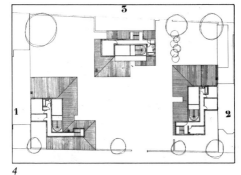

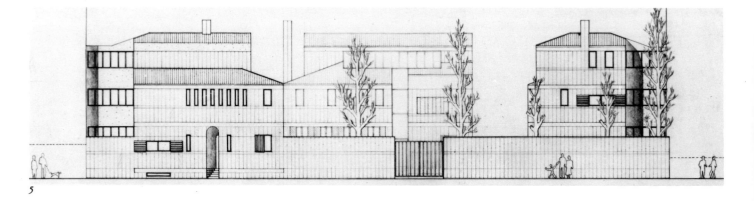

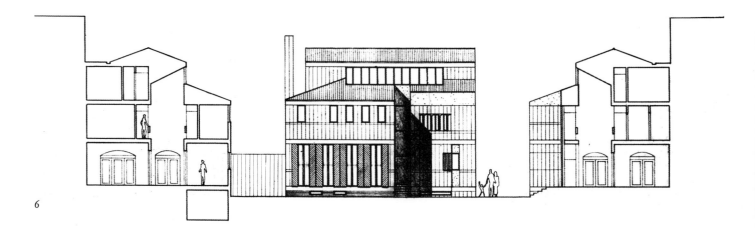

1. *Site in relation to Hyde Park.*
2. *Entrance level.*
3. *Second floor.*
4. *Attic level.*
5. *Street elevation.*
6. *Elevation of House 3, sections through Houses 1 & 2.*
7. *Elevation of House 1, section through House 3.*
8. *End elevation, House 3, with House 1 beyond.*
9. *Elevation, House 2.*

Three houses for B. Mavrolean, 1957

1958
Churchill College, Cambridge
(limited competition)

James Stirling, James Gowan
Kit Evans
Malcolm Higgs
David Gray

The open, flat and rural character of the site indicated that in designing a group of buildings as a residential College it was important to create an internal environment, 'private, enclosed and protected.'

As a first stage of building it was intended to complete an outer wall of College rooms, thus establishing the identity and territorial entity of the College. Student rooms in the outer wall are grouped about staircases which are entered off a cloister which encircles the court. The roof is also a walkway (the walls around a city) and a platform

overlooking the court, the gardens and sportsfields outside. Porticos to the street are entered on two sides of the College adjacent to outside bicycle bunkers. The second and third stage of residential buildings occur within the great court and these buildings are raised on stilts to retain the spaciousness of the court; the top floors have two-level studios with roof terraces.

The Master's house and Bursar's house are outside the walls of the great court but are connected to the College by cloistered walkways.

Family houses for College staff had to be positioned at the western end of the site and terraced maisonettes are entered from a garden court.

"A work of architecture is invariably an advertisement of a point of view. It is never either pure form or pure function; nor can it be simply a mixture of both; but always, either forcibly or feebly, it involves an act of judgement. It is an attitude taken up with regard to society, history, change, the nature of pleasure, and other matters quite extraneous to either technique or taste. Thus, a work of architecture, while always an

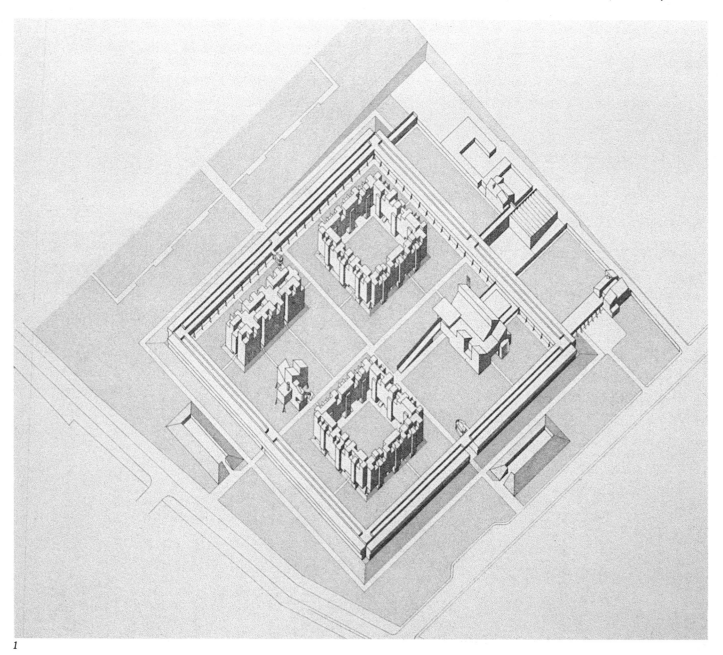

1

index to a state of mind, may quite often be construed as an illicit manifesto; and the typical work of modern architecture was until recently quite often to be interpreted in this way. Thinly disguised, it was a polemic about modernity; and for that reason it was apt to invoke all our sentiments about science, and mechanization, and the good society, and the necessity of planning, and the idea of progress, and the inexorable *zeitgeist*. Allegedly the building was innocent of all these overtones, but they were for all that a poetic medium which was the cause of half its appeal. Explicitly the building was the product of an empirical commonsense and a scientific handling of problems. But implicitly it pointed a moral. A criticism of custom, an assault upon the *status quo*, an exhortation to reform, it was put forward as an exemplary fragment of future order which had been interjected into present chaos.

"At a purely factual level, on a not very interesting site alongside the Madingly road a number of rooms of varying sizes and uses were to be disposed with some regard to convenience and some regard to order. At a more referential level these rooms were to accommodate and denote a College; and finally this College, a society animated by a common mystique, dedicated primarily to scientific pursuits, implicated with the name of a great and volatile Conservative statesman, was to stand in certain functional and symbolic relationships with the University, the country and the world.

"These problems are arranged in ascending order of complexity but are obviously inter-related at all points. Precisely how the site on Madingley road was to be exploited, how its suburban monotony was to be dispelled, how it was to be equipped with an artificial *genius loci*, all this quite clearly depended on how a College was to be denoted, how a common mystique was to be implied, whether an archetypal College could be deduced or whether a quintessence of the peculiar virtues of a Cambridge College could be distilled; and these questions in themselves became inextricably involved, and perhaps controlled, by the reasonable assumption that the buildings of a Churchill College should be in some way Churchillian-buildings perhaps big in scale, exuberant, simple, pugnacious, uncompromising and, to a degree, rhetorical.

"The scheme by Stirling and Gowan which introduces the adjective Churchillian with rather more abstracted connotations—by presenting the spectacle of an intransigent and very memorable building, conveniently leads from the problem of monument to the problem of collegiate form in general. On the whole there has been remarkable unanimity of opinion as to what a college should be. It seems to have been agreed that a college implies a courtyard and that the more courtyards a college possesses the more collegiate it is likely to become. Thus there has been in this competition what one is tempted to describe as an epidemic of claustrophilia; and, once infected by it, most competitors seem to have been satisfied to take

1. *Axonometric of completed college.*
2. *Partial elevation.*
3. *Model.*
4. *Site plan with gardens and playing fields.*

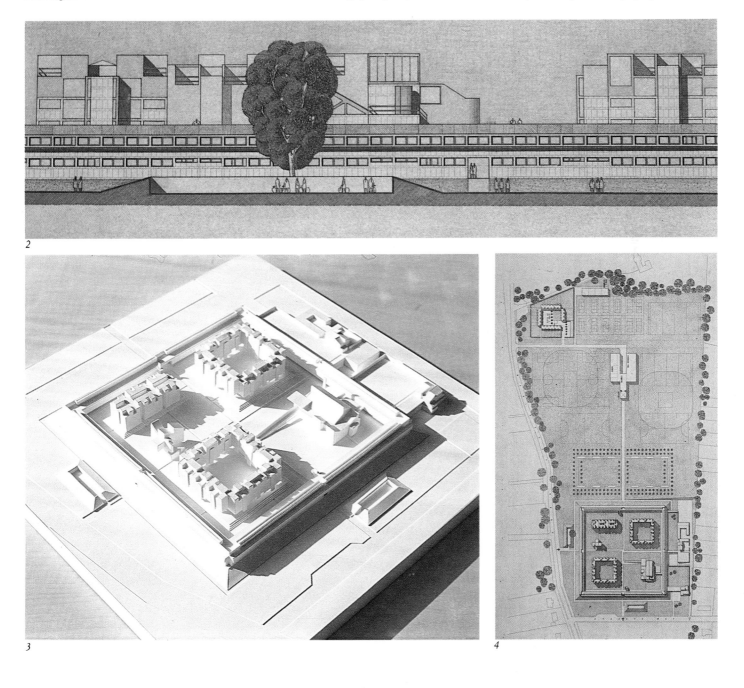

2

3

4

1. *Section, through court and dining halls.*
2. *Entrance level.*
3. *Axonometric of library.*

4. *Section through service yard and garden of Master's and Bursar's houses.*

5. *Second floor.*

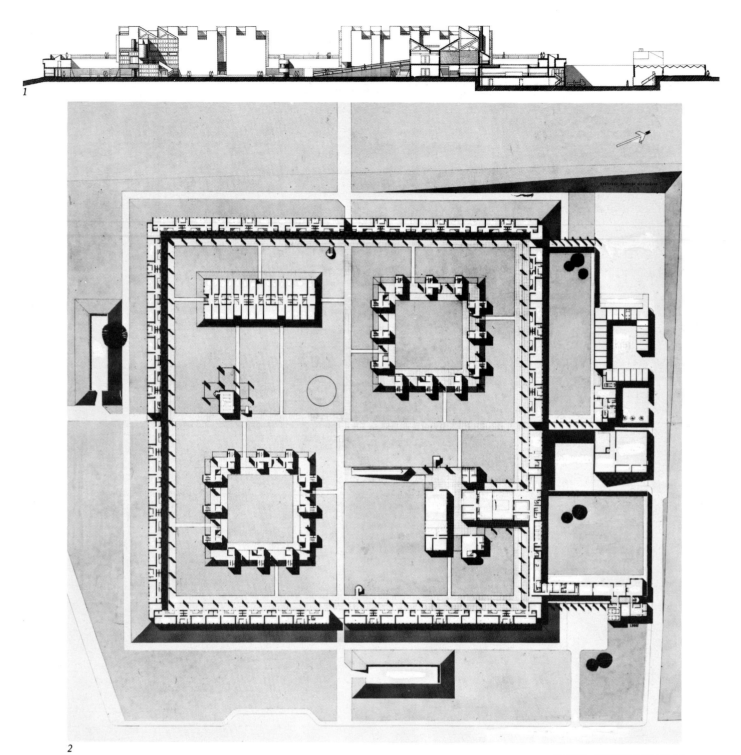

1

2

any number of courts, to press them into either complicated or casual relationship, to favour them all with an aroma of Cambridge (understood to be a demure charm), and to complete the whole with reminiscences of Le Corbusier or Scandinavia.

"But allowing that a College almost certainly should require a courtyard; and that this is a matter which, like the monumental issue, *ought* to be solved. Stirling and Gowan have perhaps come closer to a viable organization for colleges in general than have any other competitors. They have rejected the assumption that a college is simply a benign and womblike atmosphere and have insisted its form should correspond to some disposition which the mind can immediately digest. They have, perhaps somewhat obsessively, insisted that this means one courtyard and one courtyard only; but having done so they have provided a solution which as a thesis is impeccable.

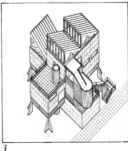

3

Churchill College, Cambridge, 1958

6. *Library elevation.*
7. *Library section.*

8. *Library plan (second floor).*

4

5

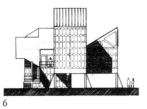

6

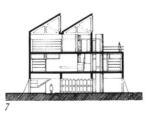

7

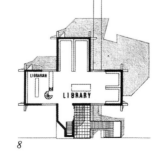

8

Churchill College, Cambridge, 1958

73

"The great problem of the college courtyard, when judged by other than picturesque criteria, is the intrusion into the enclosing wall surface of a variety of large elements, chapels, dining halls, libraries which are exceptionally difficult to bring into any relationship with the student sets which provide the basic unit of scale. Stirling and his partner present an exceptionally direct approach to this problem. In principle they discriminate between an enclosing wall of student rooms and, distributed within the space which is thus framed, a series of independent pavilions serving communal functions. The proposition is lucid and entirely convincing; but unfortunately this highly ideal classification has not received from its originators all the respect which it seems to deserve and they have, to some extent, violated their own hierarchy of significance by introducing within the courtyard, elements of the same functional value as those which they have used to enclose it.

"But, in spite of this unfortunate confusion of categories, the Stirling and Gowan scheme, as the courtyard gambit in the abstract, provides a model

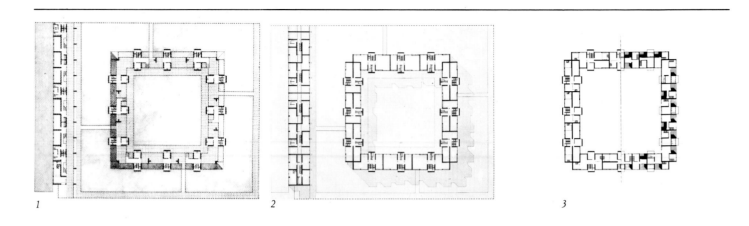

1   2   3

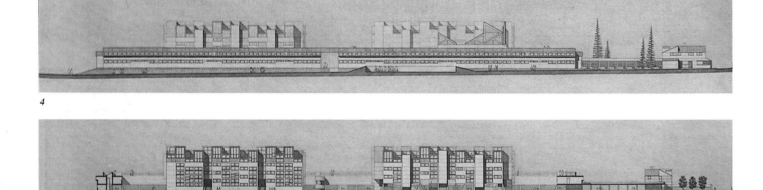

4

5

6   7   8   9   10

1. *Ground floor: outer wall and residential court.*
2. *Second floor: outer wall and residential court.*
3. *Top floor: residential court.*
4. *Entrance elevation.*
5. *Section through great court.*
6–10. *Plans and sections of students rooms and studios.*

which does deserve to be intensively studied and which will be extensively imitated.

"The Cambridge College, buttressed by, and interwoven with the fabric of a town, is for the most part always an interior. It never requires to present a continuous exterior to the world. It protrudes parts, exhibits a screen or a gate, confronts a landscape with a loggia; but it always avoids the difficulties of a complete, consistent, in the round suite of facades. In Churchill College this can scarcely be the case. The building stands free; and the problem presented is therefore infinitely more elaborate as in the case of the Gibbs building and the Palladian house in the English Park, there is a great deal to be said in these cases for a stiffening of the exterior so as to provide a definite volumetric field which will prevent all edges and definition becoming blurred. At least this is classical practice; and it is only to be expected that Stirling and Gowan, who seem to aspire to what Dr. Johnson called *'the grandeur of generality,'* should have adopted it."
C. Rowe, *The Cambridge Review,* 31 October, 1959

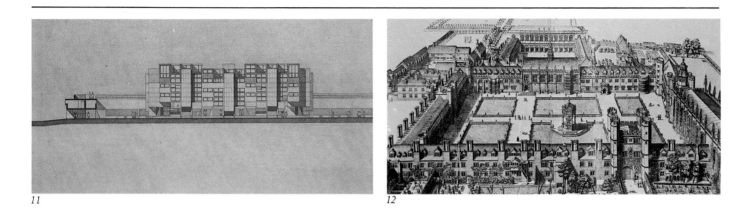

11

12

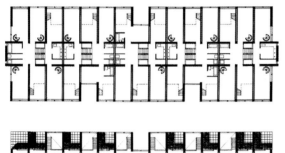

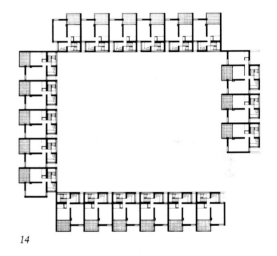

13

14

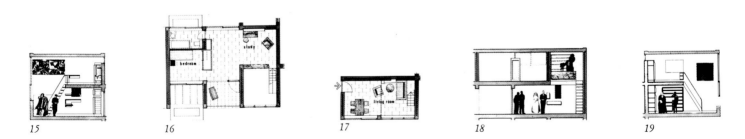

15   16   17   18   19

11. *Elevation of residential court.*
12. *Trinity College.*
13. *Upper floors of residential building with studios and terraces.*
14. *Staff housing.*
15–19. *Plans and sections of students rooms and studios.*

1958/61
School Assembly Hall, Camberwell
South London

James Stirling, James Gowan
Kenneth Davis

The school hall is situated on a bombed site adjacent to Brunswick Park Primary School, but it is separated from the school by a road which provides access to a small prefab estate. Ultimately these prefabs will be demolished and the road taken away, leaving the school playground opening onto the site of the new building.

The new building is a multi-purpose hall and activities which will take place include school assembly, gymnastics and games, and occasional use as separate classrooms. However, its main purpose is as a dining hall and kitchen, though it will also be used in the evenings and weekends as a social center for whist drives, theatricals, etc.

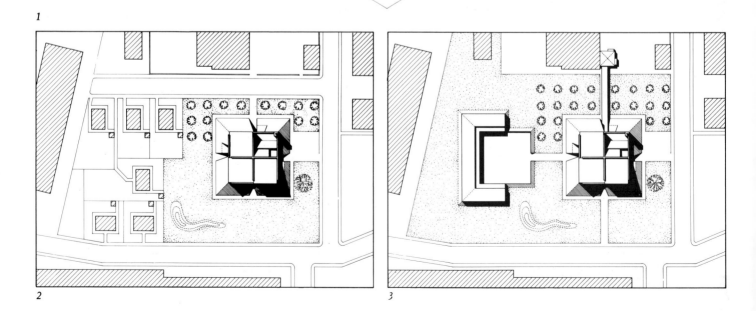

1

2

3

1. *Isometric showing roof trusses.*
2. *Site plan, first stage.*
3. *Site plan, second stage with additional classrooms.*
4. *Plan.*
5. *Studio window and earth bank.*
6. *Section through earth bank, retaining wall and studio wall.*
7. *Section.*

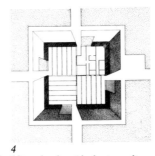

4

The neighborhood surrounding the hall is mainly residential but comprises a multitude of styles and building heights, varying from two-story Victorian to eleven-story LCC slab blocks. In these circumstances we thought it essential to integrate the new building closely with the immediate landscape; as a result the grass lawns around the hall rise up earth banks and partly engulf the building. In an effort to avoid competing in the adjoining building chaos, this solution if taken to its impractical extreme would have entailed burying the new building.

The plan is square and divided into quarters, two portions for the hall, one for the kitchen, and the

5

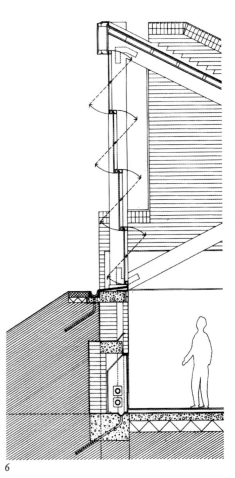

6

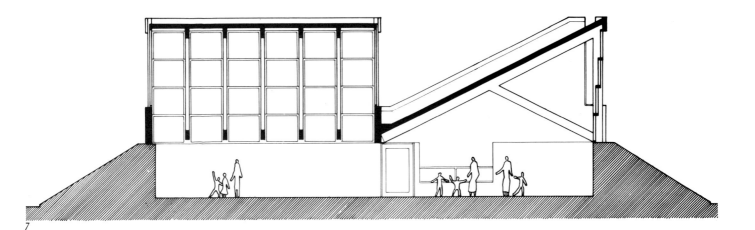

7

remaining quarter which has a flat roof for the stores, boiler house, etc. From the mid-point of the external retaining walls four RC beams span across the space onto a single column at the mid-point of the plan. Timber trusses which span between the retaining wall and the RC beams, support the roof which tilts up to let in light to the interior.

"Despite its physical neglect, buried in the particularly bleak housing estate behind Camberwell Road, it has worn very well architecturally. The modest school hall, like Churchill College uses a square plan divided into four smaller equal squares. Above three of these are steep monopitched rooflights with exposed trusses, rotated swastika fashion. The brick chimney completes the corner of the fourth square. The walls are built of white brickwork with occasional red-brick banding, and the building is connected to the ground by large grassy banks extending its geometry. This early use of decorative brick banding considerably predates the current fashion for its use by the 'post modernists.'"

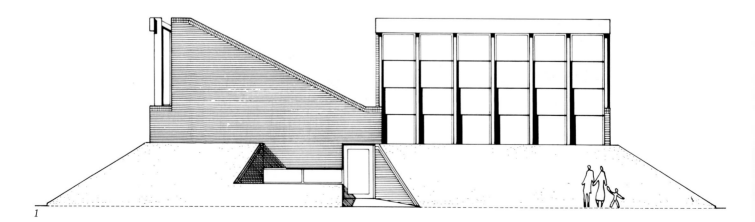

1

School Assembly Hall, Camberwell, 1958

E. Jones, C. Woodward, *The Architecture of London*, 1983

1. Elevation.
2. Exterior views.
3. Interior views.
4. Model of early scheme.

4

2

3

1959
Selwyn College
Cambridge

James Stirling, James Gowan

1

The new building (48 student apartments) was to be raised on a grass mound and act as a wall retaining the privacy of a fine garden for members of the College. All rooms would have overlooked this garden and beyond towards the Old College. On one side the wall was really a large, variously faceted window, indicating on the exterior the scale and location of the rooms within. This glazed screen was in sharp contrast with the almost windowless, backward steeping, brick walls at the rear. The irregular faceting permitted a variety of room shapes and sizes. The whole College site was to be enclosed by linear extensions of this garden-wall building.

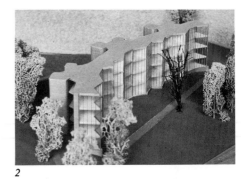

2

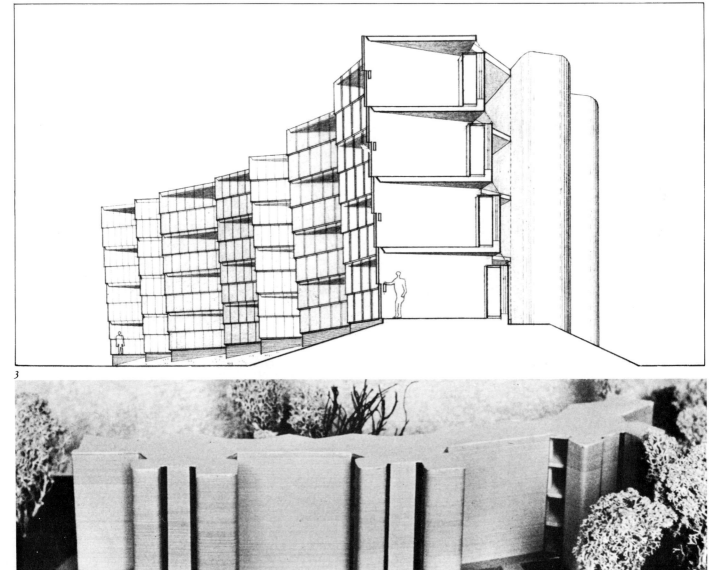

3

4

"The approach is morphological rather than methodological. Thus the profile and plan of Selwyn is as much to be accounted for by the invention of a type (i.e., stacked rooms, backed by a stair and elevator core) as it is determined by the technology adopted or alternatively by the topography of the site. In Selwyn, these last two are but the particular expression of the type, the former, seeking to exploit the cubistic reflectivity of glass and to emphasize through this, the articulation of the type in terms of a *static* service wall and a transparent *dynamic* facade: the latter, distorting the type so as to accomodate the plan to the irregular configuration of an existing college quadrangle."

K. Frampton, *Architecture and Urbanism,* Feb. 1975.

1. *Site plan.*
2. *Model—garden elevation.*
3. *Section.*
4. *Model—rear elevation.*
5. *Typical floor plan.*
6. *Sketch of existing College and new buildings.*
7. *End elevation.*

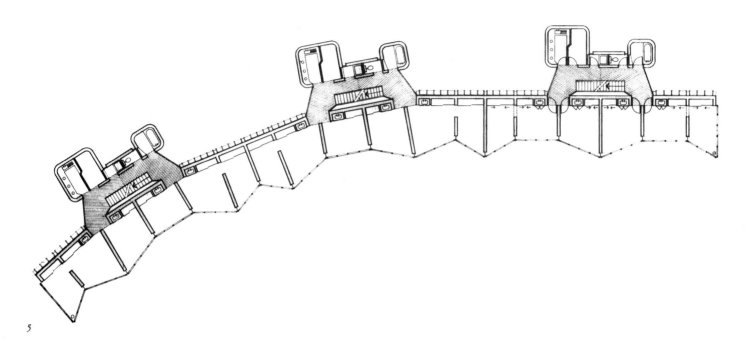

5

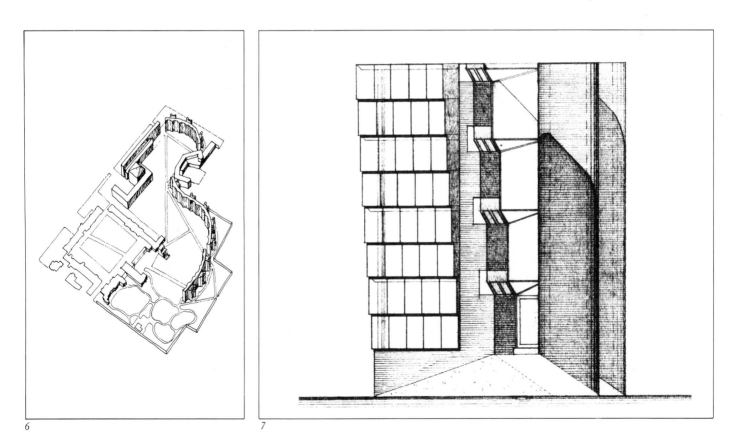

6

7

1959/63
Leicester University Engineering Building

James Stirling, James Gowan
Michael Wilford
Malcolm Higgs

Due to the smallness of the site for the first time the City allowed the University to build upwards and overlook the municipal park.

The Engineering Building comprises large ground-level workshops (heavy machinery), covering most of the available site, and a vertical ensemble consisting of office and laboratory towers, lecture theaters and lift and staircase shafts.

In the tower the form of room volumes and circulation shafts is articulated because of the unchanging nature of these spaces. The workshop instead is a non-transparent shed within which internal change can take place without external repercussion.

The aerodynamics and electrical workshops are raised above the boiler house and maintenance department and partially overhang a service road; this distribution permits vertical lifting of heavy

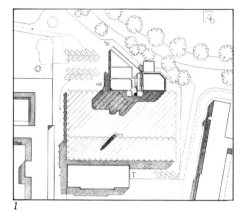

1

1. Site plan.
2. View from park—perspective.

machinery through the floor of these workshops. A similar arrangement is devised for the exchange of machinery through floor openings in the laboratories in the tower.

The roof of the workshops is an industrial one, turned diagonally across the plan to bring in north light; much of the detail design derives from this use of 45-degree angles.

The faculty required a large water tank to be supported 100 feet above ground (for pressure experiments in the hydraulics tank at ground level). The floors of administration and staff rooms are therefore carried by the structure necessary to support this tank at the top of the building.

The lecture theaters are positioned in the lower levels of the tower. The main entrance to the building is beneath the sloping underside of the large lecture theatre, which forms a portico. A ramp

2

Leicester University Engineering Building, 1959

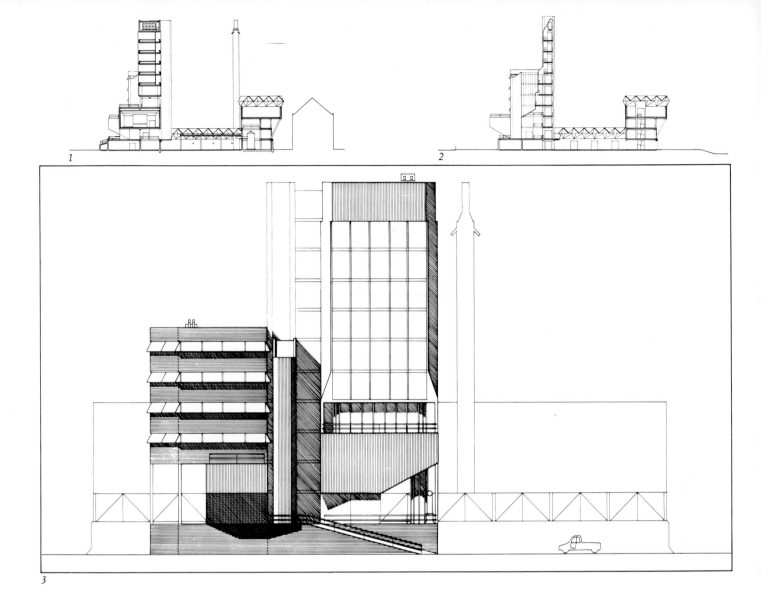

1

2

3

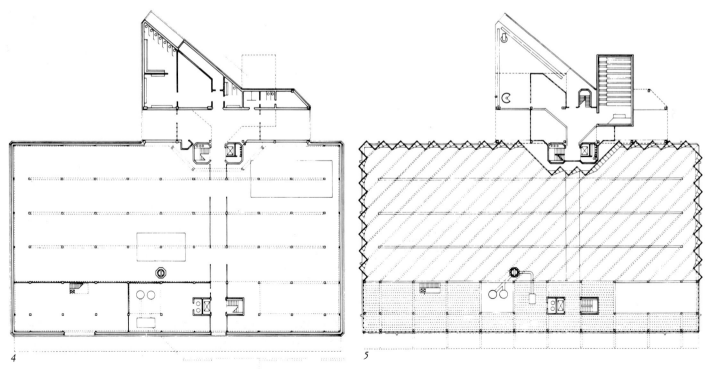

4

5

Leicester University Engineering Building, 1959

leads to the first floor entrance (on top of the podium) as well as to a spiral staircase which allows latecomers to enter the large lecture theater from the back.

The circulation lobbies in the tower decrease in size on each floor, to correspond with a lower density of occupation the higher you go in the building; hence

1. Section through entrance hall, lecture hall and offices, also through workshops.
2. Section through lobbies between stair and elevator towers and through workshops.
3. Elevation to park.
4. Ground floor.
5. Second floor with upper entrance.
6. Office tower, sixth-ninth floors.
7. Office and laboratories, fourth-seventh floors.
8. Axonometric.
9. Third floor.
10. View over workshops towards entrance.

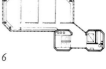

6

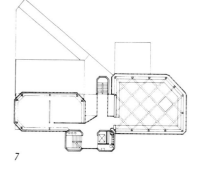

7

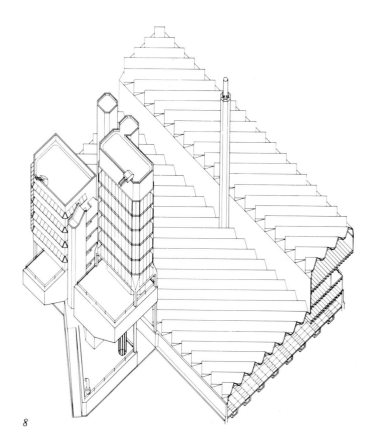

8

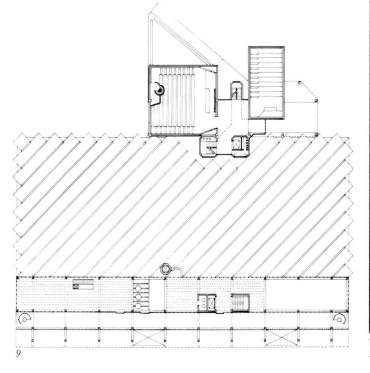

9

10

the tapering section of the glass skin sheathing these circulation lobbies.

As only one lift could be afforded in this low-cost building the bulk of student (250) movement is kept at ground level or uses staircases and ramps up to the fourth or fifth floors. The lift is used mainly by staff and secretaries going to the top floors in the building.

1. Laboratory tower.
2. Office tower.
3. Circulation diagram.
4. Entrance elevation.
5. Section through workshops, laboratories and lecture theater.
6. Workshop roof.
7. Lecture theatres.

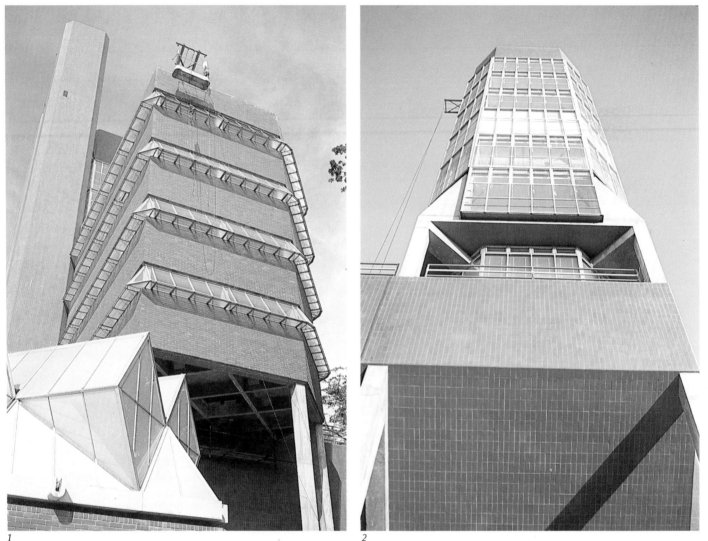

1

2

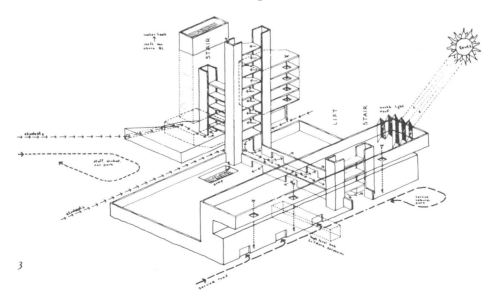

3

Leicester University Engineering Building, 1959

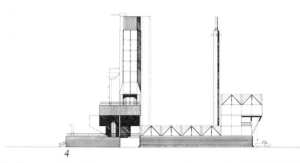

4

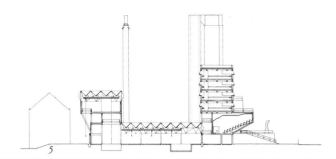

5

6

7

Leicester University Engineering Building, 1959

87

"After the New Brutalism the ability to shock became an accomplishment difficult to acquire. In the hysterical state that British architecture had worked itself into by this time, however, the quest could not be abandoned, and, in the engineering building at the University of Leicester by Stirling and Gowan, the profession was presented with its Frankenstein, amidst a concert of maidenish squeaks that have not yet died down. At the sight of this brown tiled totem, the blood ran, or rather was supposed to run, cold. Bizarre, strident, Gothic in the way that Butterfield was Gothic, the Leicester building is perhaps the most extreme example to date in modern British architecture of esthetic individualism run riot. The masochisms of its mannered form make the New Brutalism look cozy by comparison: it reaches, with the studied calculation of a Hammer films-effects man, into the repertoire of the hard Victorian ecclesiastical school of architects, translated superficially into a modern idiom in order to secure its teeth-on-edge effect. Like Butterfield's All Saints Church in Margaret Street (off Upper Regent Street), it deliberately assumes a basilisk persona. But what

Leicester University Engineering Building, 1959

have such whimsies to do with the needs of British universities today and in the future? Very little, one could submit, unless our society is so hooked in its most sophisticated spheres on this kind of historico-visual sensationalism that it cannot pursue its rational lines of enquiry without a surrounding environment that is fully turned on."
I. Brown, *Forum,* April 1972

"My first experience of Stirling was a fleeting visit to his and Gowan's engineering building at Leicester in 1968. I took against it because I saw it as old-style functionalism grossly overdone. The jutting Melnikov-style lecture theatres exposing their tilted bottoms, the exaggerated articulation of everything, and the vanity of trying to make positives out of things intrinsically negative. I was,

1. *Ground floor lobby.*
2. *Fourth floor lobby.*
3,4. *Upper entrance terrace.*
5. *Upper entrance lobby.*
6. *Lobby between towers.*
7. *Small lecture theatre.*
8. *Large lecture theatre.*

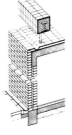

5

6

7

8

however, wrong. I was judging something as exhibitionism which was really the acting out of a deeply felt and studied thesis. Revisiting Leicester, I found the 'play' idea always coming uppermost. Here was an architect declaiming, fashioning a 'one off' rhetoric out of material anything but rhetorical; it was brilliant, arrogant play."
J. Summerson, *Architectural Review,* March 1983

"I first became aware of Leicester in 1964, while the shock waves of Kennedy's death were mingling with the growing anger of students and new tunes from the British Isles. It had the impact of a high speed auto collision, the seductive raunchiness of one of Fellini's sirens, the glow of moonlight on the Mississippi, the revolutionary glint of *Borstal Boy,* the semantic craziness of *Alice in*

Wonderland. It was an assault, a caress, a loony grin, a puckish swagger, a hot rod. It yawed up through the trees against the pea-gray sky above that English campus like a mechanical hobgoblin: gritty, not clean; dockside, not nautical; sincere, not cerebral.
"One could almost hear it clank."
C. Hodgetts, *Design Quarterly 100,* April 1976

1
2
3
4
5
6

Leicester University Engineering Building, 1959

"I say beauty 'of a sort' because the visual pleasures of this complex and rewarding building are neither those of classic regularity nor picturesque softness. Its aesthetic satisfactions stem from a tough-minded, blunt-spoken expertise that convinces even laymen that everything is right, proper and just so. It is one of those buildings that establishes its own rules, convinces

1. *Service road.*
2. *Workshops.*
3–7. *Circulation link between towers.*
8. *Section: office tower.*
9. *Section: laboratory tower.*
10. *Painting by Nils Ole Lund*

7

10

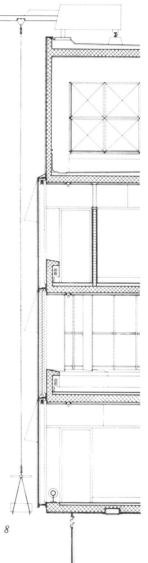

8

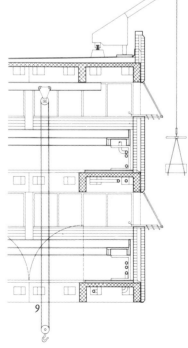

9

by the coherence of even markedly dissimilar parts, and stands upon no precedents. It rebuffs the attempts of art-historians to identify its sources (unlike some of the other modern buildings on the Leicester campus, which provide a real feast for art-historical nit-pickers), though it has in some obtuse way of its own, regained a good deal of the bloody-minded elan and sheer

zing of the pioneer modernism of the early Twenties. Largely, I think, this is because it really does seem to be a natural machine-age architecture of the sort that must have been in the minds of the Werkbund's founding fathers or Antonio Sant'Elia."
R. Banham, *New Statesman,* 14 February 1964.

1. Details of chimney capping.

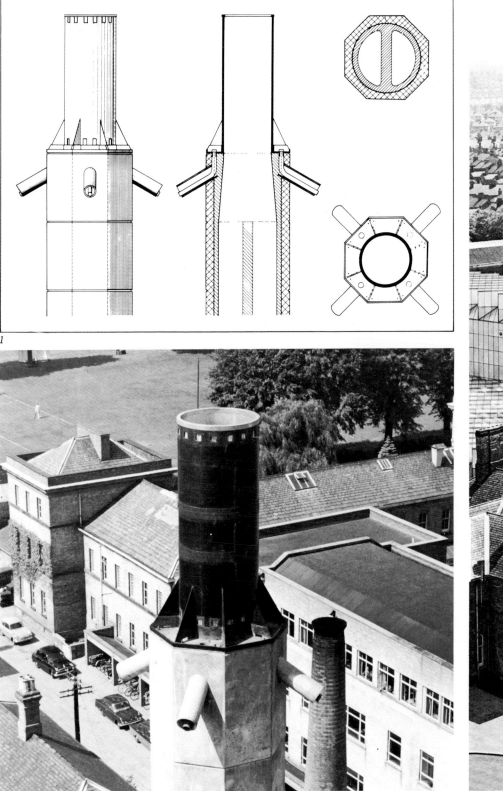

1

Leicester University Engineering Building, 1959

1960/64
Children's Home
Putney, London

James Stirling, James Gowan
Roy Cameron

For privacy the houses are sited at right angles to one another, and they stand in a walled garden. A service road provides access to the rear house and there is a screened area of hard standing for two cars.

"In the design for a children's home in South London we thought social considerations should have priority. The children who grow up in these homes are either orphans or have been taken from families where the parents cannot look after them. We wanted the new buildings to over-compensate for the lack of a real 'home.' Small in size, they are almost a caricature of the domestic house and they have the small scale of doll's houses and children's toys. The more costly decision to make two buildings instead of one was in order to reduce the size of the 'family' to about fifteen children per house instead of thirty as it would have been in a single building. We thought it important not to make the scheme institutional. Each house is looked after by a married couple who really become foster parents and, like an ordinary house, the children's bedrooms are on the upper floor. Seen from the outside, each room steps back, causing the facade to recede and articulate the bedrooms, indicating them as the important spaces within the building. Children playing in the gardens are able to identify with their own particular room."
JS, *Zodiac* 18, 1969

1. *Window and balcony details.*
2. *View from street.*
3. *View from garden.*

1

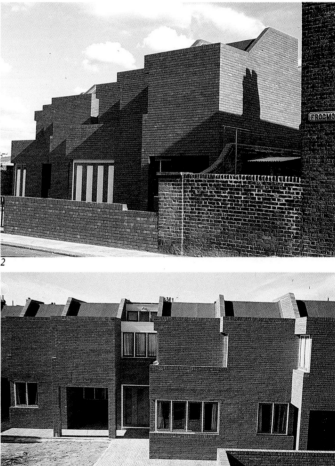

2

3

1. *Stairhall.*
2. *Ground and second floor.*

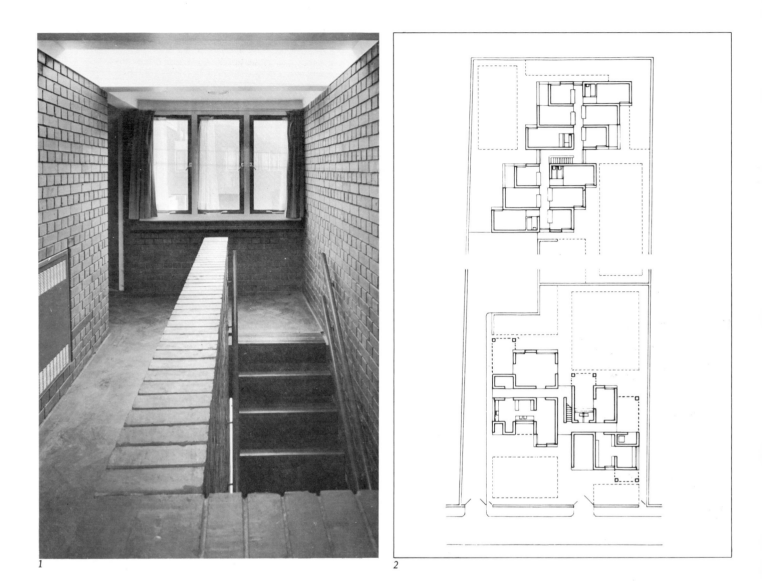

1

2

1960/64
Old People's Home
Blackheath, London

James Stirling, James Gowan
Roy Cameron
Quinlan Terry

The site was badly overlooked by terraced houses, three- and four-stories high. We consequently thought it essential to create a private garden where the residents could sit out in fine weather and not feel spied on by the neighbors. (They are very sensitive about this.) The building, therefore, was bent round a courtyard garden and kept lowest on the south and west sides allowing maximum penetration of sun and daylight into the courtyard. The corridor-route through the building is the organizing element of the plan. As it moves round the building it swells out or reduces according to location, widening where it is also the lift lobby and when it becomes the entrance hall, narrowing between bedrooms and service rooms. As it is always bending there are never long institutional views down it.

"After six of seven years designing very articulated buildings, we decided, in the old peoples' home at Blackheath, to do the opposite. Here, none of the accommodation is expressed; all rooms are concealed behind a screen of structural brick walls which wrap around an internal garden. Perhaps this is our only perverse building, and maybe, it has some resemblance to style 'a la liberté,' popular here some time back."
JS, *Zodiac*, 18, 1969

"No timorous old soul need ever feel the victim of perspective at Blackheath, the more so since the corridor is not merely a means of communication but widens and narrows to accommodate a variety of other functions. When I saw it chairs had been set up, five or six abreast, in one of the wider parts, apparently for a service.

"The polygonal plan has enabled Stirling and Gowan to remove much of the 'institutional character' (a formal concept if ever there was one, cabbage-smell excluded) that commonly attaches to such buildings: the length of corridor visible at any one time is relatively short, and disappears inconclusively round a half-corner."
R. Banham, *New Statesman*, 23 April 1965

1–3. Volume studies.
4. Courtyard and tower.

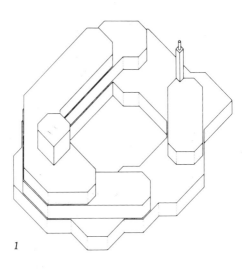

1

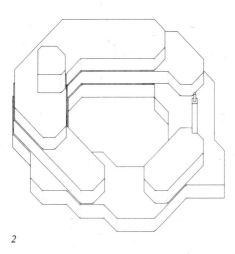

2

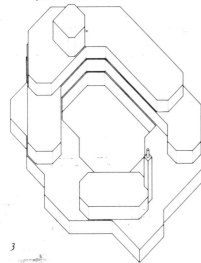

3

4

1. Section through garden.
2. Section through tower.
3. Ground floor.
4. Second floor.
5. Third floor.

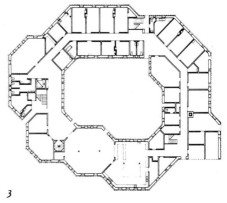

3

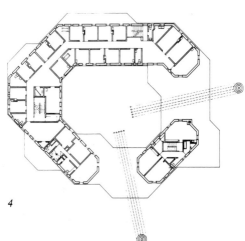

4

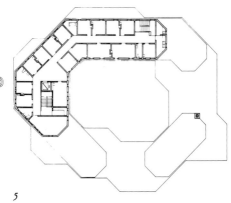

5

Old Peoples Home, 1960

1964/67
Cambridge University History Faculty Building
(limited competition)

James Stirling
Michael Wilford
Brian Frost
David Bartlett

This building was the subject of a limited competition and, apart from changes in siting, is almost the same as the original project.

The designated site included land directly west of the present building. After the competition it was found that about half the land was not available and the building had to be re-sited at short notice and turned from facing east to north.

It was necessary to provide multi-directional approaches to the History Faculty. To allow for different cross-campus circulation routes four entrances have been provided, two of which are at ground level. At the front of the building there is also an approach by ramp to the staff entrance.

The accommodation includes a reading room for 300 readers (12,600 square feet of shelving) which accounts for approximately half the floor area; the other accommodation is staff, seminar and common rooms.

The main entrances open directly into a control and enquiry area where the catalogs are housed; beyond and four feet below this level is the reading room. The book stack is on two levels and the shelving units fan radially on sight lines from the control desk, which thus has total supervision of the reading room and book stack. The control desk is also a console from which heating, lighting and ventilation is adjusted. The extract machines at the top of the glazed roof are controlled from this desk.

A variety of seating has been provided in the reading room either in specialist reading bays or at large tables in the main area. Beyond the book stack there is a continuous bench top, also for student use. The book shelf units are on two levels and the mezzanine can be approached directly from the control area or from the floor of the reading room.

The steel truss roof over the reading room has upper and lower glass surfaces with the upper containing adjustable louvres to ventilate the space formed by the roof trusses between the two skins of glass. The roof space is up to 12 feet high and, at various levels, there are catwalks providing access to the lighting installation and the extract machines as well as being used for maintenance. The under skin of glazing is translucent, producing shadowless natural light on the reading room tables. The rising chimney shape created by the sloping glass ceiling causes heated air rising from the floor to be drawn upwards and disperse through ventilators at the apex of the roof. In hot weather this process is intensified by three separate extract machines.

Inside the roof the glass surfaces are cleaned by using long arm vacuum cleaners from the catwalks. The external roof glass is cleaned by way of the gutters which act as ladders and expansion joints.

1. Side elevation.

1

The Faculty considers that close contact between the Reading Room and the other accommodation is essential and the arrangement of corridors as galleries around the Reading Room is a principal factor of the planning. The corridor windows and the lay-bys, which project into the air space of the Reading Room, allow students in the upper floors to maintain a visual but non-intrusive contact with the Reading Room.

The three upper floors of the 'L'-shaped block contain private staff rooms (two sizes) which are sometimes used for tutorials. Below, there are two floors of greater width containing seminar rooms and below this again, a wide floor containing student and staff common rooms. The smallest rooms are, therefore, at the top and the building section widens at the lower levels where the bigger rooms are located. The transition from a thin to a thick building is effected on the exterior by a stepped glass skin. In addition to the stair and lift towers at the front of the building (adjacent to and indicating the main entrances) there are fire escape stairs at each end of the 'L'-shaped block.

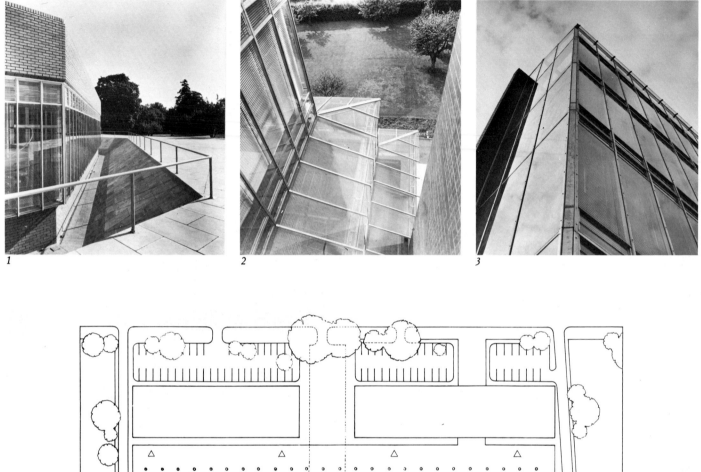

1   2   3

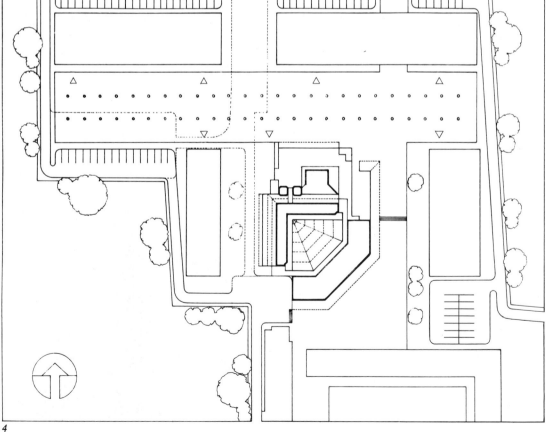

4

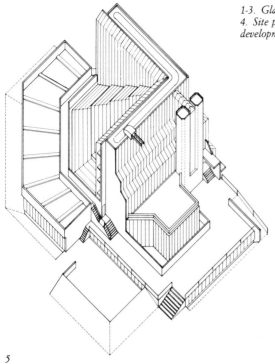

1-3. Glazing details.
4. Site plan showing existing and proposed development.

5. Axonometric.
6. Ground floor plan showing entrance, reading room and book stacks.
7. Student and faculty entrances.
8. Second floor plan showing upper entrance and student meeting rooms.
9. Secondary entrance.

5

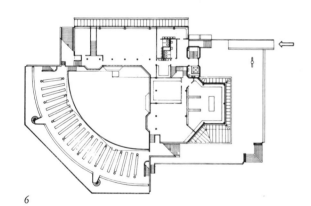

6

7

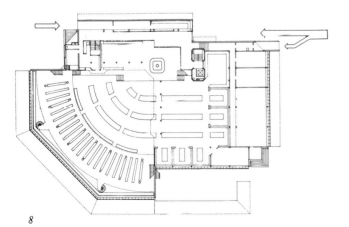

8

9

"The Cambridge history library, first seen by me in 1972, made a different impact. Here was the same rational articulation but 'over-play' had been censored and the energy behind it diverted into a redoubtable, daunting monument; enigmatic (which way round is it?); a crystal fort with a shiny brick rampart (a touch of Sant'Elia here); something of a factory, something of a conservatory. The reading room, sheltered under a monster technological awning in the angle of the two wings, whose inner flanks the awning cruelly defaced, I found difficult to take. I still do. I am only partly reconciled by seeing it as a comment on the ungentle side of history—the history 'industry,' the research production line. But the building as a whole strikes me with something very like awe."

J. Summerson, *Architectural Review,* March 1983

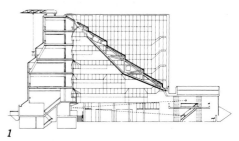

1

Cambridge University History Faculty Building, 1964

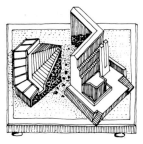

"The trouble with Stirling is that he tries to practise what he preaches. He has been able to convert the drawings into actual structures, and so we have to live with a series of monuments to the difference between theory and practice.

"The value of Sant'Elia as an architect is that he never built his futurist city. It would be pleasant

1. Section through reading room.
2. View towards entrances.
3. Fifth floor plan, showing staff rooms.
4. Fourth floor plan showing seminar rooms.
5. End elevation.
6. Third floor plan, showing seminar rooms and common room with terrace.

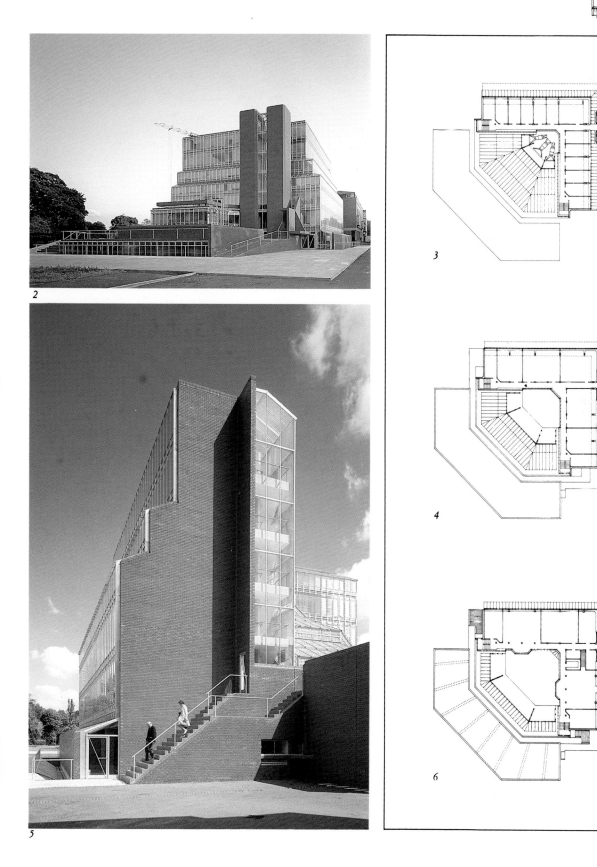

2

5

3

4

6

to say the same about Stirling. Most of Stirling's actual work is in the field of university building. But the Cambridge History Building and Queens College, Oxford show a crude disregard of the architectural ethics of the two cities; they are offensive in scale, conception and environment."
Connoisseur, July 1974

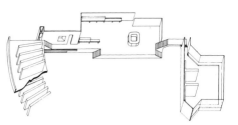

"It is like leafing through the illustrations in Andreas Vesalius's 16th century treatise on anatomy, as first the skin, then the vessels, and finally the muscular tissue itself are magically peeled away to expose the viscera. In a gesture more cinematic than architectural, the roof completes its transit and a gallery of windows bulges outward into the void of the reading room

Cambridge University History Faculty Building, 1964

as into an aquarium, enabling the visitor, now
encased in a protective capsule, to observe the
strange life of the scholars below."
C. Hodgetts, *Design Quarterly 100*

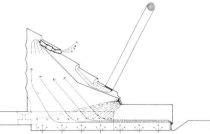

1. *Night view of reading room.*
2. *Spiral staircase connecting book stack levels.*
3. *Control desk from reading room.*
4. *Reading room from control desk.*

3

4

"The Professor of Classical Archeology in fine Roman stance, stood at the lectern and began his speech—'This building is like no building I ever learnt to love,' and finished with an impassioned plea for architects to return to the sanity of the orders. Along the way he slipped in a description of the building—'you come to the desk and you realize you are in an Edwardian hotel; either you go up to your room or you pass beyond into the tea lounge with light coming in from above and no doubt a palm court orchestra playing.' An apt description in a strange sort of way!"
JS, *RIBA Journal*, May 1965

1. *Upper level corridor.*
2. *Book stack reading table.*
3. *Reading room glazing.*
4. *Apex of lantern.*

1

2

3

4

Of a planned terrace of low-cost housing, only the first block was built. There are two apartments on each floor with the stair at rear center. An open parking garage is beneath the apartments. A ramp and stair bridge to the entrance from the sidewalk.

1. *Garage, first and second floor plans.*
2. *Section.*
3. *View from street.*
4. *View from garden.*

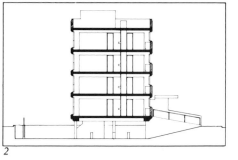

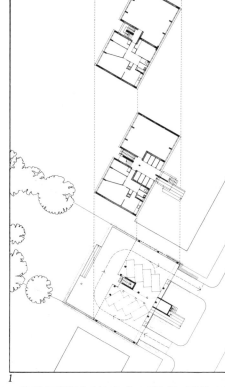

1

2

3

4

1964/68
Residential expansion for St. Andrews University
Scotland

James Stirling
Brian Frost
David Bartlett
Alfred Bews

The new buildings for St. Andrews University are in the north of Scotland where there is no local building material (not even bricks) or workmen (who have all come south). The problem was how to erect a battery of student residences as a continuous building process over a period of six or seven years. The only method which seemed possible was to design a kit of precast concrete elements to be manufactured elsewhere. These are taken to the site where they are lifted directly off lorries by mobile cranes and placed onto the building without touching ground. The factory is in Edinburgh, about eighty miles south of St. Andrews. Each building is assembled from a range of precast wall and floor units and there are about thirty-two different molds which will be re-used for the later buildings.

There are 250 students in each residence (both sexes) and the students' bedrooms are positioned in the fingers, which are pointed towards a

magnificent view of the North Sea and the Scottish mountains. The non-repetitive accommodation (i.e. dining hall, games rooms, etc.) is located in the web where the fingers join. There is a glazed promenade level about halfway up the building and, from this, internal staircases give access up or down to the students' rooms. This promenade is the main artery of circulation and is intended to be the major element of sociability. Off the promenade and adjacent to the staircases are lay-bys containing seats and vending machines. In these areas it is hoped that much of the social life in the residence will take place and, in using the promenade on route to their rooms, every student will inevitably come into contact with everyone else. On the floors above and below the promenade the staircases give onto short, unpleasant corridors (deliberately narrow and under-lit) to the students' rooms. Sometimes it is necessary to design unpleasant spaces in order to increase the usage of areas where activity is intended. There was an elementary

problem of identity inside the internal staircases— at what level does the promenade occur?—how to know when to get out. To help visually locate this, large circular holes were cut into the walls of the staircases at promenade level; not an inside/outside window in the normal sense, it is therefore different from the rectangular windows used elsewhere. The sexes change with each staircase though I don't think the University realised that, as fire exits were required onto the roof, it should be possible for the students to cross over at night unseen. The student's private room is obviously the most important accommodation in the building and every room has a window angled like an eye towards the view. This angling which is a displacement of the room articulates its position on the facade and therefore, even with a very structurally motivated scheme, we have maintained as fundamental the expression of the most important accommodation.

Jim on Jencks
Dear Sir,
Charles Jencks is all balls (AAQ, Summer 1972) if he thinks the St. Andrews Residence was designed to look like a ship, anymore than a crotch. Locals have always nicknamed our buildings, i.e., Leicester engineering—the waterworks; Cambridge History—the Glasshouse; Oxford Residence—the multi-story garage; St. Andrews Residence—the battleship; and Jencks is equally banal in using this 'significance' for his architectural historicism. I have always considered myself more a neo-classicist than an art nouveauist.
Yours,
James Stirling

Jencks on Jim
Dear Sir,
James Stirling loses his argument in the first five words (AAQ, Fall 1972) when he accuses me, metaphorically, of being 'all balls,' not only because there is more to my...anatomy than that, but really because he, like so many modern architects, would like to surpress all...metaphors

1

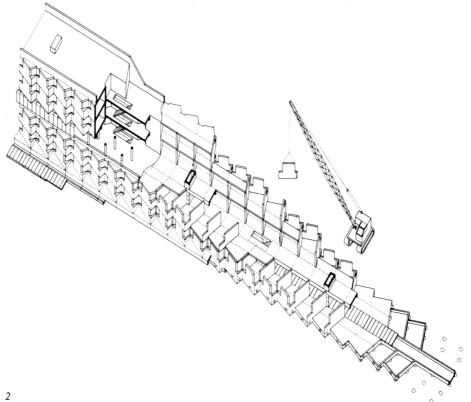

2

Residential expansion, St Andrews University, 1964

and pretend they aren't there. His reference to St. Andrew's Residence as 'a crotch' has more significance than he would like to admit, and as he cannot deny, (because I and another witness were there) at least one girl resident was highly distressed at having to enter the building 'between its legs.'

Charles Jencks

1. Main entrance from ridge walk.
2. Axonometric showing prefabricated construction
3. Building on hillside.
4. Plan: promenade level.
5. Plan: typical bedroom floor.

3

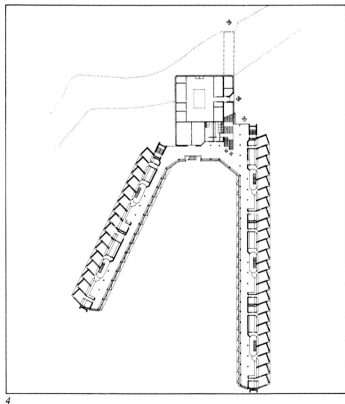

4

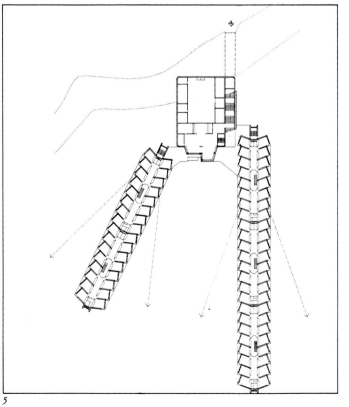

5

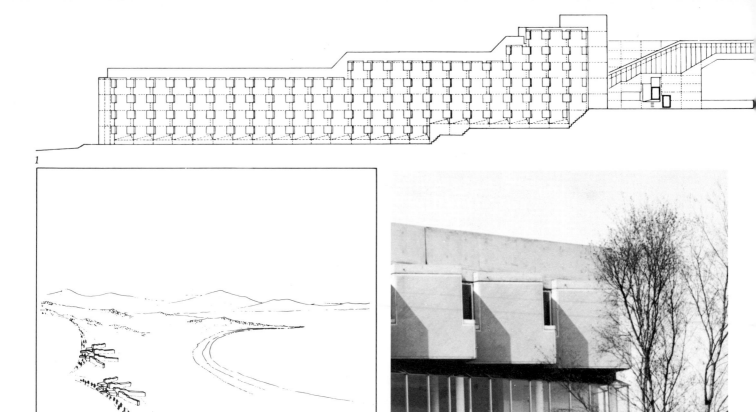

1

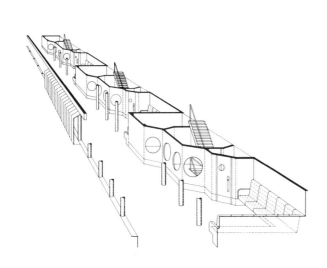

2

3

Residential expansion, St Andrews University, 1964

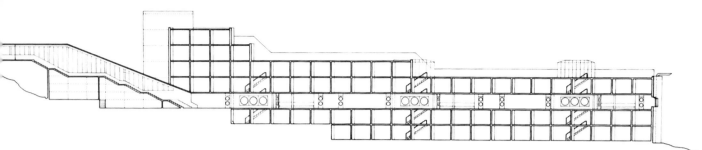

5

1. *Side elevation.*
2. *External view of promenade.*
3. *Window detail.*
4. *Section.*
5. *Grand staircase.*
6. *Entrance bridge.*

6

Residential expansion, St Andrews University, 1964

"However, the classical affinities in the basic dormitory complex will remain—the evocation of a baroque palace, the pyramidal concentration towards the centre, the diminishing of the wings towards their extremities, etc. This is hardly the first time that Stirling has gravitated towards classicism.

"St. Andrew's may be regarded as the fulfilment of Churchill, wherein that which had previously been projected as stone veneer, now appears as having been transformed into a precast concrete that serves simultaneously as both skin and structure.

"On assembly these margins serve to formally articulate the elements, while the ribbing not only masks those imperfections inherent to concrete but also serves to sharpen the shadow profile and to drain and regulate the weathering of storm water across the building's face. This three-dimensional, sensuous, raised surface almost metallic in appearance, is so superiour as to totally outclass any accepted methods for treating

1
2
3
4

1. *Side view.*
2. *Stair to promenade.*
3. *Promenade.*
4. *Dining room skylights.*

pre-cast concrete surfaces.

"This move away from site work towards factory production is no longer an isolated incident in Stirling's work. It derives from his acute awareness of the urgent need to transform, through design, an essentially craft-based industry, in order to continue to produce high quality at reasonable'cost.'

"Of greater cultural consequence is the ship as a condensation of architectonic and social ideals, for as such it emerged from the polemics of nineteenth century socialism to become one of the major paradigms of twentieth century architecture. The essential communal aspect of the *fin-de-siecle* ship resided more in its promenade deck than in its spacious saloons. This socio-sectional element,

reinterpreted, has played a substantial role in the development of modern architecture, since Brinkman's famous Spangen housing of 1920, and Moses Ginsburg's collective living units of 1927.

"In his residential collegiate work, Stirling, after Le Corbusier, has tended to both isolate and then conflate the models of the monastery and the ship.

Residential expansion, St Andrews University, 1964

Whereas the projects for both Selwyn and Churchill colleges addressed themselves, the one informally, the other formally, to traditional quadrangles as the natural and ultimate foci of their essential communality, St. Andrew's (its decks disposed to promenade rather than ambulation) delivers its 'communal pledge' to the open sea. Thus, despite its firm foundation in the site, it floats like La Tourette, indifferent to the grassy ocean of its undulating, landscaped terrain. The communal virtues of the ship and monastery notwithstanding, this self-conscious isolation (there is, for example, no evident means of access from the deck to the grass) cannot be allowed to escape our critical attention.

"Without—from the sea—the whole appears as the partly ruined *enceinte* of a Baroque city; within, it evokes an iron pier promenade transformed in time through living cellular encrustation, plunging like a transfixed dreadnought into a frozen sea; a Martello tower or a rambling Victorian sea-front mansion, from which the only exit is the solitary confinement of

1

Residential expansion, St Andrews University, 1964

one's cabin or room or upward repatriation to the pines of the high ground."

K. Frampton. © *Architectural Design* Magazine, London. Volume 40, September 1970.

1. *Precast concrete: structural assembly.*
2. *Entrance Hall.*
3. *Student study bedroom.*

2

3

Residential expansion, St Andrews University, 1964

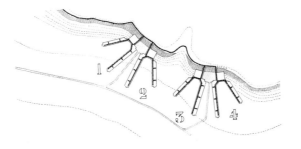

Residential expansion, St Andrews University, 1964

1965
Dorman Long headquarters

James Stirling
Michael Wilford
Julian Harrap

"If the site at St. Andrews is idyllic, then the site for the Dorman Long building must be considered satanic; positioned at the end of the steel mills and surrounded by the symbols of heavy industry—slag mountains, cooling towers, flaming chimneys, etc. Dorman Long are England's largest producers of rolled steel columns and beams and they have a long history of civil engineering from Sidney Harbour bridge to radio telescopes. They asked for the building to be of steel construction and for it to be an exposition of their standard products. Not only had the building to be made of steel, it had to be seen to be made of steel.

"The headquarters office building is fourteen storeys high, and almost 1,000 feet long. The accommodation includes many small rooms—secretaries, managers, directors etc. and areas of large spaces—drawing offices, open plan offices, canteen, library, computer centre etc. amongst others. The larger spaces are on the lower floors and this accounts for the thickening of the building section towards the ground, indicated by the splayed front. The thrust created by this splay is counter-balanced by the shafts of vertical circulation pulled out behind, which act as buttresses stabilising the total building form.

"It transpired that there was a choice of about six alternatives for the structural mesh, all using approximately the same weight of steel and all of similar cost. The choice of a particular structural appearance was therefore arbitrary, reinforcing my opinion that a design, which is primarily dependent on expression of structure is likely to be superficial.

"The structural content in architecture is likely to increase as traditional methods of construction decline and new buildings get larger and more complicated. However, I think it will be ever more necessary for architects not to rely merely on the expression of techniques for the architectural solution. Humanistic considerations must remain the primary logic from which a design evolves."
JS, *Zodiac* 18, 1969

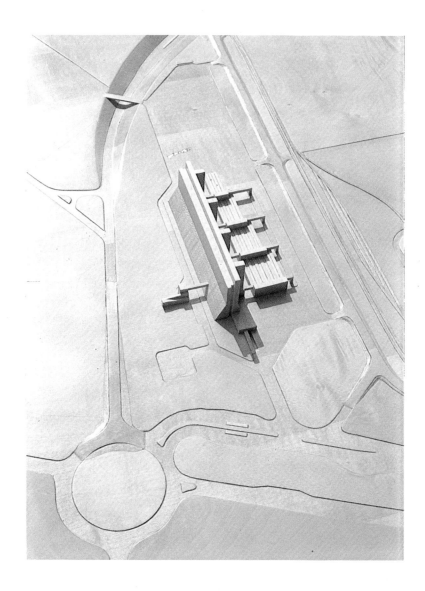

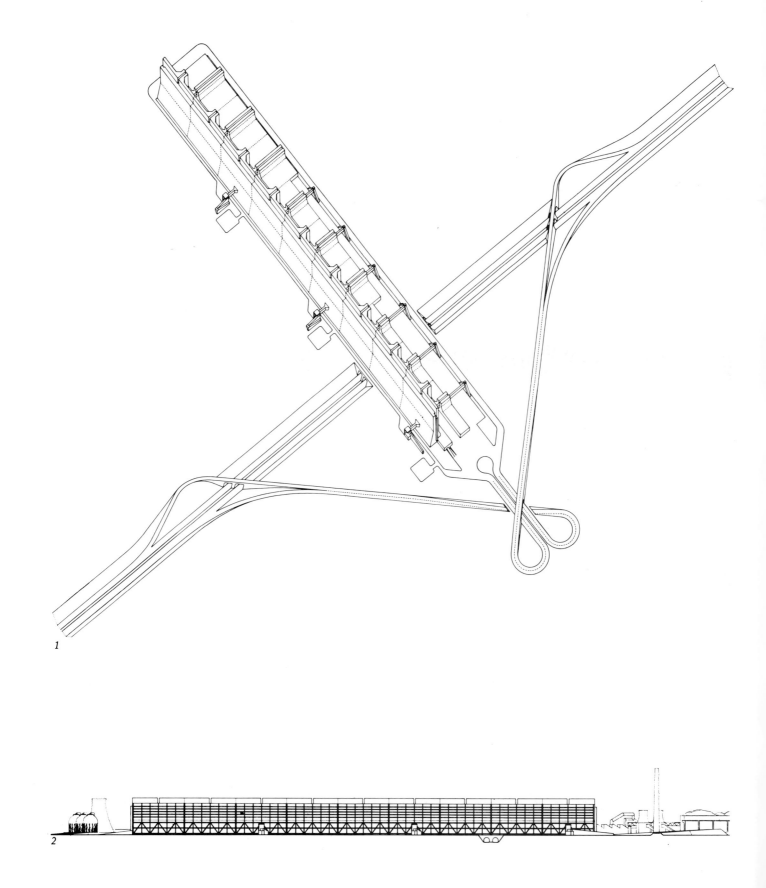

1

2

Dorman Long headquarters, 1965

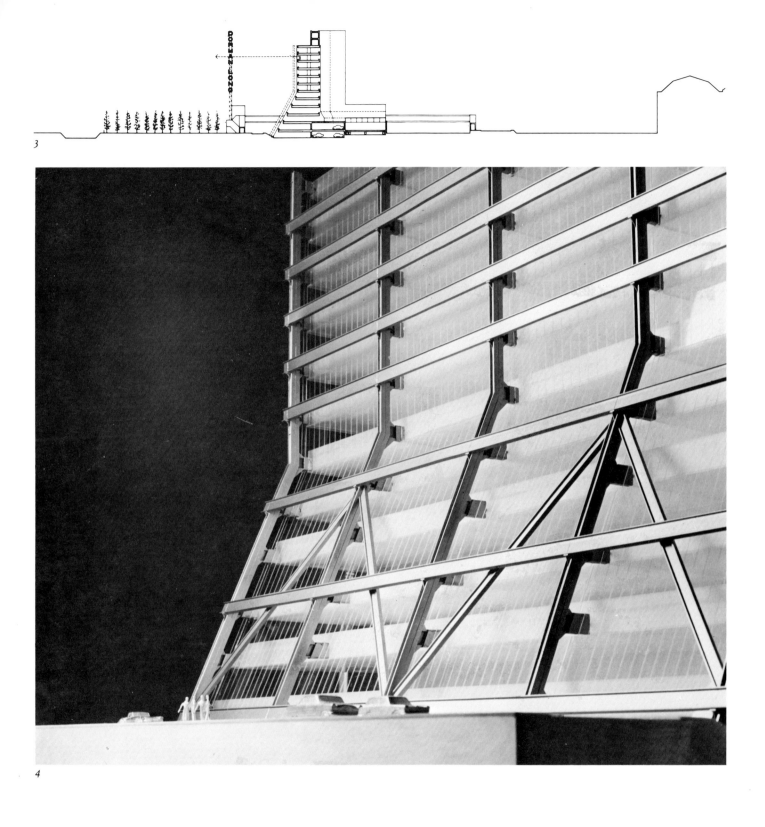

3

4

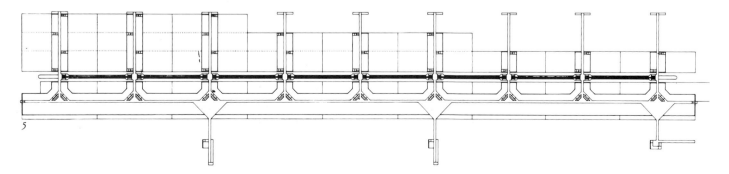

5

Dorman Long headquarters, 1965

1. External structure and office glazing.
2. Ground level plan, offices, parking and
laboratories.

3. Upper level plan, offices.
4. Entrance level plan: offices and laboratory
administration.

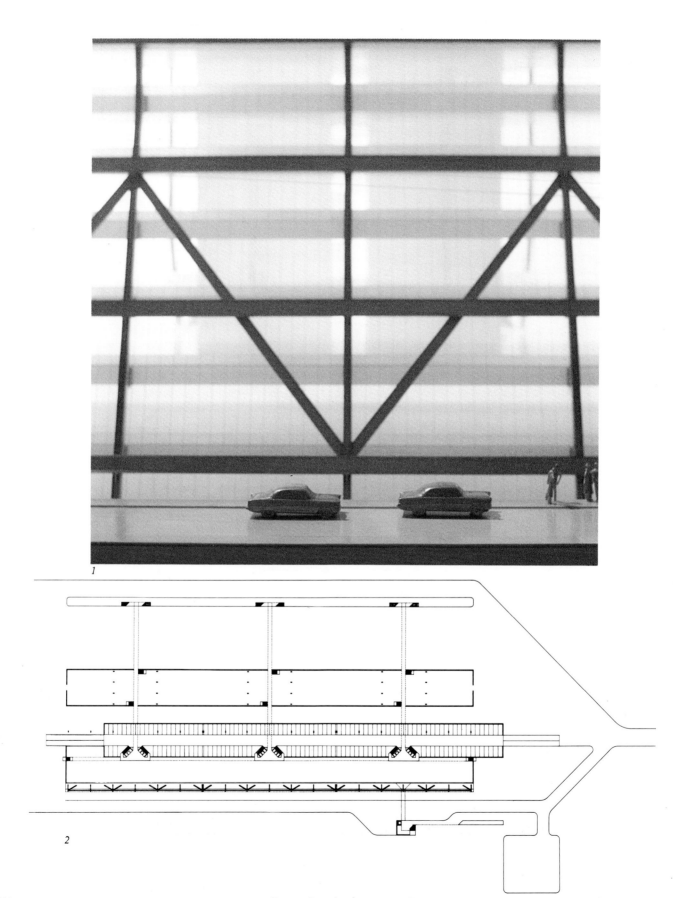

1

2

Dorman Long headquarters, 1965

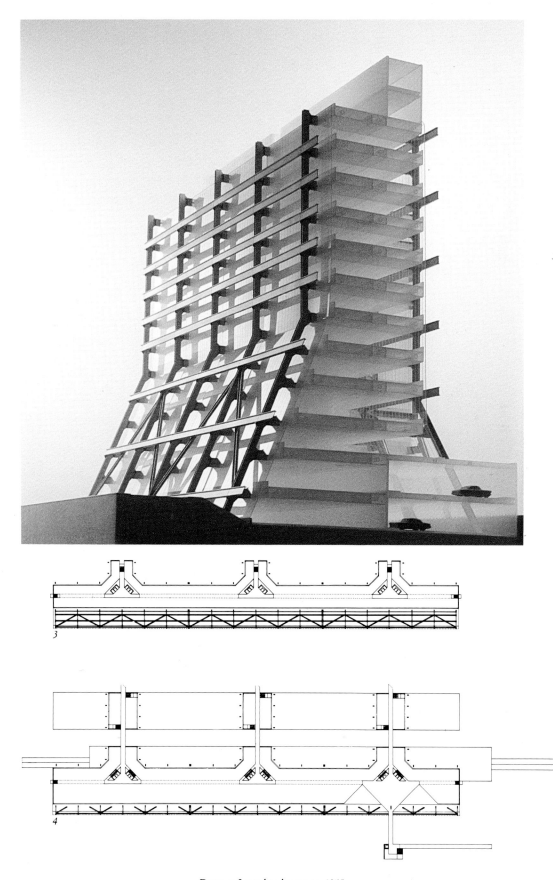

Dorman Long headquarters, 1965

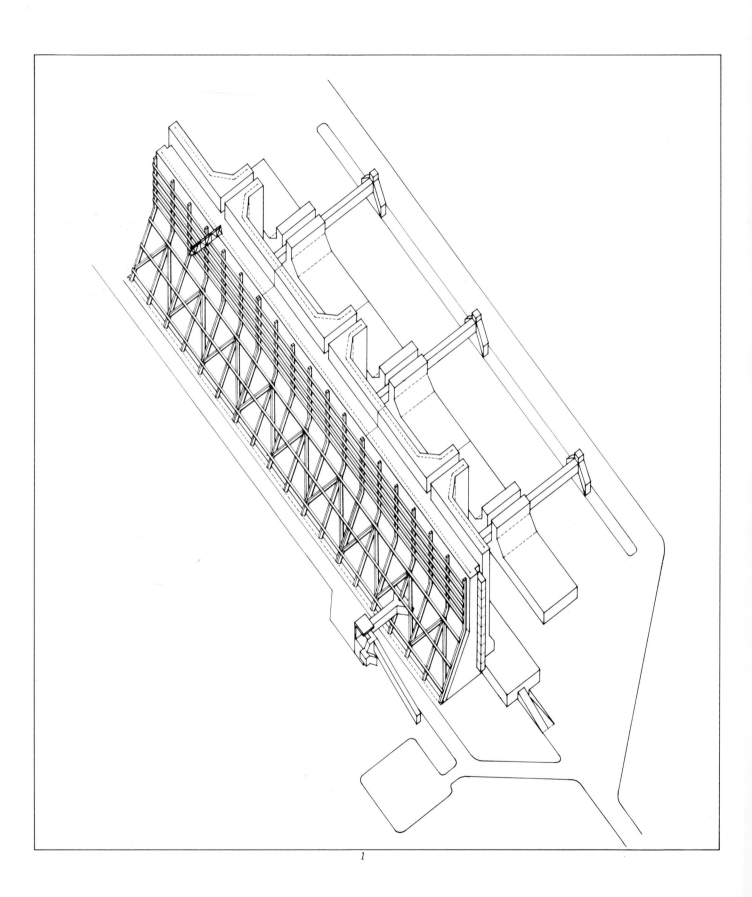

1

Dorman Long headquarters, 1965

6. External column and beam junctions.

2

3

4

5

6

James Stirling
Roy Cameron
Gunther Ismer

"The new building is a student hostel and practically all the accommodation is in single-room apartments, with separate washbasins and storage, but with shared showers, sanitation and elementary cooking areas. The exception is one three-room apartment for a fellow at the top of the building and a caretaker's flat on the ground floor—the only accommodation at that level. Half sunk in the courtyard-podium is a breakfast and lecture room.

"The site is a strange one. On one side, on the outside as it were (on the south-east) it has the suburban squalor of an asphalted municipal car-park. On the other, on the north side, a minor branch of the river Isis, overgrown by a magnificent screen of ancient trees, beyond which there is a line of meadows, more trees and the towers of Oxford.

"Of necessity, therefore, the building is two-sided, even two-faced.

"The whole mass of accommodation (the caretaker's flat and the breakfast room excepted) are held up in the air by a series of high concrete stilts. The stilts hold up a container: the tiled red

1

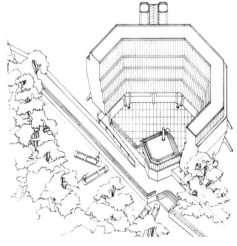

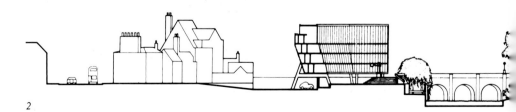

2

124

1. River walk.
2. Section, through new building, river, meadow and Magdalen College.
3. Courtyard.
4. Existing colleges and new building.

southern wall, broken only by thin bands of glazing (which light the internal corridors) and crowned by the roof lights of the duplex flats on the top storey. At two extreme points, the wall is pierced vertically by the cages of the staircase.

"The major supports, which are modified A-frames, carry a building which is tiered outward, so that the wall containing it inclines obliquely out, while the leg of the frame cuts sharply in. The main vertical circulation is enclosed in two chamfered square towers, stairs in one, elevator in the other, ducting in both. The towers are joined by a glass wall.

3

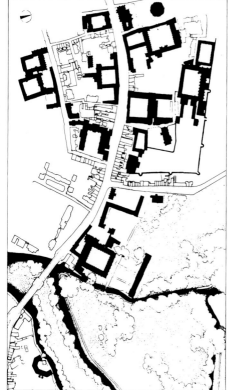

4

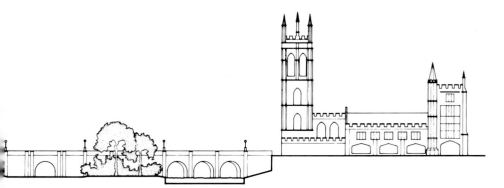

"The windowless vertical red walls of the towers rise abruptly, orthogonally, and their increasing distance from the main building as they near the ground is measurable in the glass walls which enclose the link above ground-floor level.

"The towers are at the back of the long side of the building. It has five sides: four are of equal length, the fifth is double the length. Since they incline to each other at 45 degrees, the effect is as of the five sides of a regular octagon, with one side stretched: the stretch is the entrance.

"The entry is to a circulation space round the building, a kind of cloister at a slightly lower level than the central court. The access from the cloister to the podium courtyard is up four staircases.

"Above the 'cloister' the inner side of the building is an inclined wall of patent glazing which rises to the perpendicular in the duplex apartments of the top story. The effect is of an amphitheatre for which the river with its punts, the screen of trees

1

2

3

4

1. *View towards Magdalen tower.*
2. *View from riverside.*
3. *Structure plan.*
4. *Entrance level.*
5. *View of court.*
6. *Section through breakfast room.*
7. *Sketch of breakfast room and ventilator.*
8. *Second floor.*
9. *Fifth floor.*

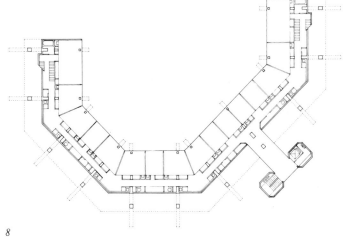

5

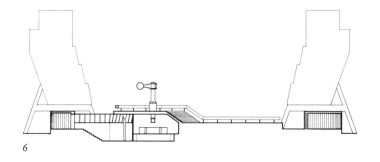

6

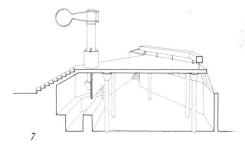

7

8

9

and the meadows beyond are the stage and the courtyard—in the Greek sense. The old cloister, the prototype of so many academic buildings, was closed on itself. The landscape—whatever there was of it, lawns, trees or market-garden—was at the centre. But this cloister is a theatre, the rooms are boxes from which you may observe the doings of any of your neighbours who has not drawn down his silver blind. What seems to me the major theme of the building is the contrast between public and private.

"The two sides of the building set it out sharply. The red brick carapace with its battered walls and narrow horizontal slits, the two bastions at the entrance. An embattled situation seen across the blank and sordid asphalt of the car-park. But on the other side, the building is a glasshouse, the projection of privacy is entrusted to the blinds alone. Stirling obviously regarded that guarantee as sufficient. The college is after all a miniature society, limited to one sex and bound by common aims and a code of behaviour. The protective enclosure against the outside world is opposed to

1

2

3

4

the transparency of the inner skin.

"The almost exhibitionist inner aspect of the cloister contrasts with the few spaces allowed to social activity under cover: the breakfast/lecture room hidden in the podium and the wide interspaces of the A-frames on the outer edge of the building.

"The roof of the breakfast room rises up several steps to form a miniature stage in the corner of the stage nearest the entrance, there is what appears at first sight an abstract sculpture, but on closer inspection turns out to be a weathercock which, in fact, acts as the ventilator of the 'open kitchen' of the breakfast room.

1. *View across river to caretakers apartment.*
2. *Riverside walk and terrace.*
3. *Breakfast room.*
4. *Entrance to cloister.*

"The Florey seems to me therefore Stirling's most mannered work. Like most mannered buildings it communicates a sense of unease through the abrupt contrast of the two sides and through more oblique features like the divided axis. The very way the entrance works, the obvious entry avoided and the direction of entry obstructed and divided by a major piece of structure disturbs and stilts the visitor's movement, which leads him to a space whose formal axis is marked for him by a weathercock/exhaust vane.

"All Stirling's virtuosity was needed to balance the divisive forces into a unified composition. Apparently the simplest of his buildings, it is perhaps the most carefully 'composed.'"
J. Rykwert, *Domus,* November 1972

"Lo spregiudicato J.S., invece di pensare come gli altri in termini di lame inclinate di cemento armatissimo, e di colossali fondazioni a scarpa, ha forse pensato ai bastoni-seggiolino che si usano in Inghilterra per assistere alle corse dei cavalli: ed ha disegnato, in sezione, delle lunghe zampe-contrafforti, che sorreggono l'edificio dal lato della contropendenza.
"A proposito delle torri, é proprio quest'unica verticale che dá l'esatta misura della contropendenza delle pareti. La torre di Pisa avrebbe la metá del valore che ha senza la verticalitá della chiesa, li accanto."
G.K. Koenig, *Casabella*, March 1975

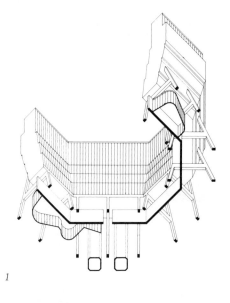

1

"The Florey Building is that huge chunk of red brick which blots out the sky as you go past St. Clements. You could mistake it for a giant water cistern. But it's not—it's a place which Queen's College built for students to live in.

"Which was very considerate of them. And generous, too. Because they commissioned a Mad Architect and gave him £400,000 to do what he liked with.

"Unfortunately, the powers that were considerate and generous enough to do all this must have been a bit on the stupid side too. For this architect was one of those characters who's out to win awards for 'distinctiveness.' And they allowed him to run amuck.

"As a result, the building which has emerged looks distinctive. After all, it was meant to. In fact, it looks as though all the bits and pieces of a giant Meccano set have been bolted together and dumped upon St. Clements."
Local newspaper, 1972

"As with its two predecessors nature is kept out. There is no place for grass, let alone a tree, in the court; instead there is a highly enjoyable conceit, a kind of machine-made tree in the form of the ventilating shaft to the breakfast room kitchen, fitted out with a wind vane and cowl. But the relationship of the building to the natural objects is not aggressive, only separate, like a submarine which has landed on the sea bed, allowing its crew to gaze at the underwater vegetation through a glass screen."
M. Girouard, *Architectural Review,* November 1972

2

3

1. *Axonometric upview.*
2. *Corridor stair.*
3. *Studio interior.*

4. *Entrance and porter's lodge.*
5. *Side stepping staircase*

6. *Section through bedroom and studio.*
7. *View across municipal parking lot.*

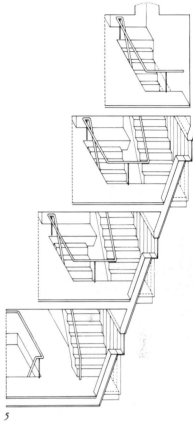

5

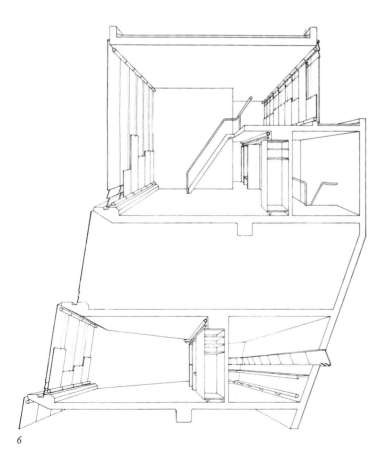

4

6

7

"We are witness to the re-emergence of a contextual concern for urban form. Paradoxically enclosing its riverside site in such a way as to ignore the outer reaches of the city, the Queen's building nonetheless displays an almost painful nostalgia for the dense quadrangular authority of Oxford's urban core. This 'gown' versus 'town' affiliation is revealed by the site plan which renders both the rivers and the collegiate buildings in such a way as to strengthen through graphic artifice, this intended link between the honorific threshold of Magdalen and the isolated form of Queen's; built so to speak on the wrong side of the bridge."
K. Frampton, *RIBA Journal*, March 1976

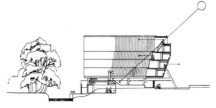

Queens College, 1966

1967/76
Runcorn New Town, low cost housing
near Liverpool

James Stirling
Michael Wilford, David Bartlett,
Julian Harrap, Peter Ray, David Gibson,
Robin Nicholson, David Falck, Tony Smith
David St. John

Runcorn is sited mid-way between Liverpool and Manchester. The Government's intention was to relieve the unemployment and shortage of housing which exists in these cities.

The terraces of housing form a series of residential garden squares that vary in size and degree of enclosure and outlook (the out-door rooms of the city; the idea of Bath, Edinburgh, etc.). All are tree planted and landscaped and contain children's play areas; the larger squares have tennis courts. These garden squares are for the use of the families which live around them. Entry is either off the access road or via a pedestrian ramp which rises from the square, to connect with public footways at second level. Pedestrians using the elevated footways are connected by bridges to the town center building at the level of shopping and entertainments. These walkways are continued south and west out of the site to link with adjoining housing areas.

The height of terraces relative to the size of a typical square (300 feet × 300 feet) is of a similar proportion to 18th century squares in Bath, Edinburgh etc. In the case of the Georgian square all terraces 'front' onto the square with public roads intervening between terrace and garden square on each of its four sides. At Runcorn the organization is an L-shaped arrangement with two fronts and two backs facing over the garden square. Access roads are on two sides only. The L-shaped arrangement also allows orientation of living spaces to the south or west. (There are no north facing living rooms). The terraces have dual aspect—the garden elevation with living spaces is visually related to the garden square used by residents, while the elevated walkways on the access (road) side overlook a neighboring square or avenue. Roads and parked cars as viewed from the garden squares are screened from sight by retaining walls, grassed banks and avenues of trees.

Views are northwards to Halton Rock (appearing above the Town Centre) and south to the hills. The site is separated from adjoining housing areas and the Town Centre by new encircling high speed roads. The express roads are acoustically screened from flanking housing areas by high earth banks and planting. These barriers, which isolate one housing community from another, produce the disturbing effect of being able to drive through the New Town—hardly seeing it.

There will be 1,500 dwellings, one third being flats for two or three occupants, one third maisonettes for four or five, and one third houses for five or six. This variety of dwelling types is contained within a building section of five stories and the ratio of family sizes is dispersed evenly throughout, thus avoiding a concentration of any particular social or age group.

To prevent noisy through traffic, the streets are planned on a cul-de-sac system.

Ground-level houses are for five to six persons and have dining/play rooms opening onto private gardens, bedrooms are above. The maisonettes for four to five occupants are entered from the elevated footways, and have living rooms opening onto large balconies, with bedrooms above. The top floors are planned as flats for two or three persons.

The footways are protected by the overhanging upper floor. Staircase towers rise from garage and parking areas to link with every floor. The stair towers form colonnades which enclose two sides of the squares.

Later unforeseen requirements, e.g. laundry, pub, shops etc., could be accommodated in the open corner space at the junction of housing terraces.

"Despite Runcorn's commitment to mass production, there is an evident attempt to recuperate the urban qualities of English neo-classical planning not only as an implied

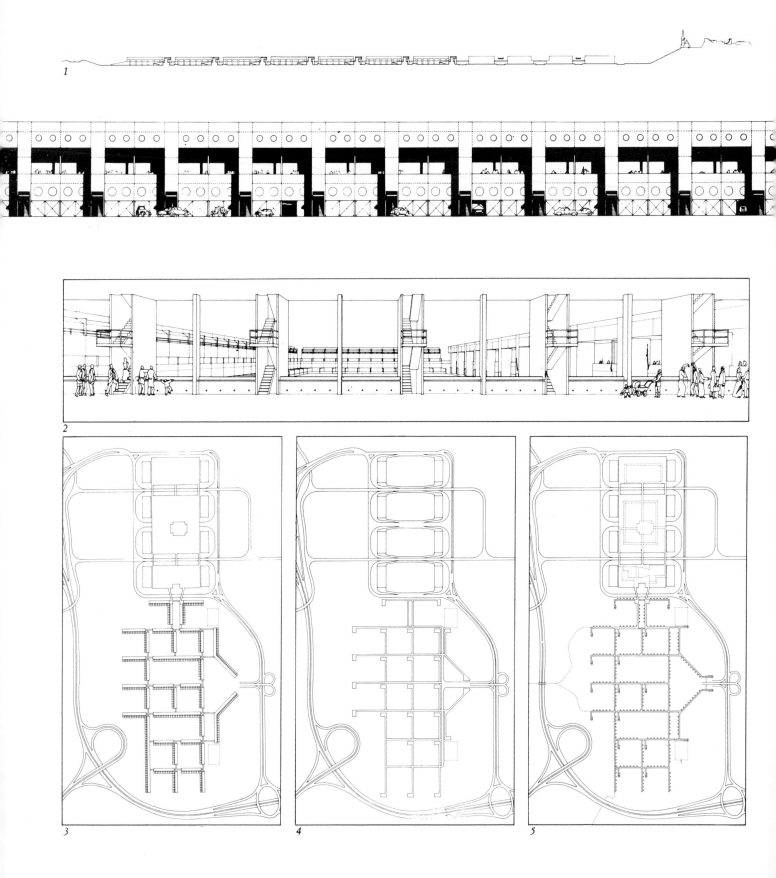

1

2

3

4

5

Runcorn New Town, low cost housing, 1967

criticism of the sterility of Zeilenbau developments but also of the inherent fragmentation of the English New Town tradition.

"The integration of historical precedent as part of the equation distinguishes Runcorn from the housing experiments of the 1920s. Runcorn posits an equality between rational design procedure and

1. *Section through housing squares, Town Center building and Halton Castle.*
2. *View from elevated walkway.*
3. *Plan of five storey housing terraces and town center building.*
4. *Plan of community roads and surrounding motorways.*
5. *Plan of elevated walkways.*
6. *Section through motorway and housing squares.*
7. *View of a garden square.*
8. *Plan showing contours and landscaping.*
9. *Early sketch of housing related to Town Center.*

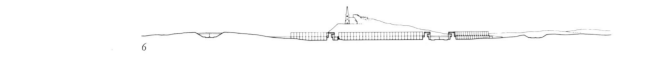

6

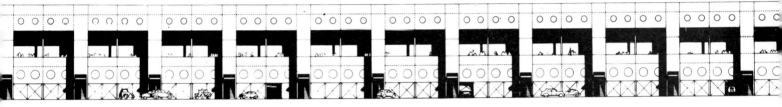

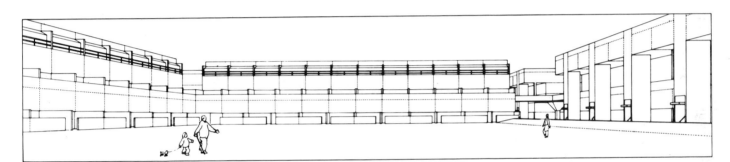

7

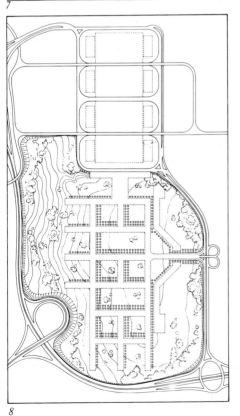

8

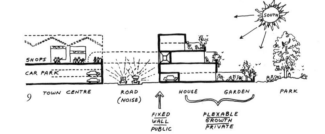

9

historical precedent as well as an interplay between quantitative analysis and intuitive response. While the ideas behind the grid may be distantly related to computer technology, the use of historical precedent can be seen as the desire for continuity."
W. Seligman, *Oppositions 7*

1. *Terraces from garden square (unlandscaped).*
2. *Corner of garden square.*
3. *Living room with furnishings.*
4. *Axonometric showing prefabricated construction.*

1

2

Runcorn New Town, low cost housing, 1967

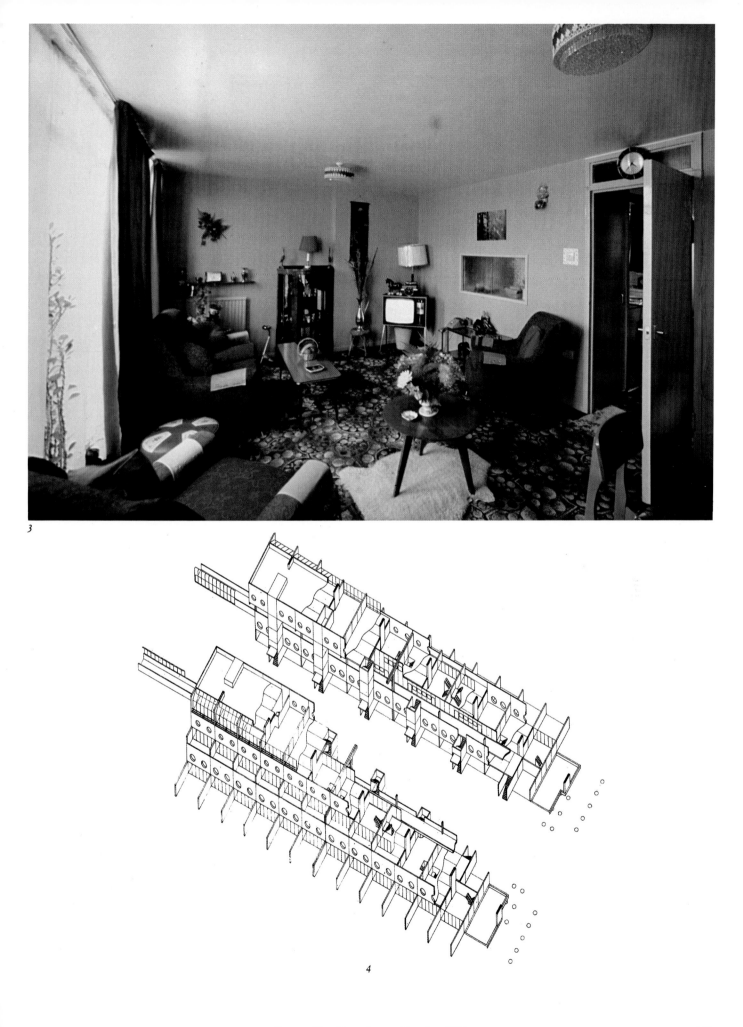

3

4

Runcorn New Town, low cost housing, 1967

1. *Isometric up view from community road.*
2. *View of corner from road.*
3. *Elevated walkway.*
4. *Isometric up view from garden square.*
5. *Ramp from garden square to walkway.*

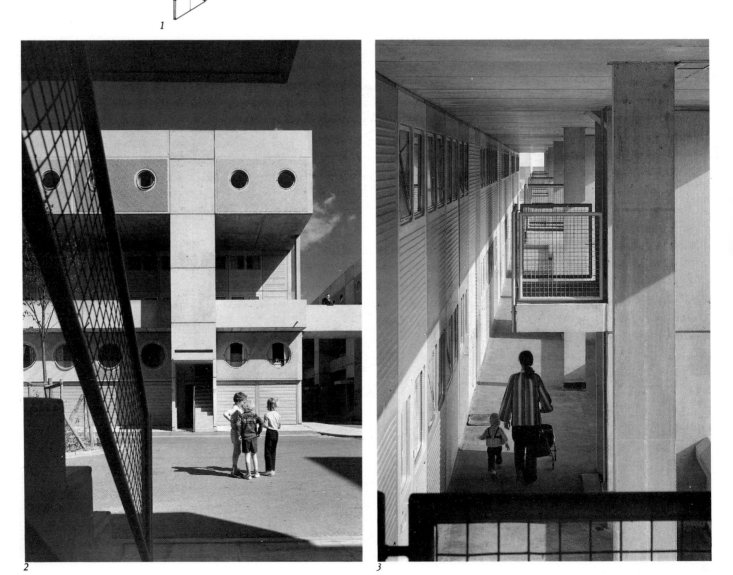

1

2

3

Runcorn New Town, low cost housing, 1967

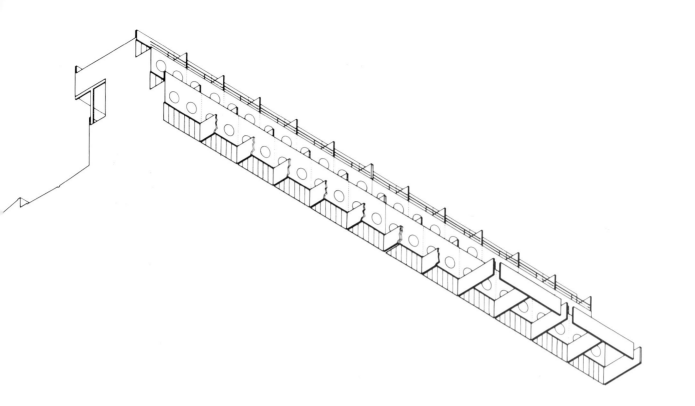

Runcorn New Town, low cost housing, 1967

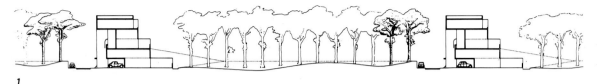

1

2

3

4

5

"Jim Stirling's designs, like those of the hi-tech school, expose the parts other architecture cannot reach.

"But the parts in question were attached to a Robert Arthur Dutch, athletic Runcorn resident and inhabitant of one of Stirling's celebrated Southgate maisonettes.

"He was found guilty of indecently and lewdly exposing himself from the distinctive porthole window to a busload of auxiliary nurses—and his defending solicitor was in no doubt about who was to blame. According to the local weekly paper, he 'slammed the architects.'

"Counsel Michael Dalling said: 'It may well be very beautiful but sometimes I think the designers should be forced to live in their designs and find out just how practical they are.'

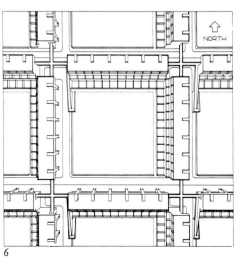

6

"Dalling told the court that the maisonette occupied by Dutch, a 36-year-old sign erector, features two unusual porthole windows which afford a full view of those appendages normally kept hidden. 'Even somebody's toes can be seen,' he said.

"'Indeed, they seem to have been designed specifically to bring such cases as this to court,' said Dalling.

"Nurse Elizabeth Dolman was a prosecution witness and had observed the breakfast time horror: 'I noticed the two port holes on the end of the row of houses. There was a man standing in the window with a hand on his head and the other outstretched, completely in the nude. It was quite a shock for me.'

1. A typical square.
2-5. View of the elevated walkways.
6. Perspective of typical square.
7,8. Sketches by R. Perez de Arce.
9. Street facades.
10. Section.

7

8

9

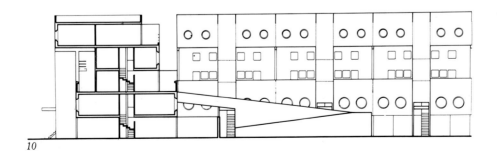

10

Runcorn New Town, low cost housing, 1967

"On another occasion he was alleged to have stood in front of the window with his arms and legs outstretched. 'He just looked like God,' she said.

"Dutch told the court: 'It never occurred to me that I could be seen.' His wife said he was 'just getting dressed.'

"This is the first time any of the houses on this £7.2 million Runcorn development has had flashing problems."
Building Design, 18 August 1981

1. *Proposed glazed walkway at corner.*
2. *Axonometric; proposed corner infill: local shop.*
3. *Plans of three housing types.*

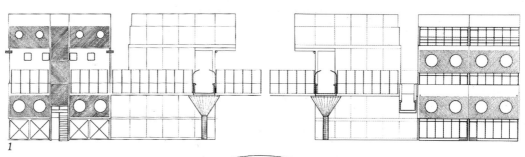

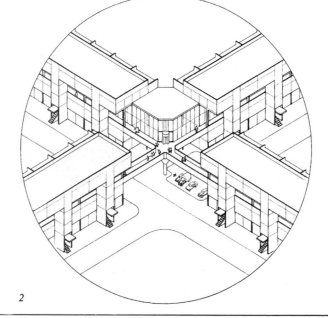

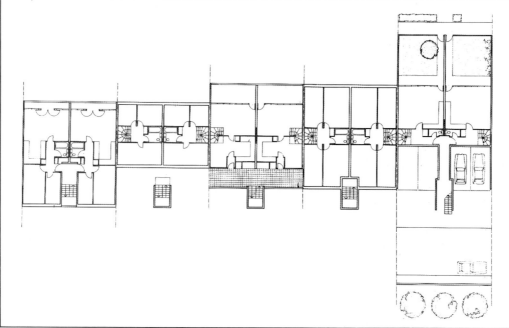

Runcorn New Town, low cost housing, 1967

1969/72
Olivetti Training School
Haslemere Surrey

James Stirling
Robin Nicholson, David Weinberg
David Falck, Barbara Littenberg

To convert a 42-acre estate to a training center, the Olivetti corporation renovated a turn of the century "Tudorbethan" manor house to a residence for students and added a teaching wing.

Two wings of classrooms, one for technicians and one for salesmen, follow the ground contours at the edge of the woods to facilitate planned extension and preserve adjacent trees. The siting splays the wings at slightly less than thirty degrees to each other. A "glazed link" from the house extends between and joins the wings. To one side of the hall at the confluence of the wings and link is a "multi-space"—an "all-purpose-everything auditorium."

Both wings contain classrooms on each floor at either side of a central corridor. A prefabricated reinforced concrete frame spans the width of the wing at the first floor and the width of the corridor above. To it are clipped prefabricated panels of glass-reinforced polyester (GRP). Four panel types are used, the molds of which remain with Olivetti for future extension of either wing.

The splayed glazed link, acts as a conservatory for the house. The floors of classrooms are at half levels to the main house, and connected to it by two ramps within the link. Floor to ceiling radiators rise at intervals beside the glazing.

The "multi-space" is subdivisible by motorized coiling perimeter walls and by motorized internal partitions which are housed in a cruciform fly loft above the space. With all partitions retracted, the total space of the hall can be appropriated and the steps at its rim used for amphitheater seating.

"It is difficult to find the exact word, 'light-hearted' has been made too serious by ponderous English attempts to excuse frivolity; 'fun' has been made miserable by people who have never enjoyed themselves in their lives; but I remember Rudolf Wittkower using the word 'festive' with strict technical accuracy to describe the swags of carved greenery between the capitals on Inigo Jones's Banqueting House in Whitehall—'as if hung there for a festival.' Something of that quality comes from the clear bright colours of Haslemere, the hints of impermanence in the plastic structure, the slightly maniac quality of Stirling's floor-to-ceiling radiators and the obsessive reiteration of the lamp-post/seaside-illuminations theme in Cullinan's balustrading. It is a quite extraordinary building in which the two architects gave Olivetti far better, in my estimation, than Olivetti deserved of them."
R. Banham, *Architectural Review*, April 1974

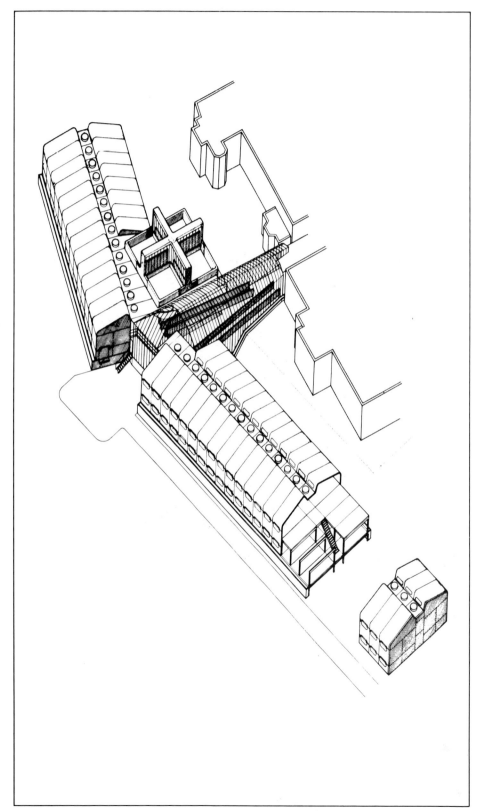

"Olivetti had left nothing to chance. They designed this June 'happening' to promote their Corporate Image located midway between technology and art. Chefs from Harry's Bar in Venice were flown in to sing as they prepared their famous risottos, 'Bellini' drinks and 'Carpaccio' filettos. You couldn't buy a Carpaccio but, if male, were given a Henry Moore lithograph. (Wives got scarves. Has Olivetti's sociologist found Women's Lib less virile in England?) A music program in the new auditorium included the Ambrosian Singers and a 'Divertimento for Olivetti machines,' composed and conducted by Tristram Cary. It wasn't quite Handel's 'Water Music' written for George I, or a Mozart opera commissioned by the Emperor Joseph II; but the idea was there. Following this was a Garden Supper Party with films by Ichikawa, lighting by 150 flickering torches, and a bonfire by tree trunks straight out of a Fellini or Antonioni.

"Part of this Training Centre resembles a blown-up piece of Olivetti equipment. Its rounded

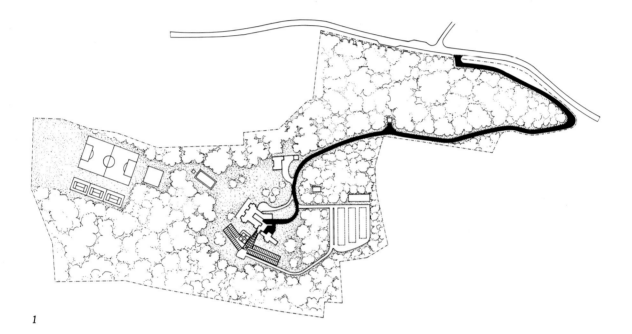

1

2

Olivetti Training School, 1969

curves and slick surface recall the 'soft-touch Divisumma 18 portable electric printing calculator.' It doesn't have the 'rubber nipples,' the new nice-feel keys of this computer; but it is vaguely sensual, especially around the auditorium which, in skin color tones, slithers and undulates its way to the ground. You want to caress and fondle this auditorium—at least as much as you want to caress and fondle any Olivetti typewriter. In part, this metaphor is sustained by the unfamiliarity of the scale. Since there is no traditional eave, and the homogeneous plastic curves over roof and wall (thus getting rid of the usual separation, including even the gutter) you see this as much like a kitchen blender as like a building.

3

4

5

"The four main elements of the new building smash into each other in a carefully careless way that is traditionally English. But they have a toughness and uncompromising quality—even a studied inelegance—which is not English at all. Had a Classicist designed it, there would be graceful separations between materials and spaces, doorways with moldings and elegant junctures.

Instead, Stirling, with his commitment to the straightforward, has just let things happen. Or so it appears until one studies the repetition of 'awkwardness.' The glass link flares out from the Edwardian mansion at a dissonant angle and frames into the two plastic wings with even more disharmony. The cruciform auditorium bites into one wing leaving wedges of twenty-two degrees. If

the wings are railroad cars, then what we see is a train accident.

"Finally the glazed gallery, a space which can be used for many activities. First of all, it is a marvelous circulation link between both wings and the mansion, a *trompe l'oeil* space which, because it flares out in three dimensions, seems

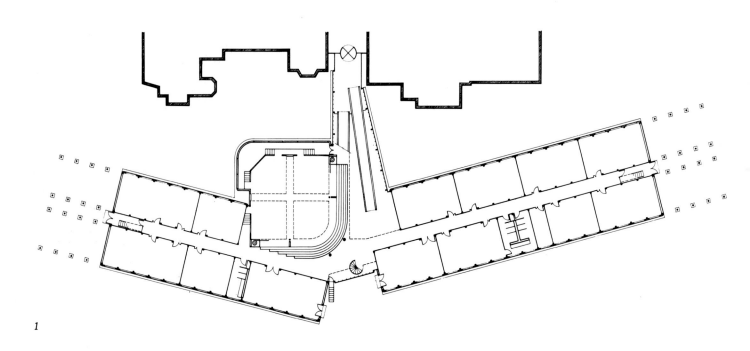

1

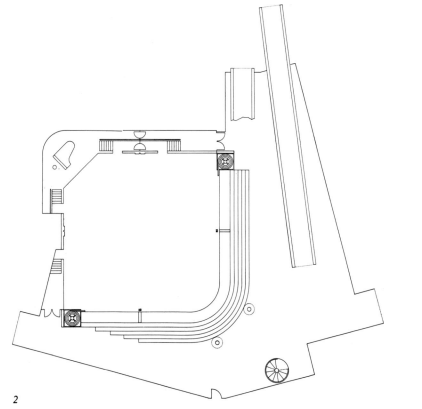

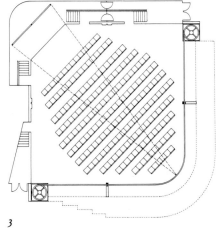

2

3

twice as long one way as the other. It is the *Scala Regia* of Bernini with a scissor ramp of Le Corbusier and glazing by Paxton—a kind of greenhouse ship's deck where grey flannel technicians can meet quietly and converse. The space is at once open to the outside wind, rain and natural elements and protected from them. Its spiky angles, filled with light and glistening, give

momentary views of greenery."
C. Jencks, *Architecture Plus*, March 1974

1. *Lower entrance level.*
2. *Multispace: and adjoining overflow areas.*
3. *Multispace: as lecture hall.*
4. *Upper entrance level.*
5. *Multispace: subdivided.*
6. *Multispace: maximum subdivisions.*

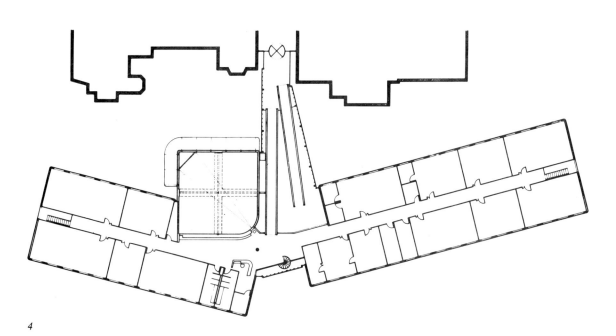

4

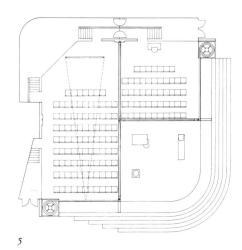

5

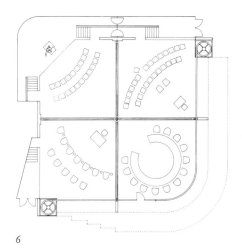

6

1. Opened multispace.
2. Lift up partitions and roof housing.
3. Section through glazed link.
4. Section through classrooms.
5,6. Views in multispace with partitions lifted.
7. Section through link.

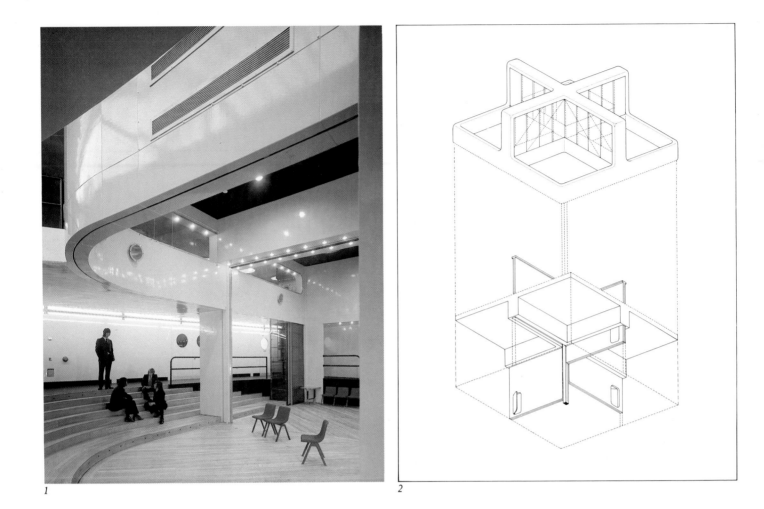

1

2

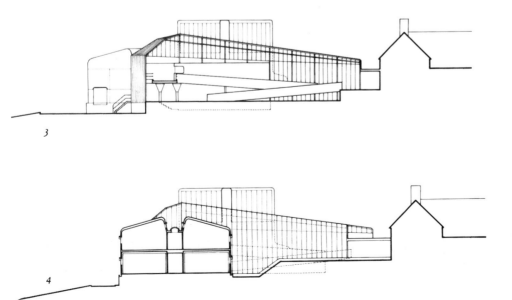

3

4

8. *Elevation towards service road.*

5

6

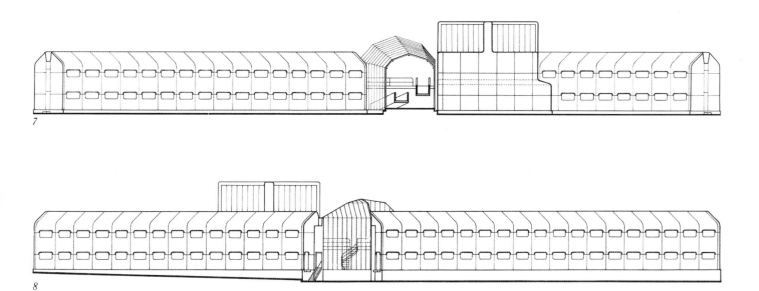

7

8

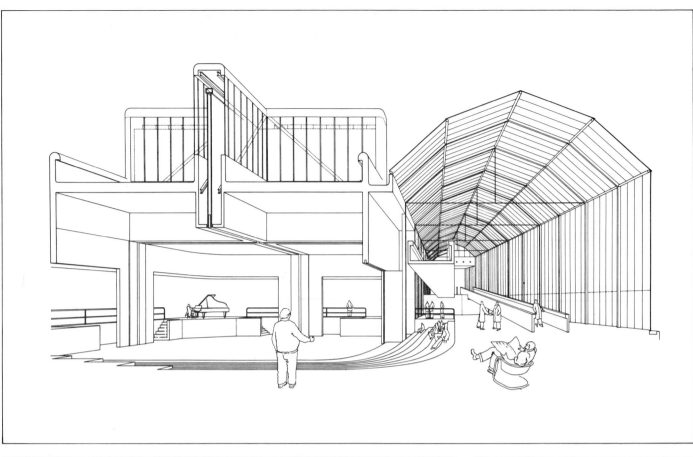

2

3

4

5

1. Multispace and glazed link to house.
2. Service entrance.
3. View into link.
4. Classrooms exterior.
5. Classrooms interior.
6. Axonometric of multispace and ramps.
7. Section through classroom wing.
8. Sketch of structural assemblage.

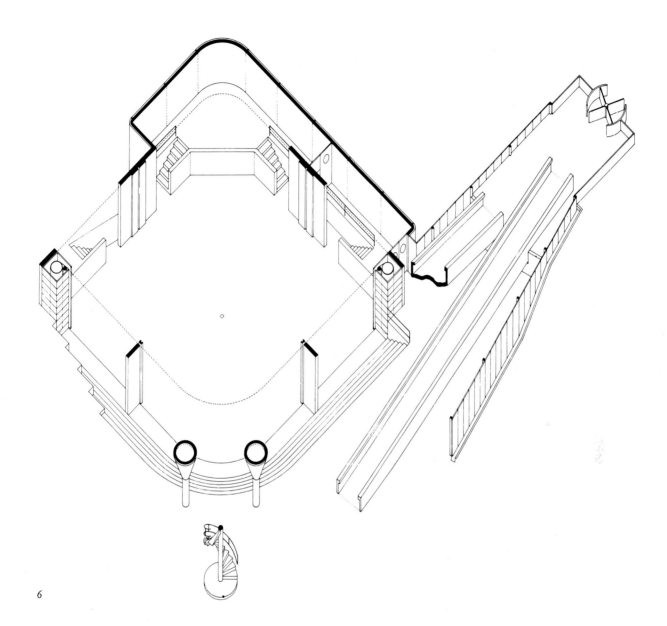

6

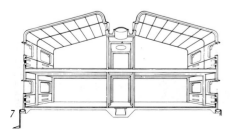

7

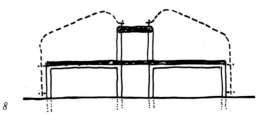

8

Olivetti Training School, 1969

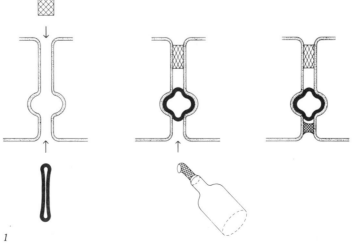

1

Olivetti Training School, 1969

153

1

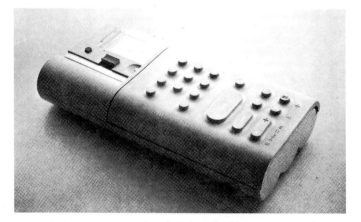

Olivetti Training School, 1969

1969
Siemens AG Munich
(limited competition)

James Stirling
Leon Krier
Michael Lehmbrock
Oswald Zoeggeler

(Extracts from Competition Report)

The complex is planned on a linear principle, so that incremental expansion can take place (two twin towers being the smallest module of expansion). The first stage is composed of three increments (six twin towers). The second stage of two increments (four twin towers), representing 60 per cent expansion (supporting a population of approximately 13,000).

The podium building is six stories and has a central core of computer research and development with the production hall at the lowest level; above this are service roads and the directors' car park, entered directly off the ringway. Adjacent to these internal roads are experimental workshops alternating with vehicle delivery areas. Above are two floors of computer research and above this is the outside 'flat-top' social valley, flanked by colonnades containing amenity areas. This elevated pedestrian boulevard, which faces south, is lined with trees and is an important feature of the new building —although a minor element in the brief, the social requirement has become a major factor in the solution. Within the colonnades are restaurants, snack bars, newsagents, tobacconists, drug stores, etc., and at the level above are social and public relation rooms required by management, i.e. library, auditorium, registry, visitors' reception, etc.

Within the podium building, and on either side of the central computer core, are six floors of accommodation with windows overlooking the water gardens between the main building and the multi-level car parks. The two lower floors are technical offices, the two middle floors laboratories and the two upper floors drawing offices.

Above the podium building and on either side of the social valley are the management office towers (seven floors of offices and a top service floor).

Their structural shafts contain lifts, staircases and service ducts. The management offices in the towers have the character of 'club land' and are of considerable spaciousness. Mezzanine floors alternate with full width floors giving double height spaces. The walls of the towers are glazed. Outside there is a full height revolving sun screen, computer programmed to the hours of the day with variable louvres adjusting to the strength of sunlight.

The training school, management headquarters and exhibition hall are combined in a single building complex north of the ringway. The upper floors coincide with the social valley level of the main building, the two buildings being linked by a pedestrian boulevard.

1. *View down shopping arcades with office towers above.*

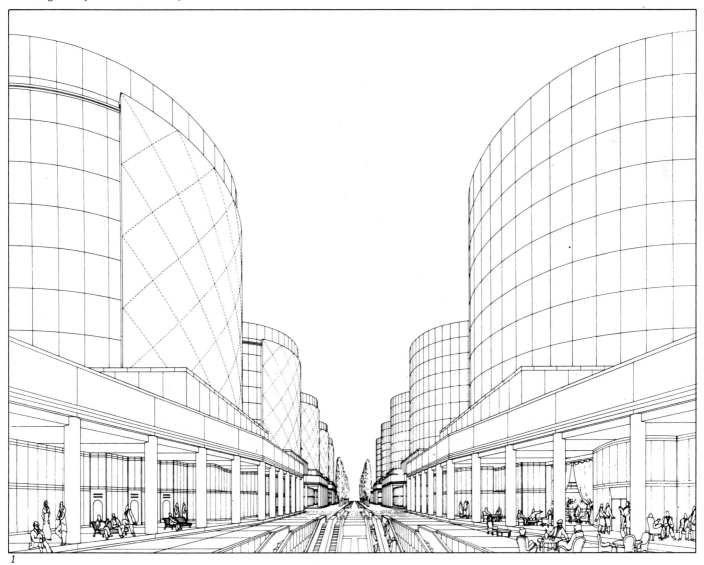

1

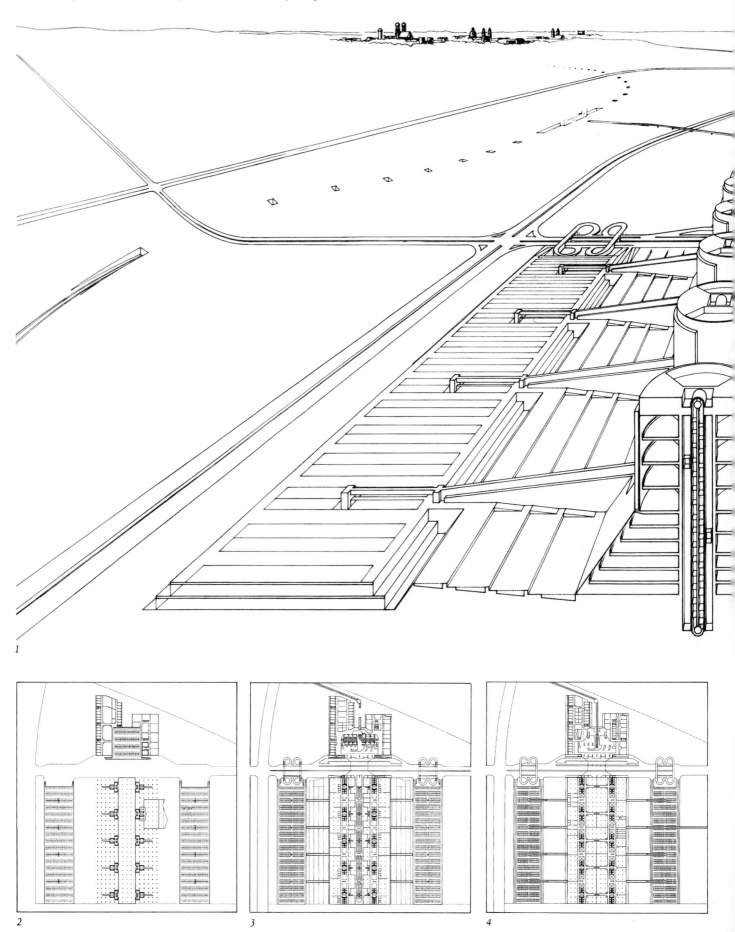

1. The proposed complex near Munich.
2. Basement: production hall and storage cellar.

3. Ground floor: internal service road, offices, visitors' parking and lecture halls.

4. Second floor; computer core, offices and exhibition hall.

1

2

3

4

Siemens AG, 1969

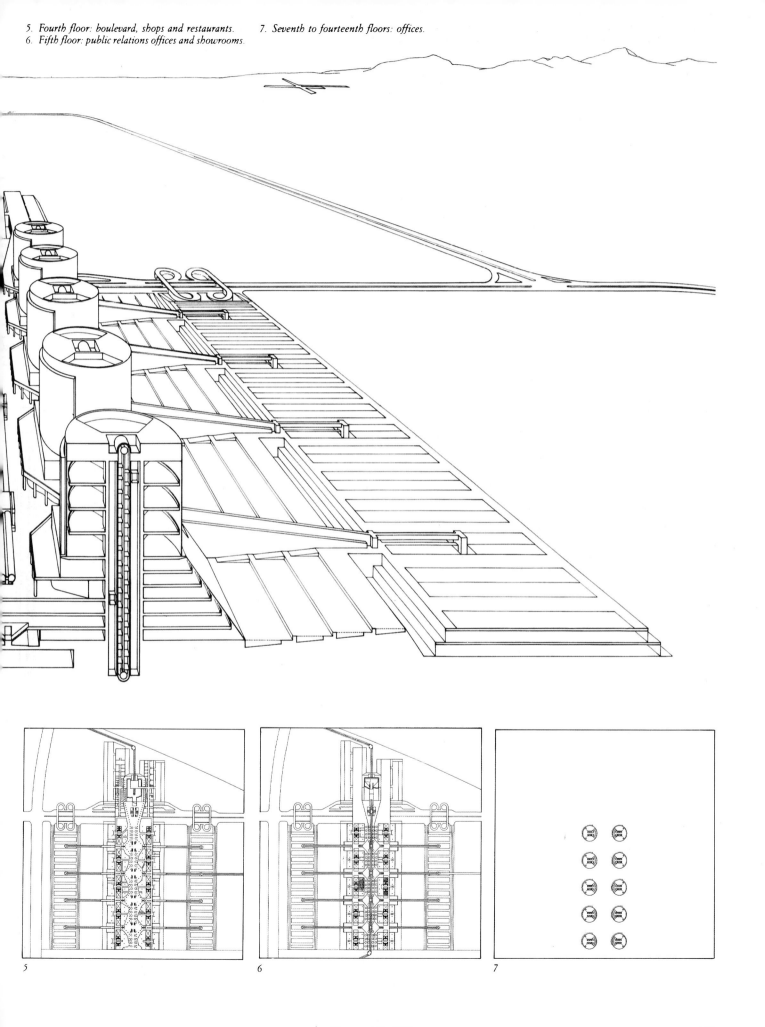

5

6

7

Arriving visitors can turn off the ringway where there are short-term parking spaces immediately adjacent to the main entrance. Inside, the entrance floor slopes gently upwards and this inclined plane provides a large area of public exhibition space.

A travelator moving in both directions connects the new building with the S-Bahn and U-Bahn subway stations. The travelator passes down the social valley between the rows of office towers, with set-down and pick-up escalators, corresponding to the plazas between towers. This tree-lined valley is considered the heart of the project, and from this area there is circulation into all parts of the building and also to the walkways leading to the multi-level car parks on the flanks.

"In the Siemens headquarters symmetrical order and neoclassical *ordonnance* is complemented by the quiet elegance of its cybernetic technique. In Siemens the pure cylindrical forms of the ten glazed office towers—each one inflected by the movement of a shallow metal sun screen, rotating silently across its periphery—establish the abstract co-ordinates of a symmetrical tree-lined axis set

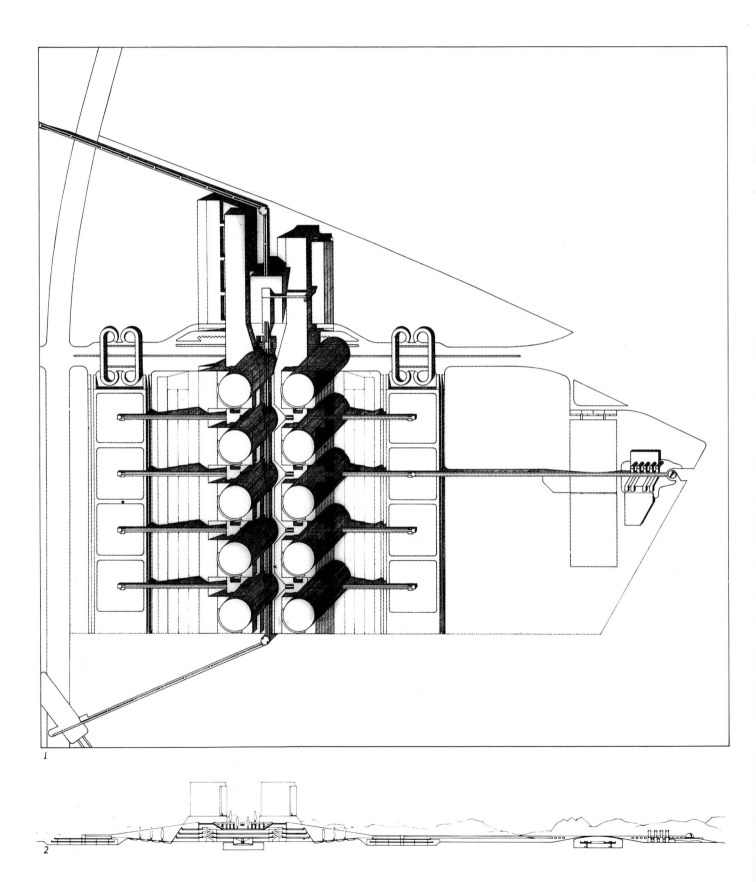

1

2

into a podium base. With Siemens, Stirling abandons his preoccupation with the modulation of expressive volumes through finely grained elements—the module of the brick and glazing bar. At the same time, these complexes emerge as 'plug-in' structures, set as free-standing objects in the open 'motopia' landscape of the 20th century. Against this ubiquitous panorama, certain associations are unavoidably aroused, depending on the specific context of both site and program. In Siemens, as in the project for Dorman Long, the metaphors are patently industrial—the 'flat-scape' megastructures of the blast furnace and the oil refinery."

K. Frampton, *Architecture and Urbanism,* February 1975

1. *Roof plan.*
2. *Cross section.*
3. *Model.*
4. *Long section.*

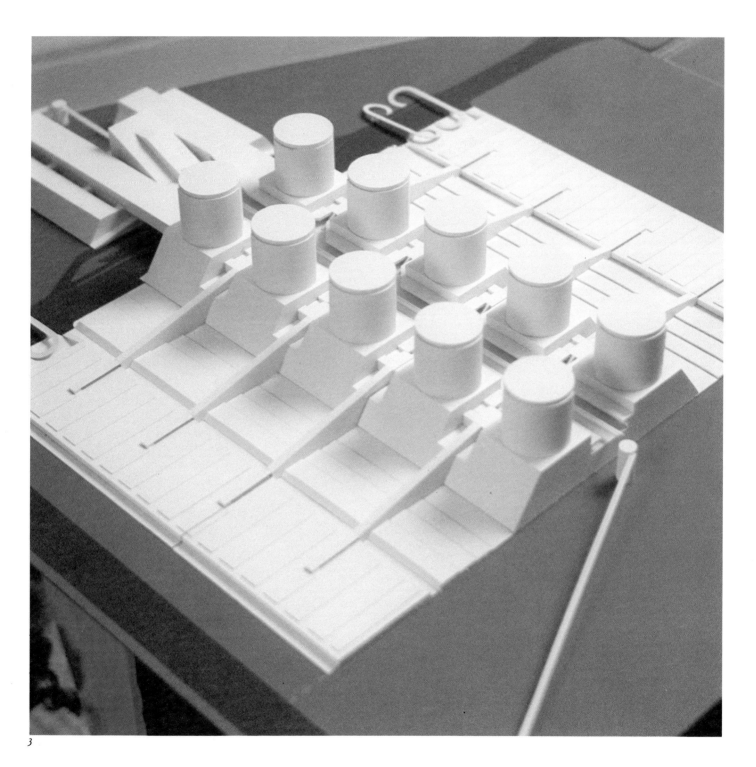

3

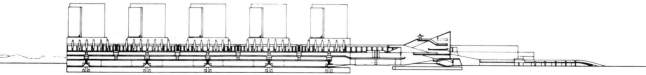

4

1. *Single increment of buildings for phased construction.*

2. *Pedestrian circulation through shops.*
3. *Model with travelator.*

4. *Partial plan: computer core, development offices and service rooms.*

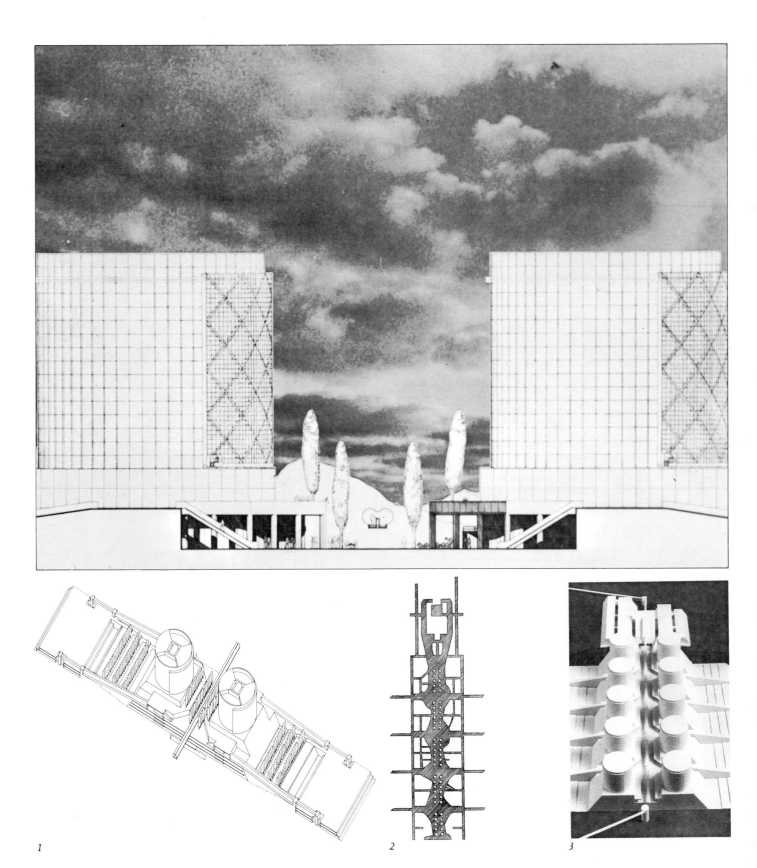

1

2

3

Siemens AG, 1969

*5. **Plan** of typical floor in office tower: managers'*
offices with typists and services on the mezzanine.

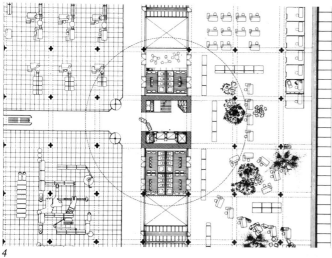

4

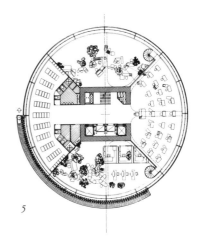

5

"Six months 'practical experience' in an architect's office was required in fourth year at Liverpool School of Architecture and it was on the occasion of informing my mother—a very reserved Scots/Irish school teacher—I had the opportunity to do this in New York, that she uncharacteristically and without warning told me I should know then—I had been conceived in New York during a voyage on my father's ship, he was the archetypal Scottish chief engineer. Consequently I have entertained beginning an autobiography—'I was conceived in a bunk on board ship, lying in New York harbour in the roaring twenties,' but as I couldn't keep that speed going, I shan't write it. Thus I sailed to America and came to spend time detailing the bookshelving for a new Gothic library in Princeton."
JS

1968
Redevelopment study
New York

James Stirling, Arthur Baker
Craig Hodgetts
Mary Jane Long
Michael Wurmfield

(Extracts from Architects Report)

The area studied is deteriorating without noticeable sign of renewal. This could well continue indefinitely until the pressures of midtown expansion build up.

The intention of this study is to propose a method of planned redevelopment which would create a balanced growth, taking into consideration the needs of the residential community as well as the necessity to encourage business.

The report considered the existing conditions, the potential land use and alternative types of development, concluding with detailed recommendations.

The purpose of Phase 1 was to establish a waterfront recreational development connected with existing residential areas.

Phase 2 related to the economic upgrading of the area through the establishment of a spine of offices along 47th or 48th street.

In Phase 3 the office spine is enlarged to a three block width accomodating further midtown growth.

In Phase 4 the renewal of the waterfront area can be completed through the demolition of the piers. The whole area back to 11th Avenue should become an extension of Riverside Drive.

"We want the terminal to achieve a design quality that will make it a symbolic ocean gateway worthy of the world's greatest port. We want it to be a focus of interest and activity that will act as a magnet to the public and relate the river and the waterfront to the city.

"We think these objectives can best and perhaps only be achieved by broadening the scope of the proposal to include related developments of the adjacent upland area, and by providing physical connections between that area and the terminal. This is the kind of unique design opportunity the Paley committee pointed to and we don't intend to let it slip by."
Mayor John V. Lindsay, 30 June 1967

1. *View of the study area from the Hudson River.*
2. *Existing land and street grid pattern.*
3. *Proposed land and street grid pattern.*

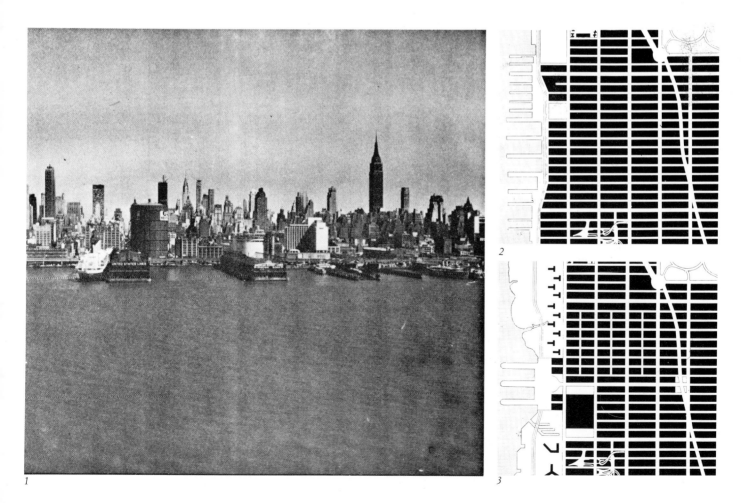

1

2

3

1969
Lima Peru, low cost housing

James Stirling
Jorge Burga
James Watkin
Eduardo Palacio

(Extracts from Architects Report)

After the "first build" by the contractor it is intended that the houses should be completed at ground level and above by house owners in self-building styles.

The growth plan drawing shows in stages of self-building a 4P house becoming a complete "one story house" (8P +), considered the most typical method of growth. Thereafter expansion takes place on the floor above, either as a separate dwelling or, in the case of a large family, as additional bedrooms and living space, in which instance part of the ground level accommodation could be used for other purposes (i.e. shop or garage, etc.).

When the house is at its smallest (4P) the kitchen, dining and living areas are shown combined. As the house increases in size to approximately 6P the dining and living areas are shown separated from the kitchen by a wall and doors. This wall (knockdown or movable) is shown in a new position when the house becomes 8P and 8P +, increasing the living space of the house as the family size grows.

Each house has two front entrance doors. One door is direct into the living area (social/traditional), the second (functional) into the house circulation area leading via the staircase and garden patio through to the service patio.

All rooms are planned with through ventilation, i.e., separate openings on opposed walls to create cross draughts.

The "first build" by the contractor takes advantage of large-scale initial production (cost and speed of erection) and is an assemblage of precast concrete wall and floor units. Party walls and outside perimeter walls are of sandwich construction and are precast units rising from ground beams incorporating window and door openings and also parapets—these are crane erected.

Roof/floor units are lightweight r.c. beams with hollow pot infill which could be man erected

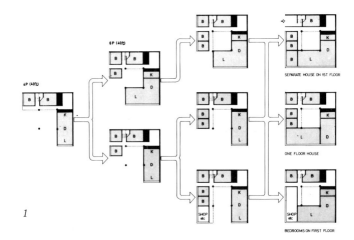

1

2

allowing self-help methods of construction to take over as expansion is required.

Just as the individual rooms of the house are grouped around the garden patio, so the various sizes of house groupings associate with differing scales of social and community space. The hierarchy grows from the individual house to the immediate neighbors by making an initial group of four houses about common party walls (and common services) grouped around the service patios. These clusterings of four house units are then grouped around a common entrance patio forming 20 or 21 houses. Thereafter this larger group becomes the basic cluster unit forming the neighborhood

3

(approximately 400 houses) and is related to access roads and car parking. There are four such neighborhoods in the allocated site area (1,560 houses) and each is separated by a public park (planted, informal garden valleys) in which are sited the schools, etc.

Flanking the approaches to the neighborhood parks and enclosing the ends of the housing areas are commercial buildings, shopping and community centers.

1. Growth plan of typical house.
2. New settlement of 10 neighborhoods.
3. A neighborhood with roads and car parking.
4. Parks with schools between neighborhoods.

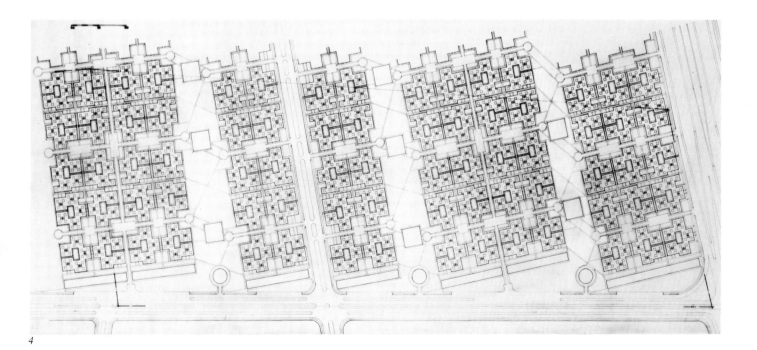

4

" 'The thing which is different about Peru is the tremendous free-for-all among house owners and builders,' Stirling reports. 'People invade the suburbs and build their own houses out of the materials at hand, and those with houses build on them outwards, or upwards. We did see quite a large housing estate designed only a matter of six years ago by a Peruvian architect. You could find only one house in every 30 like the original, and even that was barely recognizable; the other 29 bore no relationship at all to the original.

" 'The houses were extended horizontally over the garden or patio, and then went up vertically. They always seem to change the architect's windows, they put up wrought iron work, they paint them different colours. One might extend in concrete another brick. It has its own very extraordinary quality.'

"Stirling accepts that his design too may be transformed into architectural quiltwork. 'We have to allow for this, and organize it into something less uncontrolled. In a way, it is

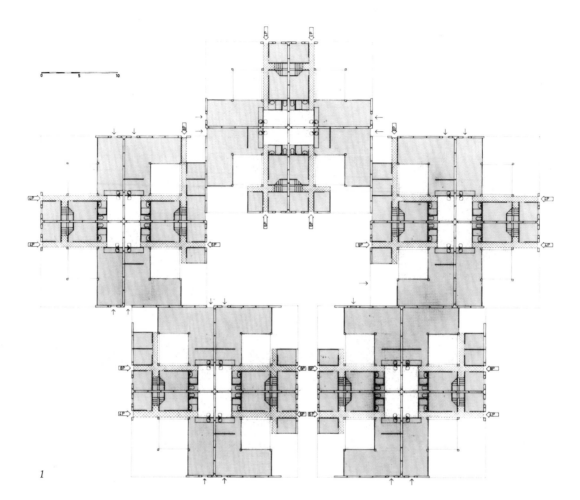

1

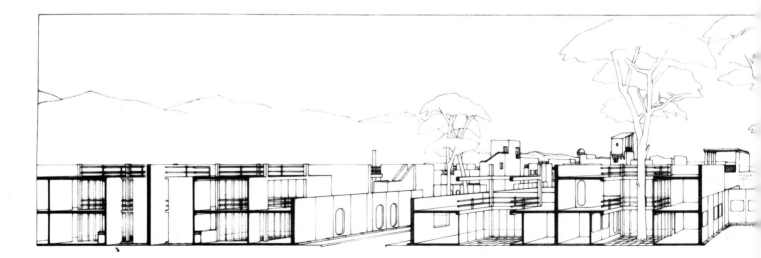

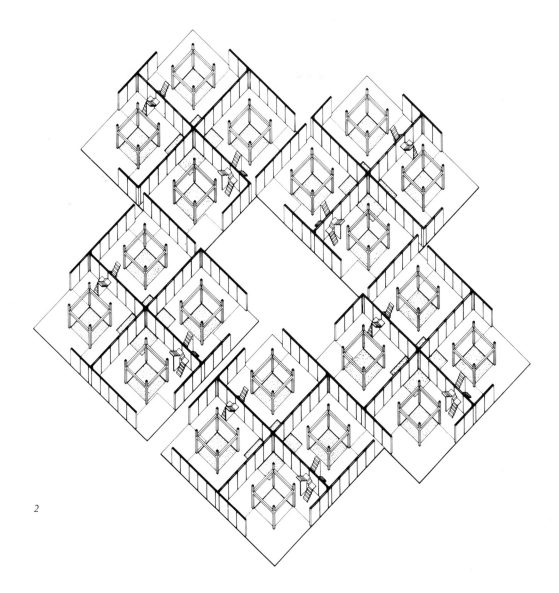

2

1. *Ground floor: basic four-house clusters.*
2. *Minimum house as built by the government.*
3. *Minimum house as developed by occupants.*

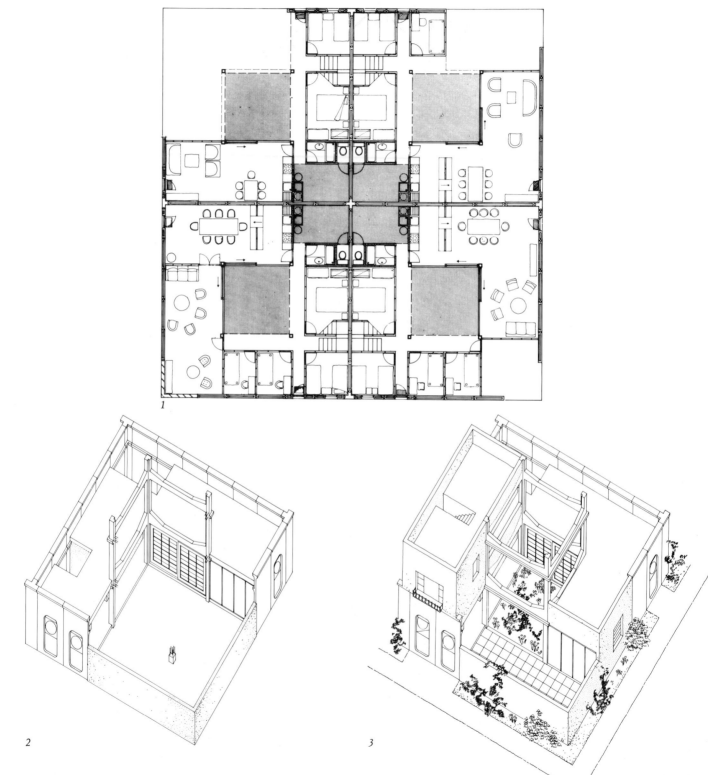

Lima Peru, low cost housing, 1969

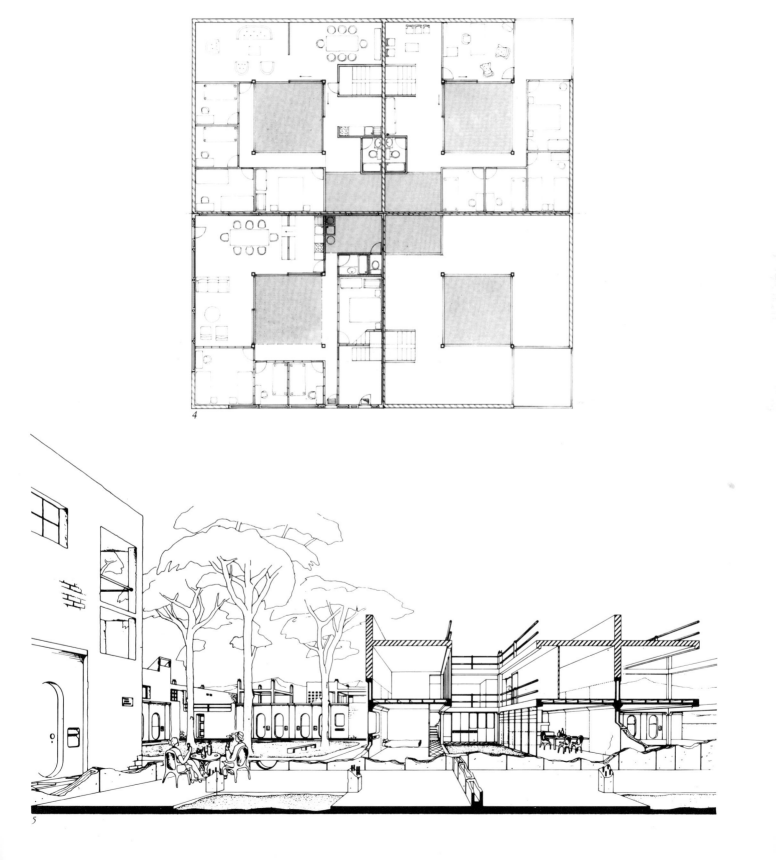

4

5

Lima Peru, low cost housing, 1969

1970
Derby Town Centre
(limited competition)

James Stirling
Leon Krier

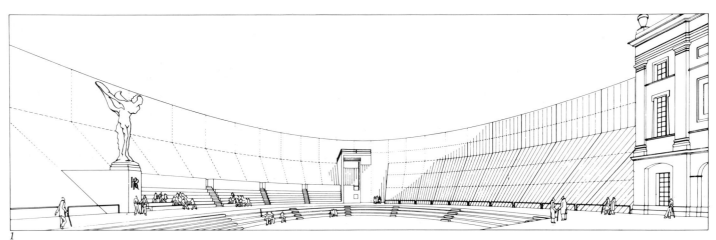

1

(Extracts from the Competition Report)

*The new building is designed as a background to
the incidents in the square. It includes:*
*A. An arena for outdoor activities, i.e., bandstand,
pop concerts, public speaking, outdoor theatre,
happenings, etc.*
*B. The staged seating backing on to the new
building and overlooking the arena.*
*C. A repositioning of the Assembly Rooms facade,
inclined to symbolize its destruction by fire and
forming a proscenium to the arena, with a hollowed
out space under for platform activities. Entry to this
hollowed out space would be from the rear through
the classical door in the facade.*
D. Repositioning of the war memorial.
E. A grouping of public telephones.
*F. The existing campanile and entrance to the
Guildhall.*
*G. The entrance canopy to the new building with
the Lord Mayor's balcony over.*
*H. The projecting ramp which is a secondary
entrance to the shopping arcade within the new
building.*

*The inclusion of these elements creates two types of
space within the Market Square: (a) an arena and
(b) a flat piazza area adjacent to the Guildhall
entrance.*

*A major element—not part of the brief—which we
have included is the arrangement of shops and other
functions along an internal shopping arcade (same
width as Burlington Arcade, London, increasing*

*in width higher up). From this glass roofed arcade
covered access can be made to the principal
accommodation, i.e., banquet halls, auditorium
halls, bars, art gallery and offices, etc.*

"The preservation of an historic facade was
suggested. Stirling tilted it back (to form a band
shell roof) definitively detaching it from a former
context and theatrically crashing it into another;
ad hoc preservationism at its most astounding,
witty and even considerate, since the facade was a
familiar but not remarkable sight."
Adhocism by C. Jencks and N. Silver

"The ruinations inflicted by saturation bombing in
the last war begin to pale before the ravages
achieved in the last twenty years through urban
renewal. Aerial photographs of town centres such
as Derby, taken between say 1920 and 1970, speak
for themselves. Derby was never heavily blitzed
but for all the difference that it has made it might
just as well have been razed to the ground."
K. Frampton, *RIBA Journal*, March 1976

"The parabola which Stirling has followed has a
high degree of internal consistency. It indeed
reveals the consequence of a reduction of the
architectural object to pure language, yet it wishes
to be compared to the tradition of the Modern
Movement, to be measured against a body of
work strongly compromised in an antilinguistic
sense. Stirling has 'rewritten' the 'words' of
modern architecture, building a true 'archeology

of the present.'

"Let us look at the design for the Civic Center at
Derby. An ambiguous and amused reference to
history is spelled out by the facade of the old
Assembly Room, inclined by 45 degrees and
serving as a proscenium to the theater which is
defined by the U-shaped gallery. The entire work
of Stirling possesses this 'oblique' character. The
shopping arcade recalls the Burlington Arcade in
London. It also brings to mind the bridge of
Pyrex tubes at the Johnson Wax building by
Frank Lloyd Wright, and perhaps even more
strongly recalls an unbuilt as well as undesigned
architecture—the shopping arcade modeled on a
sort of circular Crystal Palace which, following the
description by Ebenezer Howard, was to have
surrounded the central area of the ideal Garden
City. The Civic Center in Derby is in fact an
urban 'heart.' It is, however, part of a real city
and not a utopian model, and consequently the
memory of Joseph Paxton takes on a flavor of a
disenchanted but timely *repêchage.*"
M. Tafuri, *Oppositions 3*

1. Market Square—perspective.
*2. Inclined facade of Assembly Rooms recycled as
monument.*
3. Existing city center.
*4. Facade of Assembly Rooms preserved in
city-salvage dump.*
*5. Proposed inner city ring road and central
development.*
6. Site plan: ground level.

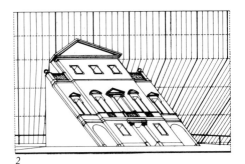

2

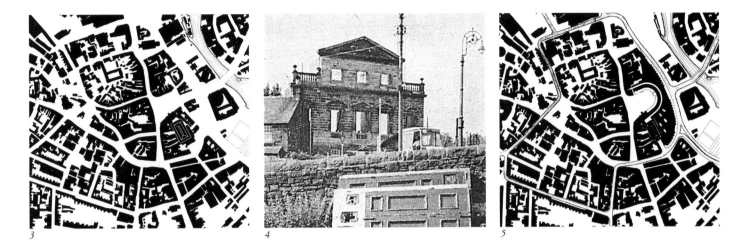

3   4   5

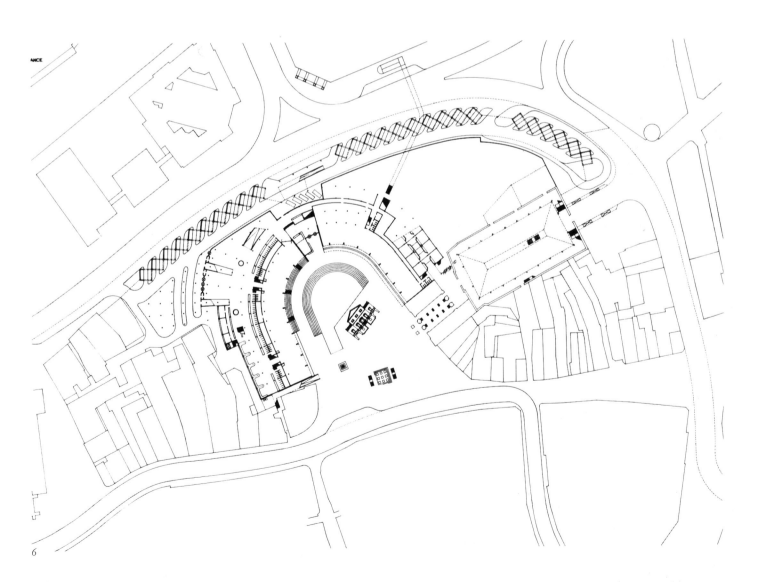

6

Derby Town Centre, 1970   171

1. *Section through Assembly Hall facade, arcade and parking garage.*
2. *Second floor plan: showing arcade, shops, upper level of foyers, banquet hall, entrance, offices and existing Guildhall.*

3. *Basement plan.*
4. *Section through auditorium, arcade and Market Square.*

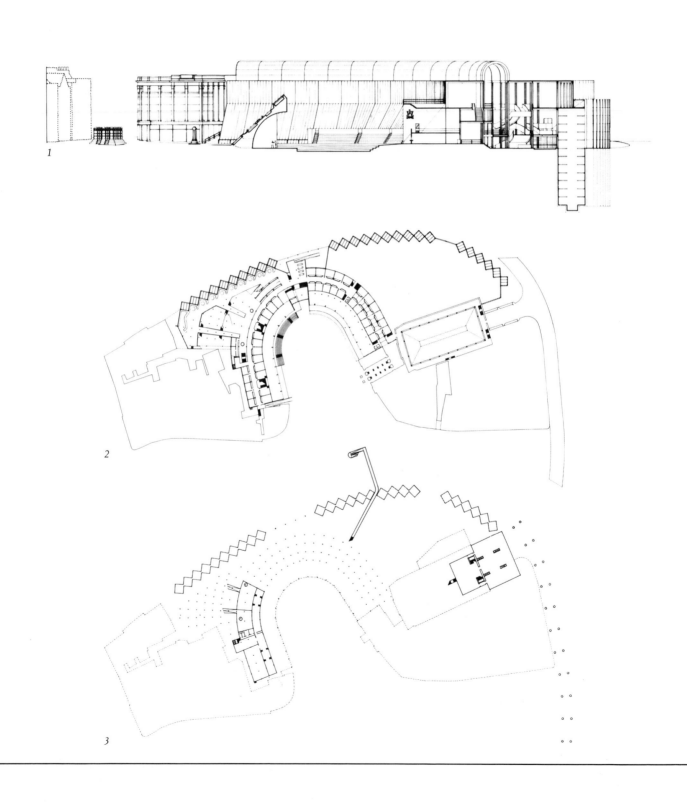

1

2

3

5. Third floor plan: showing auditorium, arcade, shops, offices, etc.

6. Fourth floor plan: showing art gallery, banquet rooms and upper level of auditorium and arcade.

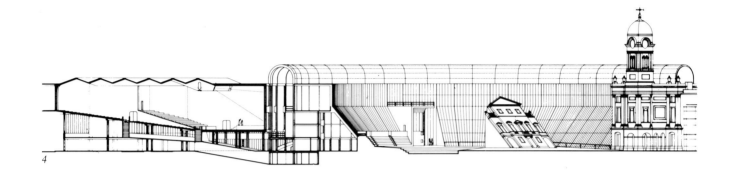

4

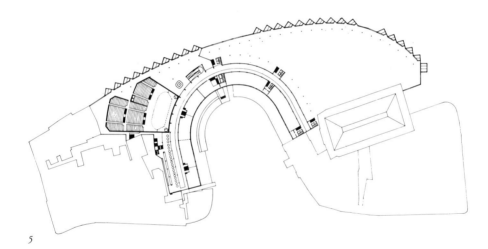

5

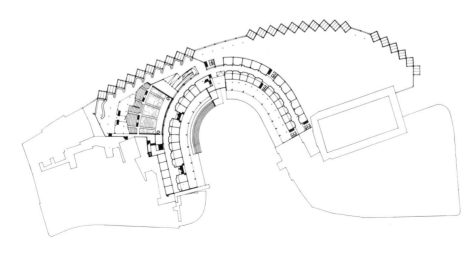

6

1. *Section through banquet hall, arcade, Market Square and offices.*
2. *Burlington arcade.*
3. *Ground floor—first phase.*
4. *Second floor—first phase.*
5. *Third floor—first phase.*

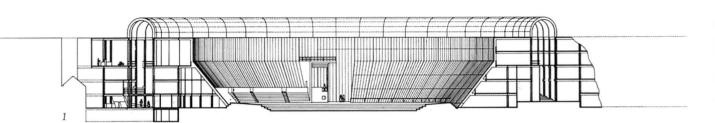

1

2

3

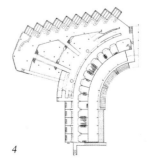

4

5

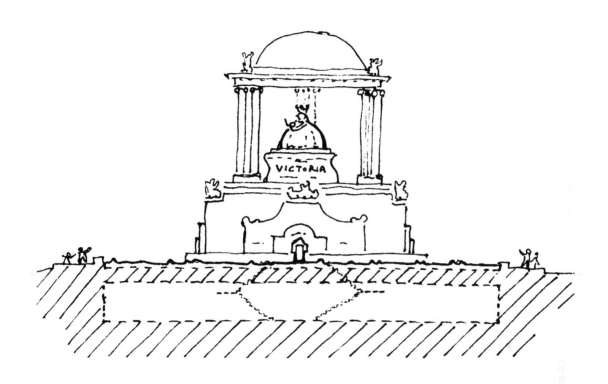

"The Queen Victoria Monument stood on a rise at the bottom of Castle Street, midway between the Town Hall and the Customs House. She looked towards neither but gazed steadfastly out to sea in the direction of the New World. She was raised on a podium and beneath her billowing skirts were located the largest public lavatories in Liverpool. All around got bombed flat and she earned the reputation of being bombproof. Soon these underground lavatories became the most popular air raid shelter on Merseyside and the site reverted to its original use for it was here that a 13th century castle had stood protecting the citizens of the Port. Thus the war, a monument and a public lavatory were combined as a (symbolic?) landmark—could therefore a public utility be a civic monument? In the Derby project we grouped the public telephones on a podium over public lavatories below;—a small monument in the new plaza." JS

7

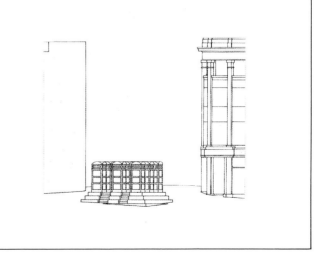

8

Derby Town Centre, 1970

Arts Centre, St. Andrews University

James Stirling, Michael Wilford
Crispin Osborne
Julian Harrap
Werner Kreis

St. Andrews University's Art Department is located in an 18th century house protected by the Scottish Fine Arts Commission. When the University decided to expand the Department, the facilities required were an art gallery for public exhibitions, a theater workshop, and studio space, for painting and sculpture.

A glazed connection was proposed between the existing gate lodges and the house: high curved wings creating a semi-public courtyard, a new outdoor room in the city.

The theater workshop was designed to vary in size and function with the use of removable partitions, housed in a fly loft above roof level.

"The idea of the city as a collage of 'types' lay behind the rational architecture conference (March 1975)...on display in the exhibition was his tiny project for an art gallery for St. Andrews, which collaged together three existing buildings, using a curved wall to create typical internal exhibition spaces and an external entry courtyard ...This collage technique, like townscape, can include historic fragments of popular conceptual reactions to a building or city. It destroys the total design, 'machine aesthetic' of the Bauhaus but retains ideal types."
G. Shane, *The Architects' Journal,* 16 July 1975

1. *St. Katherine's house and lodges.*

1

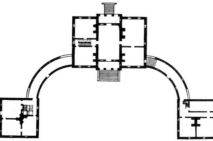

Arts Centre, St. Andrews University, 1971

1. *Section through glazing link and gallery wall.*
2. *Axonometric up view of court.*

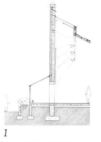

1

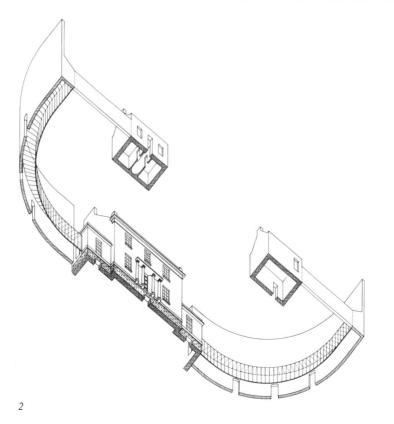

2

Arts Centre, St. Andrews University, 1971

1. *Section through gallery looking toward stage.*
2. *Axonometric of ground floor.*

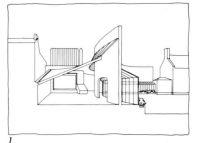

3–6. Alternate arrangements of gallery and theatre workshop.

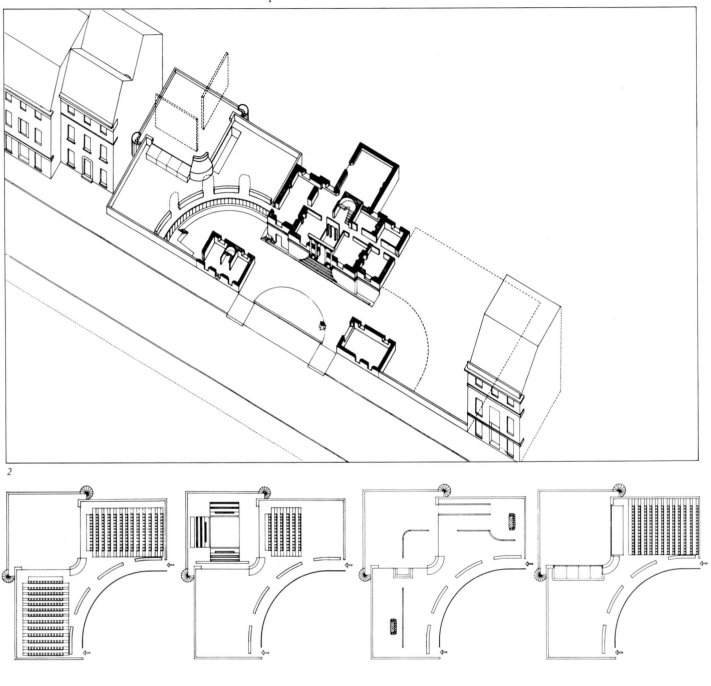

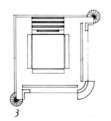

3

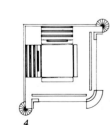

4

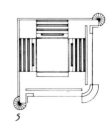

5

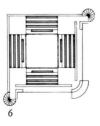

6

Arts Centre, St. Andrews University, 1971

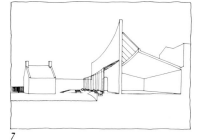

7

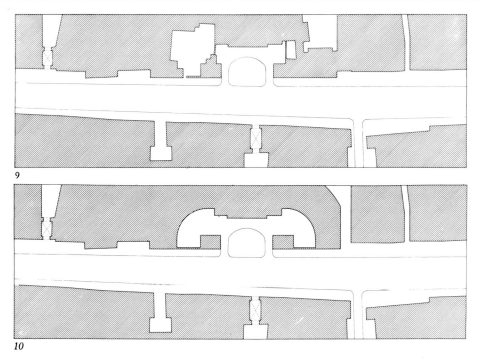

8

9

10

Arts Centre, St. Andrews University, 1971

1971
Olivetti Headquarters
Milton Keynes

James Stirling, Michael Wilford
Brian Riches
Werner Kreis
John Corrigan

(Extracts from Architects Report)

The new building is planned within the designated area of the new city of Milton Keynes. The site is in the north-west quarter of a landscaped park, the main feature of which is the existing lake. The Olivetti complex will be the only large group of buildings sited in this park. Administration offices are positioned overlooking the lake with south-easterly views of distant wooded hills. The warehouse and workshops are located behind the office building and screen the offices from the adjacent high-speed road.

Three floors of air-conditioned and open-planned offices are arranged over a sub-basement car park. A glazed concourse extends the length of the office building separating it from the warehouse, and providing access by means of galleries and staircases to all office and workshop floors, and also to the car park below. A conference room/auditorium with audio visual facilities is suspended within the concourse directly above the main entrance. The offices open on to terraces overlooking the lake and are separated from the concourse by a service zone containing wcs, locker rooms, tea areas, ducts, etc. In order to reduce circulation and disturbance to a minimum within the office areas, access to the service zone is via the galleries overlooking the concourse.

Separate vehicle access is provided to the restaurants, recreation facilities and boating club located at the southern end of the office building, so that the social facilities can be used in the evenings and on weekends.

"Here too, a simple but emerging idea. Since the Fagus factory onwards, the problem of relating workshops to an office building has been solved counterbalancing two volumes—one wide and low, the other tall and narrow—in a clever game of pure volumes, through an abstract-geometric procedure, linked to the purist aesthetics of the 1920s and 30s. J.S., inserting his volume at 45 degrees and slightly lifting it from the perimeter of the base, once again provokes a dramatic formal dissonance which, as always with him, finds a reason in landscape terms in the presence of the lake."
G.K. Koenig, *Casabella*, March 1975

1. Perspective.
2, 3. Model—views across lake.
4. Site plan.
5. Cutaway axonometric.
6,7. Model—views across lake.

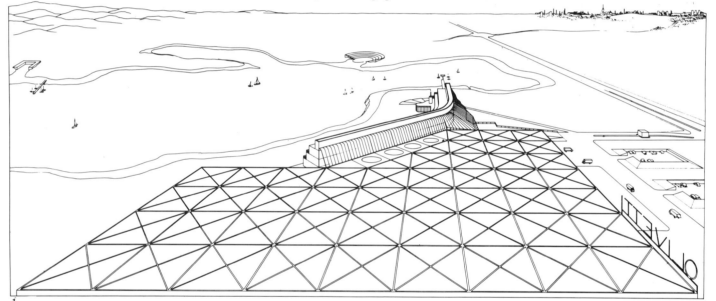

1

2

3

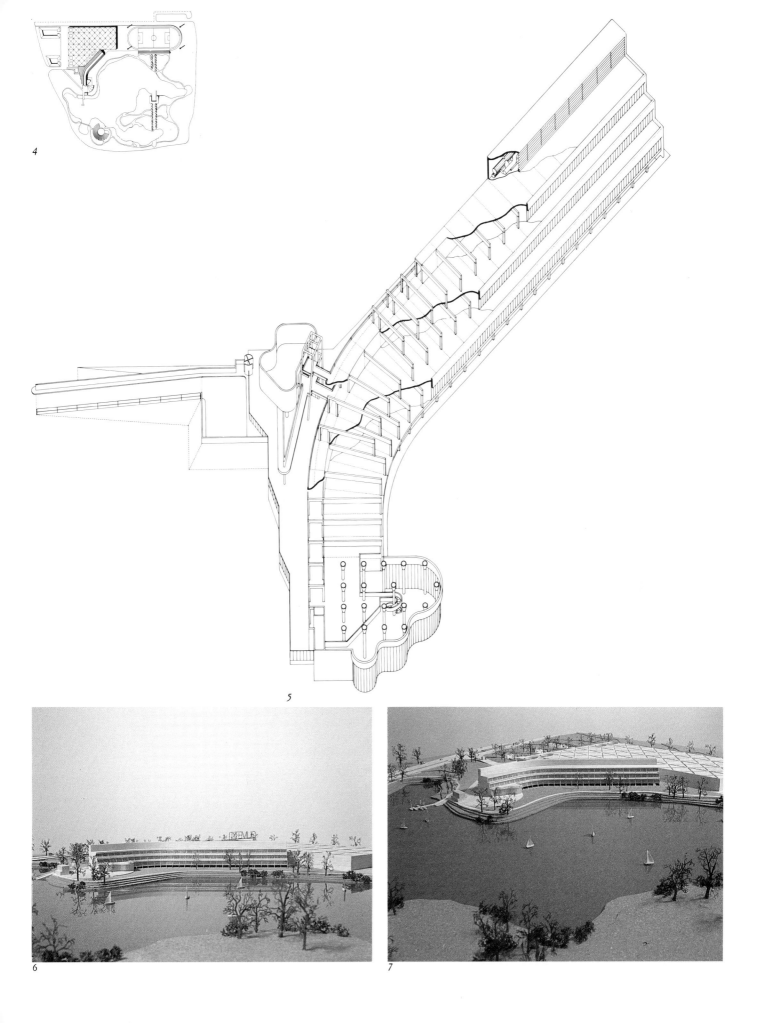

4

5

6

7

Olivetti Headquarters, 1971

1. *Ground floor plan: showing warehouse, parking,
restaurant and terraces.*

2. *Main floor plan: showing warehouse, concourse,
offices and restaurant.*

3. *Section through concourse towards offices.*
4. *Section through concourse towards warehouse.*

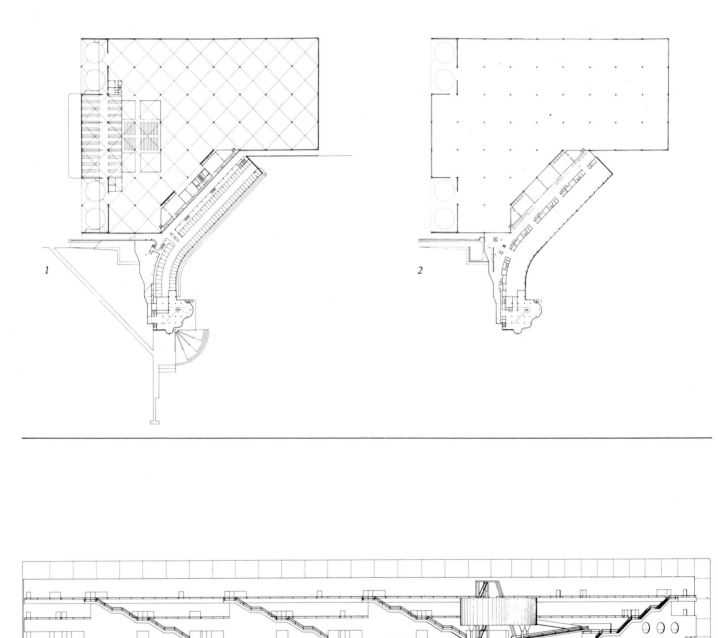

1

2

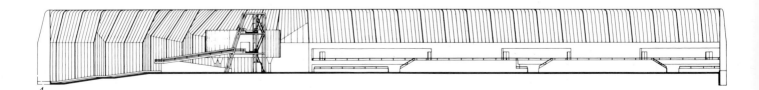

3

4

Olivetti Headquarters, 1971

1. Cutaway axonometric of concourse.
2,3. Model: views of entrance.
4. Typical office floor.

1

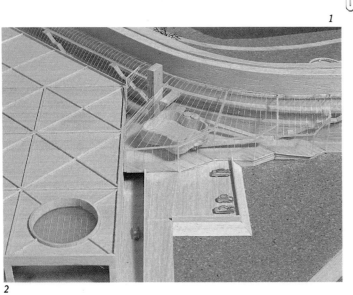

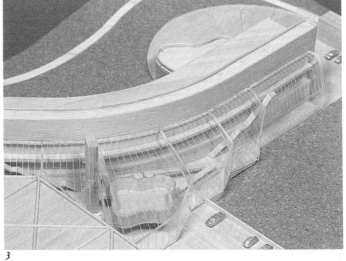

2

3

Olivetti Headquarters, 1971

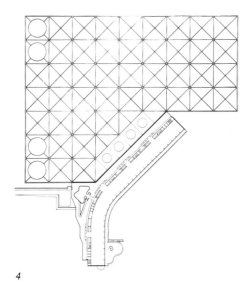

4

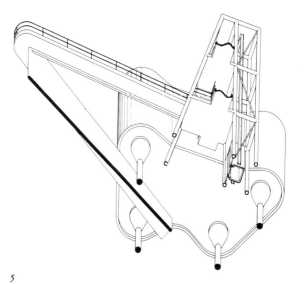

5

6

7

8

1. *Axonometric up view of restaurant.*
2. *Headquarters from across lake.*

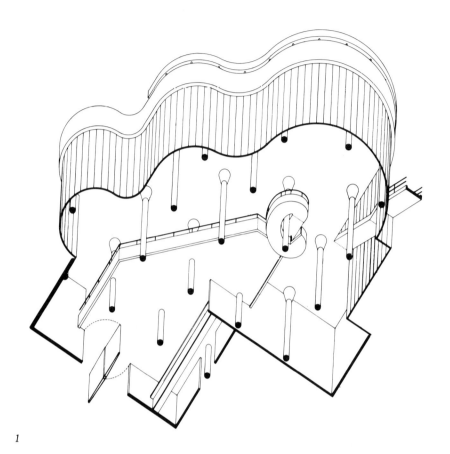

1

2

　　　　　　　　Olivetti Headquarters, 1971

Olivetti Headquarters, 1971

James Stirling, Michael Wilford
Brian Riches, Peter Ray,
Crispin Osborne, Ulrich Schaad,
David Falck

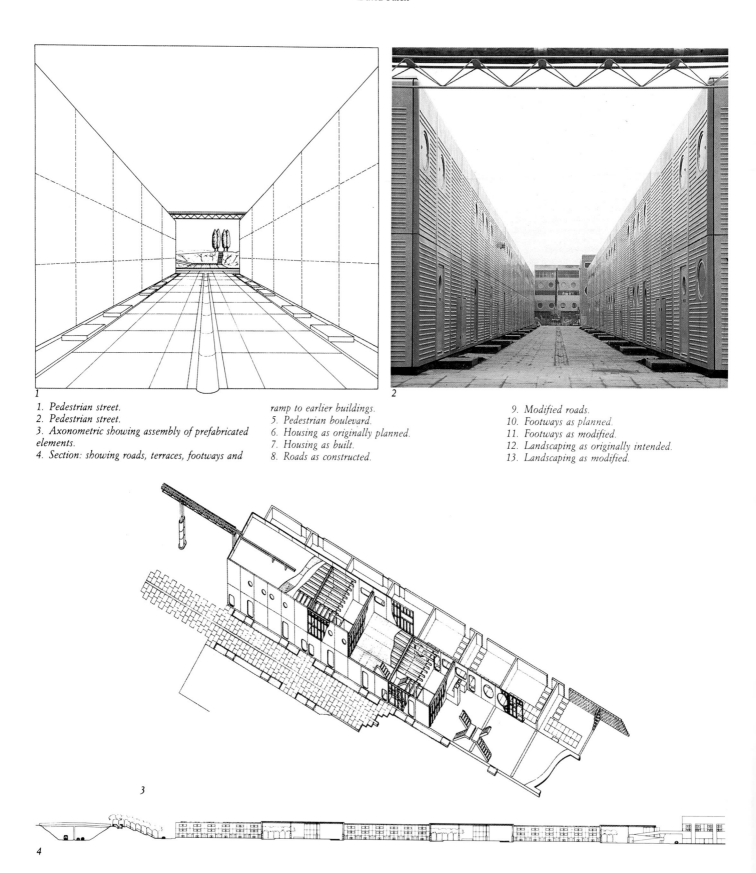

1. Pedestrian street.
2. Pedestrian street.
3. Axonometric showing assembly of prefabricated elements.
4. Section: showing roads, terraces, footways and

ramp to earlier buildings.
5. Pedestrian boulevard.
6. Housing as originally planned.
7. Housing as built.
8. Roads as constructed.

9. Modified roads.
10. Footways as planned.
11. Footways as modified.
12. Landscaping as originally intended.
13. Landscaping as modified.

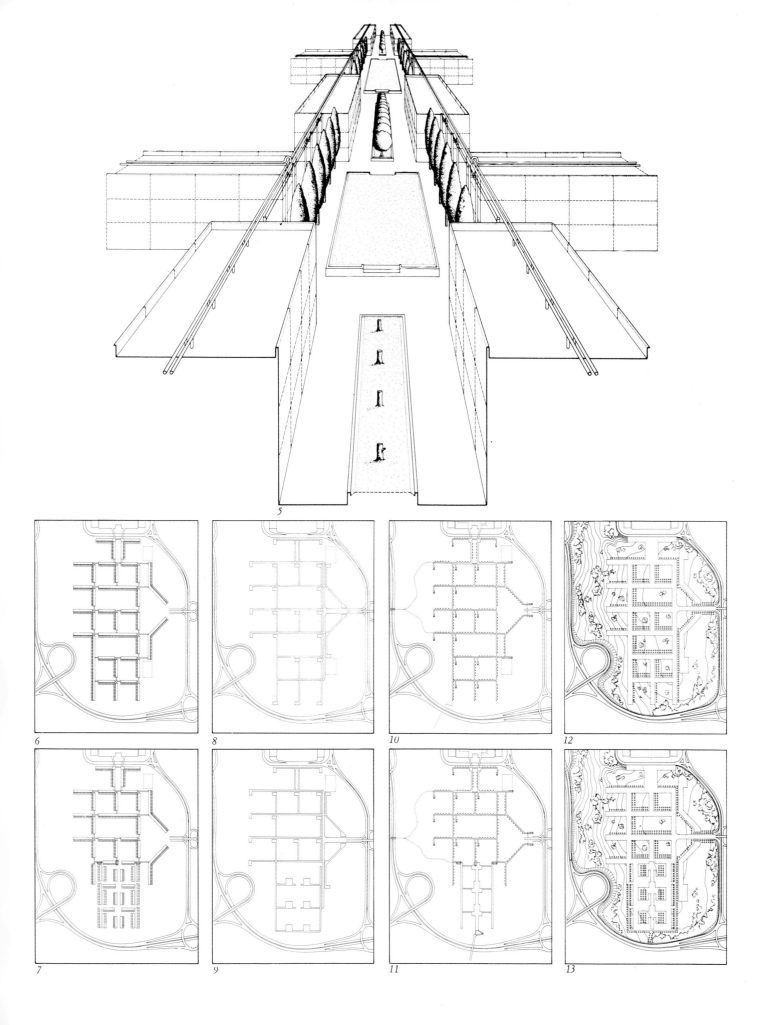

5

6　　　　　8　　　　　10　　　　　12

7　　　　　9　　　　　11　　　　　13

Southgate, housing, 1972　　　　　191

Halfway through construction of the Town Centre housing the City authorities decided to change the dwelling types, from primarily apartments to only family houses, each within a garden. As all roads and underground services had been built we had to fit the new proposal to the existing layout. A new district heating system was required and this was constructed across the roofs of the new houses.

"The latest and probably final part of the Town Centre housing at Runcorn is almost finished. It is low-rise housing with gardens: about 250 two and three storey dwellings arranged in terraces around squares.

"It is the same planning configuration as the massive portholed concrete terraces which form the greater part of Southgate. Unlike those five- and six-level terraces the low-rise housing is made from GRP panels. Panels are banded vertically in contrasting colours.

"It is as if the brightly coloured GRP-clad maisonettes of the first stages have been unplugged from the concrete supports structure

by some megastructural hand and laid out on the ground in a corner of the site next to the railway.

There is a nice, colourful, cheap and cheerful air about in the squares which are mostly planted out in grids of trees. It is not the way the Runcorn landscapers would have done it but six or seven years will tell us whether Stirling's abandonment of the irregular-equals-nature argument has been vindicated.

"In the squares the brightly coloured GRP more or less comes off. Deliberate or not it is two fingers to the bureaucrats who insist that architecture should be dignified and banal and colourless to match, perhaps, the weather. In front of each dwelling there is a tiny front yard offering a modicum of privacy behind not very high blockwork walls.

"But round the back it is straight Butlins: long rows of corrugated plastic walls with the occasional service pipe running up the walls and across gaps between rows of houses.

"Meantime back at the megastructure everybody is settling into their great squares with a remarkable degree of satisfaction."
S. Lyall, *Building Design*, 12 August 1977

1. *View down pedestrian street.*
2. *Three story terraces with gardens.*
3–6. *Plans of two story and three story housing terraces.*
7. *Section showing pedestrian street and public gardens.*

8. *Corner detail of GRP panels.*
9. *Two story and three story terraces along pedestrian street.*
10. *Pedestrian streets and public spaces.*

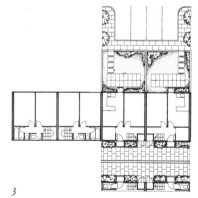

1

2

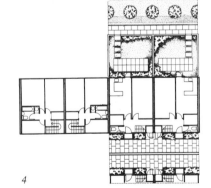

3

4

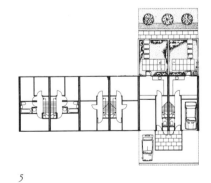

5

Southgate, housing, 1972

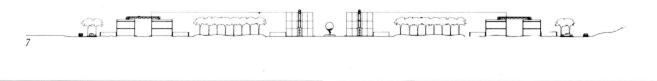

7

8

9

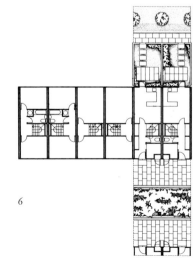

6

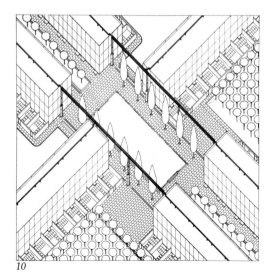

10

Southgate, housing, 1972

195

"The second phase buildings are two storey or three storey high terrace houses. They correspond to well-established types, although their constructional system, and in particular, their 'fabric,' is entirely unusual. Here the courts become more secluded communal gardens, the street pedestrianised, and the parking access occurs in each court in the open. District heating ducts run at roof level and span from one terrace to the next on metal frames. This feature, which is a result of cost considerations, has the effect of raising services to the quality of a monument and, as in the Centre Pompidou, the architecture seems to be stated as a celebration of technology."
R. Perez de Arce, *Lotus 36*

Southgate, housing, 1972

1975
Museum for Northrhine Westphalia
Düsseldorf (invited competitor)

James Stirling, Michael Wilford
Russell Bevington
Robert Livesey
Crispin Osborne

(Extracts from Competition Report)

The new Museum (Modern Art) is intended to be a 20th century container for contemporary works of art and an integral element in historic Düsseldorf. The design of the new building is meant to harmonize the diverging forms of the St. Andreas Church, the monumental Land-Court building, the houses along Neubruck Strasse and the civic buildings on Heinrich Heine Alle. In addition to this (perhaps impossible) task it is hoped to achieve an architectural appearance that is as individual as the older buildings in contrast to the oversimplified appearance and overblown scale associated with modern architecture (i.e., the box, the slab).

Only the south west corner facades of the old Library are retained where the appearance in Neubruck Strasse is important for that street. Nevertheless our attitude to the surrounding urban context is to infill and to preserve. All facades in Neubruck Strasse and Heinrich Heine Alle are retained, without compromising the functional working of the new building.

The Grabbeplatz will continue to be surrounded on three sides by existing roads, consequently we have raised the plaza to protect it from motor traffic (increasing its potential for outdoor exhibitions, etc.). This raised platform allows for an increased pedestrian scale (i.e., relative to the Land-Court building) and a less costly carpark (reduced excavation), and its height allows connection to the municipal art gallery across the road via a footbridge.

To the north the Grabbeplatz is extended with a pedestrian walkthrough to Ratinger Mauer and this walk is enhanced by a series of architectural events which include a reference to the Old Town wall and a circular garden with enclosing curved wall.

The pavilion on the plaza is sited on the axis of Muhlen Strasse and it marks the entrance to the new Art Gallery, the start of the Ratinger Mauer walkthrough and the way down to the underground carpark. It is also a sheltered area for those waiting for buses and coaches and provides a place for people to congregate. It is perhaps a much

smaller scale alternative to the entrance steps of the Metropolitan Museum, (New York) or the portico of the British Museum, (London). As an object the pavilion has a similar relationship in the Grabbeplatz as the Schlossturm has in the Burgplatz. It makes reference to the small freestanding building (the original art gallery) which in previous times was sited in the Grabbeplatz and has a relationship to the pavilion corners of the adjacent Land-Court building. There is also an association with the neo-classical gatehouses which mark the entrance to the park from Heinrich Heine Alle. The Pavilion would have a glass roof—using diffusing glass and the covered area beneath would be flooded in shadowless light.

1. Site plan: Rhine and Burgplatz to the left, Grabbeplatz and City park to right.

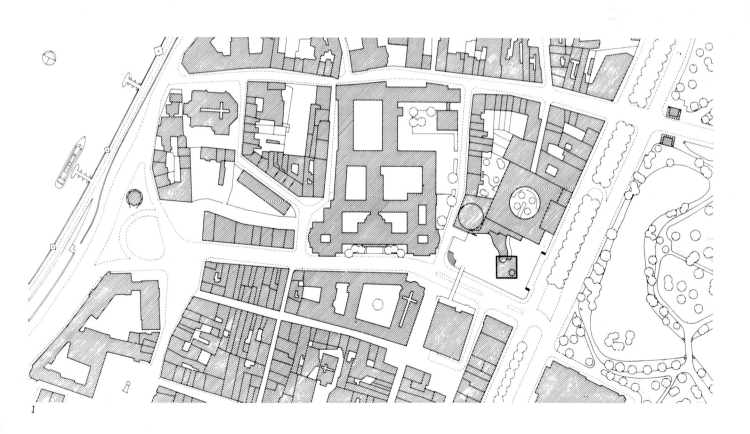

1

"...Stirling literally celebrates the extension of the Ratinger Mauer, as a right of way, by creating a metaphorical city wall, through which to represent both the line and the presence of the old city Mauer...This metaphorical wall is fully integrated into the most prominent feature of Düsseldorf; namely the entry portico on the Grabbeplatz, which not only 'represents' the gallery as a whole, through its axial alignment with the main thoroughfare of Muhlen Strasse, but also counters as an urban symbol the free standing Schlossturm that articulates the space of the Burgplatz, overlooking the Rhine...This same 'empty' top lit portico—an ironic comment possibly, as to the consequence of all museum culture—also stands as a metaphor for the actual genesis of the institution, since its free standing location on the Grabbeplatz refers to the pre-war site of the original art gallery that previously occupied the square...This endless layering of meaning on top of meaning seems to permeate the entire structure. Thus the organic glass envelope to the entry foyer, which cascades freely down, in contrast to the frontality of the portico, serves not only to reveal

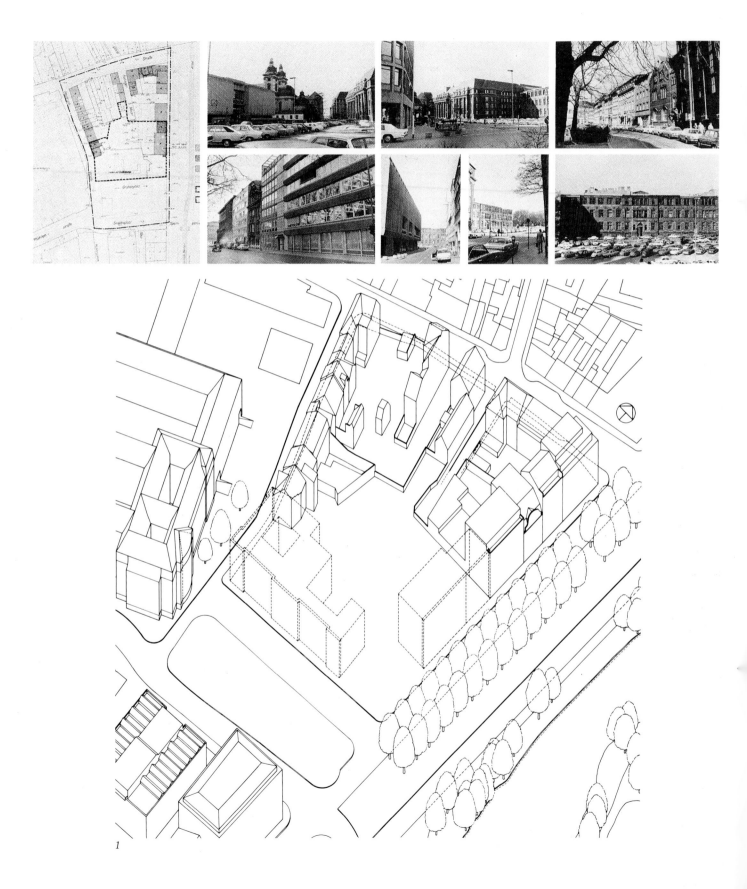

1

Museum for Northrhine Westphalia, 1975

the public life of the institution, but also to effect a 'surreal' transition between the main mass of the gallery and the gutted shell of the library... Finally where the square plan of the portico echoes the square plan of the whole and where the cubic mass of the portico volumetrically inverts the cylindrical void of the circular garden, the figure ground references at Düsseldorf attain, at least for Stirling, a level of unprecedented complexity."
K. Frampton, *RIBA Journal,* March 1976

1. *Axonometric of existing buildings.*
2. *Axonometric of old and new buildings.*

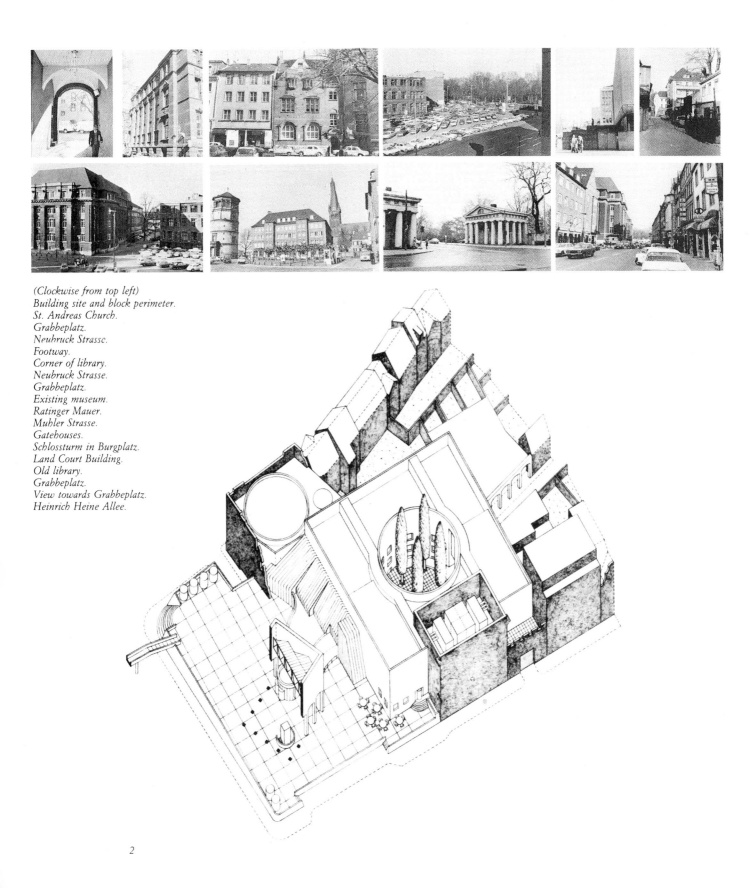

(Clockwise from top left)
Building site and block perimeter.
St. Andreas Church.
Grabbeplatz.
Neubruck Strasse.
Footway.
Corner of library.
Neubruck Strasse.
Grabbeplatz.
Existing museum.
Ratinger Mauer.
Muhler Strasse.
Gatehouses.
Schlossturm in Burgplatz.
Land Court Building.
Old library.
Grabbeplatz.
View towards Grabbeplatz.
Heinrich Heine Allee.

2

"Both 'representational' and 'abstract' were present in this competition project, where a neo-classical type entrance pavilion is, as it were, pulled out from a circular void to symbolise and represent the whole museum which, to minimise its impact on the historic centre, is otherwise buried in the city block.

" 'Neo-classical' as there are several such buildings nearby and because I think there is an identifying association still attached to 19th century museums. The main building may be 'abstract' but the pavilion is more 'representational,' that is to do with tradition, history and familiarity, and maybe archeology and memory as prior to the war a

building of about the same size had stood on this actual spot for centuries and within it were exhibited the city's art treasures."
JS, *Lecture 1981*

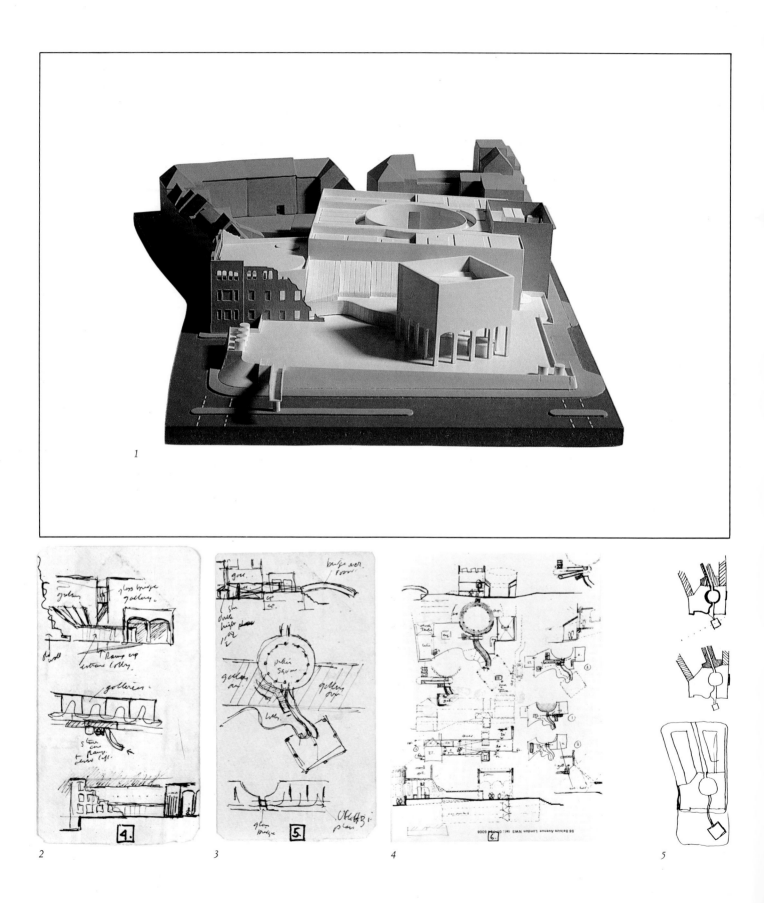

1

2   3   4   5

1. Model: *view of new Grabbeplatz.*
2-6. *Concept sketches.*
7. *Entrance level.*

8. *Gallery level.*
9. Model: *view from Neubruck Strasse.*

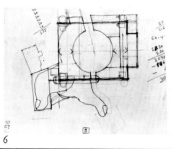

6

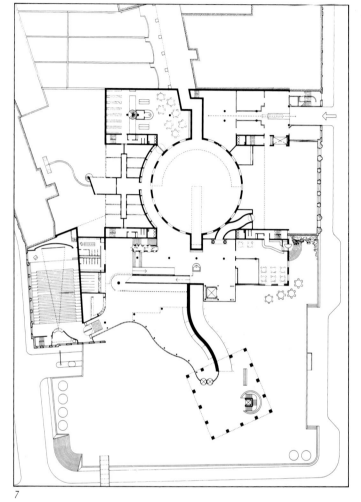

7

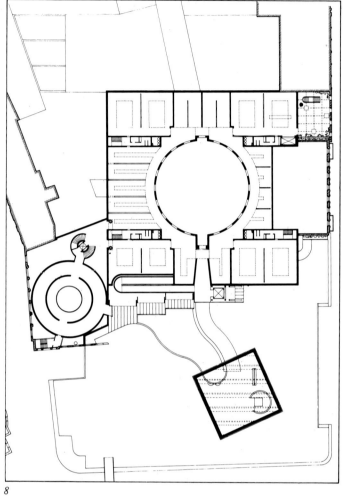

8

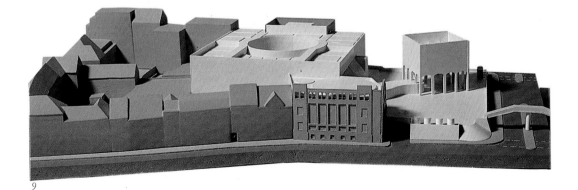

9

1. *Axonometric of entrance circulation.*
2. *Aerial view of site.*
3. *Model: building in context.*
4. *Isometric upview of garden and pavilion.*
5,6. *New building in city model.*
7. *Model: building in context.*

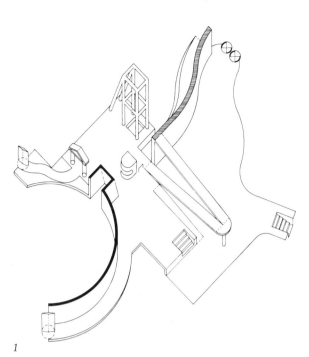

1

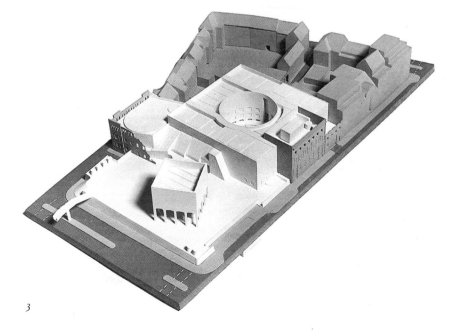

2

3

Museum for Northrhine Westphalia, 1975

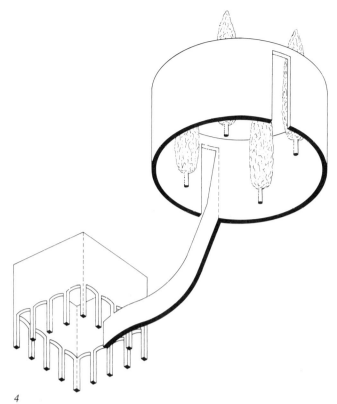

4

5

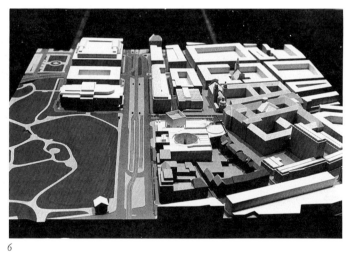

6

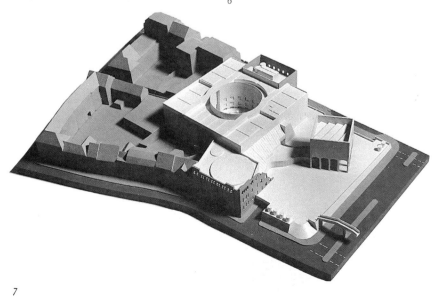

7

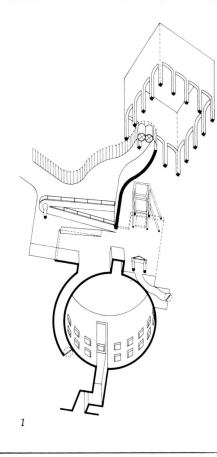

1

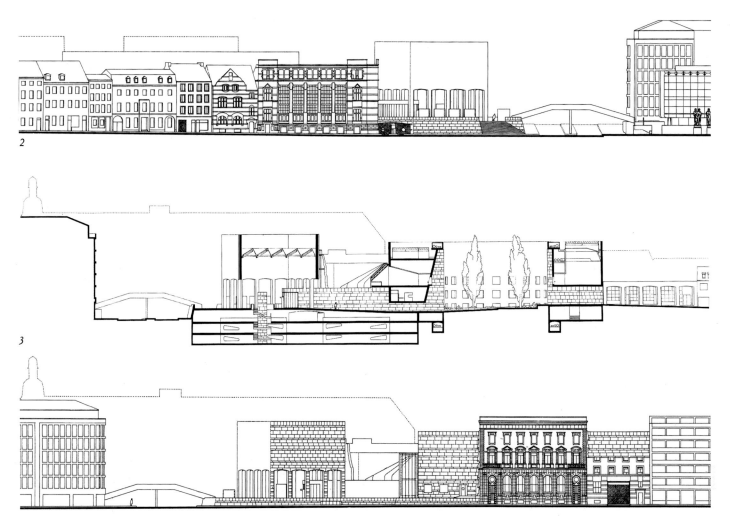

2

3

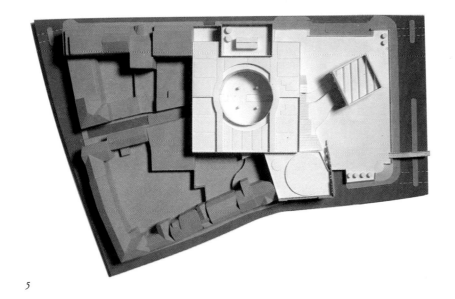

5

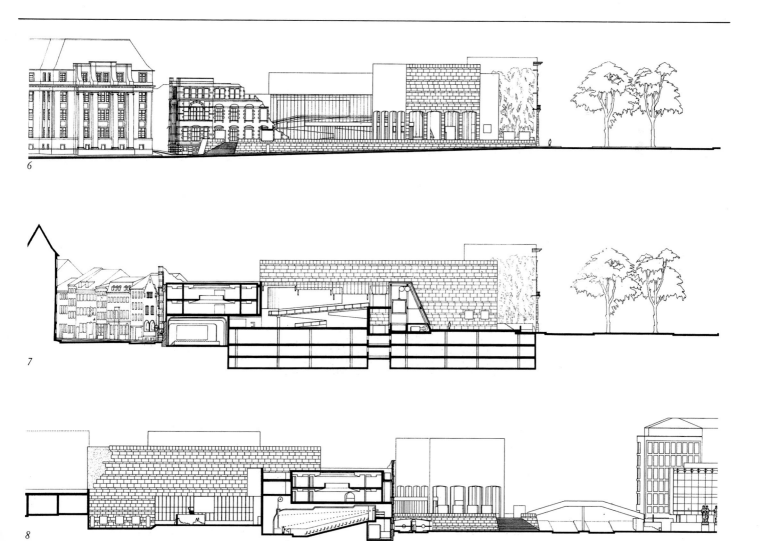

6

7

8

Museum for Northrhine Westphalia, 1975

1. *Up view of gallery laylight.*
2. *Public footway through garden and pavilion.*
3–6. *Concept sketches.*

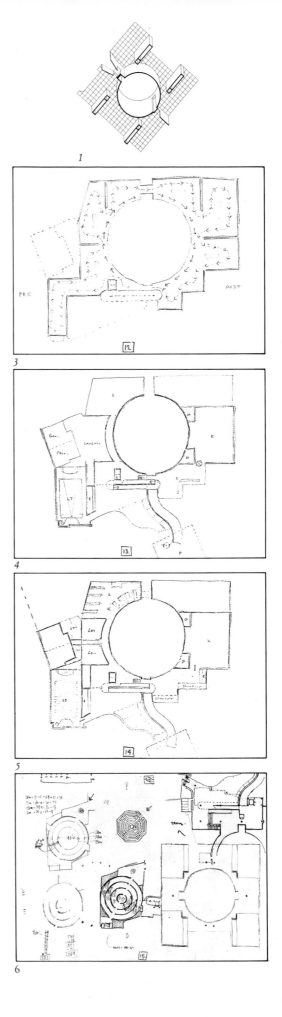

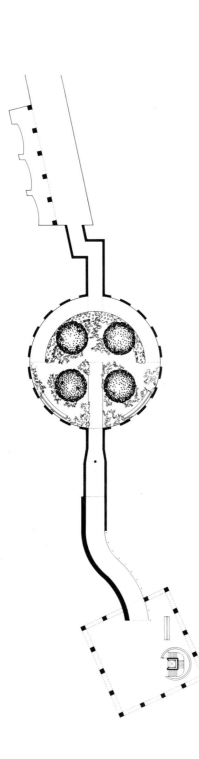

2

Museum for Northrhine Westphalia, 1975

1975
Wallraf-Richartz Museum
Cologne (invited competitor)

James Stirling, Michael Wilford
Russell Bevington
Robert Livesey
Werner Kreis
Ulrich Schaad

(Extracts from Competition Report)

Our proposal for the sites north and south of the Hohenzollern bridge is to develop them in a way that will frame and unify the separate monuments of the cathedral, the railway station and the Hohenzollern bridge; to seek integration and find an urban resolution for the railway area—"an urban vacuum a quarter of a century after the war." The new buildings designed for both sites (Breslauer plaza to the north of the railway tracks and Museum plaza to the south) are grouped and massed in deference to the cathedral and in response to the gateway aspect (drawbridge) of the Hohenzollern bridge crossing the Rhine on the axis of the cathedral.

Gateway buildings (monumental) are positioned on either side of the bridge. Semi-enclosed within these buildings are circular plazas overlooked by museum/river edge related shops. The equestrian

1

statues of Wilhelm II and Freidrich which for many years stood in the open at the approaches to the Hohenzollern Bridge are repositioned in these plazas. The gateway buildings are like civic balconies or city doors overlooking the Rhine; from them ramps incline down to the river promenade and green zone along the river edge.

The "no man's land" of railway tracks has been screened visually and acoustically from both Museum plaza and Breslauer plaza by retaining walls which also support elevated footpaths. We have treated the edge of the railway zone like a tree-lined canal bank or river edge. Toward the river edge the height of new buildings increases to be more in scale with that of the bridge; however this is at point further removed from the cathedral.

1. Aerial view of the Cathedral railways and bridges.
2. Model: view from railway tracks.

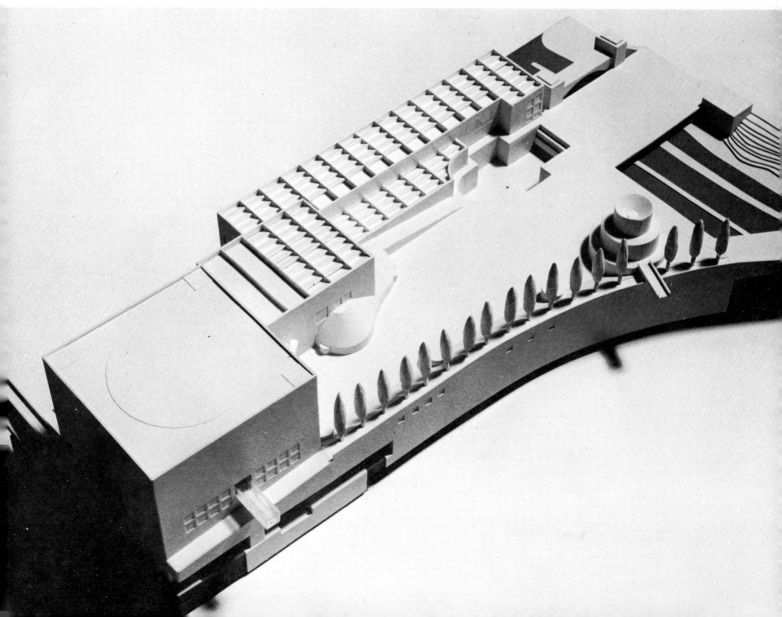

The new museum can be approached on foot from the Dom Platz and railway station on a continuous plaza. The museum can also be approached from the Rhine promenade and river edge green zone by a large ramp which arrives in the circular plaza.

The building is in three parts: a long gallery wing; an intermediary entrance building; and the gateway/auditorium building. The physical appearance of the plaza is determined by a series of architectural elements, including a "lean-to" entrance hall (the shop on the corner), the sloping roof/ramp over the entrance gallery descending on the axis of a sunken sculpture court, the inclined tubes of free spanning escalators and a ziggurat (electric sub station) marking a footbridge crossing from Breslauer Platz.

In the outer entrance hall (peristyle) there is a large sales counter with museum information, advance booking, etc. Two ramps lead to separate foyers, each with cloakrooms.

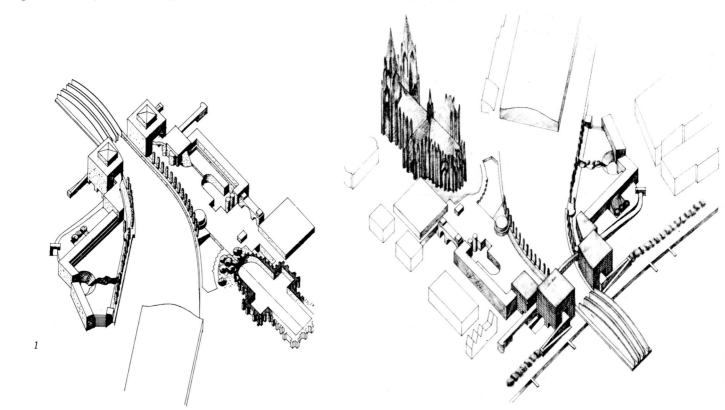

1

2

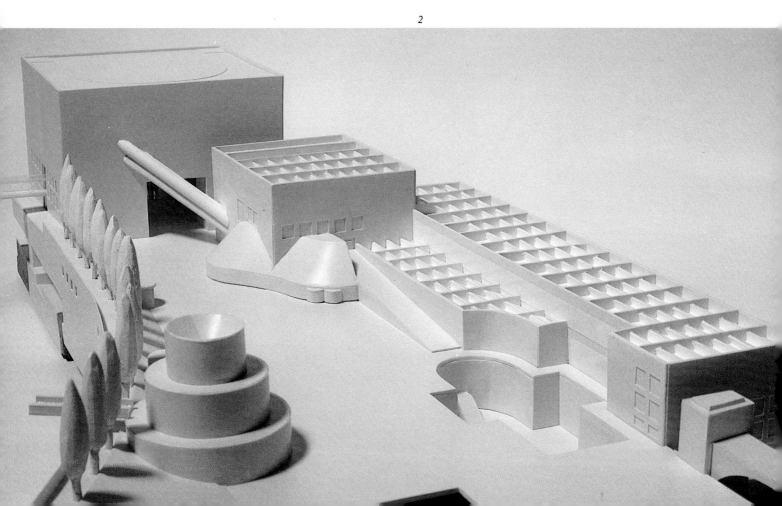

1, 2. *Axonometric sketches.*
3. *Model: view from the Cathedral.*
4, 5. *Hohenzollern Bridge 1945.*
6. *Axonometric: of gateway, gallery and entrance building.*

4

5

6

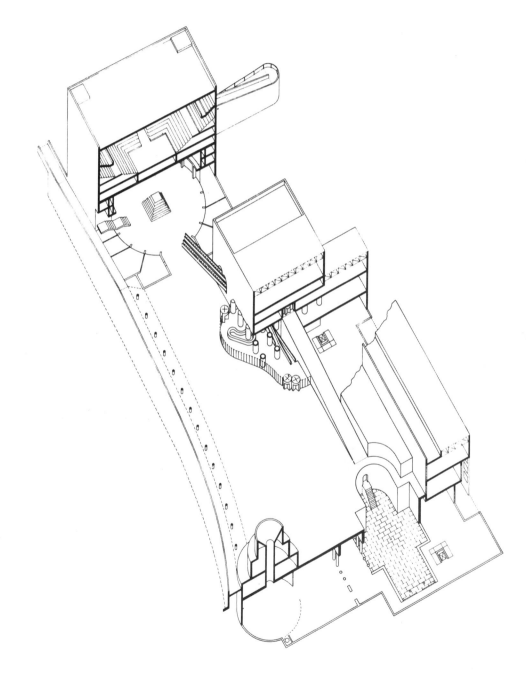

1. *Section through lower gallery and sculpture garden.*
2. *Plan: level two.*
3. *Plan: level three.*
4. *Plan: level four.*

5. *Model: view of entrance plaza.*
6. *Plan: level five.*
7. *Plan: level six.*
8. *Plan: level seven.*

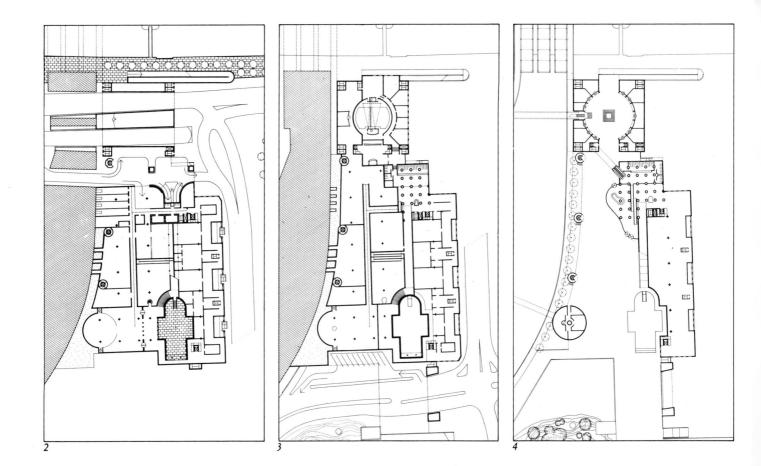

1

2

3

4

210   Wallraf-Richartz Museum, 1975

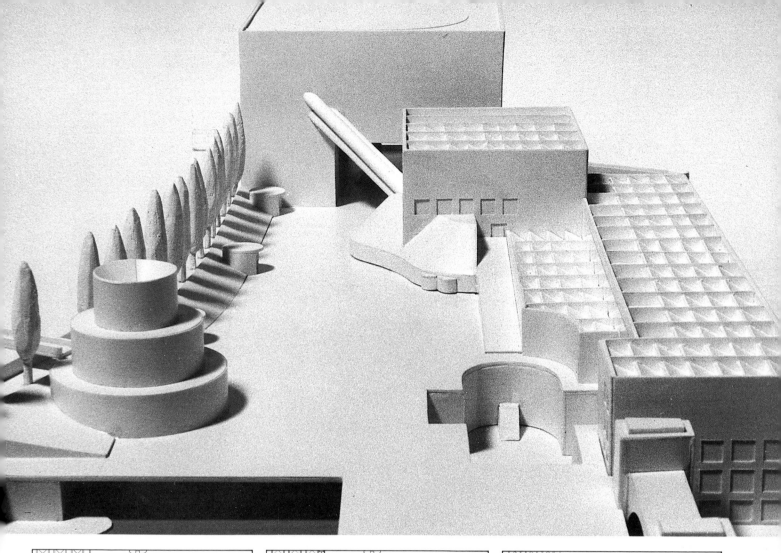

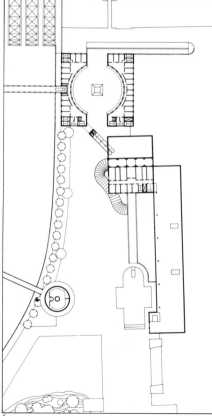

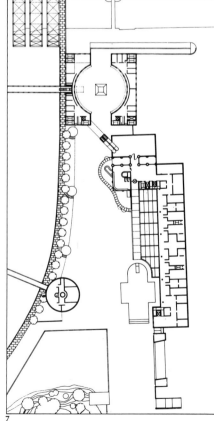

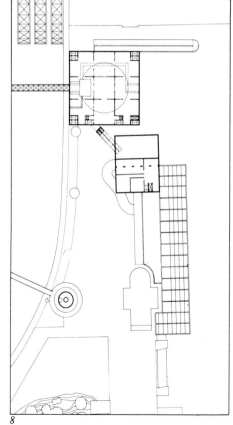

6

7

8

Wallraf-Richartz Museum, 1975

From the upper foyer, escalators rise to the multi-purpose auditorium.
From the lower foyer there is entrance to the museum galleries.

The long gallery wing is approached via an internal passage and is planned on three levels, each with a linear arrangement of partition walls linking vertical circulation cores at either end. The partition layout of galleries varies, but all relate to the principle that on each floor access is down a side lit gallery off which visitors proceed into larger and more flexible top lit or artificially lit spaces.

"For Stirling, the ideal form is a ledolcian object-in-the-round, carefully placed into its context in an almost ancient-Greek fashion. The objects themselves, in the case of the Cologne project, are vaguely reminiscent of interwar Italian designs like Aschieri's *Museo della Civiltá Romana* (a building which, if better known, could easily become a cult object). Stirling, while appearing to give only lip service to the spatial context of Cologne, subtly proposes a system of local

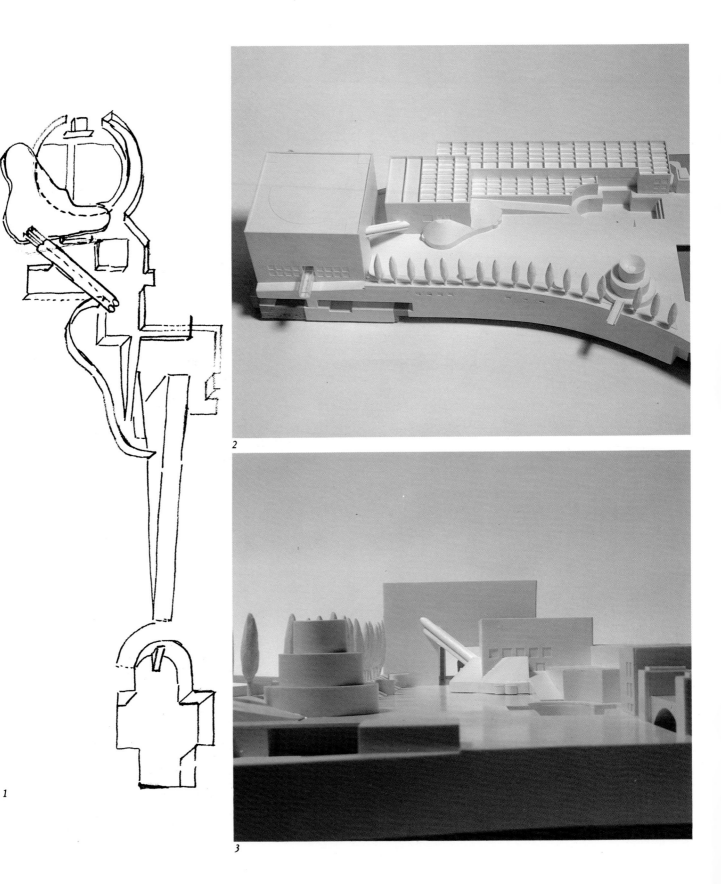

1

2

3

Wallraf-Richartz Museum, 1975

1. *Concept sketch.*
2. *Model: view from railway.*
3. *Model: view from Cathedral.*
4. *Model: view from river.*
5. *Wilhelm II enclosed in new building.*
6. *Wilhelm II in the open.*
7. *Axonometric of entrance hall and sculpture garden.*
8. *Entrance plaza.*

4

5

6

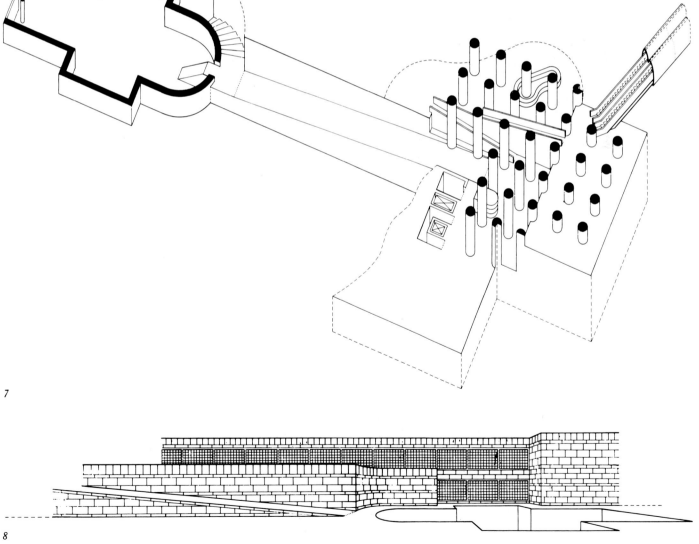

7

8

symmetries that requires the most minor of deformations of his two 'propylea' pavilions—deformations that show the ultimate fragility of otherwise robust, solid blocks.

"Ultimately, it is the idiosyncrasies of Stirling's buildings that make them so appealing. His ability to absorb influences and to throw them back fresh has kept him at the forefront of an avant-garde that he bitterly denies."
T. Schumacher, *Skyline*, April 1978

"The Cathedral is very much the most important feature of the setting, creating as it does its own universe and typography and compensating for the losses of geographical and historical identity occasioned by the modern pedestrian precinct that has replaced vast areas of the town centre such as it existed prior to the war. It seems altogether appropriate that Cologne whose present physical aspect embodies both the growing pains of the industrial transformation of Europe and the destruction of prewar European civilization, should become the locus for a new architecture

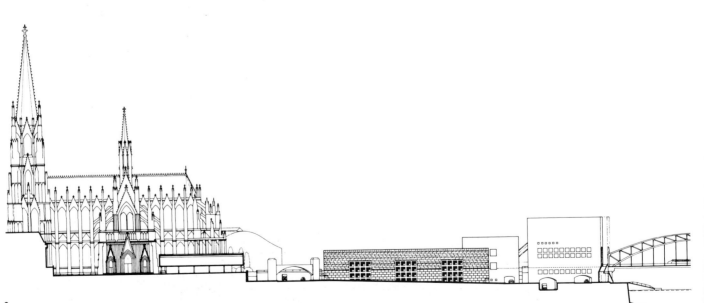

KÖLNER
Informationsblatt zur

1

2

Wallraf-Richartz Museum, 1975

having its roots in the beginning of the nineteenth century. For it is now clear that Schinkel is back, for all his having been combined with the post-Corbusian motifs and other private elements of the Stirling canon. Notably, the gateway/auditorium building appears to be a reference to Schinkel's Altes Museum in Berlin (1822-30, badly burned out in 1945). The reasons

for the validity of such a citation are long: suffice it to say here that the Cathedral site, much trodden by history, is a modern-*romantik* Acropolis of sorts. As such it is a world away from simple and unambiguous conceptions, such as the South Bank development, London, or the simplistic monuments at Chandigarh and Brasilia."
D. Stewart, *Architecture and Urbanism*, July 1976

1. *Site plan: plaza level.*
2. *Elevation of new buildings between the Cathedral and the Rhine.*
3. *Site plan: roof level.*
4. *Elevation of new buildings from the Rhine.*

DOM

Turmbesteigung

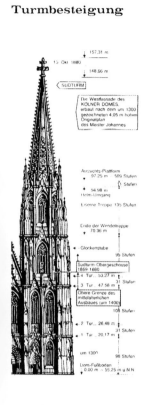

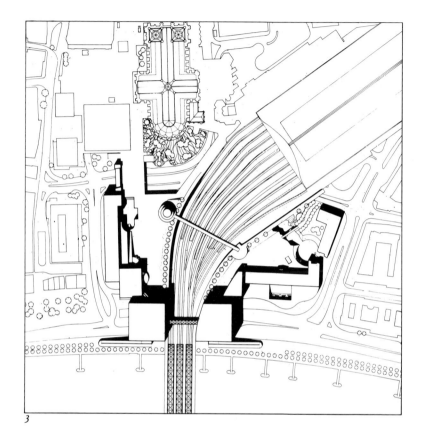

3

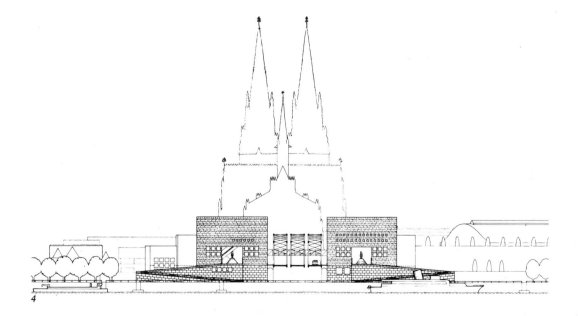

4

1976
Government Centre, Doha
(limited competition)

James Stirling, Michael Wilford
Russell Bevington
John Tuomey

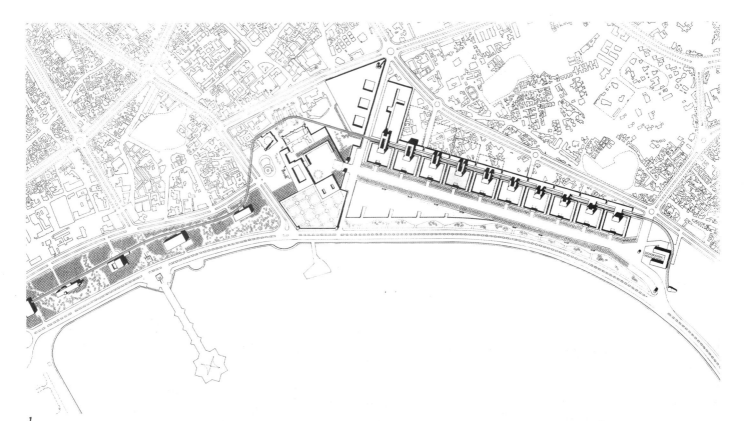

1

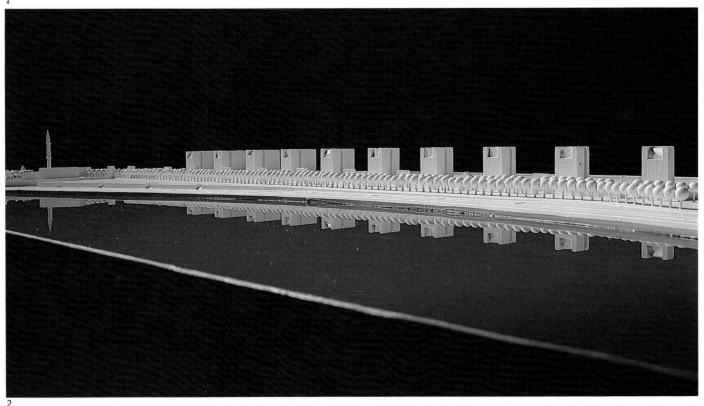

2

An objective was to emphasize the position in Doha of the Ruler's Palace while proposing at the same time a dynamic and prestigious Government Centre appropriate to Quatar's developing status. These qualities were to be apparent when viewing the Center from the Corniche, from the bay or from the air, and when experienced as a working environment by the Emir, his Ministers, employees and visitors. A further objective was to establish a visual and working relationship between the Palace and Government buildings.

New Ministry towers were sited along a tree-lined Mall connecting the Corniche to the Palace. Each Ministry had a distinctive entrance gate leading into a private courtyard enclosed by shaded arcades.

1. Site plan.
2. Model: view from bay.
3. Model aerial view.
4. Model view of Corniche and Ministry towers.

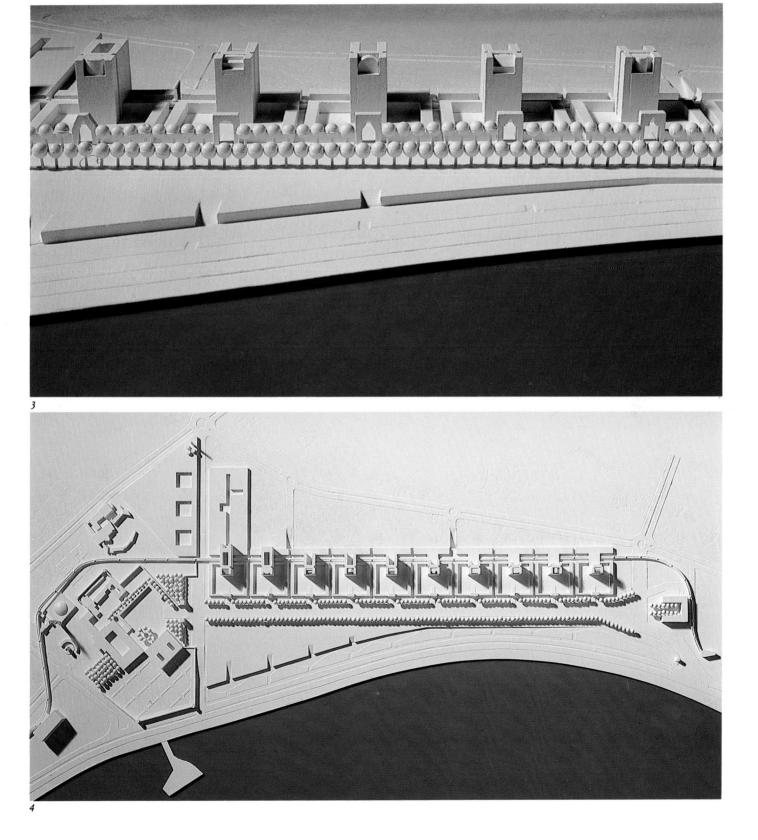

3

4

Courtyards were individually landscaped with different pools and water gardens. The upper level of this arcade overlooked the Mall providing a balcony for viewing motorcades and processions and allowing views of the Bay. There were also public arcades between each courtyard providing shaded walks for citizens crossing the Government Centre on route to the promenade. These prevented the line of new Ministry buildings from becoming a barrier between the town and the Corniche.

Each Ministry was accomodated in a thirteen story building.

The height and width of the Ministry facades were constant but, as each Ministry required a different volume of accommodation, the buildings varied in depth.

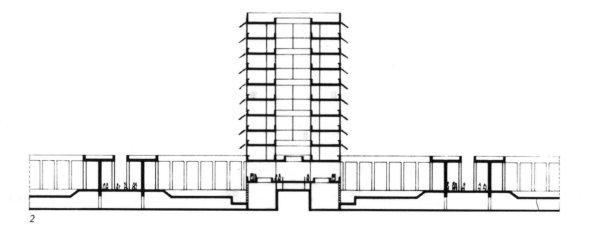

1

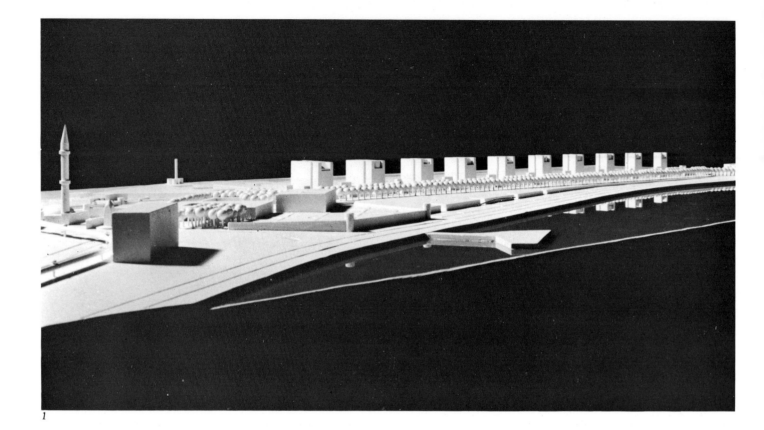

2

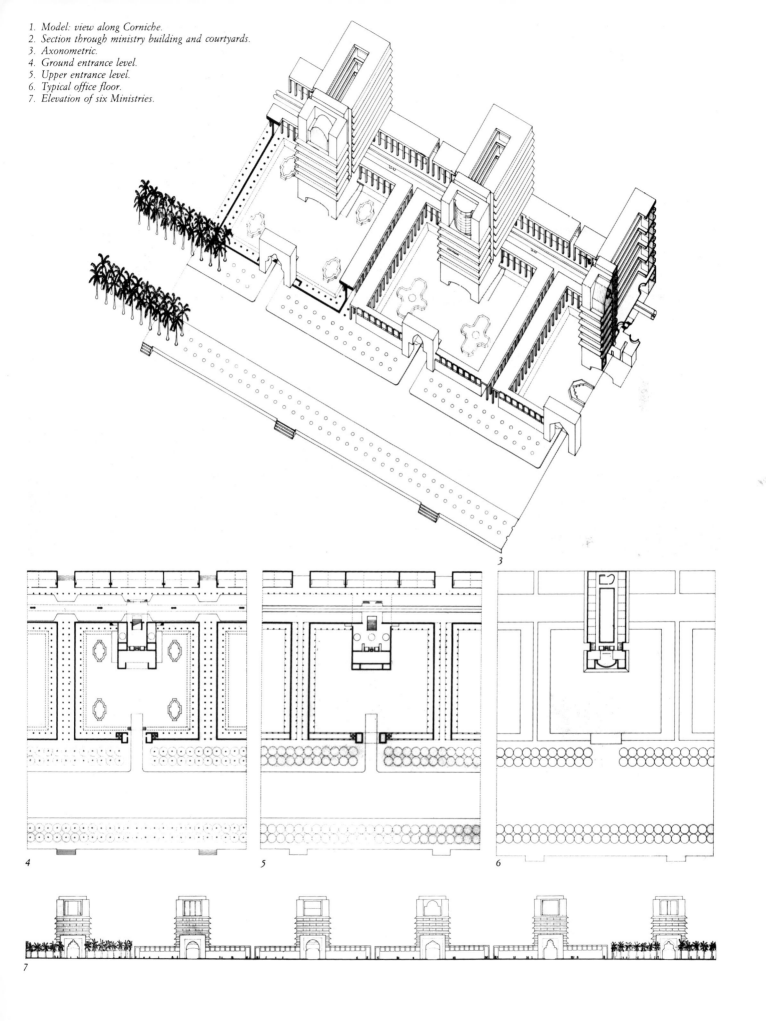

1. *Model: view along Corniche.*
2. *Section through ministry building and courtyards.*
3. *Axonometric.*
4. *Ground entrance level.*
5. *Upper entrance level.*
6. *Typical office floor.*
7. *Elevation of six Ministries.*

3

4   5   6

7

Government Centre, Doha, 1976

1976
Regional Center, Florence
(national competition)

James Stirling, Michael Wilford
Russell Bevington, Ulrich Schaad
John Tuomey, Barbara Weiss
in collaboration with
Castore, Malanima, Rizzi (Florence)

(Extracts from Competition Report)

Characteristics of the site are the flat damp valley of the Arno which is given to flooding (tragically in 1966), the overlooking hills of Monte Morello and the approach of Florence's ugly outer edges. Coupled with these is a need to preserve as much of the valley as a green zone for Florence which suggested a compact and protected group of buildings set in the landscape. Buildings for the Regional Headquarters of Tuscany and a Judicial Court building in conjunction with residential, commercial and professional office accommodation are required.

The new complex is positioned down hill from Castello, to allow a pole of urbanism to develop that is not entangled with the out buildings of Castello. Nevertheless, strong connections are developed between Castello and the new center. The "stone garden" which is nearest Castello is a threshold, a front doorstep, for the sequence of

buildings which make up the complex—"garden/ gateway/island." From this threshold there are walkways through the woods connecting with the new railway station and important streets in Castello including the avenue which leads to the Villa Reale. The "stone garden" is the upper surface of a large underground carpark and has a grid of small scale planting and stone/gravel texturing related to the gardens of the Villa Reale. Positioned over the way up from the carpark is an entrance pavilion that serves as portico to the enclosed bridge which spans to the "gateway" and defines the beginning of the walking approach to the new center.

Approach by car, bus or rapid transit is through the "gateway"—a cluster of buildings made up of the hotel and three commercial office towers. This element is, in a larger sense, a gateway to the movement in the valley and the approach to Florence from the west; it would also be the entry

to the new University of Florence when built. At lower levels, this "gateway" becomes an interchange with roads, ramps, car-parking and garaging, also bus and taxi drop offs. Below ground level there is provision for a rapid transit line and station to be built if and when it is extended from Florence. All levels of this interchange are connected by escalators which rise to a commercial plaza from which there is entry to shops, banks, offices and the hotel. From this plaza an enclosed bridge provides a walkway to the new center—"the island"—and this walkway-galleria has flanking spaces allowing market stalls to be set up and also the selling of newspapers, flowers, tobacco, etc.

1. The Arno Valley with the City of Florence showing public spaces and parks and including the new development (upper left).
2. Site plan: The Regional Center in relation to Castello.

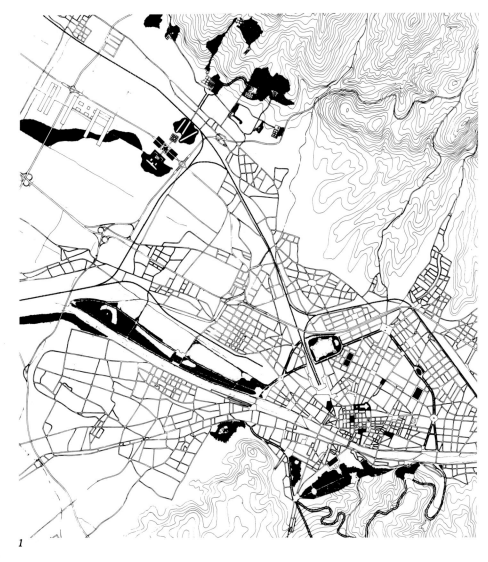

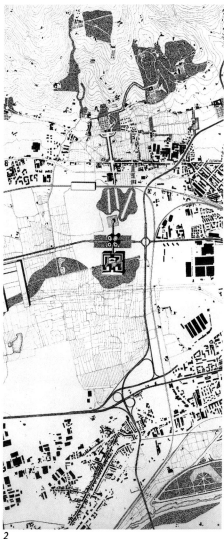

1

2

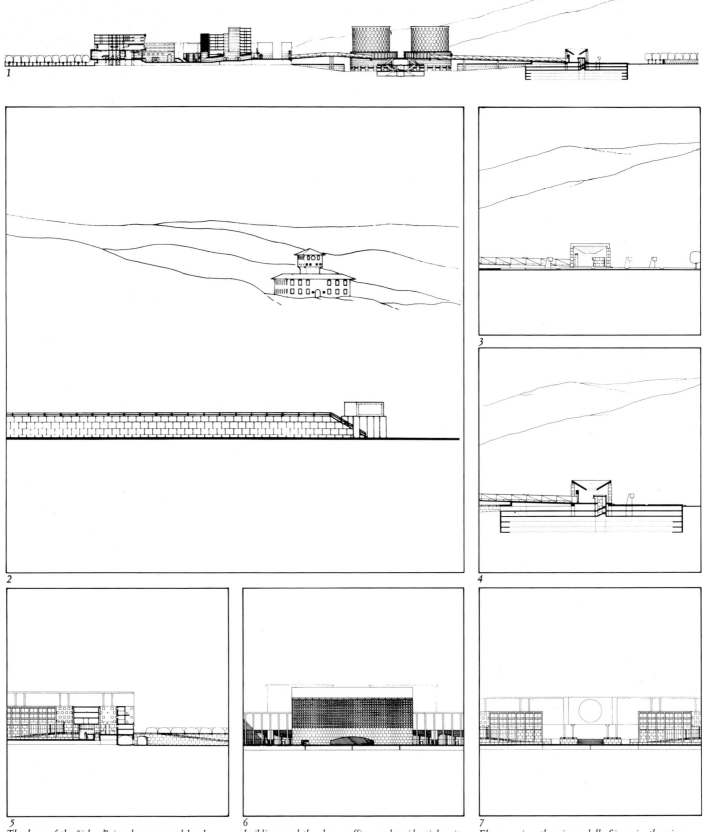

5
The base of the "island" is a large ground level carpark divided by fire walls into parking zones. The service roads and zones provide access and parking for all living and working on the "island" and there are frequent stairs to the plazas and buildings above. The Regional and Judicial

6
buildings and the shops, offices and residential units are positioned in relation to several plazas and pedestrian "streets" at varying levels though all are connected by colonnades and terraces. The relationship of buildings to urban space is of similar proportions to some of the famous spaces of

7
Florence, i.e., the piazza della Signoria, the piazza SS. Annunziata, etc. A "mix" of office and residential units and shopping, restaurants, bars, etc., should keep these plazas active throughout the day and evening. On the flanks of the "island" are four levels of studio apartments. Beneath these

1. *Section through 'Island,' 'Gateway,' 'Garden'*
2. *Roman wall.*
3. *Entrance pavilion.*
4. *Garden—car park under.*
5. *Pedestrian street.*
6. *Regional Headquarters.*
7. *Judicial Building.*

8,9. *Gateway.*
10. *Gateway plaza.*
11. *Colonnade.*
12. *Island.*
13. *Regional Headquarters.*

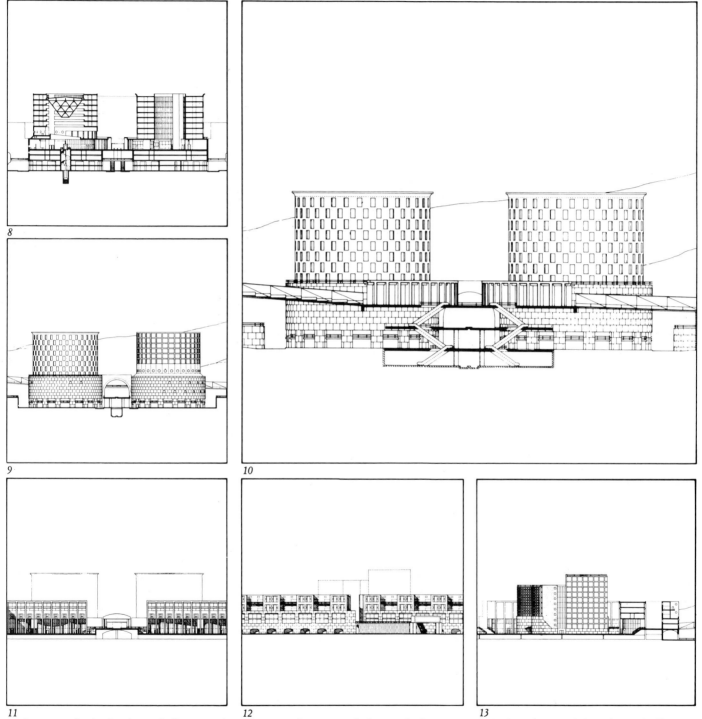

8

9

10

11

12

13

studios are two levels of professional offices entered from pedestrian "streets." The central plaza is flanked by colonnades behind which are shops, and in the floors above is a mix of apartments and professional offices. The Political and Judicial buildings face each other across the central plaza.

The surrounding site was laid out in the first century B.C. and a Roman grid superimposed on the valley has influenced the subsequent development of fields, dykes, roads, etc., this being still visible today. A Roman grid line runs through the central plaza and this antique sign has been

utilized to position and shape the new buildings. Walkways from the "island" into the adjoining fields and woods are along "Roman walls" that correspond with this grid.

"The project is defined as a composition of three

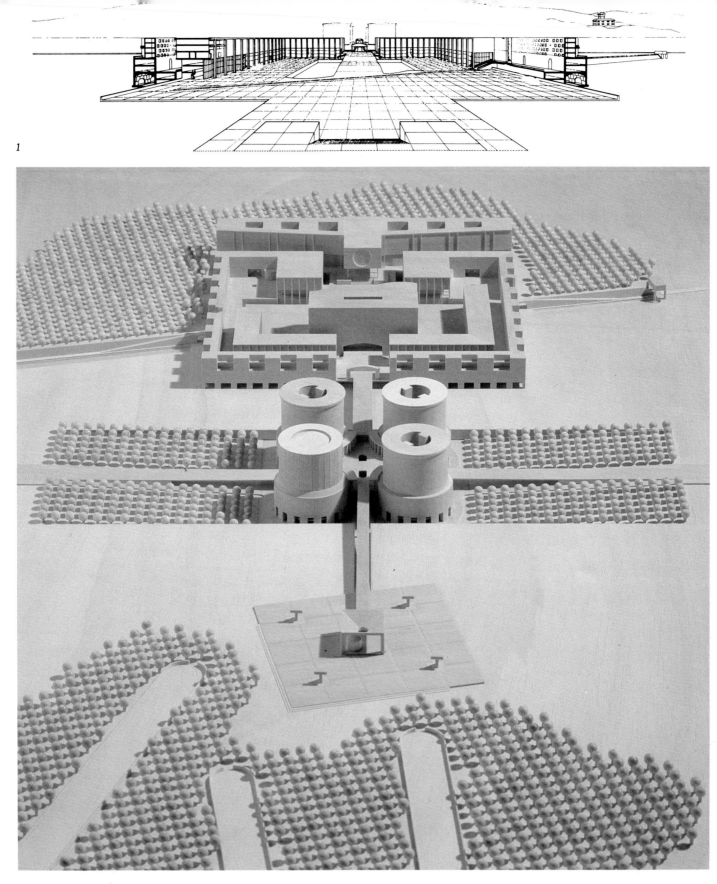

1

architectural objects strung along a route which coincides with the axis that focuses on the area of the villas and the hills.

"As is written in the report, the integration of the residential area which the station of Castello and

the area of the villas is not made in the physical sense of continuous building but through a critical historical reading of pre-existing elements and through the proposal for a system of greenery very closely integrated with the built structures.

"This decisive opposition to the built city, taking for a scale and for a formal reference point the elements of the landscape, explains the volumetric and plastic emphasis of the proposed architecture: much in the same way to that done by Stirling in the project for the AG Siemens in Munich (a

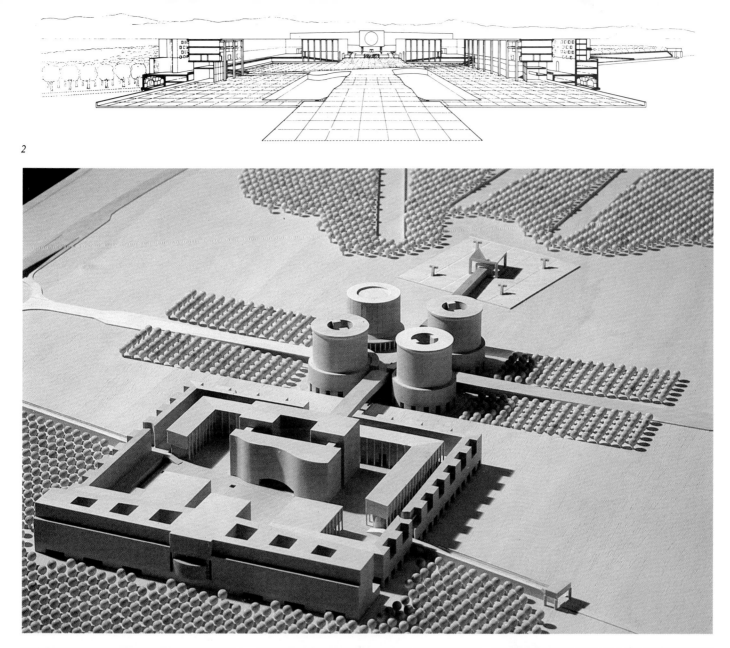

2

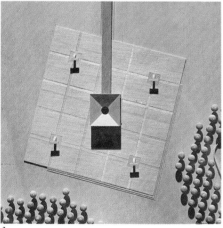

3

4

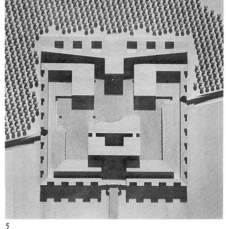

5

great formal event in an unbuilt plain) and contrary to the interventions by the same architect for central functions within the spaces of a built city (i.e., the project for the centre of Derby).

"Stirling builds a privileged landscape for his architecture—almost like a strongly defined architecture by Francesco di Giorgio or one by Laurana in a Renaissance landscape.

"Historical allusions and re-use of elements of his own formal experience mix in defining this architecture."
G. Muratore and A. Villa, *Casabella*, March 1978

1. *Perspective towards Arno Valley.*
2. *Perspective towards Castello hills.*
3. *Garden.*
4. *Gateway.*
5. *Island.*

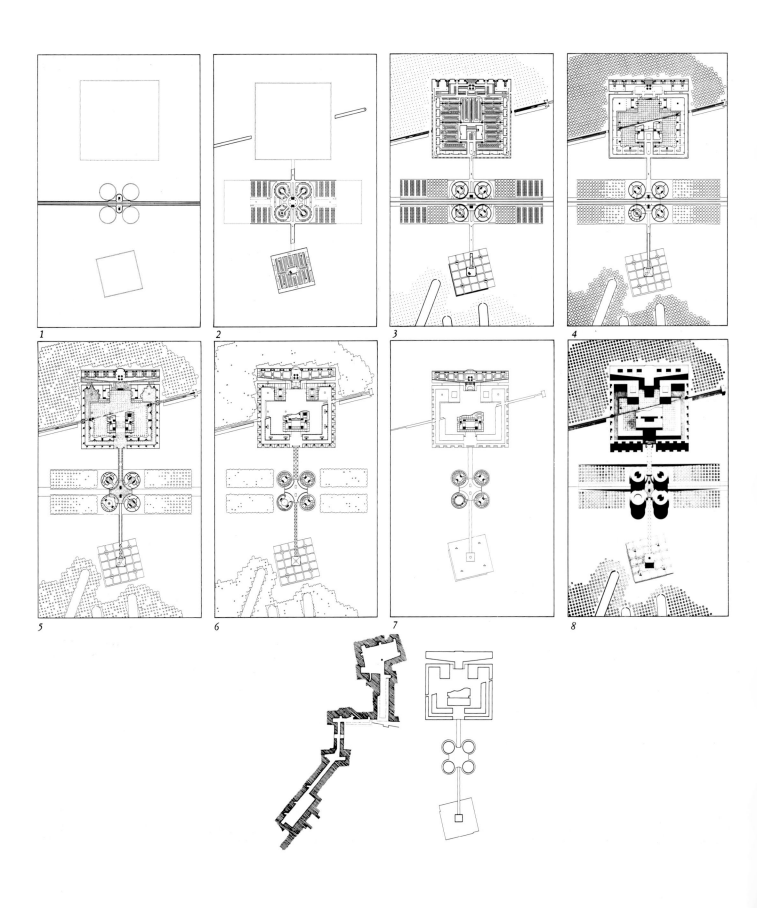

Regional Centre, Florence, 1976

1976
Meineke Strasse
Berlin

James Stirling, Michael Wilford
Ulrich Schaad

(Extracts from Architects Report)
A contextural remedy
Objectives

1. To repair the street from post war damage done to it by modern architecture and commercialism (i.e., the new multi-level parking garage). To restore the street to a pleasant mixed, residential character by the inclusion of a new building interposed between the garage and the pavement. This new "contextural" building will accommodate small shops and a restaurant at pavement level and professional offices and maisonette type studio/apartments in the middle and upper levels.

2. To allow the multi level garage to function properly, but to conceal its gross overscaled appearance. To repair the corner between

Meineke Strasse and Lietzenburger Strasse that has diminished to a one story petrol pump station. In turning the corner to make a non-disruptive transition between Meineke Strasse and Lietzenburger Strasse by designing the corner as a hinge.*

3. To use the established language of the street (i.e., types of windows, entrance doors, gables, balconies, etc.) and the traditional materials of the old buildings (i.e., masonry, rendering, etc.).

4. The new building includes architectural elements of veneer (blind facade), portico (house form), gateway (garage entry), hinge (corner transition) and secondary elements such as passageway, e.g. the

pedestrian entrance to the garage and the entry to a new urban garden, (which is a reconstruction of the single special condition occurring on the old side of the street) to be used by the restaurant.

1. Prewar.
2. Post-war.
3. New proposal.

"Stirling exemplifies the extent to which a new building must form part of a 'patchwork' so that, by making amends for the gap which it fills, it can contribute to the process whereby the disjointed fragments of the city find new coherence. In this way, out of the scattered chaos, a unified environment is reconstructed.

1   2   3

"The streetline was broken up to make space for a sterile monument, the reasons for whose existence as a multi-storey car park were as scant as its respect, as a piece of aggressively modern architecture, for the historic unity of the environment.

"Stirling's apartment block begins with a plain elevation. At the point where the circular stair-shaft of the car park abuts on the old houses, where the grid pattern of the large building suddenly takes over from the old residential block, Stirling seeks a soothing intervention. He is doing what has been proscribed for decades in the name of the functionalist ethic; he is disguising the grid with a perforated facade; he is providing a mask behind which the brutal reality of the car park nevertheless remains fully visible, repeatedly peeping out where least expected and even exposing itself in all its nakedness on the upper storeys. We mistrust the 'architecture of masks' and fail to appreciate that the intention, so playfully presented, is by no means to conceal things with such devices, but rather to dramatise

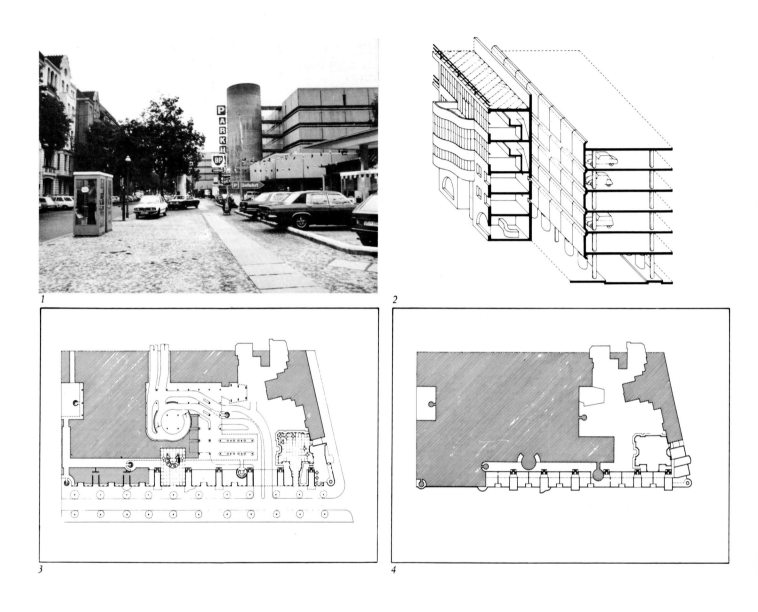

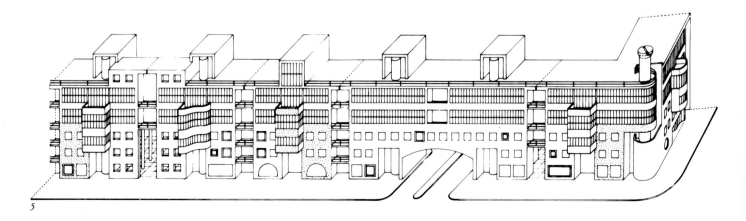

and emphasize the problem. So the building acquires its 'face,' a 'faccia,' a 'facade.'

"As we move along the building, the architecture becomes increasingly dense. Amidst the jostle of so many bays, shop-fronts, doors and windows, a passage threads its way into the world behind. Then the elongated section of the building takes over, spanning the entrance to the car park like a bridge. The bands of windows shoot forward to the street corner, across the intervening obstacle of a final bay, to end in a monumental corner-piece—a column (in reality a lift-shaft) which seems, like a spindle, to wind the entire building around it.

1. *Post-war multi-level parking garage.*
2. *Section through existing garage and new building.*
3. *Plan at street level.*
4. *Typical upper level.*
5. *New buildings and entrance to garage.*
6. *Existing street frontage.*
7. *Proposed street frontage.*

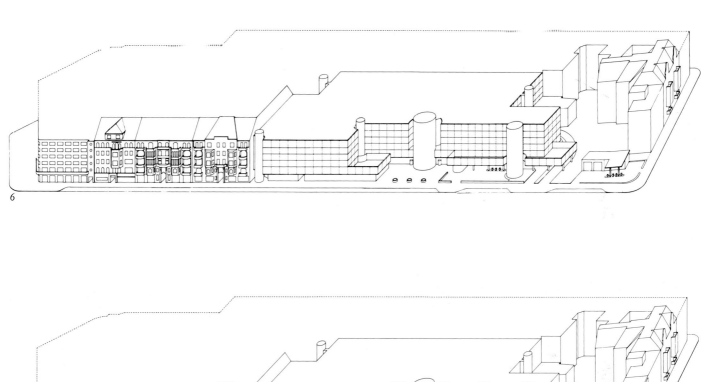

6

7

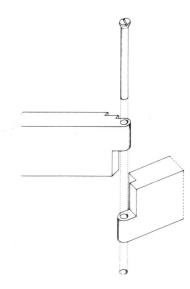

"In this way, the banal petrol station has become something; an urban situation full of life. The meeting of two streets is no longer an uneventful occurrence. Stirling's corner gives a lead into the Meineke Strasse, and with the help of a standard building element—a stair- and lift-shaft—creates an emphasis which could paradoxically be described as an unmonumental monument.

"When an environment is repaired, a street once more becomes a street, and when living is again made possible, a unity is simultaneously created which can be responded to visually, which we can experience as characteristic of how towns should be, as a recognisable place. Such a place could be—beautiful."
H. Klotz, *Berliner Morgenpost,* 18 January, 1977.

Meineke Strasse, 1976

1977
UNEP, Headquarters
Nairobi (unfinished)

James Stirling, Michael Wilford
John Tuomey, Peter Ray
in collaboration with
Giancarlo De Carlo and Mutiso Meuezes (Nairobi)

The Headquarters for the United Nations Environmental Programme was to be located on a 100 acre site outside Nairobi. The brief required that the new administration buildings "should exemplify the environmental policies of UNEP and be responsive to local conditions." Accordingly, low energy, low rise (two and three storeys) buildings were considered. Also included were Council and Conference facilities. A windmill park and a solar lake were incorporated in the landscaping of the site.

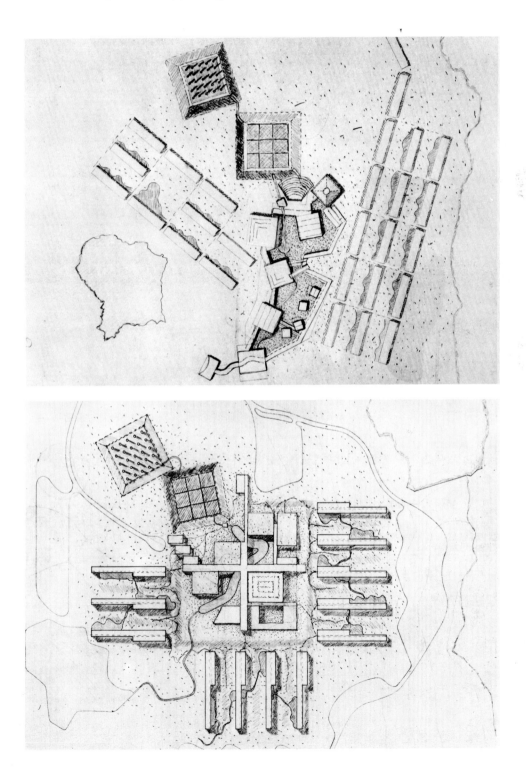

1977
Revisions to the Nolli Plan
Rome

James Stirling, Michael Wilford
Russell Bevington
Barbara Weiss

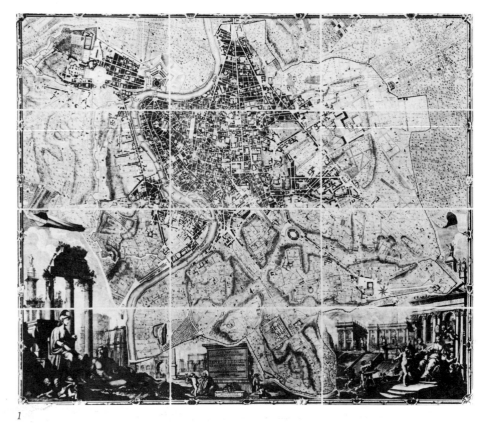

1

Stirling presents a city of spatial neutrality, characterised by the spatial indefiniteness of modern urbanism, although far better than most. Stirling also represents for the entire enterprise an underlying conscience of modernity, lest we forget where we are."
A. Chimacoff. © *Architectural Design* Magazine, London. *AD* 3/4 1979 'Roma Interrotta'.

Revisions to the Nolli Plan of Rome (fig. 1)
The MFA Solution
(and notes towards the demise of the post war planning profession)
Megalomania is the privilege of a chosen few. Piranesi who made his plan in 1762 was surely a Megalomaniac Frustrated Architect (MFA) as also Boullee, Vanbrugh, Soane, Sant'Elia, Le Corbusier, etc., and it is in this distinguished company as an MFA architect that we make our proposal.[1] The megalomaniac architect is at his most frustrated in regard to projects designed but not built. So the initial decision was to revise Nolli's plan incorporating all our unbuilt works. Soon we were trying to incorporate the entire oeuvre[2] and in order to sustain momentum a rigorous method was necessary. Therefore the selection of projects (fig. 3 and 4) is limited to those appropriate to aspects of context and association either to the circumstances of 1748 (fig. 2) or to JS projects at the time they were designed—sometimes to both. Projects are disposed in prototypical ways with wall buildings related to, or reinforcing the Gianicolo and Aurelian walls. Sometimes topography has influenced the choice with hill buildings on the Gianicolo slope and water edge buildings along the Tiber. There are projects which have a parallel relationship to built form contexts. There is also an interchange of monuments, e.g., JS birthday-cake in lieu of Garibaldi. A selection had to be made of existing

"Rowe and Stirling present two different kinds of urban worlds, they share a kinship of plan organisation; both employ collisions of grids and juxtapositions of geometrically clear urban elements. (Rowe offers a city of spatial hierarchies, of streets, boulevards and squares, of clearly defined public spaces, of potentially identifiable neighbourhoods in a wholly traditional plan.)

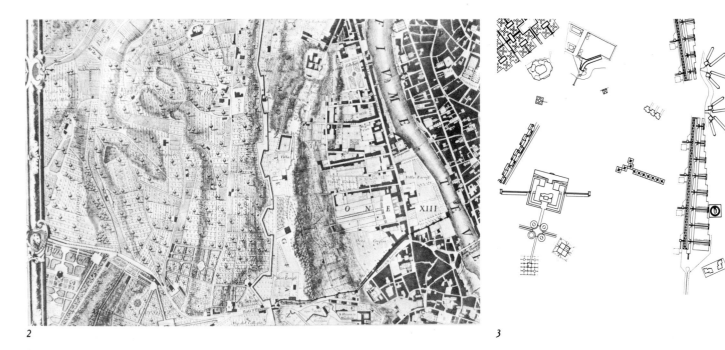

2

3

buildings and places essential to preserve/ integrate/intensify, and this, along with contextural, associational, topographical, prototypical, typological, symbolical, iconographical and archeological considerations has helped integrate JS projects (also S&G and JS&P projects).[3] However there was a larger objective; of achieving with our proposal a similar density of environment to that evolved via history. Thus our MFA (Master of Fine Architecture) solution is an alternative to the buildings and surroundings now existing and would, perhaps, accomodate a not dissimilar quantity of working and living areas, institutions and public spaces, etc. Comparison is therefore invited (fig. 4).

This 'contextural-associational' way of planning is somewhat akin to the historic process (albeit timeless) by which the creation of built form is directly influenced by the visual setting and is a confirmation and a complement to that which exists.[4] This process may be similar to that of "Collage City,"[5] (and the teaching of C. Rowe) and the working method of a few architects (e.g., O.M. Ungers) and stands in comparison to the irrationality of most post-war planning—supposedly "rational" but frequently achieving a reversal of natural priorities (surprisingly it's now realized that "New Towns" have a debilitating effect upon old towns which they were intended to enhance by relieving pressure). A typical sequence of "rational" planning is firstly the design of sewers/services, "part of the infrastructure," the routing of which dictates the layout of roads. This, in turn, dictates the disposition of buildings and an abject environment results—particularly in relation to housing, the last in the chain of events, which frequently ends up with the budget run out and finance for housing reduced to a minimum. At

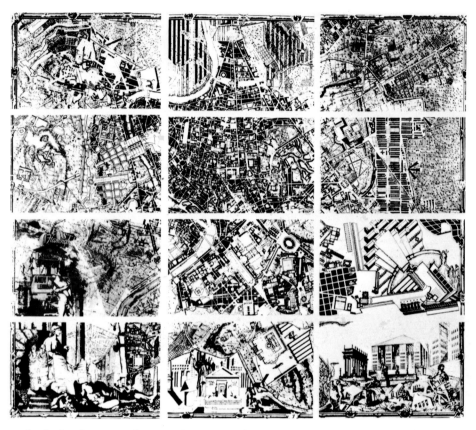

another level is the post-war destruction by planners[6] of magnificent 19th century cities, e.g., Liverpool, Glasgow, Newcastle, all in the name of "progress," which means demolition of "out of date"

buildings and replacement with the lethal combination of urban motorways and modern (commercial) architecture here termed "block modern." (cf. blockhouse, blockhead, blockbuster,

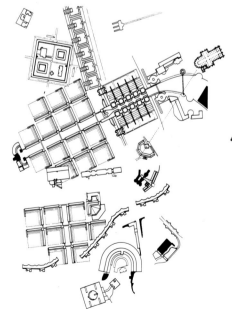

4

blocked). Expediency and commercialism corrupt the possibility of quality in urban design and irrational procedures and reverse priorities seem the "stock in trade" of the planning profession. Thus cities have lost their identity and townspeople are numbed with problems of memory while their children grow up in kitschplace and junkland. Disbandment of the planning profession in the U.K. at least must surely be considered, (with exception perhaps of an honorable role as Conservors of our Resources). Until the last war urban design was relatively well done by serious (i.e., not commercial) architects and it is preferable to return to that situation.

Revision notes... and Instructive Itinerary for a guided tour of the new Gianicolo area:

a) Residents in Rome may now enjoy the new autostrada connecting them directly from the Oratorio dei Filippini and Chiesa Nuova (fig. 7) to the Via Aurelia. From the Toll entry station—a giant vacuum cleaner (fig. 5) sucks up the overload

5

6

7

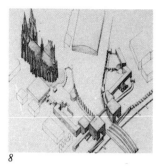
8

9

10

11

12

13

14

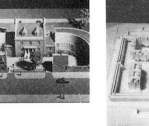
15

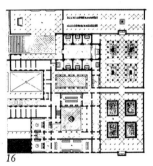
16

17

18

19

20

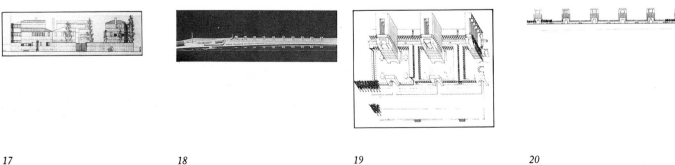

of cars from off the streets of Rome. This autostrada, here termed *Vacuum Strada*, passes under the Tiber and Gianicolo Hill. Note similar relationships in the Cologne project 1975 (figs. 8 and 9) of the Hohenzollern Bridge and railways crossing the Rhine (now the Tiber) on the axis of Cologne Cathedral[7] (now the Oratorio). Here the railway has become the autostrada and the *Bahnhof* the Toll station.[8]

b) The irreparable urban separation usually occurring between river banks (as between Westminster and South Bank) has here been overcome by construction of a platform over the Tiber in the spirit of a Place de la Concorde (fig. 6)—so wide as to be more in the nature of a land crossing than a bridge. (Such a platform, alas, could have been a meaningful objective of the Festival of Britain 1951). The (plat)form of the Siemens project 1969 (fig. 10) with its grand avenue and flanking water gardens, seemed appropriate to the site and required functions. This complex includes a shopping center, office towers and multi-level carparking, all easily accessible by residents on both banks of the Tiber.[9]

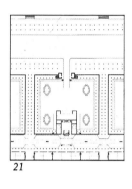

21

22

23

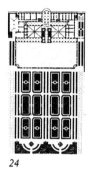

24

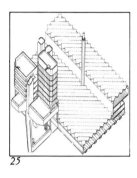

25

26

27

28

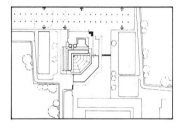

29

30

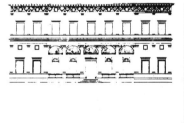

31

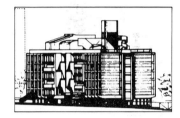

32

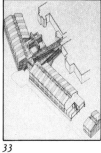

33

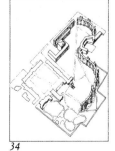

34

35

36

c) The Siemens complex is closely connected to a new housing community which spreads over the flanks of the Giancolo. (Runcorn housing 1967, fig. 11 and relationship to Town Centre building—"Shopping City"). Housing terraces are grouped around neo-classical squares with the increment of the house used repetitively to constitute the wall (of the palace, cf. Nash). The terraces are interconnected by bridges, which cross over Vacuum Strada and also to the slope of the Gianicolo. The student residential area to the North and Campus to the South are linked by these elevated walkways.

d) The axis of Vacuum Strada is focused on the Villa Lante (fig. 12), Giulio Romano's early project that contains some of the personal qualities of his better known works. The Villa is preserved and its importance intensified (in the manner in which the 18th century house generated the plan for St. Andrews Arts Centre 1971, fig. 14). The curved flanking wings of the extensions create an outdoor urban room.[10]

e) A winding path running along the crest of the Gianicolo Hill from the Porta S. Pancrazio to the Vatican, connects the Villa Lante (Arts Centre) to a new student community (St. Andrews dormitories 1964, fig. 13). Entrance is from the Gianicolo wall (North Haugh) into the buildings via long descending stairs. Each residence is planned with splayed legs and angled windows, giving every room a view across the Eternal City (Scottish mountains.) Between the legs of each building the sloping hill becomes a partly enclosed garden for the private use of residents.[11]

f) Nearby is a male residential college (Churchill College 1958, fig. 15) incorporating the Convent of S. Onofrio (fig. 16). "As a first stage of building it was intended to complete an outer wall of College rooms, thus establishing the identity and territorial entity of the College. Student rooms in the outer wall are grouped about staircases which are entered off a cloister that encircles the court. The roof is also a walkway, the walls around a city..."[12]

g) Near Churchill College is located the residence of Basil Mavrolean, a Greek shipping millionaire who had a reverence for Winston Churchill. (His London residence, project 1957, fig. 17, was also to be sited near Churchill's.) A walled compound with three houses, one each for his sons and himself, was proposed; his is the central house. From the compound there is a short walk to the reinstated Porto Leonino landing steps and ferry across to the new shipping terminal opposite (New York study 1968). From there departs a public monorail to the Banco di S. Spirito (Broadway).

h) Along the Tiber (Doha gulf) are aligned the buildings of eleven new ministries (Government Centre Doha 1976, figs. 18 to 22). The programme required each ministry to have its own personality yet office floor areas were similar. The Minister's suite at the top of each tower overlooks the waterfront.[13] Entry into arcaded courtyards is from Via Lungara. The layout incorporates the Palazzo

Salviati (fig. 23) and Sangallo's facade. The courtyards are individually landscaped with different designs of pools and water gardens. The upper level of the arcade overlooks the Via Lungara (New Mall of the Corniche) providing a balcony for viewing motorcades and processions by employees and allowing views of the Tiber (Doha gulf).

i) Continuing along the Via Lungara, the road rectified by Jules II, one reaches the new University Campus. Entrance is from the Palazzo Corsini (fig. 24), the 18th century re-adaptation of the previous Palazzo Riario. In these premises Christina of Sweden founded in 1700 the literary group of the Arcadia. Today it houses part of the collection of the National Gallery of Ancient Art. The monumental staircase is at the core of the plan; from it departs the main axis of a formal garden which has been extended and slightly realigned ending at the foot of the bigger-than-real JS on a birthday cake (fig. 26) which has replaced Garibaldi on a horse (fig. 27). This garden has positioned on its edges a Department of Engineering (Leicester 1959, fig. 25), and an Arts Department (Sheffield 1953, fig. 28) including a School of Architecture, also a History Faculty (Cambridge 1964, see also West Road site plan which proposed that future academic buildings be grouped around a garden, figs. 29 and 30).

j) Across Via Lungara from the Palazzo Corsini and facing over the Tiber (river Cherwell and Angel Meadow) is a new student residence (Queens Oxford 1966, fig. 32). The axis on Magdalen Tower is here focused on the Oratorio dei Filippini. The Tiber edge, today a busy road separating the Farnesina from the river, is returned to a more primitive state, with the addition of a public walkway and mooring for punts/ships. From this walkway a ramp leads into the new building. A stepped terrace in the courtyard creates a high point for viewing and declamations and at this level there is a rotating emblem.

k) The Villa Farnesina (fig. 31) is located in the same beautiful garden on the Tiber. It was originally built by Peruzzi for the wealthy family of Agostino Chigi. "All the qualities of a villa, palazzo and theater would be found under one roof." Today the building is used by the Accademia dei Lincei and the National Print Collection. An extension to the Farnesina is required and a glazed conservatory links the old and new buildings (Olivetti, Haslemere 1969, fig. 33). The junction of the tapering conservatory with the villa occurs on a corner thereby least affecting the Peruzzi facades.

l) Parallel with the Aurelian wall is a wall of student housing (Selwyn College 1959, fig. 34). This linear building has a continuous north facing glass window and on the back, close against the Aurelian wall (fig. 35) are towers of vertical circulation. Similarly the Aurelian wall incorporates a high number of watch towers and presents a continuous walkway along the crest. The wall of new building is broken in two places, at the Porta Settimiana and to allow walking connection up the

Bosco Parrasio steps into the area of Trastevere.

m) Entering Trastevere from Via della Lungara one is confronted with a corner/facade building designed to reinforce the frontage of Strada della Scala and the east side of Piazza delle Fornaci (Meineke Strasse Berlin 1976, figs. 36 to 39). "To repair the street from post-war damage done to it by modern architecture and commercialism (the multi-level parking garage in Meineke Strasse) and restore it to a pleasant mixed residential character by the inclusion of a new building interposed between the garage and pavement... The new facade allows the Church of S. Maria della Scala (garage) to function properly while concealing its gross overscale appearance... The corner had been designed like a hinge to make the transition between Strada della Scala (Meineke Strasse) and Piazza delle Fornaci (Lietzenburger Strasse) less disruptive... To use the established language of the street (i.e., types of windows, entrance doors, gables, balconies, etc.) and the traditional materials of the old buildings (i.e., masonry, rendering, etc.). The new building includes architectural elements of veneer (blind facade), portico (house form), gateway (church/garage entry), hinge (corner transition)..."[14]

n) The street leading to the Ponte Sisto passes through an area of medieval alleys and buildings. A new building comprising shops, offices and a bank (figs. 40 to 42) has been designed in a manner to preserve important historic buildings (the Alt Mill and Renaissance gable in the Marburg project 1977, fig. 43). The colonnade which separates and unifies the old and new structure leads towards the bridge. "the interspace between the new building and the old mill is designed as a meandering pedestrian passageway similar to the many footways in Rome (Marburg)..."[15]

o) Continuing further into Trastevere one reaches a new piazza (Derby Town Center 1970, figs. 44 and 45). The edges of medieval urbanism are here reordered to define a central space and the focusing elements (the inclined Assembly Hall facade at Derby, fig. 50) is the Entrance Pavilion to a new Museum (Düsseldorf Kunstgalerie 1975, figs. 46 and 47). The new piazza with its shopping arcade and civic accommodation, represents a secular alternative to the Piazza S. Maria in Trastevere, the religious center point of the area for many centuries.

p) The new Museum of Architecture contains, as its main feature, Bramante's Tempietto. This may be seen in the circular garden of the museum in a setting similar to the one originally intended by Bramante. Serlio describes the unbuilt setting around the Tempietto, as intended by Bramante, to be "a concentric circular colonnade incorporated into the interior of the present courtyard."[16] The relationship of the two concentric circular elements—Tempietto and courtyard (fig. 48)—is the expression of Renaissance religious symbolism. A public pedestrian walkway (Ratinger Mauer in Düsseldorf) connects from the entrance pavilion through this circular garden and up to the famous

Fontana Paolina (fig. 51). Not far from the Museum are the Steps of the Arcadians (fig. 49), the quarters of a group of poets who aimed to "return poetry to the purity of classical tradition."[17] The steps lead also to another area of housing and to the University.

q) The road out of Rome towards Tuscany passes through the Porta S. Pancrazio, one of the city's main gates. The Gianicolo walls were built by Pope Urban VIII (1623–44) according to Renaissance military design, though keeping in mind the specific contours of the hill. Complementary to these a new wall of buildings is proposed (Dorman Long 1965, fig. 52). These walls along the crest of the hill separate the historic area from the Campagna Romana. The form of the new buildings reinforces the defensive/protective function of the Gianicolo wall whilst absorbing the post-war development which has occurred in the area around via Gregorio VII. Vehicular access is from Vacuum Strada and there is multi-level carparking at lower levels with lifts to office floors above. To facilitate personnel movement in these large buildings a moving pavement at first floor level interconnects all lift towers.

r) On Via Aurelia a few kilometres from the Porta S. Pancrazio and near to the branching of Vacuum Strada is located the new Administration Center for Rome (Florence project 1976, fig. 53—architects Castore, Malanima and Rizzi in collaboration with JS&P). The city intends to vacate its Regional and Judicial Offices from the various Palazzi in the historic area and give these buildings over to residential use. The design of the new center relates to the concept "garden-gateway-island" (fig. 59). The garden of the Villa Doria Pamphili is a threshold, the front door step, to a sequence of new buildings; it is also the upper surface of a large underground carpark. Positioned over the "way up" from this carpark is an entrance pavilion (The Villa Pamphili, figs. 54 and 55), which serves as portico to the bridge spanning to the "Gateway." The Gateway (fig. 56) is a group of buildings which include a hotel and three office towers; it is in the larger sense a Gateway for the approach to Rome/Florence from the west and by Vacuum Strada to the new developments on the Gianicolo hill. At lower levels, the Gateway becomes an interchange with roads, carparking and metro stop. An enclosed bridge leads to the island. The base of the island is a large ground level carpark with frequent stairs to the piazzas and buildings above... The Regional and Judicial buildings and shops, offices and residential units are positioned in several piazzas and pedestrian streets at varying levels though all are interconnected by colonnades and terraces (fig. 57)... The relationship of buildings to urban space is of similar proportions to those in Florence, i.e., the Piazza della Signoria (fig. 58), the Piazza SS Annunziata, etc., and a "mix" of offices and residential units plus shopping, bars, etc., should keep these places active throughout day and evening...[18]

s) To the north a new park and lake have been created for public recreational use. The site around the lake is landscaped according to the tradition of 18th century English gardens, including the careful positioning of architectural follies (cf. Stourhead, fig. 60), such as a group of stiff Dom-ino Houses (1951) and an Expandable House 1957, fig. 61) and a model Village (1955, fig. 62) and many more, all connected by footpath around the lake. The most picturesque site along the water edge is occupied by the Castle (Olivetti Milton Keynes 1971, fig. 63) which has generous sports facilities and its own pier for sailing. The island in the center of the lake has on it a small pavilion (house on the Isle of Wight 1956). Bordering on this luxurious estate is a rural housing commune (Lima 1969, fig. 64) consisting of house clusters grouped around central patios. The Via Gregorio VII leads back to Rome.

Footnotes

1. "Architects used to need kings and dictators to liberate their megalomania, but now they do a better job themselves. They think that they are given large sums of money to play games with, just as a child or a Rembrandt for that matter is given a cheap box of paints. So Gropius flees Hitler and inflicts the Pan Am building on New York. Stirling inflicts the glasshouse on Cambridge. Lloyd Wright's houses are notorious hell to live in. Even Saarinen foists his protege's unbuildable Opera House on Sydney. The common factor is a complete disdain for the people who have to live with it (God help me, I'm going to have to live with the glasshouse!). All this is in the authentic tradition of Vanbrugh and Gilbert Scott. Nothing matters to these men but their reputation in the art-histories. They are not so much undemocratic as anti-democratic: structural fascists. The astonishing thing is that Hitler was a failed painter. Stalin a failed divine. Had they been failed architects, they would have shed blood, not in rivers, but in oceans."
H. Brogan, The Cambridge Review, October 1968.

2. 30 out of 60.

3. Stirling and Gowan projects—Isle of Wight House 1956, Three houses for B. Mavrolean 1957, Expandable House 1957, Churchill College 1958, School Assembly Hall 1958, Selwyn College 1959, Leicester University Engineering Building 1959, Old Peoples Home 1960, Childrens Home 1960. JS and Partner (Michael Wilford) projects— Olivetti HQ 1971, St. Andrews Arts Centre 1971, Düsseldorf Museum 1975, Cologne Museum 1975, Meineke Strasse Berlin 1976, Government Center Doha 1976, Regional Centre Tuscany 1976 (with Castore, Malanima, Rizzi), Dresdner Bank Marburg 1977.

4. "The collection (in a building) of forms and shapes which the everyday public can associate with and be familiar with—and identify with— seems to me essential...the total building could be thought of as an assemblage of everyday elements recognisable to a normal man and not

only an architect. For instance, at Oxford it was intended that you could recognise the historic elements of courtyard, entrance gate towers, cloisters; also a central object replacing the traditional fountain or statue of the college founder. In this way we hoped that students and public would not be disassociated from their cultural past..." JS Lecture, 2nd Iran International Congress of Architecture, Persepolis 1974. See "Connexions" Architectural Review, May 1975.

5. "Collage City," Colin Rowe and Fred Koetter, Architectural Review, August 1975. Also Warehouse Press and MIT Press.

6. Employed or commissioned by Central Government or Local Government.

7. "Despite obvious preference of location this most important site (in Cologne and adjoining the Cathedral) has been criss-crossed by high speed roads which together with service roads cover much of the ground surface of the building site." Report by City Authorities to the Architects for the new Museum—such is testimony to the Planners' Art.

8. "The triangular plaza of the Cologne project is here a more valid modern alternative than the 19th century creation of the Corso Vittorio Emanuele, as the Cologne project retains the plaza's original shape. This plaza is dominated by two religious buildings, however the Oratorio dei Filippini prevails, because of 'the extraordinary density and intensity of the image, which makes Borromini's insertion the true protagonist of the surrounding space.'" Portoghesi, Roma Barocca.

9. The Roman left bank has always had a character of its own. The medieval quarter, Trastevere, had and still has a definite working class status, while the Gianicolo area slowly developed as the "suburban" home of the wealthy and the location for many convents and monasteries. Today it also houses Rome's main prison, Regina Coeli—("The police successfully prevented the demonstrators from reaching the Regina Coeli prison, which is on the Trastevere side of the Tiber, by blocking all bridges. This caused additional traffic chaos." The Guardian, 7 March 1977.) The Siemens crossing spans from the tightly knit fabric of the right bank to the Via Lungara, approximately at the location where today exists the Ponte Mazzini. Siemens incorporates the courtyard of the Convent of S. Giacomo and is an attempt to urbanize the area west of the Tiber.

10. "The idea of the city as a collage of 'types' lay behind the Rational Architecture Conference (March 1975)...On display in the exhibition was his tiny project for an art gallery for St. Andrews, which collaged together three existing buildings, using a curved wall to create internal exhibition spaces and an external entry courtyard...This collage technique, like townscape, can include

historic fragments of popular conceptual reactions to a building or a city. It destroys the total design, 'machine aesthetic' of the Bauhaus but retains ideal types." G. Shane, *The Architect's Journal,* 16 July 1975.

11. For sexual allusion, see C. Jencks, *Architectural Association Quarterly,* 7 September 1972. Also follow up letters from JS and Jencks.

12. From architect's report.

13. From architect's report. "The floor area of each Ministry building can be independently increased by horizontal extension of the towers in the direction away from the waterfront. The height of all towers therefore remains constant, signifying the programme requirement that physically the architects should not indicate any Political—Ministry—hierarchy."

14. From architect's report.

15. From architect's report.

37

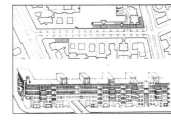

38, 39

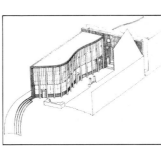

40

41

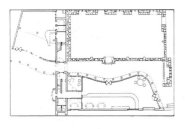

42

43

44

45

46

47

48

49

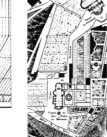

50

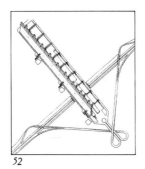

51

52

53

16. Portoghesi, *Rome of the Renaissance.*

17. Portoghesi, *Roma Barocca.*

18. From architect's report.

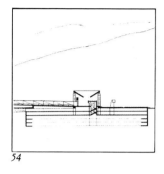

54

55

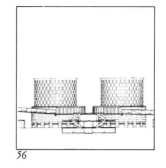

56

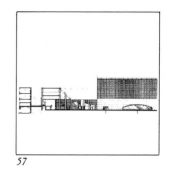

57

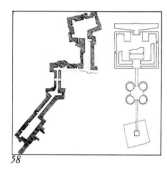

58

59

60

61

62

63

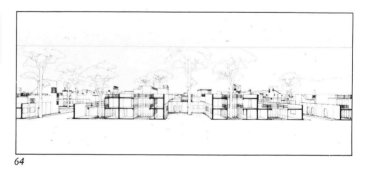

64

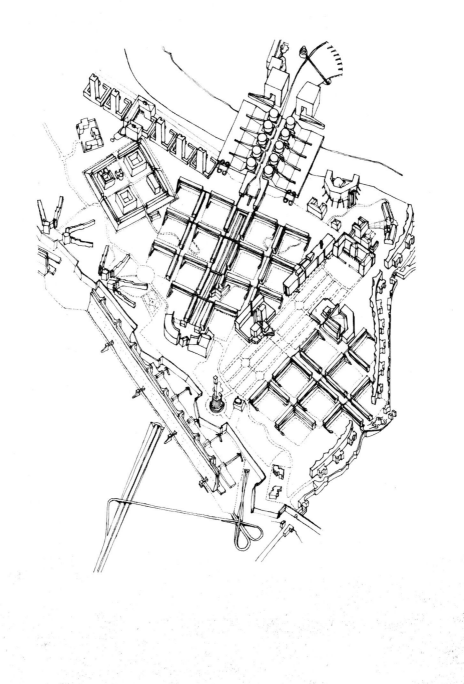

Revisions to the Nolli Plan, 1977

1977
Dresdner Bank
Marburg

James Stirling, Michael Wilford
Ulrich Schaad
Russell Bevington

The new building replaces an existing, modified and ruined one that presently flanks Pilgrimstein. It will contain a Bank at ground level with offices above. At third floor level there could be self contained professional offices. The new construction will be orientated towards the Medieval mill, and away from the heavily trafficked street. The space between the new building and the old mill is designed as a meandering pedestrian passageway similar to nearby footways in Marburg.

The arched niches in the facade to Pilgrimstein are a 'memory' of the arches under the clock tower which was recently cut in half to make way for road widening.

The exterior of the old mill (16th century) should be converted to its original form as far as practical. The old mill could house a museum/gallery or restaurant, alternatively, classroom/studio space for education/art purposes or dance or a small scale theater.

"The most satisfying aspect of the project seems to be the solution whereby the pedestrian is received within the winding colonnade and led through the service spine into the inner courtyard without having to follow a fixed route. Because the tight space of the courtyard is animated by the

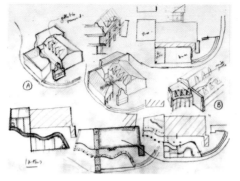
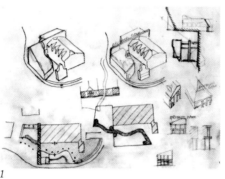

1

movement of the facade itself: the courtyard narrows and widens and, transversally, along the rear side of the voluted pediment, leads to the lower level of the square in front. The pediment itself is left free, because it is treated like a stage flat and, since it is an 'historical work of art,' constitutes a highly effective decorative piece for the square and the courtyard. It is here that one finds what might be called the aesthetic centre of the composition considered as a whole. The movements of the volutes are echoed by the movements of the facade of the bank building.

"Stirling's irony wins out just because he relativizes the venerable tone of the historical moment itself. The voluted pediment with its huge slabs no longer represents a parenthesis between two symmetrical wings, but becomes almost superfluous and even more beautiful when read as a stage flat. Jutting out over the pavement, the facade of the main building is completely closed: narrow windows keep out the aggressive presence of the surrounding world, here represented by heavy motor-car traffic."
H. Klotz, *Lotus 18*

1. *Preliminary sketches.*
2. *Sixteenth century.*
3. *Nineteenth century.*
4. *Twentieth century.*

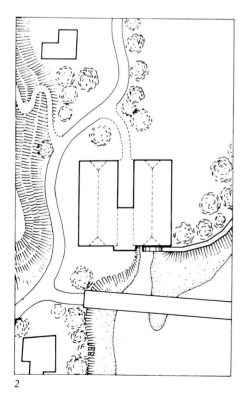

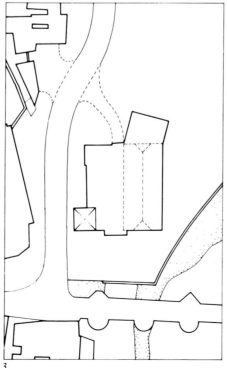

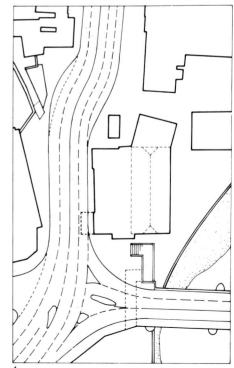

2

3

4

1. *Axonometric up view.*
2. *Ground floor.*
3. *Second floor.*
4. *Structural diagram.*
5. *View from river.*
6. *View towards river.*

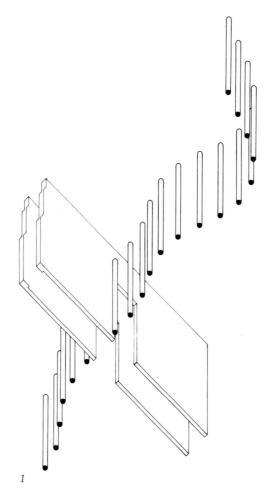

1

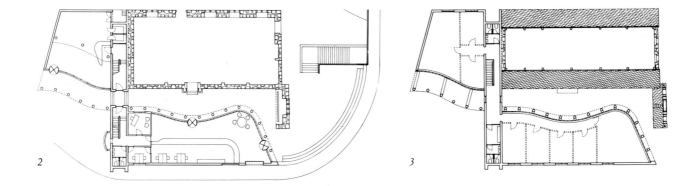

2   3

Dresdner Bank, 1977

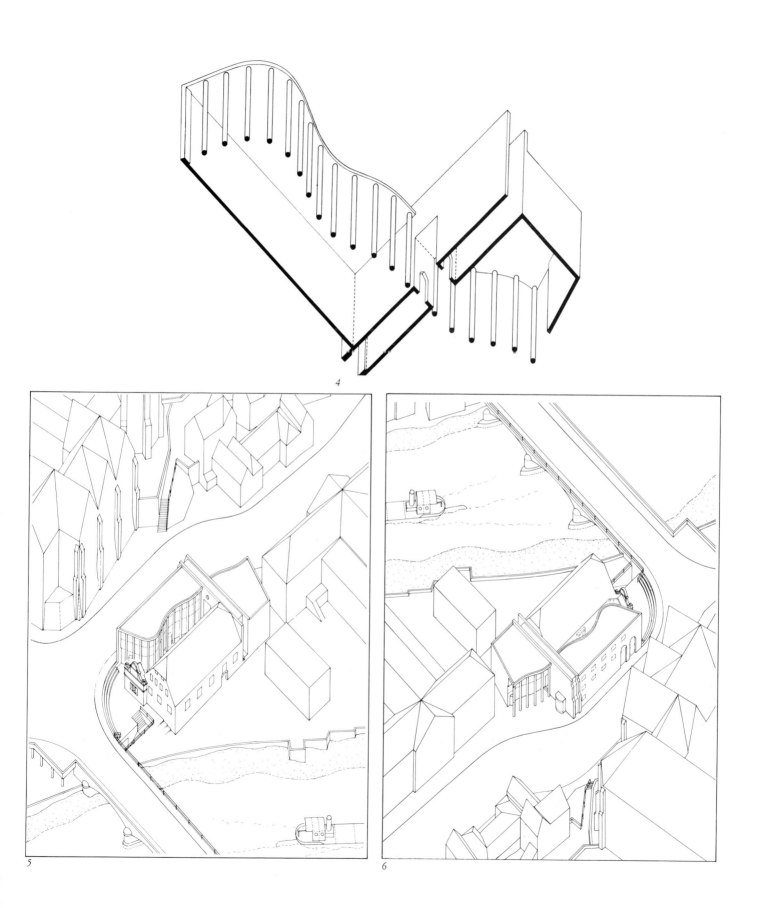

4

5   6

Dresdner Bank, 1977   243

1. *Clock tower corner, 1920.*
2. *Pilgrimstein.*
3. *Clock tower corner, 1977.*
4. *View down Pilgrimstein.*
5. *Renaissance gable.*
6. *University Building opposite.*

1

2

3

4

5

6

Dresdner Bank, 1977

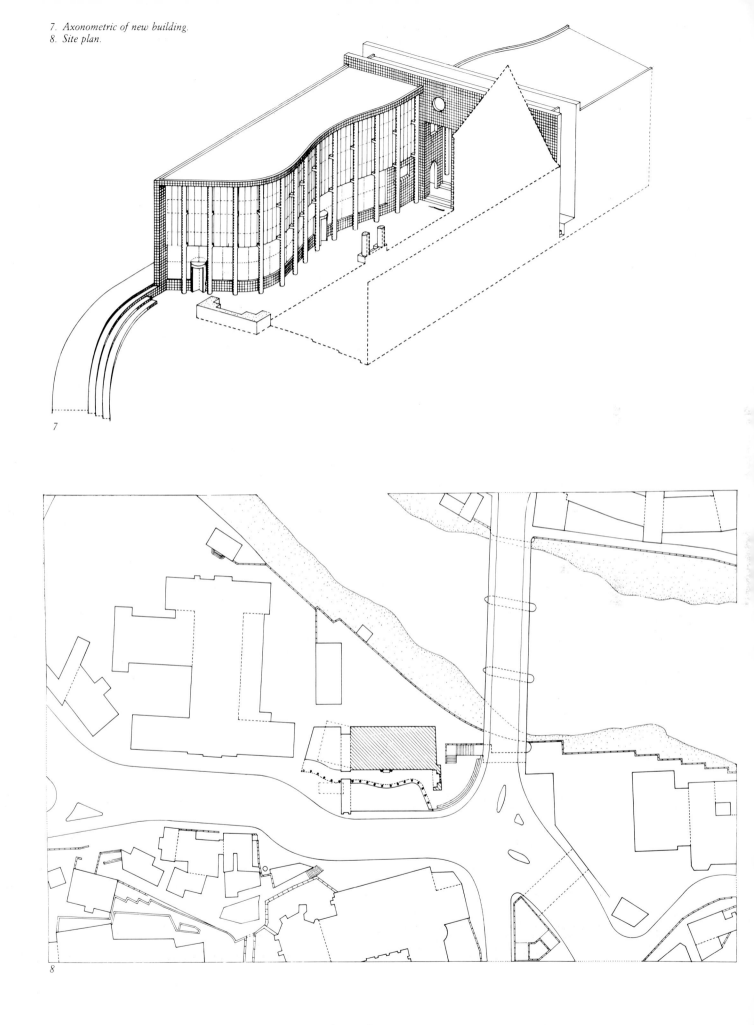

7. *Axonometric of new building.*
8. *Site plan.*

7

8

Dresdner Bank, 1977

245

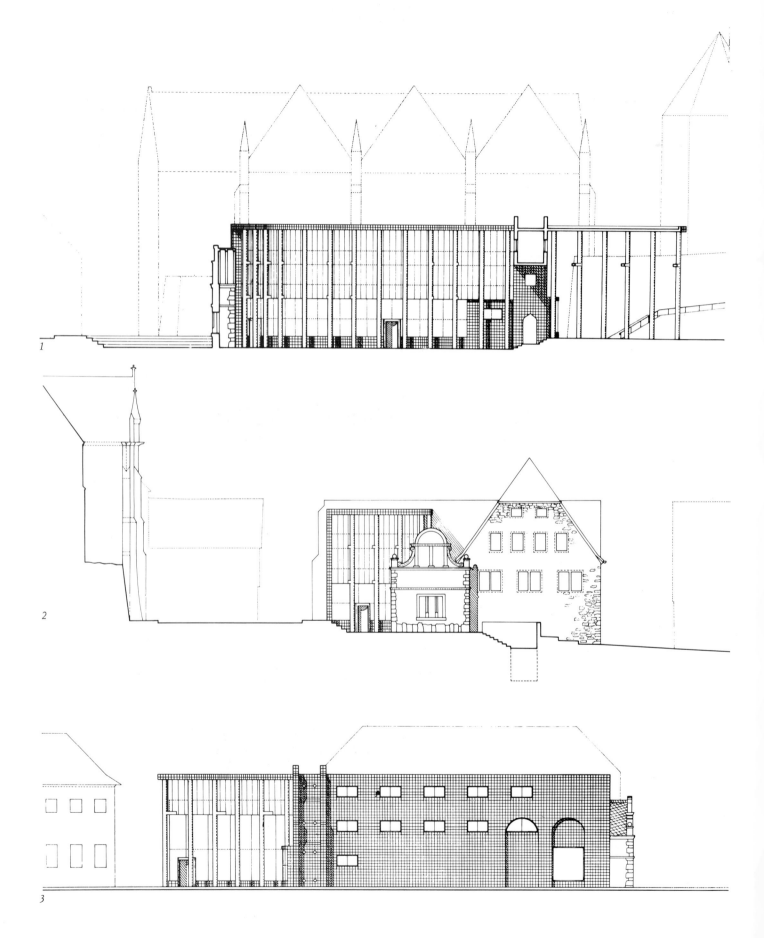

1

2

3

1977
Housing Study for Muller Pier
Rotterdam

James Stirling, Michael Wilford
Alfred Munkenbeck
John Tuomey

The redevelopment of Muller Pier on the River Meuse is required, as existing harbor facilities have become obsolete. The City of Rotterdam wanted proposals as to the use which this pier (natural land) could be put. Our suggestion was to build an urban housing neighborhood.

800 apartments varying in size from one to six persons are distributed throughout, providing intermixing of age groups and family sizes with the

largest apartments located near the ground. Each apartment has a balcony as well as the use of the residents' garden. The dwellings include single floor and duplex units with enclosed access galleries on every third level, serviced by elevators from ground level.

Shopping and community facilities are located at the northern end of the pier. A cafe/restaurant is located at the southern end with a panorama of the harbor.

The residents' garden includes landscaping with shrubs, lawns, footpaths and fountains as well as areas for tennis, football and other sports. A tree lined promenade provided along the water edge and would be accessible to the public as a city amenity.

1. Axonometric of proposed development.

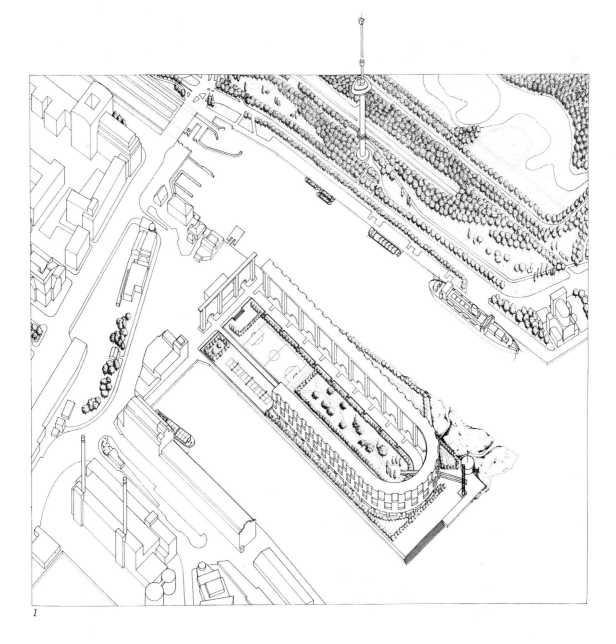

1

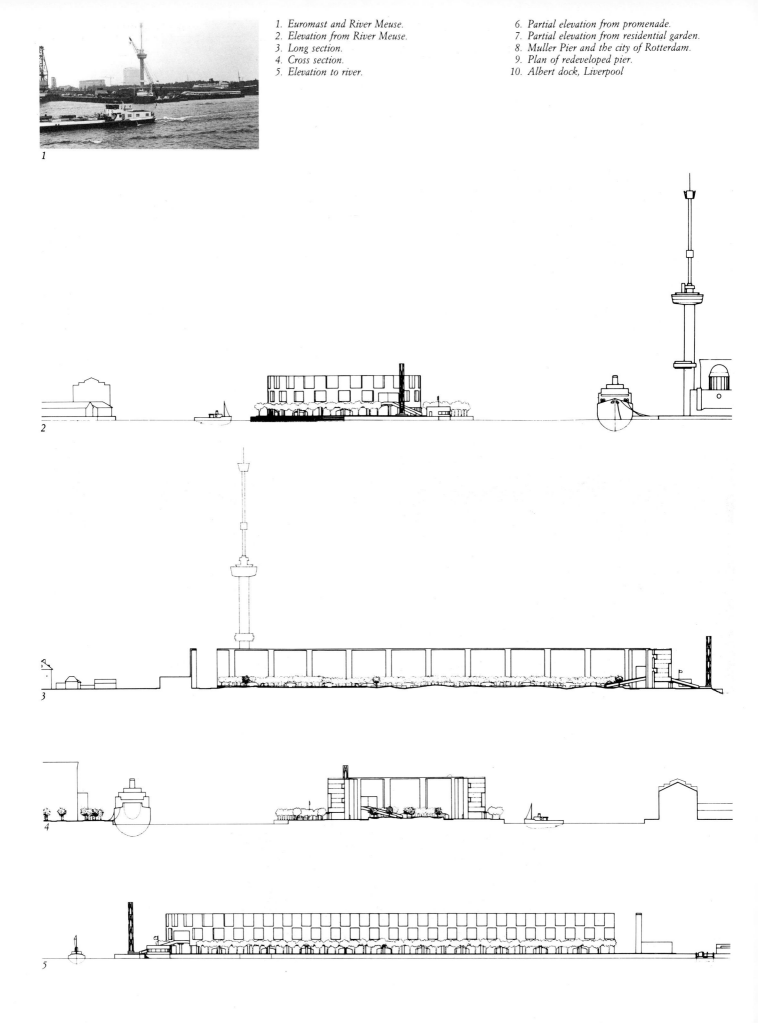

1. *Euromast and River Meuse.*
2. *Elevation from River Meuse.*
3. *Long section.*
4. *Cross section.*
5. *Elevation to river.*
6. *Partial elevation from promenade.*
7. *Partial elevation from residential garden.*
8. *Muller Pier and the city of Rotterdam.*
9. *Plan of redeveloped pier.*
10. *Albert dock, Liverpool*

Housing Study for Muller Pier, 1977

6

7

8

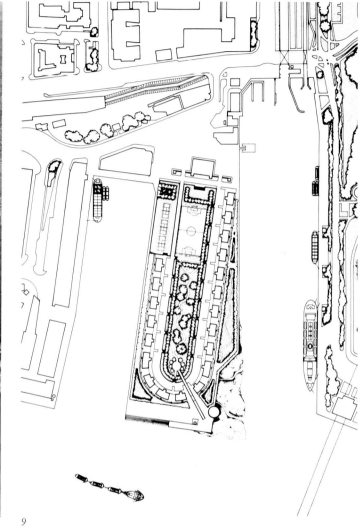

9

10

1978
Institute of Biology and Biochemistry
University of Tehran (unfinished)

James Stirling, Michael Wilford
Peter Schaad
in collaboration with
Burckhardt & Partner (Basle)

*The building cross section was a formal
representation of the natural valley and used the
contours to provide sequential entry. Linear
buildings overlooked three central gardens. All
accommodation was grouped in several zones
arranged in parallel across the site.*

1. View of site.
2. Site plan.

3. *Massing diagram.*
4. *Preliminary sketches.*
5. *Axonometric.*
6. *Basement level.*
7. *Lower garden.*
8. *Lower and central gardens.*
9. *Lower, central and upper gardens.*
10. *Cross section through site.*

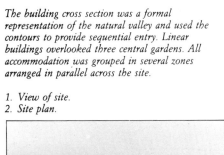

1

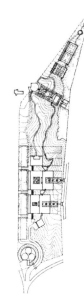

2

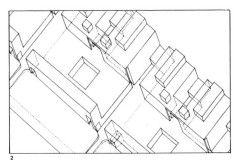

3

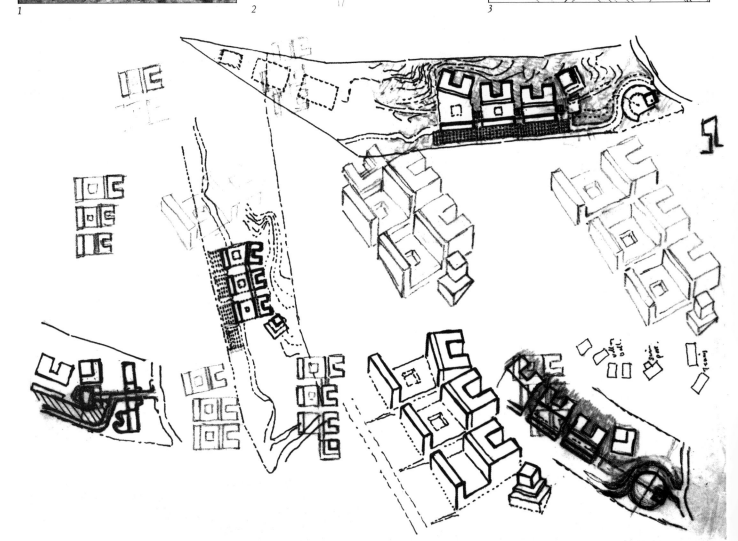

4

250

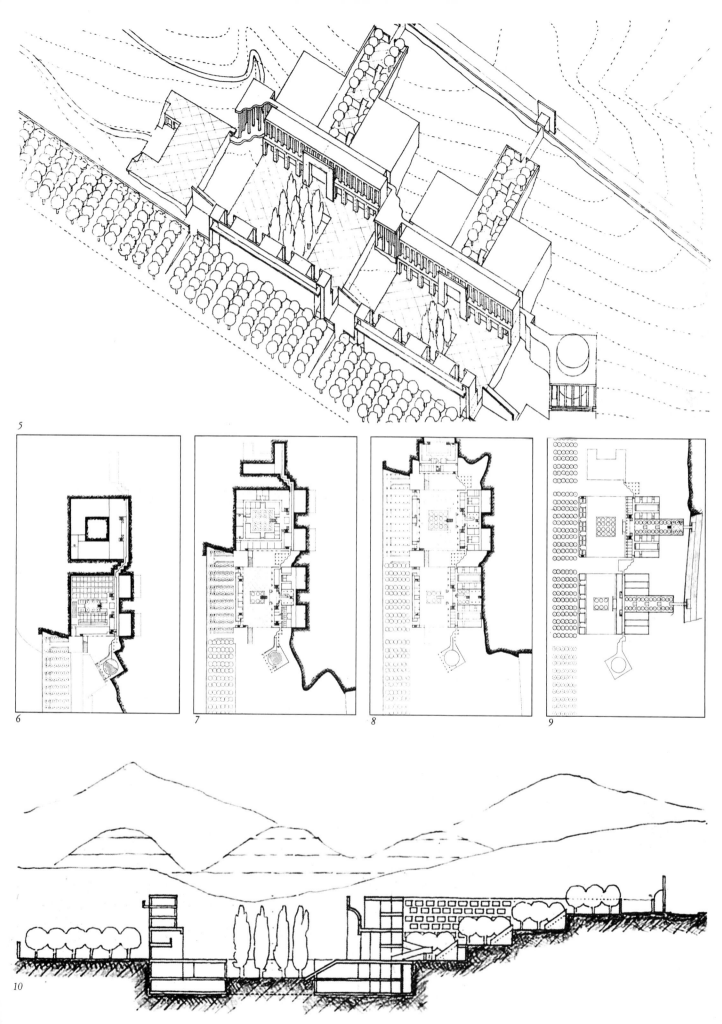

5

6

7

8

9

10

Institute of Biology and Biochemistry, 1978

251

1977/83
Staatsgalerie New Building and Chamber Theater

Stuttgart, Germany
(Limited Competition)

James Stirling, Michael Wilford

London Office:
Russell Bevington, Ulrich Schaad, Peter Ray, John Cannon, Alexis Pontuik, John Cairns, Alfred Munkenbeck, Shinichi Tomoe, John Tuomey, Markus Geiger, Paul Keogh, Ulrike Wilke, Peter Schaad, Chris MacDonald

Stuttgart Office:
Siggi Wernik, Tommi Tafel, Rudolf Schwarz, Pia Riegert, Laszlo Glaser, Jochen Bub, Heribert Hamann, Christian Ohm, John Rodgers

Letter in Architectural Design 9-10-77
Sir:
For the first time since the 50s an architectural competition entry has aroused controversy not only among architects, but also among the interested public, splitting the architectural scene into opposing groups like a bombshell.

Immediately after the news that the Stirling project was to be built was released, there were scornful letters in the local press by architects (including Frei Otto) describing his design as inhuman and totalitarian.

What is the controversy all about?

The jury had chosen an architectural and urban design concept which is quite "alien" to the architecture to be found in this part of Germany. Stirling's U-form layout plan with the centrally placed drum-shaped sculpture garden and the public walkway leading through this sculpture garden uses historic architectural elements—he cites elements of the traditional museum (there are even elements of Schinkel's museum in it.) At the same time his work is not traditional, but conceptually new and fascinating. His design is strong and decisive.

The essense of this very heated controversy is very fundamental to the path "modern" architecture is

1

taking. Behnisch, Frei Otto and other, less well known, architects presently producing our day to day architecture in Germany, follow the concepts of "non-determinism," producing "light weight," "open," "democratic" and "non-offending" buildings. To this view of architecture, integration into historic context only exists as soft and bending architectural forms—being generally accepted as both adequate and modern. It is only within this conceptual framework, that competition entries vary to produce endless variations on the same theme. This generally accepted harmony was violently intruded upon by Stirling's astute architectural statement. In discussion he said he was sick and tired of the boring, meaningless, non-committed, faceless flexibility and open-endedness of the present architecture.

Stirling's main opponent (apart from Frei Otto's statement to the local press) was Prof Behnisch—the third prize winner and architect of the Olympic buildings in Munich. He attacked Stirling's design as being purely formal—architecture becoming art itself, with shapes borrowed from Palladio, without meaning apart from pathos: "Can one imagine Picasso's goat grazing in the drum shaped sculpture garden?"

He associated Stirling's design with the totalitarian approach, especially with Staufian architecture—and even with the Tannenberg memorial, a Nazi monument. He suggested that the design sacrificed

the importance of art objects that were to be exhibited in the museum for the sake of architecture, and went on to call the design academic and inhuman.

Stirling's supporters emphasised both the urban design quality of the project and its architectural quality. Stirling is said to have ignored aspects of contemporary town planning concepts by organising forms, shapes and open spaces in such a way as to produce a perfect integration into the existing fabric and a vivid spatial rhythm. The formal concept, they point out, cites historic elements rather than using them in an unintellectual way—and by doing so, a new architectural approach seemed to be created.

With regard to the accusation that Stirling's architecture was "totalitarian," Professor Duttmann asked: "What does democratic architecture look like?"

Finally, the representative of the Staatliche Hochbauverwaltung said that "the Ministry had decided to commission Stirling with the building because he had set impulses to architecture which had not been received during the last 20 years."

The controversy is not over yet, and hopefully the discussion on which way architecture should go will continue.

With kind regards,
Margret Maier-Reichert
Horst Reichert
Stuttgart

"A compositional method that can master eclecticism is difficult to find: Stirling at last offers us one. It is to establish a massive, obvious and deliberate prime element. The large "U" of the galleries is unequivocal. The fourth side is then filled (less densely) with the exotic elements that

2

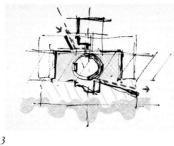

3

tempt you to stop and look. The centre is heroically etched-out. Opposite the entrance a ramp and elevator leads directly to the exhibition rooms of the Staatsgalerie extension. Fifteen rooms. In series. Simply arranged with a traditional opened-flank door space from one to the next. Naturally as well as artificially lit, the ceiling is in the form of a total lay-light, and the glass is deliberately misted, so that you will be aware of the roof structure but not too distracted by it. There is little that one can say about it.

"It should answer very directly the complaint made by many museum directors that primadonna architects impose too much upon the galleries, and it retains (via the ceilingscape) just enough of the delight in structural substance to remind future generations that it *is* in the end a twentieth-century building.

"I once heard Frank Newby, who has been the engineer for several of Stirling's key buildings, explain the maturing of his structural abilities. In Leicester, he had to be taught that structure could perform across three dimensions and that concrete could be used plastically. In Cambridge, there were sophisticated metallic objects to be designed—also in three dimensions. 'But at the Florey building, Jim had learned all he needed— he came to me with a clever piece of structural thinking all of his own.' Now, quite simply, clever structures bore him.

"Which leads me to a major clue. Stirling becomes bored. This happens to him in social circumstances, and certainly in architectural circumstances. So the design of a very large building such as this reflects his reaction to several layers or scales of boredom. But he is Master enough of the situation to recognise that mere playfulness and trick piled upon trick would be disastrous. So the essentials are straightforward. The planning diagram is

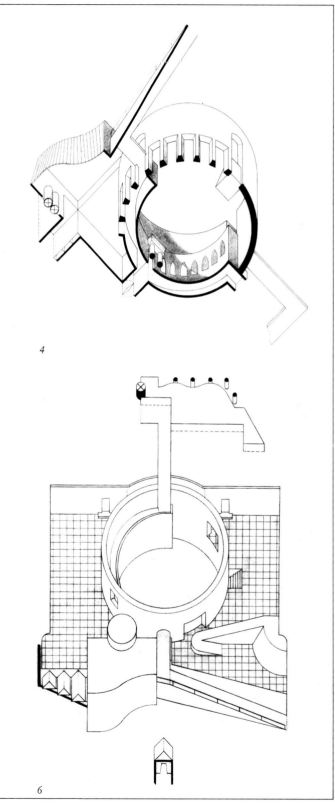

4

6

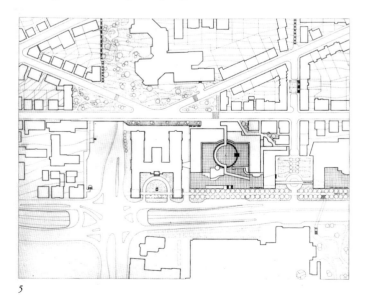

5

1. *Administration entrance and library.*
2. *Entrance level.*
3. *Section through car park, circular court and administration.*

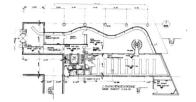

1

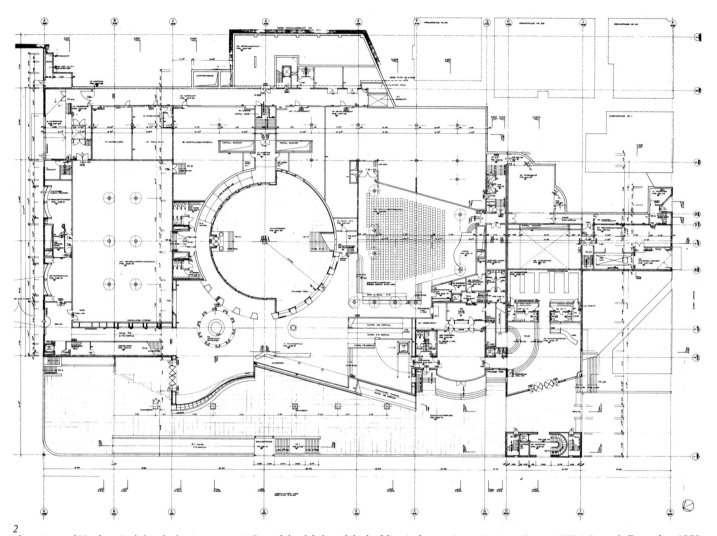

2

(almost) out of Neufert. And then he begins to create the town."

"He describes the Staatsmuseum complex as 'urbanism', and presents us with a solution that is more concerned with the process of gradual unfolding than stylised deployment.

"One of the delights of the building is the way in which the lower public floor presents a whole range of internal plazas; each with its own identity. They all seem to be likely venues for a friendly encounter, a quiet gaze, a rendezvous or a spot lecture.
P. Cook, *Architectural Review,* March 1983.

Stephen Games, *RIBA Journal,* December 1980
On site at Stirling's Staatsgalerie
Journal: How's the work going?
Foreman: There are some builders and formwork carpenters on this site who've been working on building sites for 25 or 30 years and they've never seen anything like it. When they first saw the

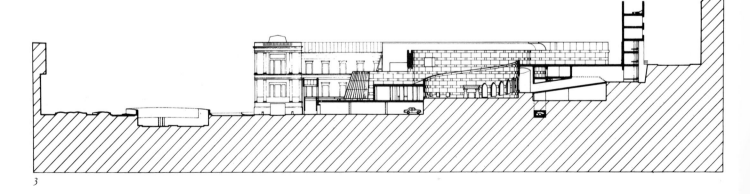

3

4. *Directors office and administration.*
5. *Gallery level.*
6. *Gallery entrance, public footpath, cafe, and theatre entrance.*

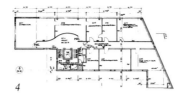

4

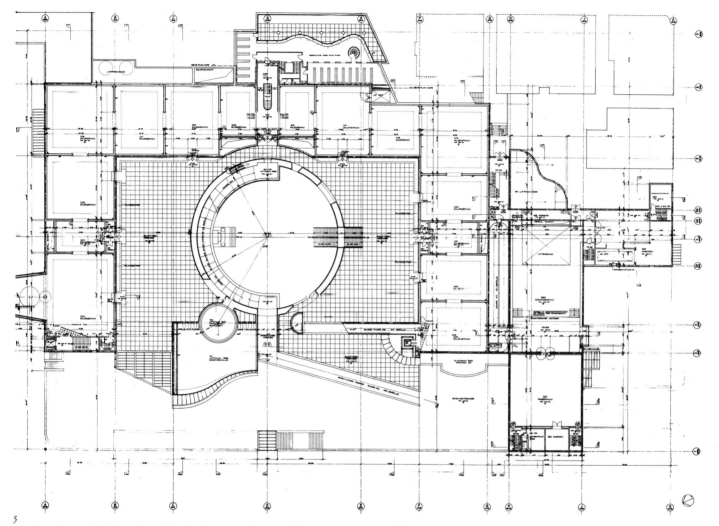

5

drawings they said "What is this rubbish?" but now it's up they stand back and admire. They say "I built that". They're very proud of themselves.
Builder: I think it's very bombastic architecture, fascist architecture. You know the Zeppelinfeld that Speer built for the Nuremburg rallies—where a hundred thousand people crowded together to chant "Hitler, Hitler"? That's what Stirling would like to do here. I think he'd like to appear in the middle of the hall here and for everyone to salute him.
Foreman: I think he got the idea for the Staatsgalerie from a building in a village not far from here. It's about 100 years old and it's also circular in plan and with round windows.
Builder: I think he got the idea from all those English castles.
Foreman: We see him occasionally—always dressed the same in dark blue suit, light blue shirt and black tie. And always a sloppy old pair of Hush Puppies that look as if they're coming apart.

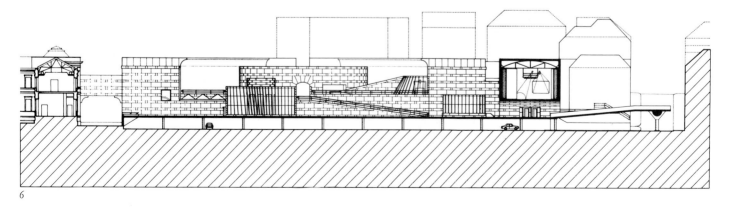

6

1

2

He always wears them. And he wanders around, giving orders.
Builder: Reminds me of Mies van der Rohe—he used to behave like that.

Stirling, the outsider, intuitively recognises the essential character of the location; in contrast, the local architects respond to Stuttgart as a city of commerce—their baggage of formal typologies and planning strategies prevents them from seeing it as Stirling does. The accusations of Fascism and totalitarianism levelled at his work are irrelevant. As practitioners of an architecture continually adapted to the needs of industrial production, bureaucratic procedure and economic necessity, they should have thought twice before using such labels—people who live in glass houses should behave more circumspectly.
J. Waldren, *Architect's Journal,* 22 December 1982

"The third invited German competition we did win.

Some inter-relating characteristics of old and new are:

A All existing buildings are retained preserving the street character of the area. Suttgart was bombed out and even more destroyed by post-war reconstruction so preservation of as many buildings as possible was an important requirement of the competition. Where new buildings come to the street, such as the theatre service wing on Eugenstrasse and the museum administration on Urbanstrasse, they have the scale and alignment of adjoining old buildings.

B The old gallery (1837) is neo-classical, and U-shaped in plan. There is a semi-circular drive to the entrance and at mid point of the forecourt was a classical urn, replaced in the 19th century by a man on a horse. The new building is also U-shaped and instead of the semi-circular drive there is a circular courtyard.

The man on a horse is reiterated by a taxi drop off pavilion with banner, also on the axis of the plan.

C   The new theatre wing duplicates the wing of the old gallery (similar scale and materials) and they semi contain forecourts with entrances that front onto the boulevard;

"Mandatory to the competition was the inclusion of a 3 metre terrace fronting Konrad Adenauer Strasse containing a large car park. Also a public footpath a short-cut across the site, a democratic request in many German competitions—which unfortunately does not help maintain the entity of the city block.

"I hope this building will evoke an association of Museum and I'd like the visitor to feel it 'looks like a museum.' In its built details it may combine traditional and new elements though old elements are used in a modern way, for instance, the histrionic coving is not a cornice used throughout, but only defining the sculpture terraces. Similarly

3

4

5

there are assemblages of constructivist canopies which define a hierarchy of entrances.

"I include a plan of Schinkel's Altes Museum representing the 19th century Museum as a prototype. They have attributes which I find more appealing than those from the 20th, for instance a parade of rooms, as against freely flowing space; also even when small they have a certain monumentalism—in the City it's essential to have a hierarchy of landmarks,—a city without monuments would be no place at all. For me monumentalism is nothing to do with size or style, but entirely to do with *presence*—thus a chair could be monumental—I have several.

"And it's no longer enough to do classicism straight, in this building the central pantheon, instead of being the culmination, is but a void—a room like non space instead of a dome—open to the sky.

"The axiality of the plan is frequently compromised, set piece rooms conjoin with the

Staatsgalerie New Building and Workshop Theatre, Stuttgart, 1977

free plan and the public footpath meanders either side of a central axis—thus the casually monumental is diminished by the deliberately informal.

"The ambivalence of the front corresponds to the ambiguity of the boulevard (Konrad Adenauer Strasse is more an autobahn that a street). Instead

1. *View into circular garden*
2. *Upper and lower terraces*
3. *Public footpath*

1

2

3

of a facade the front recedes, presenting a series
of incidents adjacent to the walking movement,
into, through, and across the building.

"In addition to Representational and Abstract;
this large complex I hope, supports the
Monumental *and* Informal; also the Traditional
and High Tech."

JS lecture 81.

1

2

3

4

Staatsgalerie New Building and Workshop Theatre, Stuttgart, 1977

1978
Bayer A.G. PF Zentrum
Monheim (limited competition)

James Stirling, Michael Wilford
Alexis Pontvik
Alan Levitt

(Extracts from Competition Report)

Buildings are sited with the intention of creating an idyllic research and development center. It is hoped to achieve an arcadian setting for the whole complex with perhaps similar building-to-land relationships as was achieved in the 18th century with the large country house (or Schloss) and its attendant outbuildings set amid picturesque landscape.

Laboratory complexes are positioned radially around a landscaped park and each is planned as a group of buildings around internal gardens. The entrance facades which overlook the park would be completed in the first construction phase and the 150 percent future expansion requirement is provided by extending the complexes in an outward direction—increasing by whatever amount in any time phasing. The identity of the center buildings and the integration of laboratory complexes would be established at the outset and be preserved through all stages of expansion. Overall we hope to avoid the institutional and architecturally we are attempting to achieve a visual integration of the sophisticated/technical with vernacular/rusticated.

"Each laboratory complex is symmetrically organised on a grid of pedestrian circulation routes and these major elements are deployed in a formal arrangement fronting a horseshoe avenue, from which they radiate away without regard to orientation. The avenue, with its adjoining canal, defines the edge of a landscaped park, the focus of which is the U-shaped tower of the administration building. Circulation to the central administration building from the laboratories is across this park rather than by the defined routes of enclosed walkways.

"Stirling's scheme has greater and more formal impact from the road but reveals less. The symmetrical, blind walls of the parking structures screen the view of the park and flank the entrance plaza in front of the imposing central administration building. Entry to the site is between two lodges, placed symmetrically on the axis of the administration building.

"On each side of the administration block pavilions with colonnades projecting into the entry plaza form entrances to the wings which contain the library, exhibition hall, tropicarium, cafeteria and dining rooms, fronted by a pergola overlooking the park. A conference centre is located in the base of the administration block. Curving, sloping ramps connect the plaza with the park.

"The towering U-shaped administration building is at the focus of the composition; its plan form reflects that of the park and the avenue. The whole central complex is a symmetrical composition, grand in scale in an austere neo-classical style, with ashlar stone-facings, fat pure-cylindrical columns and a huge semi-cylindrical cornice to the main tower but otherwise no mouldings, architraves, or entasis.

The entrances to the laboratory complexes are defined by large pedimented aedicules with stepped glazed roofs which straddle the avenue and by bridges over the canal to the park. From these pavilions runs the main organising element of each of these complexes, which contains the primary circulation routes and social and communal facilities arranged around an atrium, each of differing form, lending identity to each complex. Running off from these central elements are the three-storyed, heavily serviced laboratory blocks.

The communal areas are a neo-classical hybrid of modern and old, with cylindrical concrete columns and taut sheets of glazing with Italianate vernacular details, such as exposed timber rafters and roman or ceramic tile roofs. The end walls of certain spaces, like the library in the chemistry block, are in a more formal finish of ashlar stone facing in two-toned horizontal bands. The laboratories themselves are rendered externally, again in two-toned horizontal bands. Each block of laboratories is straddled by a huge table-like structure of shiny blue metal (enamelled steel of anodised aluminium). The 'legs' at each corner are the fresh air supply ducts and the 'table top' walls above the roof enclose the plant and are punctured by louvred circular vents. The result is to give a huge scale where each three-storey block of laboratories reads as a single unit, the identity of each storey being suppressed by wide bands of colour absorbing the windows. This forms quite a contrast to the more delicately scaled atria and communal areas, where Stirling intends that staff and visitors 'should feel that what they are experiencing is more akin to a sequence of Florentine courtyards and gardens than the entirely functional environment of an anonymous research centre.'"
P. Buchanan, *The Architect's Journal,* 16 January 1980

Stirling has identity
From Georg Weiler

Sir: I am disappointed that your reviewer found James Stirling's entry for the German research competition sinister and dismaying (*AJ,* 16 January 1980, pp. 112–114). As a former research fellow at the foundation who was aware of the progress of the competition (though not involved in the decision-taking), I can only say that of all the entries it was Stirling's that impressed the centre's future users as a stimulating place in which to meet and work.

Your reviewer called the design militaristic; well, at least its description demands adjectives! The other entries (which I hope you will publish for comparison) failed to spark any qualitative response, so uniform and unmemorable were they in their spatial constitution. Their *image fixe* seemed to be that of the post-war secondary school. As a layman, I need "recognition handles," entrances, walls, windows of distinctive design, by which to identify different institutions. Architects may be able to distinguish one network of small-scale courtyards from another; I find it difficult and confusing.

I would suggest that after 50 years of determinedly neutral and unmemorable architecture, a design with such a positive identity should be welcomed. Particularly at a time when urban proliferation makes the need for recognisability all the greater.
Georg Weiler, Imperial College, London SW7,
The Architect's Journal, 6 February 1980.

1. Schloss Solitude, Stuttgart.
2. Site plan.

1

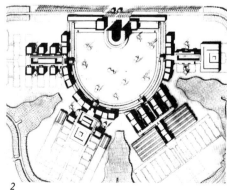

2

1. The Bio-1 Complex.
2. The Bio-2 Complex.

3. Central services complex.
4. Chemistry complex.

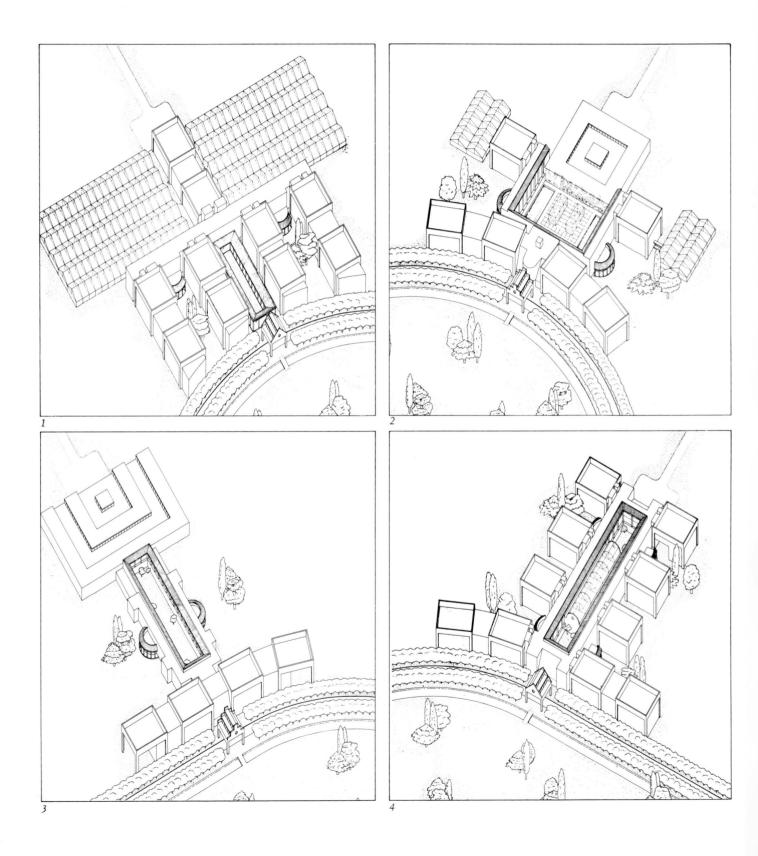

1

2

3

4

5. View towards park.
6. View from street.

5

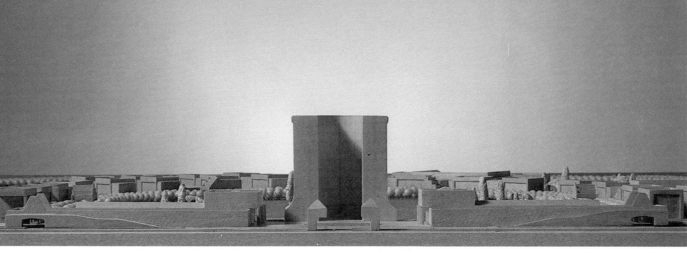

6

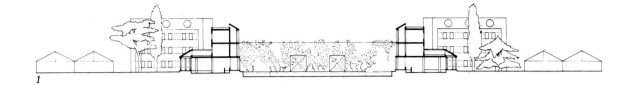

1

2

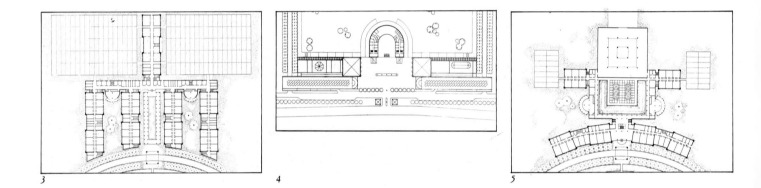

3 4 5

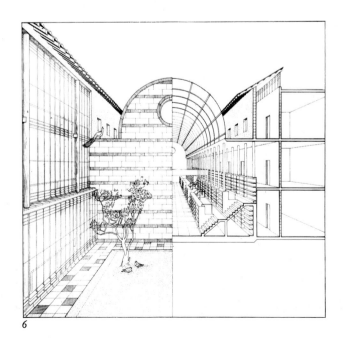

6

Bayer A.G., 1978

7. Chemistry complex: section through library.
8. Central services complex: section through social lounges.

9. Plan Chemistry complex.
10. Plan Central services complex.

11. Model, view of whole development.
12. Elevation of offices and central buildings.

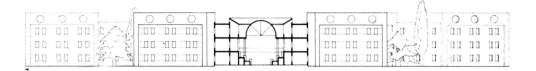

7

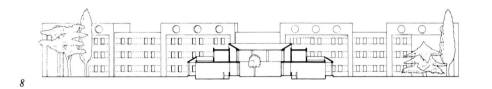

8

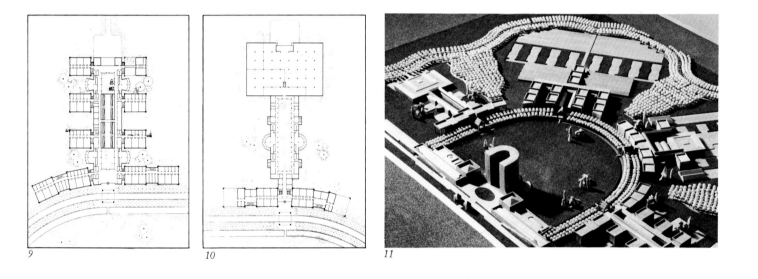

9

10

11

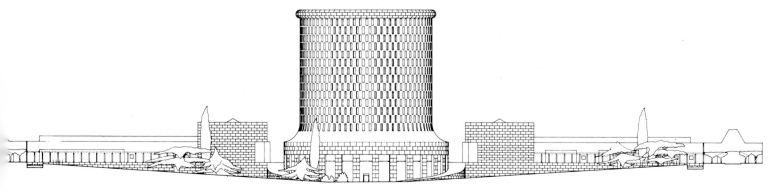

1. Bio-1.
2. Chemistry complex.
3. Bio-2.
4. Central services.

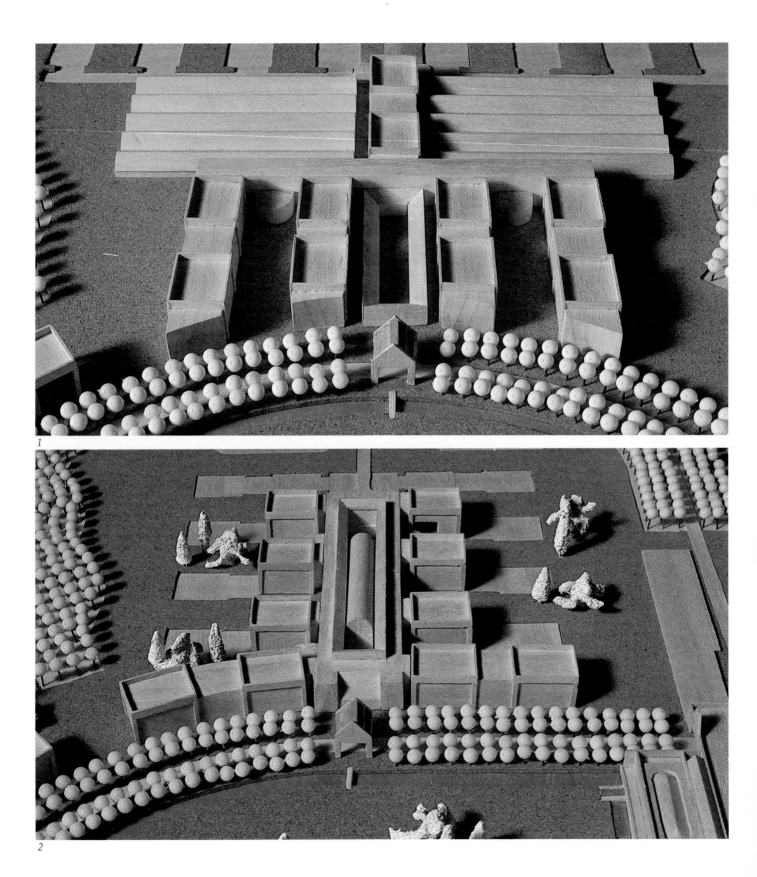

1

2

Bayer A.G., 1978

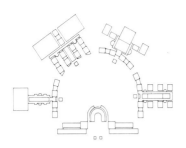

3

4

1. *Elevation Bio-2.*
2. *Section Bio-2.*

3. *Perspective of social lounge (vernacular) and laboratory (technical).*

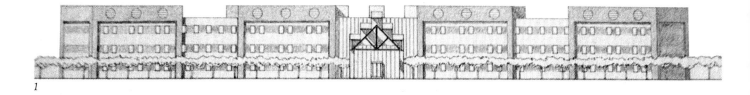

1

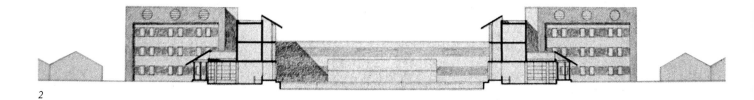

2

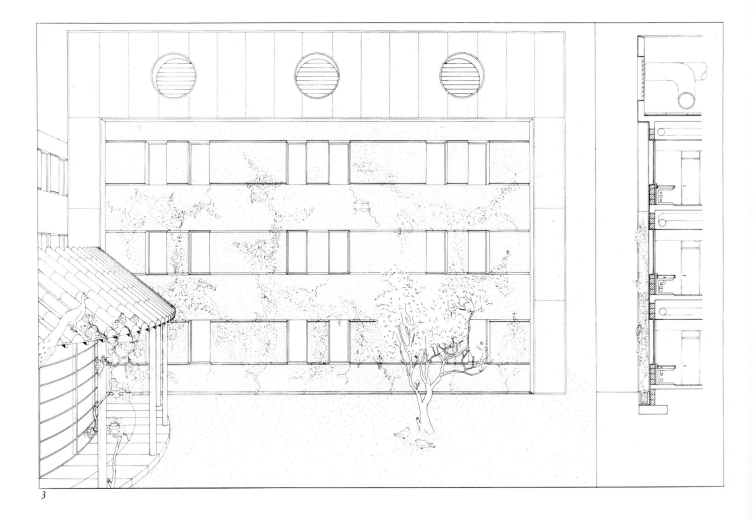

3

Bayer A.G., 1978

1978
11 Townhouses
New York

James Stirling, Michael Wilford
Robert Livesey
Mark Rosenstein

The requirement was for the design of eleven luxury townhouses, the whole to be five stories high and built over an existing underground parking garage. In anticipation of development above, the garage included in its roof structure (at ground level) a parallel row of structural beams on 18-foot centers to support the party walls of the houses to be built on top.

We used the beam spacing to plan an 18-foot wide (thin man) house alternating with a 36-foot wide (fat man) house, the latter on three floors with an independent apartment on the two upper floors; since the lower house was on three levels, it did not contain a lift. With alternating 18-foot and 36-foot widths, we were able to plan three varieties of dwelling. The movement backwards and forwards of the street facade expresses the house within the terrace, and bay windows, studio glazing, balconies, etc., indicate the more important spaces within. This is similar to the surface projections—windows, entrances—on traditional New York town houses which exist around the site and give the streets on the upper East Side their particular quality.

"The grouping as a whole balances depth and surface well—the fronts go in and out, playing mass off against void like the heavy limestone mansions that once controlled Fifth Avenue.

Inside, the floor plans are especially varied and intricate; what appears to be the facade of one house may in fact contain pieces of another, for Mr. Stirling has borrowed spaces within the overall grouping to create complex, interlocking floor plans.

"Elements in one house's facade carefully balance those in another, and it is easy to see how each scheme was conceived as a group; the houses would be weaker as single units."
P. Goldberger, *The New York Times*, 16 June 1980.

1–4. Studies of bay windows and entrances.

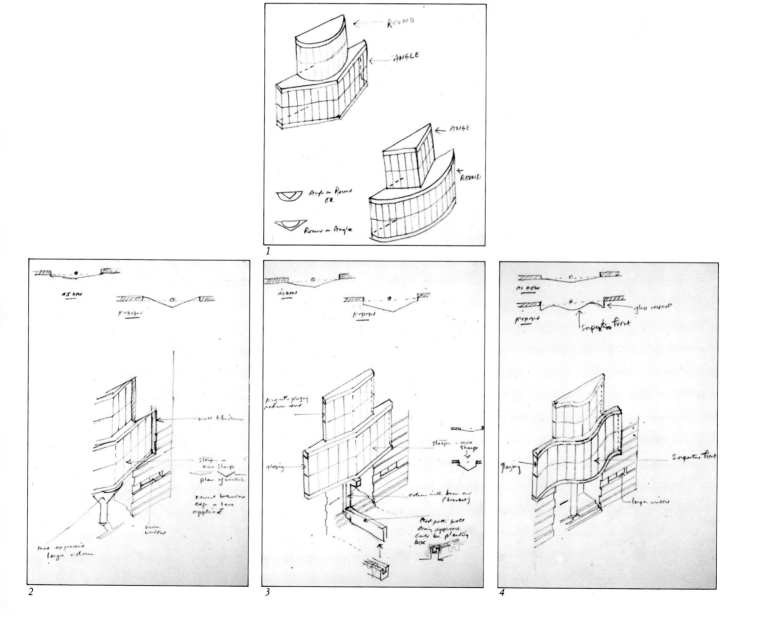

"To New Yorkers, row house facades were a
vertical message describing the social order—
private floors above, public rooms centred over
the service level—legible to the passersby in a way
apartment houses never could be. Unlike later
apartment monoliths which created side street
valleys and avenue hilltops, the carpet of three to
five storey structures preserved the original
topography of the city."
C. Gray, *International Architect 5,* 1981

1. *New York Townhouse.*
2,4. *Preliminary sketches.*
3. *Upper East Side Street.*

5. *Section through new townhouses with existing garage below.*
6. *Cut away axonometric.*

1

2

3

4

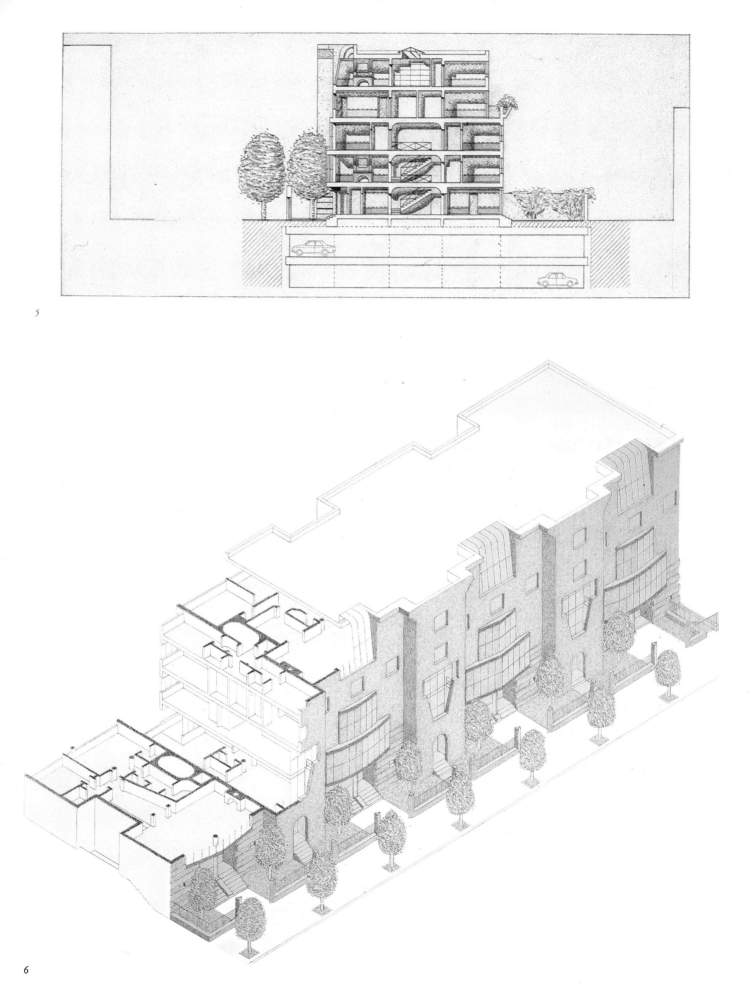

5

6

11 Townhouses, 1978

1. *Ground floor.*
2. *Second floor.*

3. *Third floor.*
4. *Fourth floor.*

5. *Fifth floor.*
6. *Diagrammatic section.*

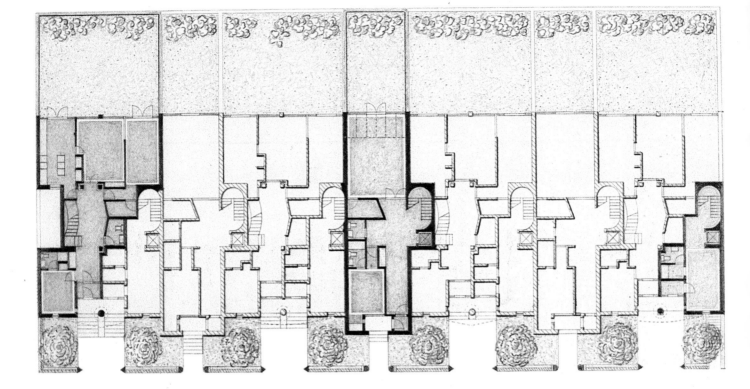

1

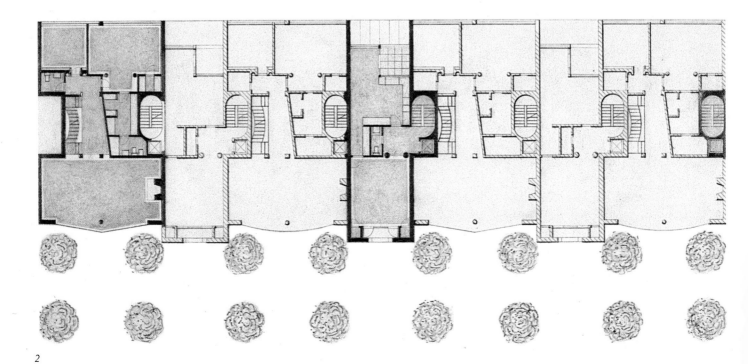

1. *Ground floor.*
2. *Second floor.*

3. *Third floor.*
4. *Fourth floor.*

5. *Fifth floor.*
6. *Diagrammatic section.*

2

11 Townhouses, 1978

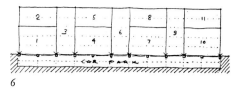

6

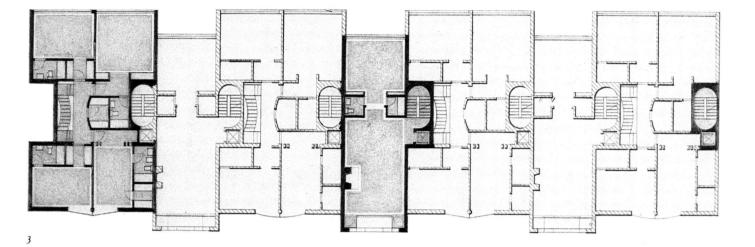

3

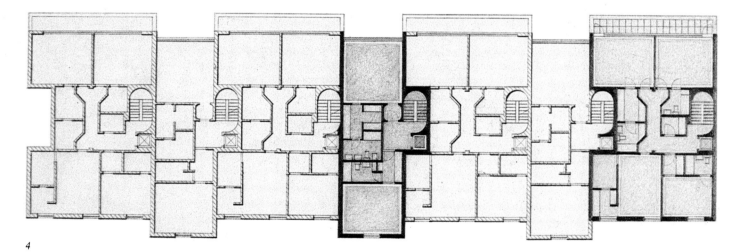

4

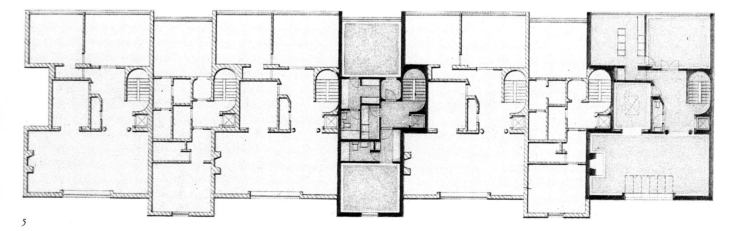

5

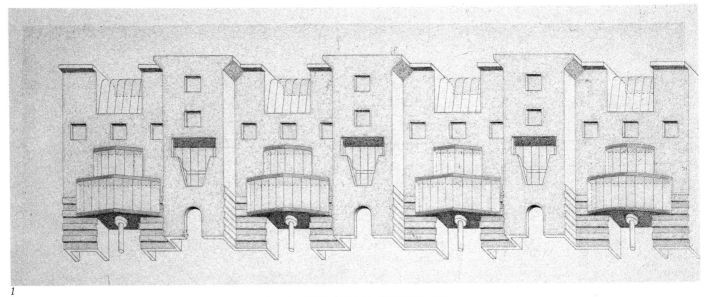

1

2

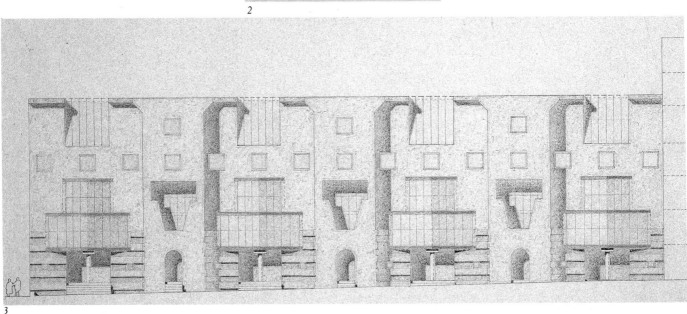

3

1979/81
Extension of the School of Architecture, Rice University
Houston

James Stirling, Michael Wilford
Alexis Pontvik, Paul Keogh
in collaboration with
Ambrose & McEnany (Houston)

(Extracts from Architects Report)

The new building is L-shaped and interlocks with the North Wing of Anderson Hall. It is also consistent with Cram, Goodhue and Ferguson's original strategy of supplementing the narrow buildings of the central quadrangle with linked blocks facing outwards towards the loop road.

The new wing forms a three-sided courtyard with a garden facing west. The intimate quality of this courtyard contrasts with the central quadrangle and the large green to the west.

Internally, a spacious double story circulation gallery and central exhibition/jury space integrates the new wing with the existing building and is the focus of the School. The gallery is centered on the existing risalit on the courtyard facade of Anderson Hall. A new entrance is positioned at the north-east corner and opens directly into the gallery, mirroring the existing entrance. The gallery bridges over the exhibition/jury space at second floor, stopping short of the semi-circular ends to provide visual connection between levels at the entrances. These areas are rooflit by lanterns which also register the terminations of the gallery on the exterior of the building.

The exhibition/jury space can be adapted for various activities by means of large sliding doors. Enclosed exhibitions or lectures for a seated audience of approximately 200 can be arranged simultaneously with closed or open juries. The combined area can accommodate large exhibitions and receptions. Glazed doors provide access into the courtyard

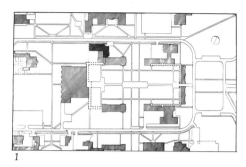

1

garden which could function as an extension of the exhibition space for receptions and parties.

The design of the new facades maintains sympathy for the existing campus style. The treatment of masonry and window openings makes reference to the style of Cram, Goodhue and Ferguson's original buildings.

This is not so much an act of self-denial as one of candor: the architectural climate is at last ripe to the admission that some problems acknowledge relatively dull solutions. Stirling's building, like Caesar's wife, is above suspicion and in playing no one false plays Stirling true. With architects as clients, and their school as project, this is no small triumph.
M. Sorkin, *Arts & Architecture,* Winter 1981

"I went to Rice to see the building but couldn't find it"
Philip Johnson

The special spaces of the spine further the distance from exterior treatment by appearing to be, from their articulation, nearly as a separate construction placed within a shell. That is, the assemblage of paired stairs, bridge and lozenge-like ends whose curved glass surface appears to be a volume sitting within the entry porch, all combine to read as a large furniture element within a volume defined by a contrasting building envelope.
P. Papademetriou, *Global Architecture Document 5*

It is, in fact, both original and joyful, and it is difficult to spend any significant amount of time in the building and on the Rice campus and believe that the Architect should have done much of anything else.

Within the L-shape that the building's plan takes, the Architects have created a pleasant garden court, like many of the aspects of this building something that one might think had been there for a generation. But once again, the goal is not to create a sustained illusion—there are curious cone-shaped skylight towers, like little rockets, on the roof, and the entrances are through round bays of glass, all of which make it clear that this is not a building constructed in the 1920's. But these details never take over and control the

1. *Campus master plan*
2. *Sketch of new wing and courtyard through existing colonnade*
3. *Photograph of new wing and courtyard through existing colonnade*

2

3

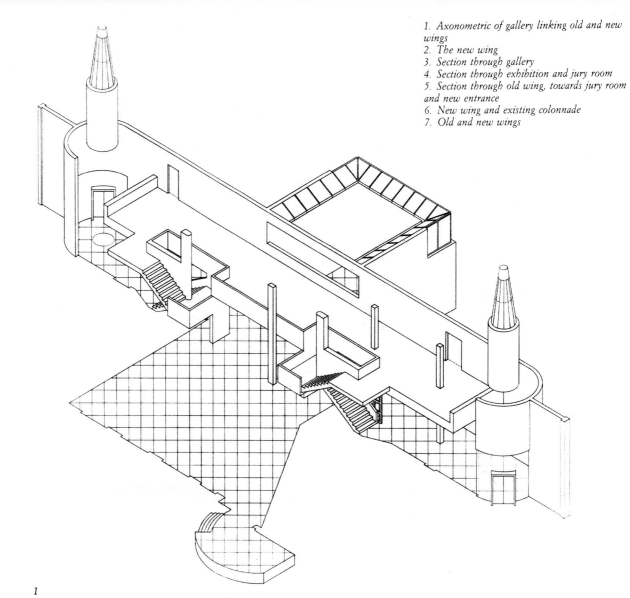

1

2

Extension of the School of Architecture, Rice University, 1979

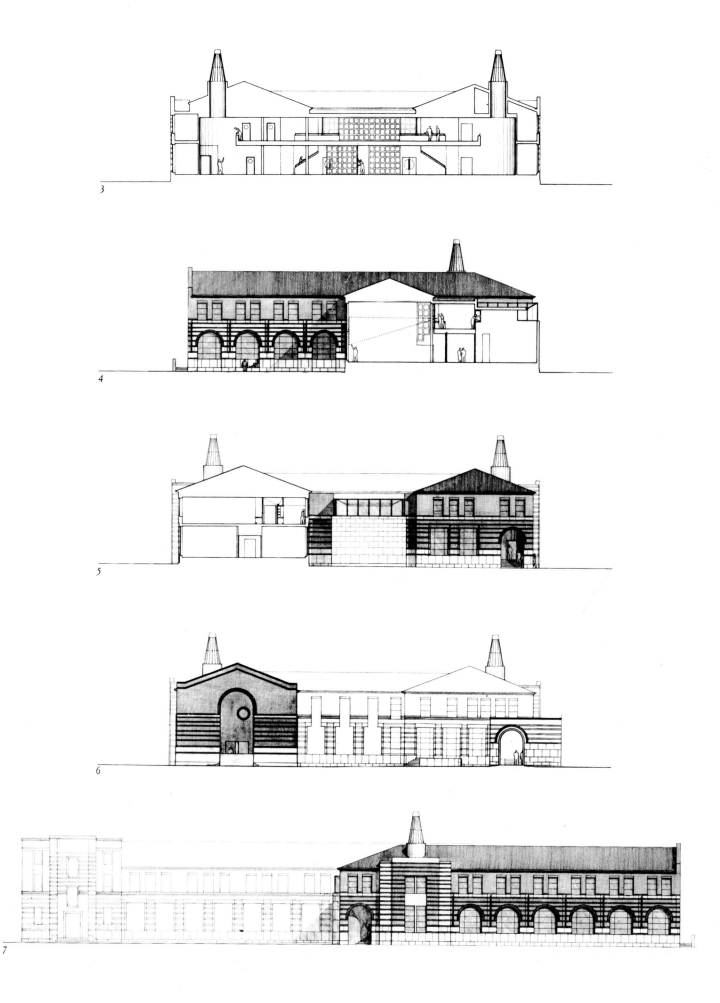

3

4

5

6

7

Extension of the School of Architecture, Rice University, 1979

building—the central idea is the continuity with what has come before.

It is no surprise that the building is fairly popular with students—it is far pleasanter to be in than most architectural schools, and indeed, in its restraint it offers a lesson that most buildings in which architecture is taught eschew.

P. Goldberger, *New York Times,* 12 March 1983

1. *Anderson Hall before extension*
2. *Ground floor, old and new buildings*

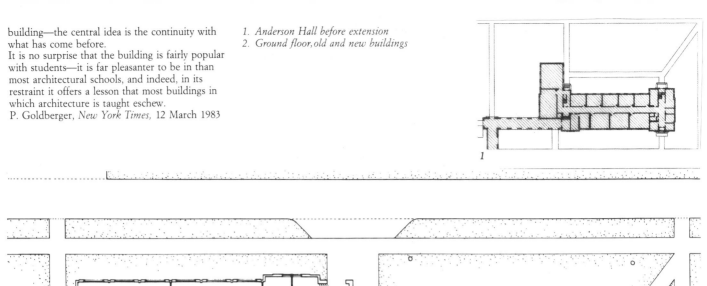

1

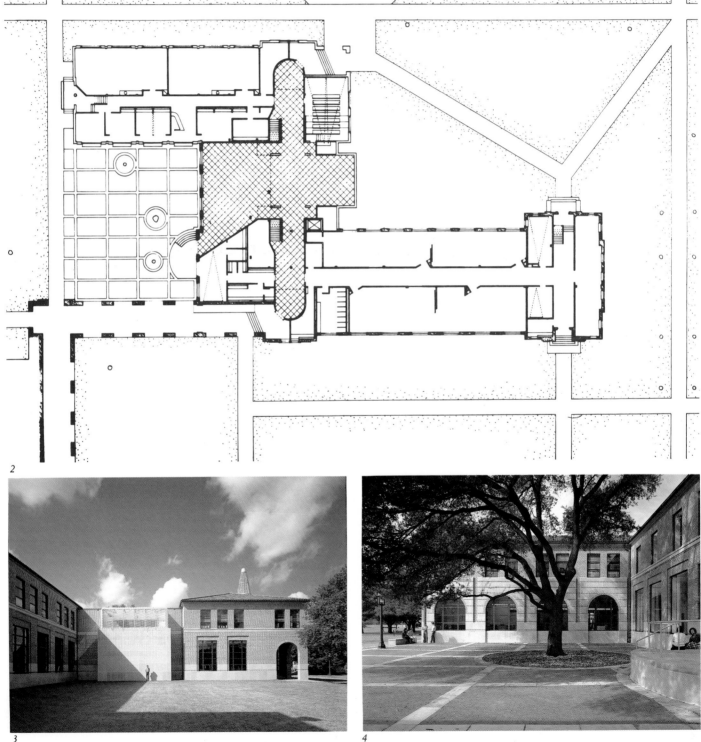

2

3

4

Extension of the School of Architecture, Rice University, 1979

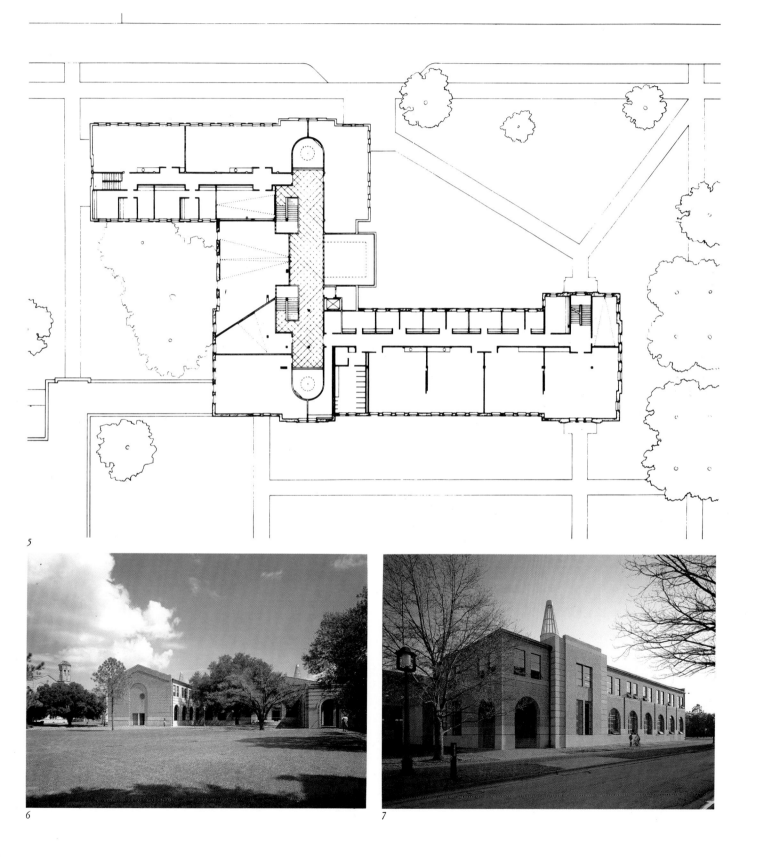

5

6   7

Extension of the School of Architecture, Rice University, 1979

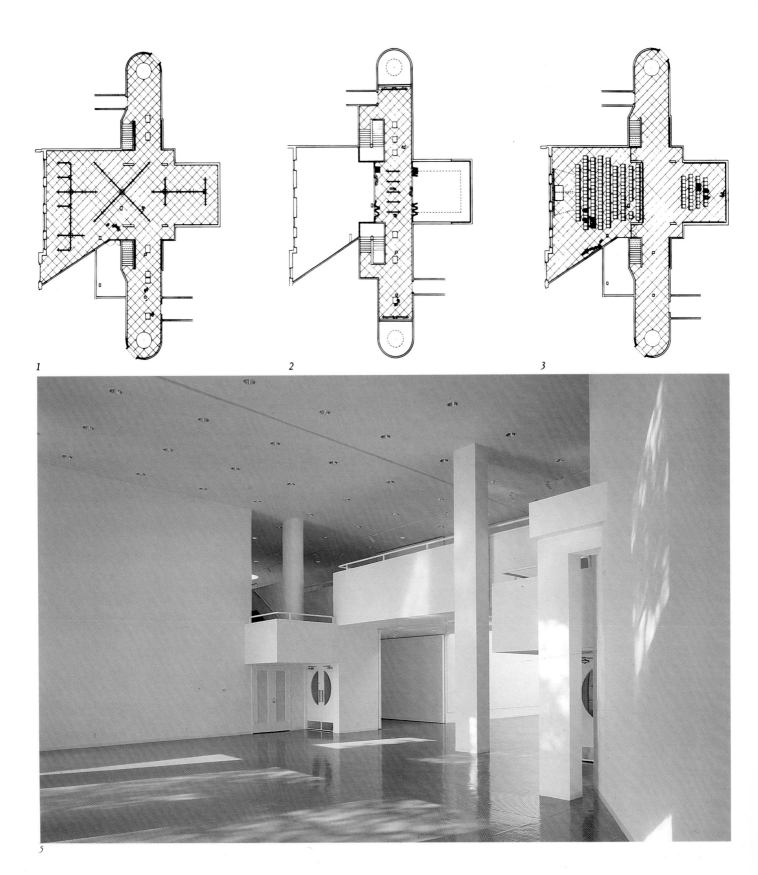

1   2   3

5

      Extension of the School of Architecture, Rice University, 1979

6. Exhibition space in use.
7. View of gallery.

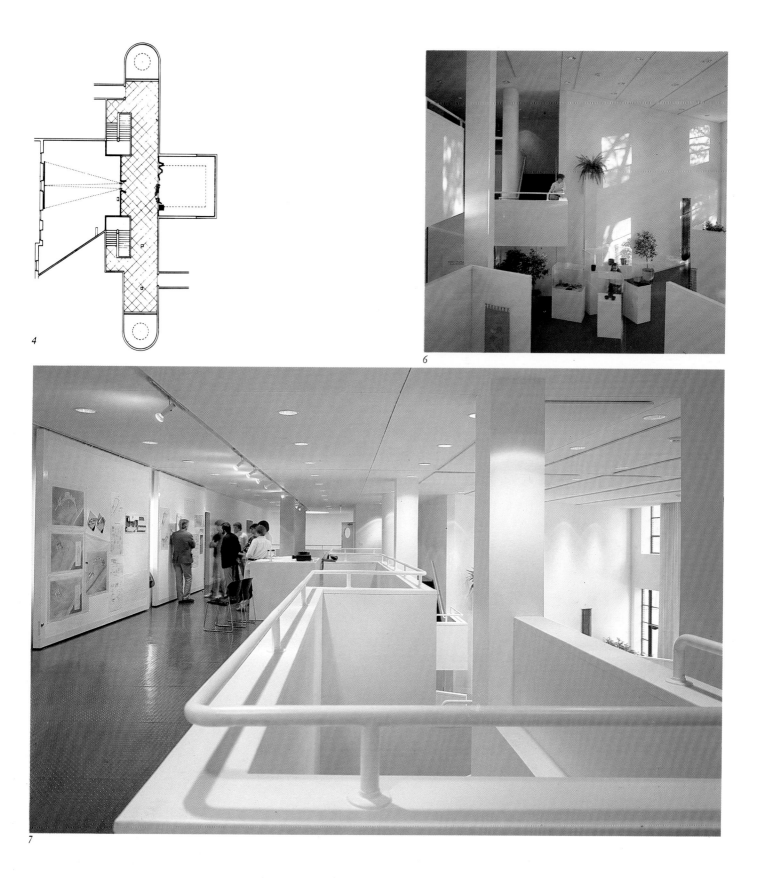

4

6

7

Extension of the School of Architecture, Rice University, 1979

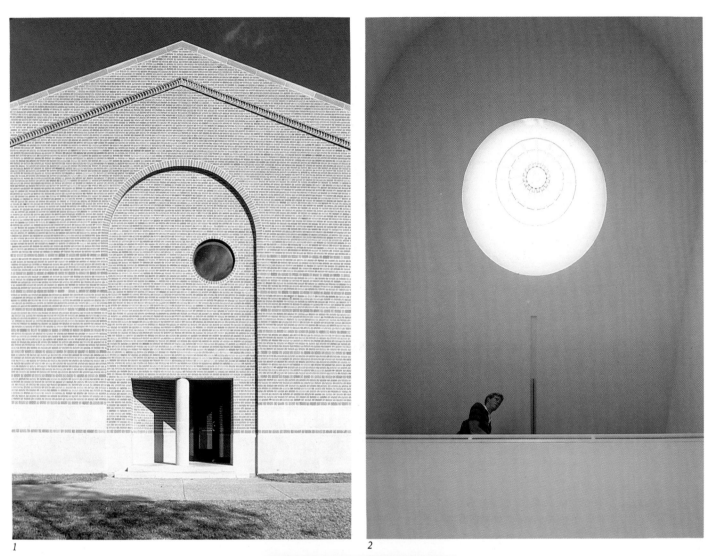

1

2

3

Extension of the School of Architecture, Rice University, 1979

1979
Wissenschaftszentrum
Berlin (limited competition)

James Stirling, Michael Wilford
Walter Naegeli
John Tuomey
Peter Schaad

(Extracts from Competition Report)

The primary need of the Science Center is for a great multitude of private offices in which individual and small group work can happen. Conference rooms, directors' rooms, secretaries' rooms, administration offices, etc., are also required. A special concern is how to find an architectural and environmental solution from a programme mainly composed of repetitive offices. The rational office solution usually produces banal box-like buildings. Much of what is wrong with post-war urban redevelopment lies in the uniformity of these rationally produced office blocks and they may be the biggest single factor contributing to the visual destruction of our cities in the post-war period.

An additional problem here is the requirement to preserve the facade and larger part of the old Law Courts building (19th century, Beaux Arts and huge in scale).

Our proposal is to use the three Institutes of the Science Center (Management, Social and Environment) plus the building for future
expansion to create a grouping of three or four relatively independent buildings, all of which are similar but different. The architectural form of these buildings may relate to familiar building types and the whole group of buildings, old and new, is perhaps more akin to a college or university precinct. With this proposal, each of the three Institutes could have its own identifying building. Each Institute has two directors with complementary staff and a binary organization seems fundamental. As the new buildings are planned from a symmetrical basis, allocation of rooms should adapt to this dual organization rather well.

The new buildings cluster round a central garden of an informal character and the single large tree in the center of the site has been preserved. The loggias and arcades which overlook this garden also have a relationship with the cafeteria, the existing building, conference facilities, etc. The cafeteria is at garden level in the Management Institute. The conference facilities are at ground level in the Social Institute. The car park is at basement level in the Environment Institute. Free standing in the garden is the library tower with a reading room at ground
level having views into the garden.

With this concept of several buildings each of differing form, informally related to gardens and the existing building, we hope to make a friendly, unbureaucratic place—the opposite of an institutional environment, even accepting that the building programme is for a multitude of offices and the design of a single complex.

Deutschlands Architekten sind aufgescheucht: Ihr Britischer Kollege James Stirling hat die moderne Baukunst zum Irrtum erklärt; zur Belebung der verödeten Umwelt empfiehlt er Rückgriffe auf Bauformen aus zwei Jahrtausenden. Erste Erfolge: In Stuttgart baut er ein monumentales Museum, in West-Berlin ein stilreiches Wissenschaftszentrum. Die Fachpresse meldet: Die Tendenz, ein neuer Historismus, breite sich aus "wie ein Buschbrand".
Der Spiegel, 7 July 1980

1. *Model, view into garden*

1

"Gerd Neumann, a German critic, has discovered Athenian eclecticism in the different shapes (Gerd Neumann, 'James Stirlings Spree-Athen "Eklektizimus"!?' Bauwelt 14 April 11, 1980, pp. 575–77). The preserved building is the Parthenon, the octagonal library is the Tower of the Winds, the amphitheatre semi-circle is the Odeon of Herod, the long institute is the Stoa of Attalos, etc.

Again, however, the reading can be polyvalent and Schinkel and Adam precedents be found. The building thus becomes, like 19th-century Berlin, something of an enigmatic conjecture on the past, powerful because it characterises different institutes in different ways, disturbing for its nightmarish recollections, interesting for its urban spaces and perplexing for its classical distortions."
Architectural Design 5/6. 1980

"There is a church, a stoa, a campanile, an amphitheatre and a fort or castle. Each is articulated in plan only, seemingly extruded from the ground, and cut off and terminated simply with a square sectioned cornice. What is the significance of these forms and how were their relationships determined?

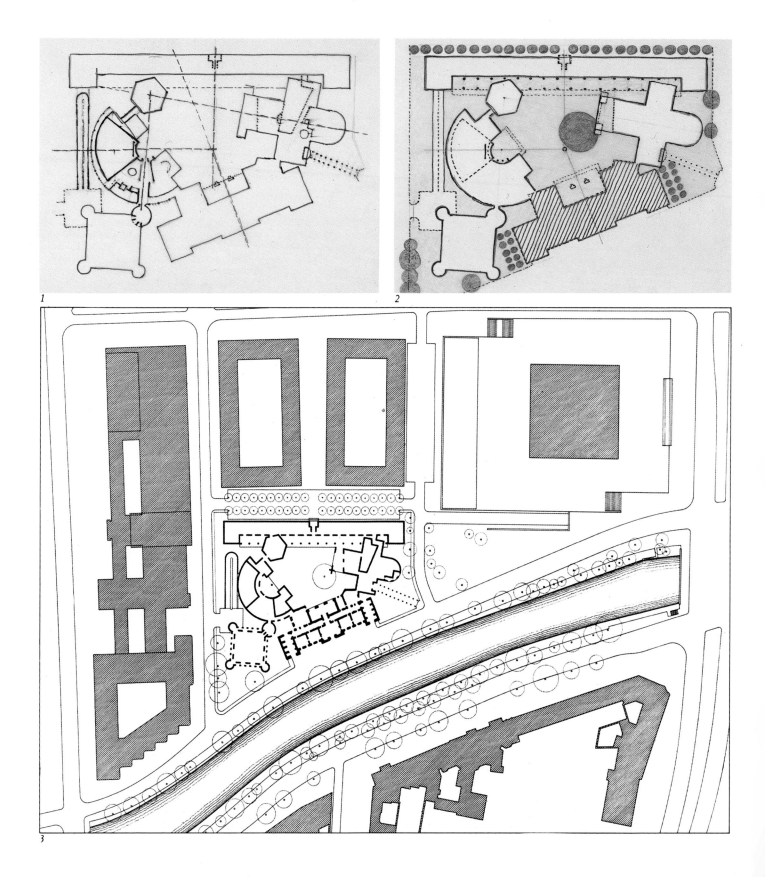

1

2

3

"There are vague reminiscences of Pisa. The church and campanile here are in similar relationship to the church and baptistry in Pisa (the campanile replacing the baptistry while still alluding to the tower); the diagonal path across the grass to the entrance in the rear of the transept is very similar; and the stoa could perhaps be the cemetery moved closer to collide with the other two elements. There may be something in this, but it leaves much unexplained.

"Further investigation reveals that every face, centrepoint and other important crossing is

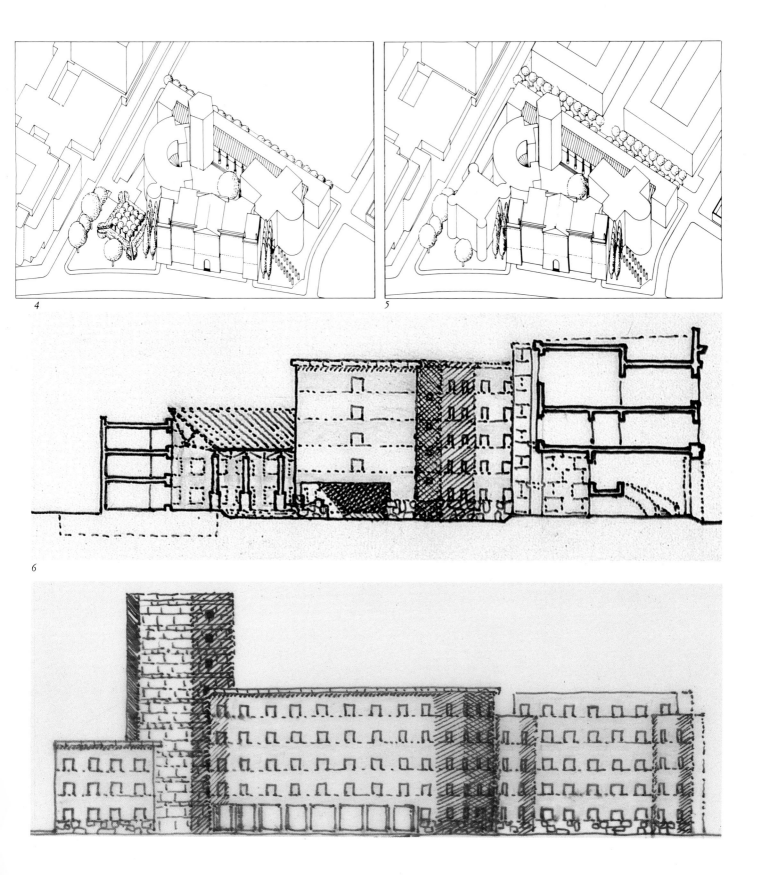

4

5

6

generated by lines, either connecting significant points on the existing building and then projected; or connecting a point on this building with a significant point on the site; or connecting significant points of the new building.

"Some of these generating lines are shown plotted over a ground floor plan. They resemble, at a small scale, the leylines that once connected ancient monuments and topographical features in the British landscape, or perhaps some of the generating lines used by medieval masons. However, though this system of lines explains and controls the placing of the buildings it does not explain their forms: only that of the theatre seems to have some functional justification in that the form accommodates the fanning lecture theatres. Perhaps the forms also have an esoteric derivation that is less apparent than the leylines. In any case, this project seems not only further indication of the demise of Functionalism, but perhaps also that in these transitional and confusing times Big Jim is resorting to magic."

P. Buchanan, *Architectural Review*, April 1980

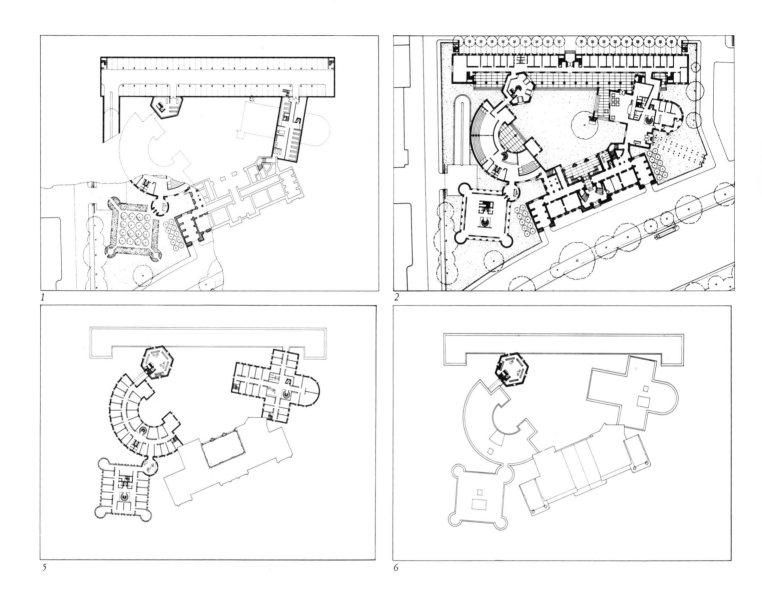

1

2

5

6

1. *Basement plan.*
2. *Ground level.*
3. *Second floor.*
4. *Third floor.*
5. *Fourth/fifth floors.*
6. *Roof plan.*

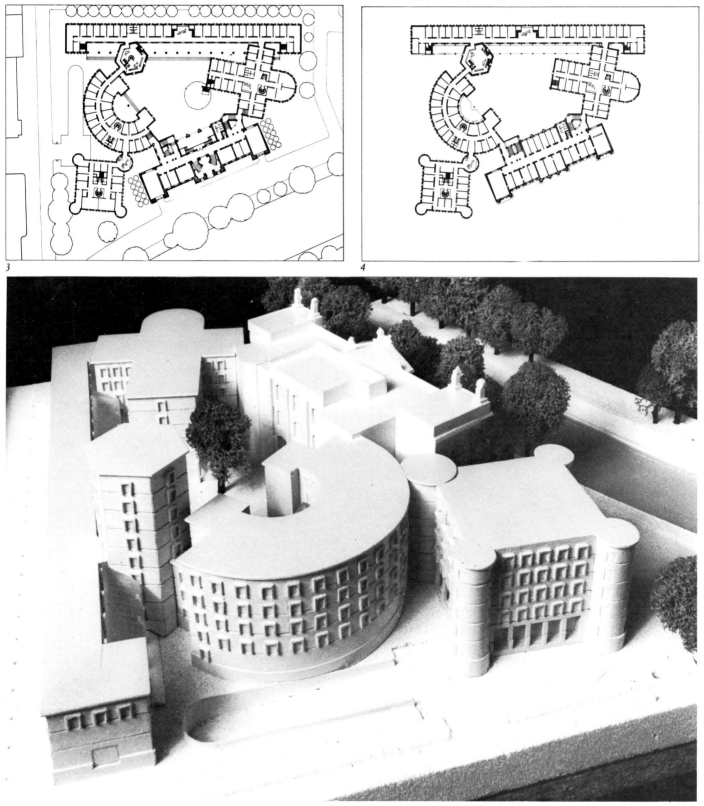

3

4

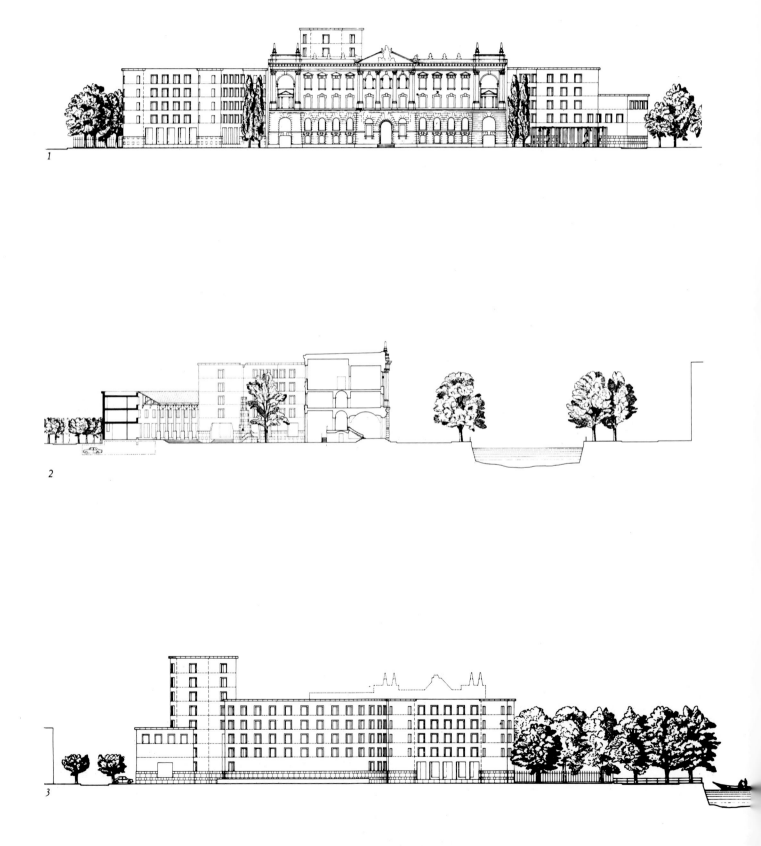

1

2

3

Wissenschaftszentrum, 1979

1. Street elevation
2. Section through garden and existing building

3. Street elevation
4. Section through garden and new building

5. Section through existing building and garden
6. Elevation towards Mies Van der Rohe Museum

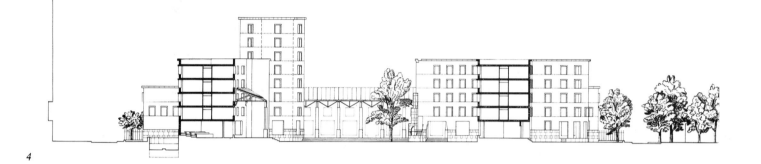

4

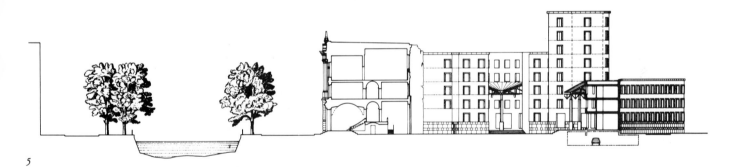

5

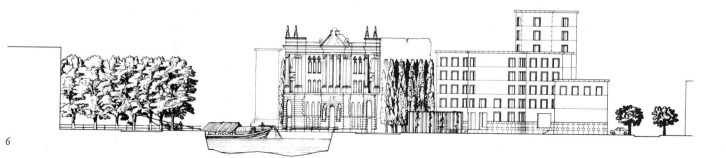

6

1

Wissenschaftszentrum, 1979

1979/84
Fogg Museum New Building
Harvard University

James Stirling, Michael Wilford
Ulrich Schaad
Robert Dye
Ulrike Wilke
in collaboration with
Perry, Dean, Stahl & Rogers (Boston)

(Extracts from Architect's Report)

The new Museum will occupy an L-shaped site across Broadway from the present Fogg Museum. It will house the Museum's collections of oriental, ancient, and Islamic art, and provide space for special exhibitions, offices, curatorial and service departments, storage, classrooms, and library collections. Nearly 11,000 square feet of galleries will be created, an increase of more than 75 percent over the gallery area of the existing Fogg. The principal facade will be on Broadway, facing the north wing of the present Fogg. The main entrance, centered in this facade, will be marked by a glass entrance lobby and two columns, set into a paved forecourt.

A continuous brick facade runs along Quincy Street and curves at the corner to continue down Cambridge Street. Windows are placed functionally, according to the requirements of the rooms.

The new building will be one of the largest at Harvard open to the public on a regular basis. It will contain a public lecture hall and galleries both for temporary exhibitions and for the Fogg's permanent collections.

Visitors will enter from Broadway, through a glass lobby, into a formal entrance hall. Stairs at either side of this entrance hall will lead to a lecture hall on the lower level. A skylit staircase will rise through the center of the building to all gallery levels. Its walls will be polychromed in harmony with the exterior. To the left of the stair will be the five office levels of the building, while to the right will be three levels of public galleries. Architectural fragments from the Fogg's collections will be mounted in the walls of this staircase.

1. Preliminary sketches.

1

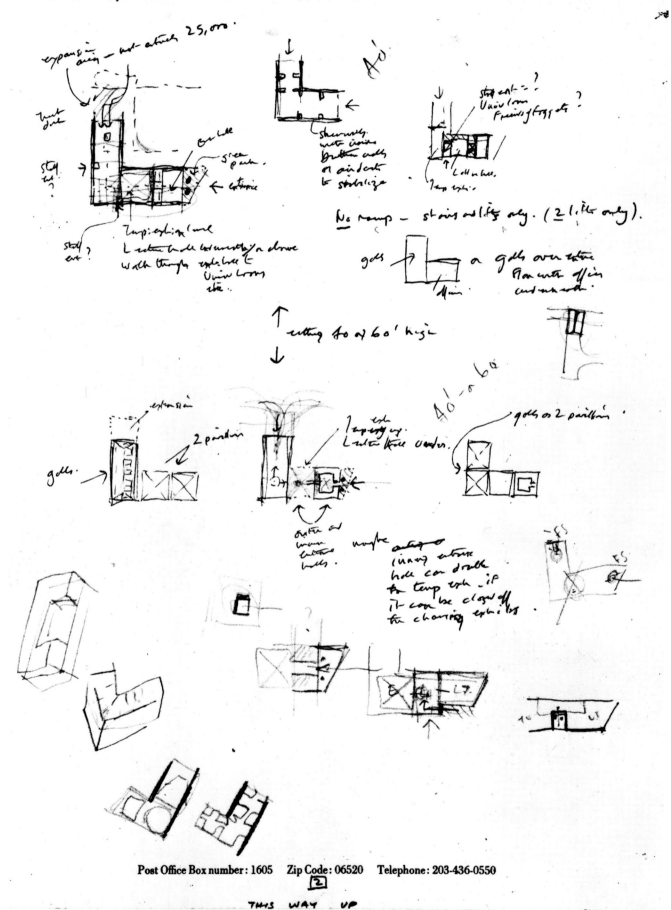

Post Office Box number: 1605   Zip Code: 06520   Telephone: 203-436-0550

2

THIS WAY UP

1

"The oscillating fortunes of a plan to expand Harvard University's Fogg Art Museum have seemed worthy of a paperback suspense thriller in which The Millionaire, David Stockman, Mephistopheles and Lassie intervene in the affairs of a venerable art institution. The drama has tested patience, raised tempers, occasioned lapses of professorial circumspection and also gained coverage in the national press, which has given the story substantial—and unwanted—publicity."
S. McFadden, *Art in America,* April 1982

1. *Preliminary sketches.*
2. *Site plan.*
3. *Entrance level.*
4. *Gallery level.*

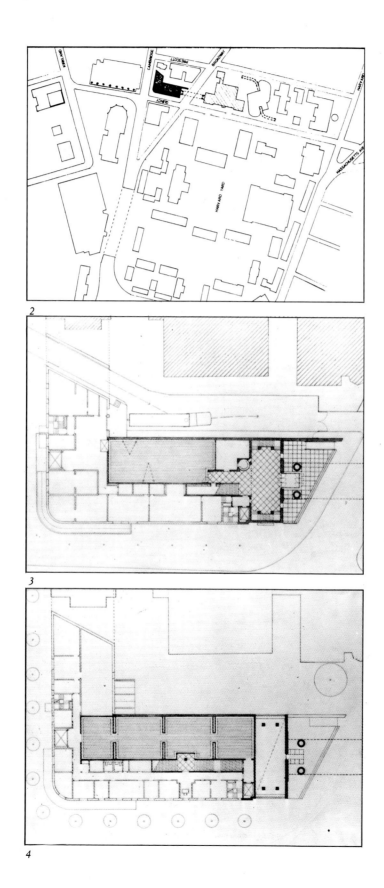

2

3

4

"We have lived with the villa and the palazzo for a long time now. From Pliny to Palladio, from Potsdam to Princeton, the suburban villa has offered retreat from the urban world to a contemplative natural setting. The villa we know today tends to be informal, like the life it houses. The palazzo, by contrast, is the prototypical urban building. Hemmed in where the villa is free-standing, the palazzo is recognised not by its roof but by its wall. Its architectural assignment is not to dissolve the barrier between inside and out, but to establish a strong separation between them. Where the villa turns outward to its open site, the palazzo is inward looking. Where the one may be casual, the other is disciplined and formal. The first belongs to the garden; the second to the street. These buildings are in our memories. We recognise them readily whether they are historical monuments in Europe, or everyday structures in Cincinnati.

"Their very typicality may have rendered them unremarkable, while their age and tradition made them appear old-fashioned, if not obsolete,

3

especially in the last fifty years when architects largely abandoned such prototypes. Recent decades have given Boston and Cambridge a collection of landmark structures that consciously avoid fitting into any such comfortable recesses of collective memory. It is therefore of some interest that the two latest architectural projects of note in Cambridge are a villa and a palazzo. In the Fogg project, Stirling has recovered the wall separating inside and out, and the primary opening in that wall, the front door... Where the Academy with its more open site utilised a loose assemblage of discrete rooms and open spaces around a central hall, the Fogg addition isolates and emphasises every part of the building, without a trace of the freely flowing space of modernity. The

1. *Entrance hall (day).*
2. *Entrance hall (night).*
3. *Cut away axo.*
4. *Section through entrance hall and upper gallery.*
5. *Section through offices, staircase, galleries and lecture hall.*
6. *Section through entrance hall, staircase and lecture hall.*

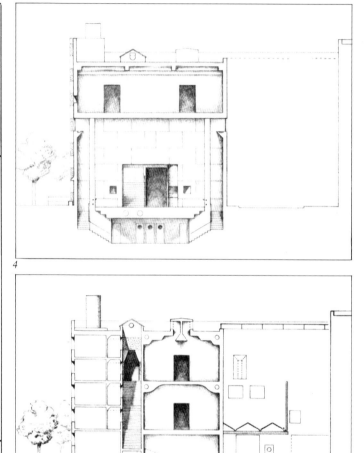

MAY 6TH 1987

DEAR JIM, I SAW TODAY YOUR VERY FINE DESIGN FOR THE FOGG MUSEUM WHICH IS OF COURSE EX-BITED IN THE FOGG, WHICH IS IN-CIDENTALLY WHERE I BOUGHT THIS CARD! IT REALLY IS A SMALL BEAUTY THIS BUILDING. IT WAS VERY MOVING TO LOOK AT THE DRAWINGS FOR THIS BUILDING IN THE FELIX WARBURG ROOM & TO REALISE THAT THE TWIN COLUMN THEME WAS RIGHT THERE IN THE ROOM ITSELF! AND EVEN MORE THAN THE TWIN COLUMNS THE CLERE-STOREY WINDOWS WHICH ALSO SUGGEST THE UPPER PART OF THE STAIR SHAFT WHICH RUNS THROUGH THE ENTIRE HEIGHT OF THE STRUCTURE. I LIKE EVERYTHING ABOUT THIS WORK; THE TWIN COLUMN ENTRANCE, THE HIGH ENTRY HALL, THE DESCENT INTO THE LECTURE HALL, THE TEMPORARY EXHIBIT-ION SPACE, THE LONG ESCALATING STAIR & ABOVE THE TOP LIT EXHIBITION SPACES. (ALL) I HAVE ONLY ONE RESERVATION! WHICH IS (AS IF YOU COULDN'T ANTICIPATE IT) THE LONG FACADE! WHAT FOLLOWS IS AN IMPERTINENT PETITION! PLEASE, PLEASE RECONSIDER FACADE! THE TWO COLOUR BRICK IS FINE, BUT IN ITSELF IT DOESN'T OVERCOME THE NO DOUBT DELIBERATELY "SHOCKING" DISORDER OF THE FACADE. WHAT I DON'T UNDERSTAND IS THE RATHER SIMPLE & EVEN BANAL PRINCIPLE WHICH DETERMINES THE FACADE; NAMELY EVERY WINDOW IS IN THE MIDDLE OF ITS RESPECTIVE INNER WALL! I THINK THAT THIS IS A RATHER FEEBLE PRINCIPLE BECAUSE ① FACADES ARE REPRE--SENTATIVE & THERE SHOULD BE A DISJUNCTION BETWEEN INNER & OUTER ORDER ② THE ROOMS COULD BE CHANGED SUBSEQUENTLY, ETC. PLEASE MAKE A SLIGHTLY MORE ORDERED PATTERN. ITS A GEM! IT WOULD BE A PITY TO "SPOIL" IT. *

LOVE TO MARY O'CONGRATS

FROM KENNETH FRAMPTON (LOVE FROM SILVIA).

Upper Deck, 1929
Fogg Art Museum, Harvard University

4

5

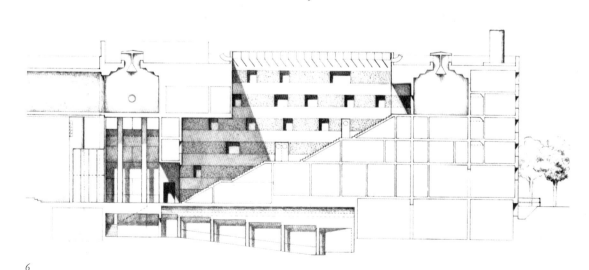

6

disconnectedness of this planning serves a very different purpose from that of the Academy, for here the goal is to establish a sequence of spaces that will continue via a bridge over Broadway into the galleries of the old Fogg, to conclude in the Fogg's gracious Renaissance revival courtyard. The dramatic proportions of Stirling's vestibule and stairway establish a momentum which, with allowance for browsing along the way, will carry the visitor to the top floor and back to the front of the building to cross into the old museum. Stirling has designed a building whose culminating space is across the street, in another structure. This link across Broadway, is problematic... however, he has designed an addition that will work with or without its bridge; no doubt he had in mind the fate of Michelangelo's plan for the Laurentian Library in Florence, a building Stirling's powerful spaces recall. There the final room which visitors would have reached after passing through the tall vestibule and the long narrow reading room, was never constructed, leaving the existing mannerist spaces with a brilliant, if unintended, tension."

G. Wolf, *New Boston Review,* October 1981

1

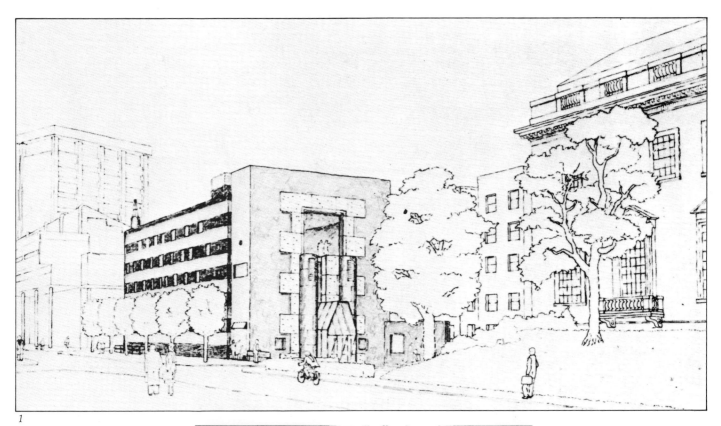

2

"In this project Stirling shows us that it is not always necessary to say everything all the time. An *avoided cadence* or *elusion* is often more enigmatic than an enigma soaked in silence. But only great masters will not get lost in the uncertainties that wait at the bottom of the infinity of experimentalism. As Palladio used to say, one should be 'guided by natural inclination.' Stirling makes this quality

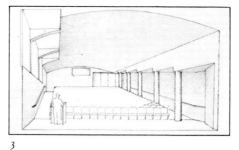

1. *View down Quincy Street*
2. *Staircase View*
3. *Lecture hall*
4. *Entrance detail*
5. *Quincy Street: detail*
6–8. *Elevation studies*

3

4

5

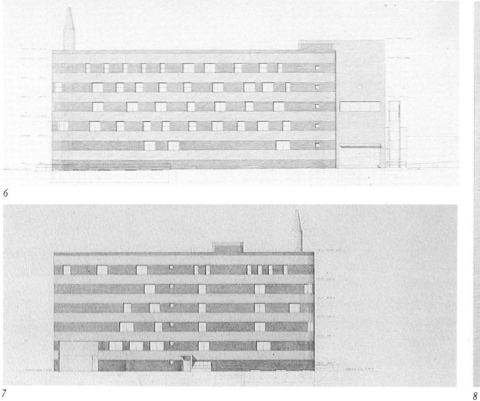

6

7

8

Fogg Museum New Building, 1979

evident by demonstrating his unaffectedness once again by taking up distant and apparently incompatible chords, to then submit them to his delicate volumetric catastrophes.
M. Scolari, *Casabella,* May 1982

1. *Entrance without bridge.*
2. *Entrance with bridge.*
3. *Bridge, entrance and entrance hall.*

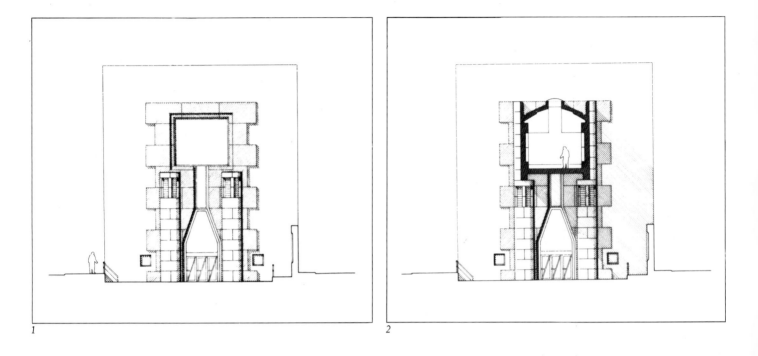

1

2

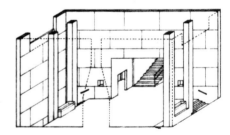

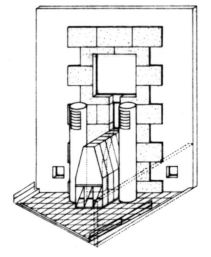

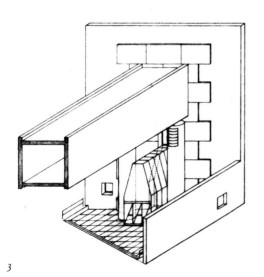

3

Fogg Museum New Building, 1979

4. A "possible" bridge/gallery over Broadway,
elevation.
5. Section.
6. Plan.

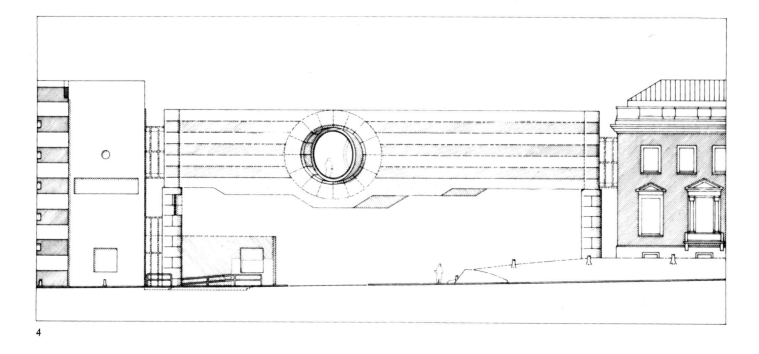

4

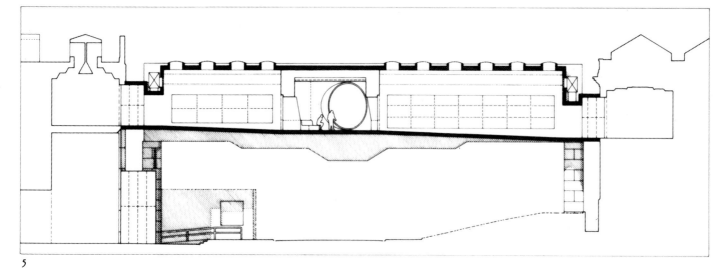

5

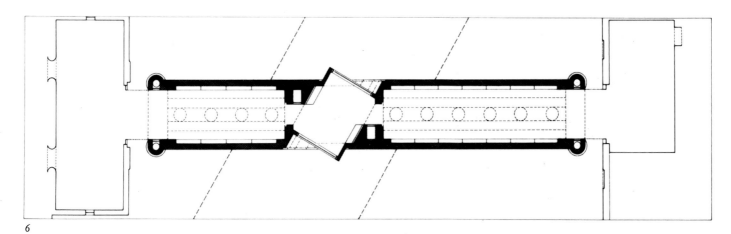

6

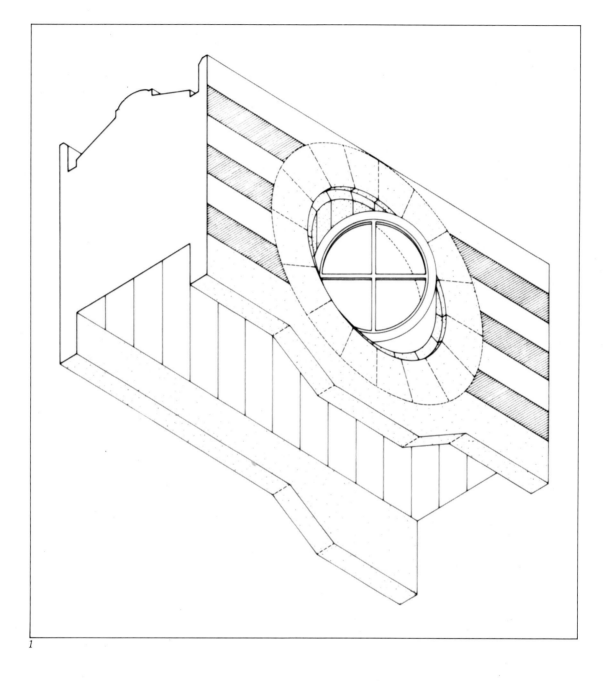

1

Fogg Museum New Building, 1979

1980/85
Clore Gallery (Turner Museum) Tate Gallery
London

James Stirling, Michael Wilford
Russell Bevington, Peter Ray,
John Cannon, John Cairns,
Robert Dye, Lester Haven,
Walter Naegeli, Sheila O'Donnell,
Richard Portchmouth, Philip Smithies,
Stephen Wright

(Extracts from Architects Report)

The Clore Gallery is the first element in the development of the Queen Alexandra Hospital Site for use by the Tate Gallery. Certain visually important buildings of the hospital complex should be retained and integrated with the new buildings. The retention of the Lodge with its counterbalancing relationship to the Medical College to the south-west preserves the contextual setting of the Tate and maintains the symmetrical balance of the Gallery about its entrance portico. Nevertheless, the Clore Gallery will have its own identity and be clearly seen from Millbank across the gardens of the Tate.

The new building is designed as a garden building (extension to the country house) with pergola and lily pool and a paved terrace with planting and sheltered seating. It is L-shaped with a gallery wing connecting to the existing building immediately behind its pavilioned corner. The shorter wing returns towards the river on the line of the existing Lodge. Setting back the new building and matching its parapet to that of the Tate allows the pavilioned corner, with its greater mass and height, to maintain its architectural significance while leaving

the symmetry of the Tate frontage undisturbed.

The entrance of the new building does not face towards the river (avoiding competition with the main building), but sideways towards the Tate portico and the shoulder of the Tate—an architectural conversation between the new entrance and the pavilioned corner across the sunken terrace is intended. The existing cornice is carried across the principal facades of the new building and stonework details of the Tate walls are carried partially onto the building. The garden facades have panelling of stone with rendered infill (stucco). Towards the Lodge the panels are infilled with brickwork to match. The service facades are in light

colored brickwork with colored metal window elements.

The upper level contains the galleries and these are at the same level as those in the Tate, allowing uninterrupted flow of visitors to and from the main building. Daylighting will be through roof lanterns. A bay window off one of the galleries is a place to pause, and rest one's feet and enjoy views into the garden and across the river.

Non-exhibition spaces located in the lower level include the entrance hall, lecture theater, staff facilities, paper conservation department, plantroom, etc. In the entrance hall there is an information and cloaks counter, and a showcase containing the Turner relics (his model ships, palettes, glasses, snuff box, etc.). There is also a public reading room overlooking the garden which is fitted with a pantry where drinks and sandwiches can be prepared for evening functions.

"Sir John Summerson, curator of the Soane Museum and himself a RIBA Gold Medallist, is

1. *Upview of garden/riverfront elevation with viewing window, pergola and seats.*

1

intrigued by Stirling's design: He told the AJ: "It's a funny building, but no funnier than Soane, who would have enjoyed that deep slot that the stair goes up in—and so would Soane's friend, Turner. I like the complexity, the play of layers. It's full of intriguing allusions—1930's 'modernist', German neo-classicism, 'low tech' and so on. The great shock is the Newgate-type prison wall cut away with a pair of scissors. It's all a bit mad which is what people say about the Soane Museum. It's just the thing for the Tate, and the sooner it gets built the better."
Architect's Journal, 15 July 1981

"To show breaks and transitions Stirling has used several Modernist compositional techniques. He

1,2. Site plans before and after extension.
3. Viewing window: studies.
4. Axonometric (up) of viewing window, entrance, and reading room window.
5. Axonometric (down) of entrance terrace.

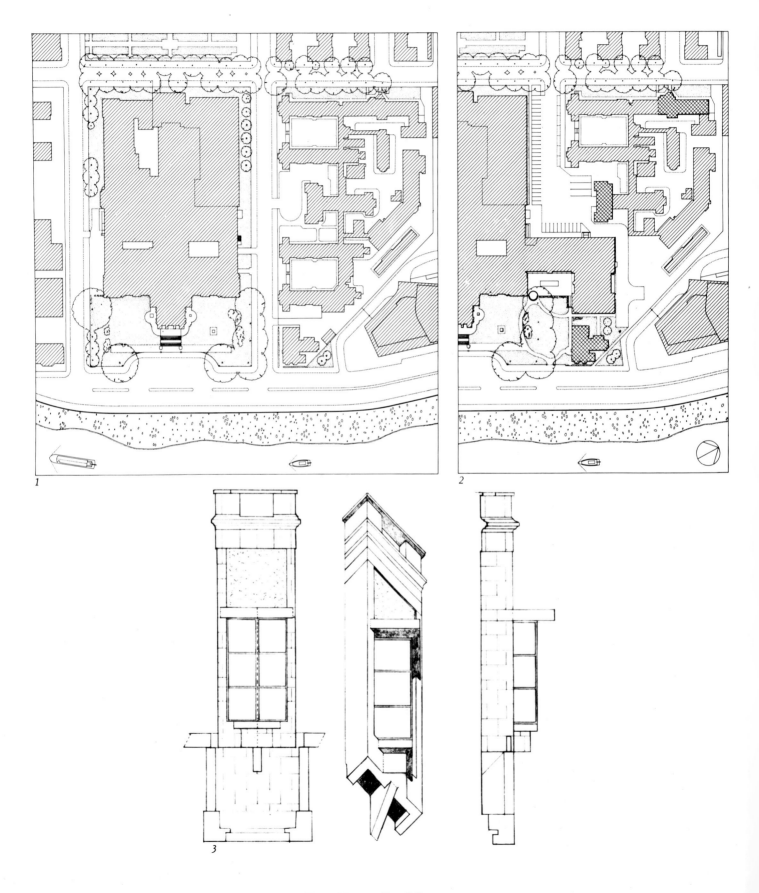

1

2

3

(Turner Museum) Tate Gallery, 1980

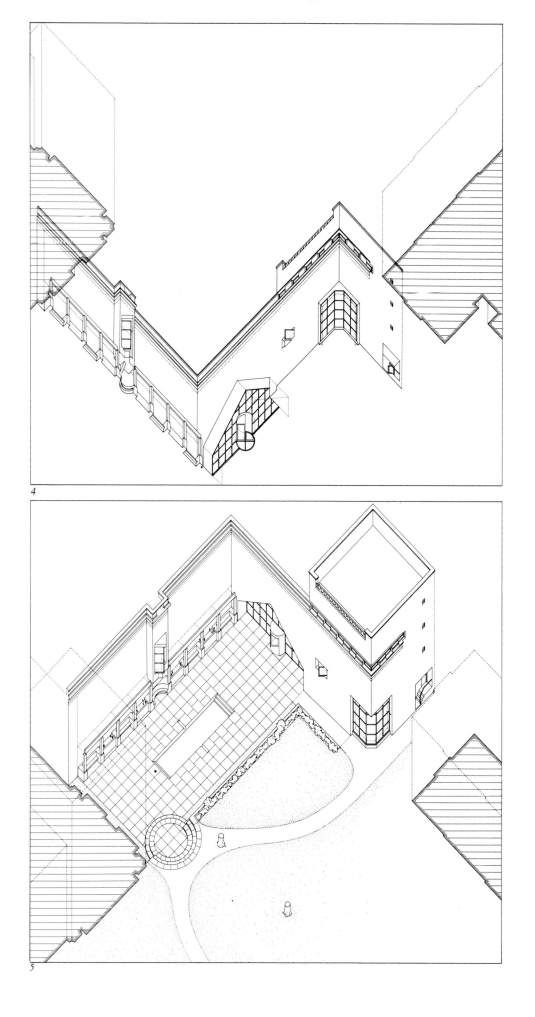

4

5

(Turner Museum) Tate Gallery, 1980

ends the infill square bays with a quarter beat and then elides them into the next theme; or he suddenly cuts them away abruptly.

"A clear separation of surfaces to accentuate depth and function is allowed. The square glass wall is sunken back twice, at the entrance and corner public reading room, to become a reference plane which unites similar activities-in this case, a view of the garden. The most unusual and therefore controversial aspect of the whole building is the treatment of this corner. Four odd things happen at once. A funny window pivots out (shades of Marcel Breuer's Whitney Museum?). The brick infill steps up to the right and then suddenly jumps over space to hang. Brickhanging.

The glass wall behind chamfers back to avoid these falling bricks and the entablature quickly changes sex.

"Stirling can show the square wall pattern as an ordering system, not as substance. Like a Renaissance application of pilasters, this square 'order' is conceptual rather than real structure: the

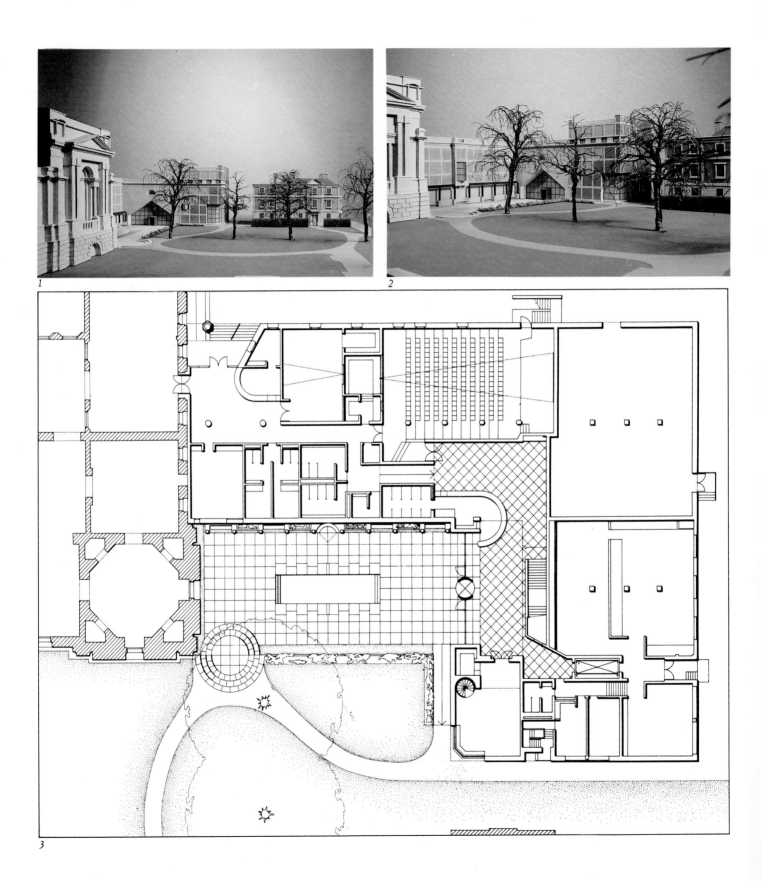

1

2

3

　　　　(Turner Museum) Tate Gallery, 1980

cantilevered pattern makes this clear. A single external window, and view of the river, is thoughtfully provided for relief from this unremitting experience of art and architecture. After this feast of vintage Turner and Stirling the cultural gourmand will relish it. The beauties of eclecticism are those of flexibility, variety and depth. An eclectic building of Borromini can respond to various opposite buildings in a site, can change character, even mood, with different functions, and relate fully to a complex, cultural past. This the Clore Gallery, the first major cultural commission in London since the National Theatre, will do.''

C. Jencks. © *Architectural Design* Magazine, London. *AD* 1/2 1982 'Free-Style Classicism'.

1,2. *Model: garden facades.*
3. *Entrance level.*
4. *Gallery level.*
5,6. *Model: garden facades.*

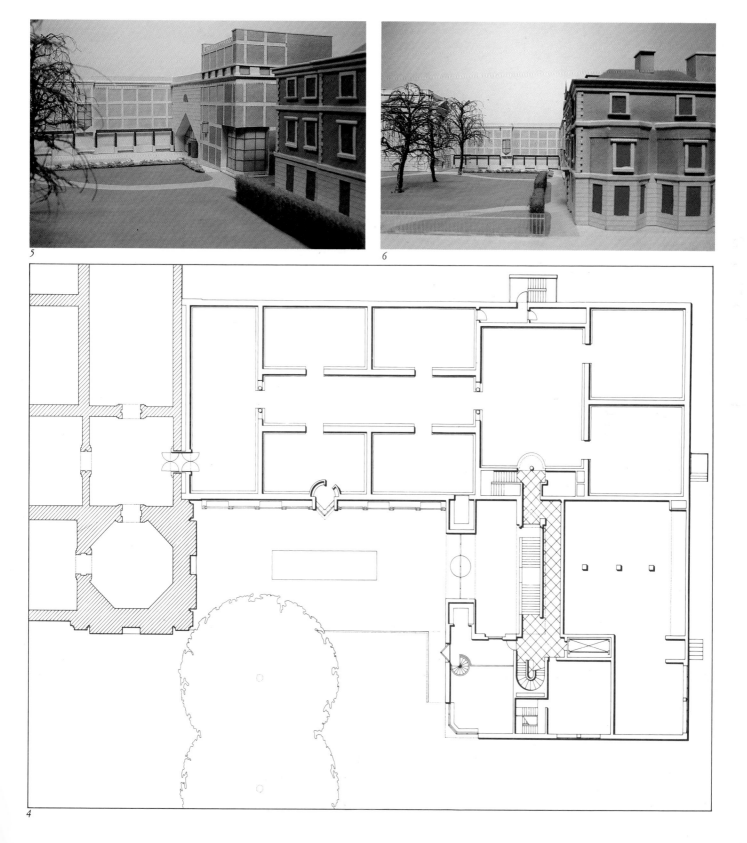

5

6

4

"James Stirling is an architect whose work provokes such paroxysms of fury among such a range of critics that he must undoubtedly be getting at least something right. When Roger Scruton for example used this page recently to attack modern architecture—"after CND and the Argentines, the greatest threat facing Britain today"—he claimed that Stirling's was the ample figure he had in his sights.

"It was Stirling who designed the remarkable Cambridge University history library; in the eyes of right-wing Spectator readers, a far more unforgivable sin than any amount of developer's hit-and-run hackwork.

"From the opposite end of the political spectrum, the monumentalism of recent work has stirred some defenders of orthodox modernism to accuse him of "fascism". His columns, massive masonry and formal planning all smack of Speer and the Third Reich, they claim. Stirling's champions are equally given to overstatement. The American Philip Johnson has called him "the world's

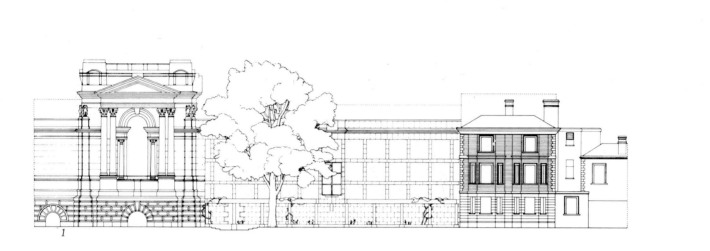

1

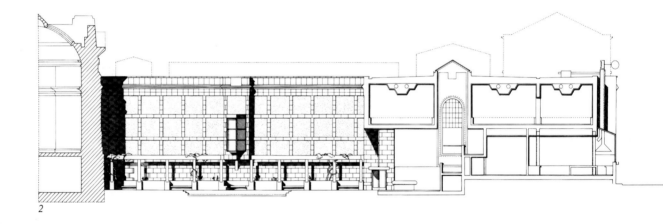

3

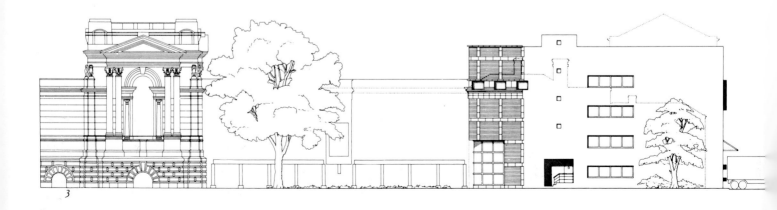

2

greatest living architect".

"It has taken all of Stirling's highly developed sense of irony to survive. What other serious, 57-year old professional would have the nerve to allow himself to be photographed for the cover of a colour supplement building a sandcastle, kitted out with bucket, spade and knotted handkerchief?

Stirling's greatest claim to attention, however, is his remarkable ability to go on inventing style after style, which legions of imitators go on struggling to reproduce years after the master has moved on to other things.

"He began with a couple of essays in Brutalism, dabbled with system building, tried high tech, and

1. *Corner of the Tate Gallery, new extension and existing Lodge.*
2. *Section through sunken terrace and entrance.*
3. *Side elevation towards lodge.*
4. *Section through Galleries and entrance elevation.*
5. *West elevation.*
6. *Elevation to service road.*

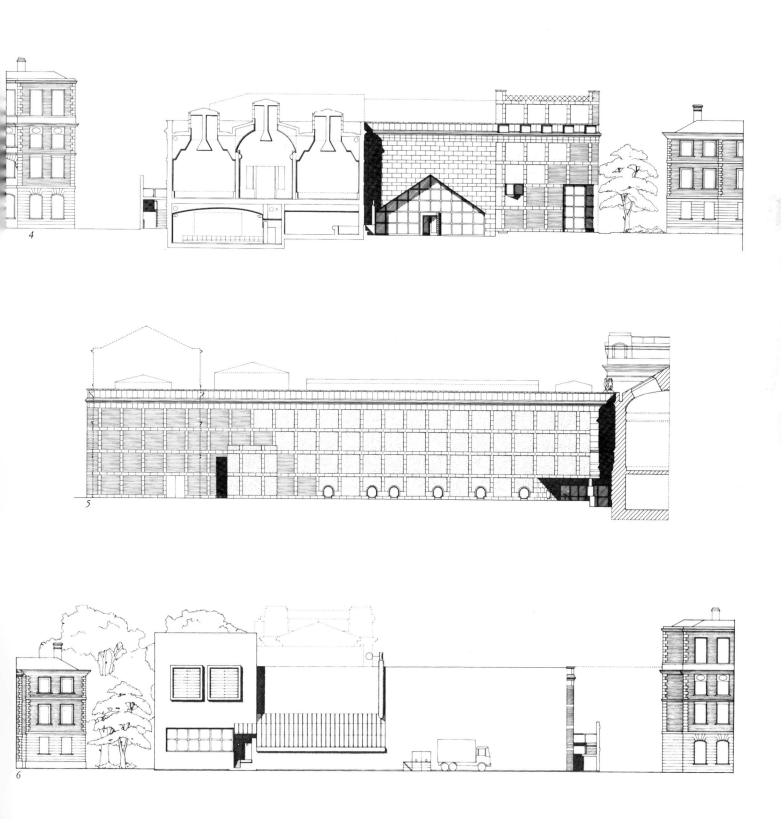

(Turner Museum) Tate Gallery, 1980

is now ransacking history for inspiration. And still he gives every impression of being about to move on yet again always well ahead of the field. He is, in short, an original; and originals are never comfortable to have around.

"Today the Queen Mother unveils the foundation stone of the new Clore Gallery, being built to house the Tate's Turner collection. It is his only prominent commission in London to date, occupying a conspicuous position overlooking the Thames, attached to the Tate's existing facade.

"Despite Stirling's enormous reputation overseas, measured by many commissions in West Germany, Italy and America, he has built nothing at all at home since 1976. It is as if Graham Greene had been writing exclusively in Spanish for the past 10 years.

"But Stirling will have much more impact in the long term. He is the first major architect of the 1960's to have come to terms with the historical legacy of architecture. He is unselfconscious about

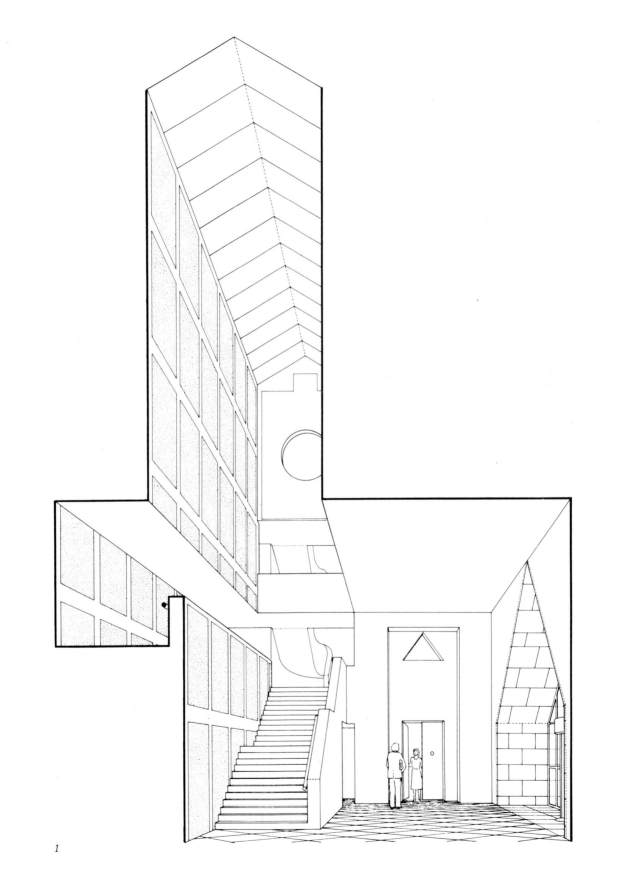

1

(Turner Museum) Tate Gallery, 1980

working with the planning principles of the past. But he is also mature enough to recognize that the heroic period of modern architecture in the 1930s is equally a part of our heritage.

"All of this sounds like a huge burden for one small L-shaped building in Millbank to carry on its shoulders. Judging by the drawings of the scheme now on show at the Institute of Contemporary Arts, it is more than equal to the task. Stirling has treated every facade in a different way: anathema to the early modernists who made a fetish out of consistency, but highly appropriate for a building whose guiding intentions are respect for context.

1. View towards reading room and entrance.
2-5. Working drawings: external wall sections.

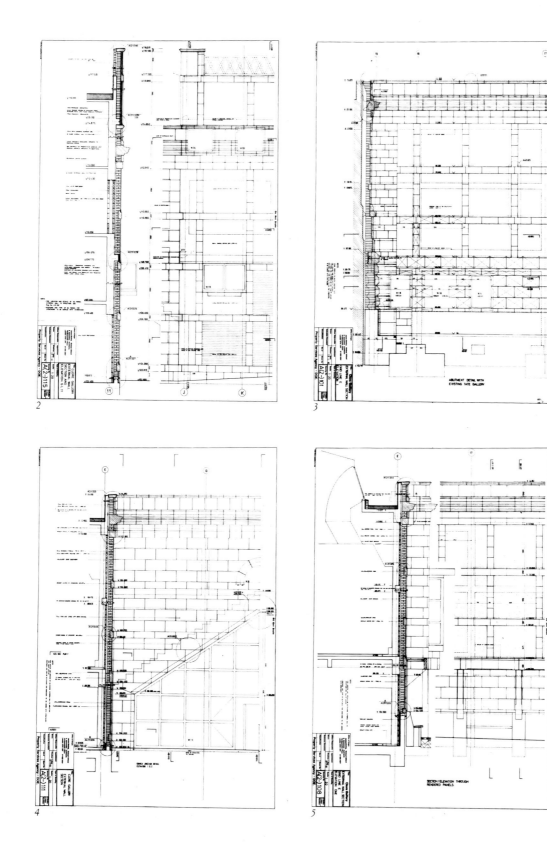

2

3

4

5

"So the main facade is classically inspired, with a central bay window, a colonnade and solid masonry walls, in deference to the character of the Tate itself. But there is also a brick-faced wing, nearest to an adjoining brick-built Edwardian structure, as well as a 'modern' service entrance, free of historical mannerisms. At the corners the different approaches collide with one another in almost surreal fashion.

"Inside, the gallery space has a formality that would have gladdened the hearts of the National Gallery's trustees whose search for a 'basilica' created so many problems for the entrants to the National Gallery extension competition."
D. Sudjic, *The Times*, 19 April 1983

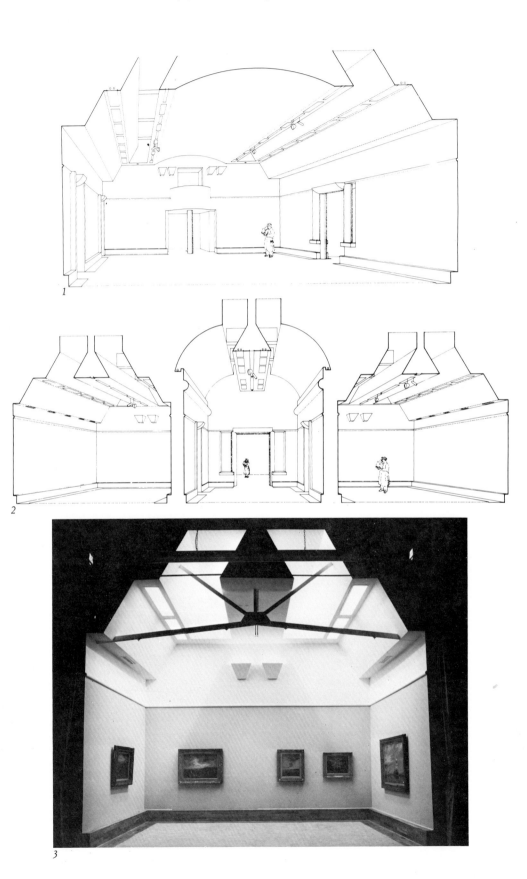

1

2

3

The unveiling of the foundation plaque for the Tate Gallery's Turner extension — was rather a low key affair. Stirling himself seemed to be trying to suggest he didn't know what the fuss was about either. He certainly didn't buy a new outfit to greet the Queen Mother, appearing in his habitual blue shirt, sack o'potatoes style grey suit, scuffed blue suede shoes and woolly scarf. It was a chilly day and while the gathered throng froze the royal personage was warmed by two discreetly placed warm air heaters behind the Louis Quinze chair (was this a purposeful historical reference or was it the only suitably regal chair they had?) From the back of the crowd the plaque itself looked like grp trying to look like bronze; with rather inelegant graphics

1. *View of Gallery.*
2. *View of central and side galleries.*
3. *View of full scale model room.*
4. *Upview of entrance elevation.*

4

(Turner Museum) Tate Gallery, 1980

311

it compared ill with Big Jim's beautiful drawings arranged for the QM's inspection. She put a brave face on it as Stirling explained them to her but without wishing to underestimate her grasp of the complexities of architectural draughtsmanship, a worm's eye view axonometric or whatever is not the easiest of styles to comprehend.
RIBA Journal, May 1983

(Turner Museum) Tate Gallery, 1980

1980
Extensions to the Music School
Theater Plaza and Ministry Offices
Stuttgart

James Stirling, Michael Wilford
Russell Bevington
Ulrike Wilke
Thomas Tafel

(Extracts from Architects Report)

Proposals for the Development on Urbanstrasse Behind the New Parliament Offices on Konrad Adenauer Strasse

Site Planning Objectives

A.   To incorporate the competition winning solution for the new Parliament building in every detail, as if its presence on site was that of an existing building. Similarly to include the competition proposals for carparking, access, etc., including a new footbridge across Konrad Adenauer Strasse.

B.   To include the JS/MW designs for a Concert Hall and Schools of Acting and Opera. Also for a "Theater Plaza" on the lower level of Eugenstrasse, and the positioning of a Ministry of Sports and Culture on Urbanstrasse.

C.   To preserve as many existing buildings as possible maintaining the street character of Urbanstrasse, particularly with a new Ministry/Art Gallery building.

D.   To activate the interior of the city block with a footpath arcade. This footway is flanked by a music shop and commercial gallery. The entrance is from Urbanstrasse through the new Ministry building and it terminates on the cafe terrace which adjoins the new Parliament offices and Concert Hall.

Concert Hall

A.   848 seats are provided on three separate levels thus avoiding the appearance of a large area of seats on a single slope.

B.   The ramp which rises from the entrance foyer has standing space to allow viewing of a performance in an intermittent and casual manner, i.e. students from the acting and opera school coming in for a short stay. This ramp and standing wall is considered as part of the auditorium, it would have carpet on floors and walls and be artificially lit.

C.   The entrance foyer is planned as a space in which small musical or acting events can happen without blocking circulation to the Concert Hall.

D.   The tea making/drinks room adjoining this foyer could also provide service to the outside tables on the terrace (under the suspended canopy).

E.   The loading bay to the Concert Hall is off Eugenstrasse opposite the service entrance to the Chamber Theatre. This should allow mutual use of vehicles and equipment and perhaps interchange of service personnel.

F.   The end of the Concert Hall closest to Konrad Adenauer Strasse has a buffer zone comprising fire stairs, ducts and control rooms, an area of acoustic separation from traffic noise.

Schools of Opera and Acting

A.   Are planned on the 3rd and 4th floors overlooking the 'Theatre plaza' from which there is an entrance that is also used by artists performing in the Concert Hall.

B.   The Schools have close connection to the Concert Hall and its side stage which would be used by students when convenient.

Commercial Art Gallery for the City of Stuttgart

A.   The Gallery is entered from Urbanstrasse into a middle level containing foyer, cloaks, tickets, etc. This entrance (13 feet high) is planned as a free space receiving daylight from a central laylight, and opening onto a sculpture garden which has landscaping, high walls and a covered loggia.

B.   The basement has three exhibition rooms and a lecture/film theater with seating for approximately 130 people which could be extended into the gallery space if a larger lecture space was considered essential.

C.   The upper level of the gallery is planned as a sequence of spaces around the central laylight—these exhibition spaces could be daylit.

New Ministry building for Sports and Culture

A.   This building is planned in four levels on Urbanstrasse. At ground level there are four commercial art galleries entered directly from the street.

B.   The location of conference rooms at every level creates a displacement of the central corridor thus preventing long, institutional views down this corridor which at mid point has a bay window with seating adjoining a tea room.

1. Section through exhibition space.
2. Elevation to Konrad Adenauer Strasse.

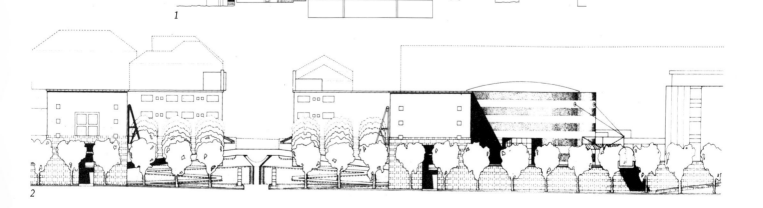

1

2

1. *Parking garage*
2. *Theater garden terrace and foyer to Concert Hall*
3. *Commercial galleries, acting school and auditorium*
4., 5. *Ministry offices, acting school and auditorium*
6. *Axonometric of Cafe terrace and Concert Hall arch*
7. *Elevation to Concert Hall and section through Ministry building*

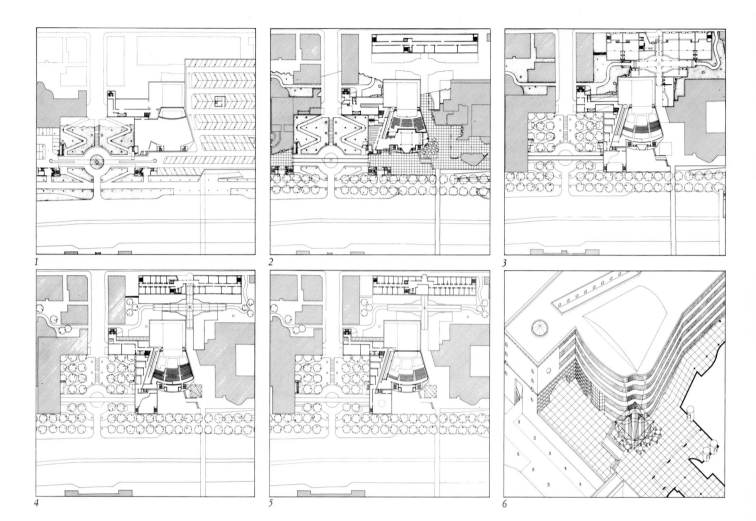

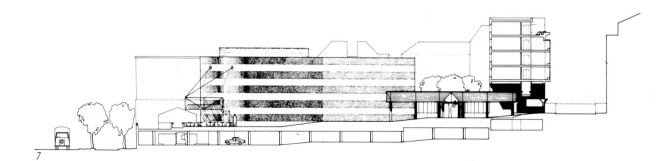

Extensions to the Music School and Plaza, Stuttgart, 1980

1980
Extension of the Chemistry Department,
Columbia University
New York

James Stirling, Michael Wilford
Richard Portchmouth, Christopher McCormack,
Ulrike Wilke, Jeffrey Averill
in collaboration with Wank, Adams and Slavin. (New York)

The site on Broadway and 120th Street is at the top left corner of the campus. It is occupied by the Gymnasium, the roof of which is the outdoor "ground level" for this part of the campus. Our problem was how to make an air rights building over without piercing the Gymnasium with new structure.

A characteristic of McKim, Mead & White's campus plan is that there are gaps between buildings and an impenetrable wall is not presented to the adjoining neighborhood. To have merely added to the Chemistry Department with the large amount of accommodation required could have resulted in a new building extending and connecting with Pupin

(the Physics building) thus producing a continuous wall of building around the north west corner of the campus which would have been untypical and perhaps seen as hostile to the neighborhood.

1. Columbia University; plan of campus.

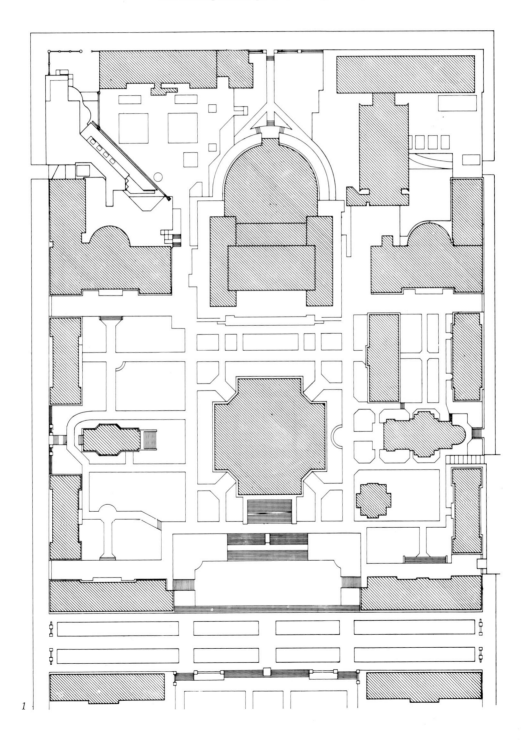

1

When the Gymnasium was constructed, four heavy engineering columns were positioned to allow an air rights possibility. We have made use of these, but also found we could site new structure along the Broadway boundary and that it was possible to drop a structural pylon (and freight elevator) into the service yard behind the existing Chemistry building. This minimum of structural supports has necessitated a bridge type structure, positioned to slew half the floor area diagonally back into the campus, which permits a gap between the end of the new extension and Pupin. This slewed-back wing will reduce the area of outdoor terrace in this part of the campus where it is too extensive and under-used.

1. Plan: entrance level.
2. Plan: typical floor.
3. Plan of gymnasium and engineering columns.
4. Perspective: view from campus.

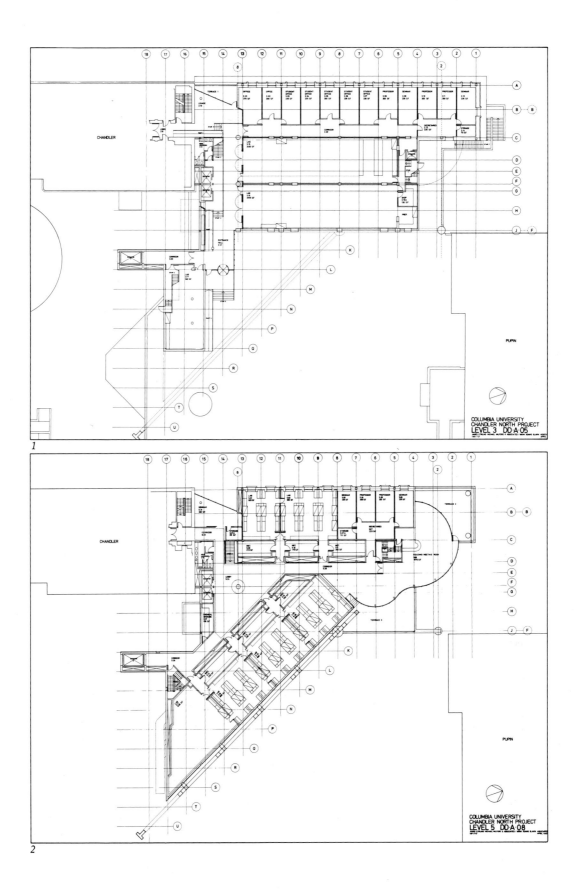

Chemistry Department, Columbia University, 1980

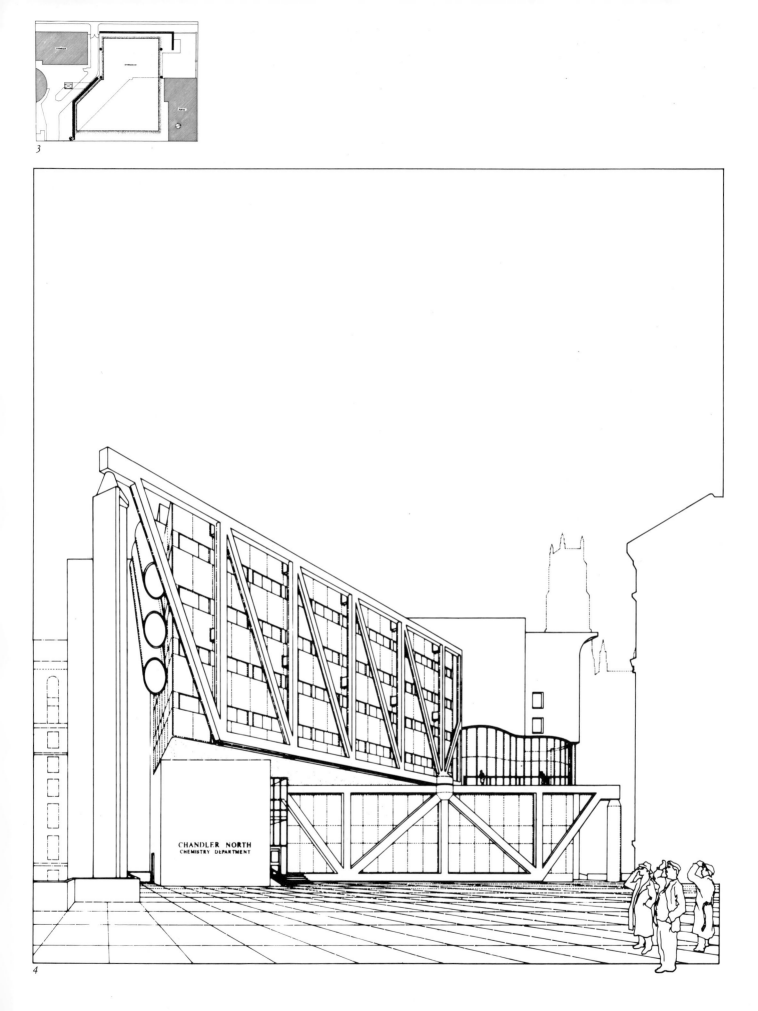

3

4

CHANDLER NORTH
CHEMISTRY DEPARTMENT

Chemistry Department, Columbia University, 1980

317

The new extension combines the masonry appearance of McKim, Mead & White's buildings (particularly along the Broadway frontage), with an engineering truss and lightweight panel appearance relative to spanning the Gymnasium. A lower steel truss spans across the Gymnasium and onto this rests an upper truss which carries laboratories. The trusses meet on a pin joint which can accept movement and expansion.

The new accommodation is mainly laboratories, instrument rooms and offices, though at the junction of the diagonal and Broadway wings overlooking the gap, there is a social lounge/reading room which has views inwards across Columbia and outwards towards Riverside.

The splayed plan created by the diagonal wing makes, internally, a triangular lobby adjacent to the lifts. This area is centered by a large flared column with circular ceiling coving and concealed uplighting. This center is at the crossroads of corridors serving the existing building and the new extension.

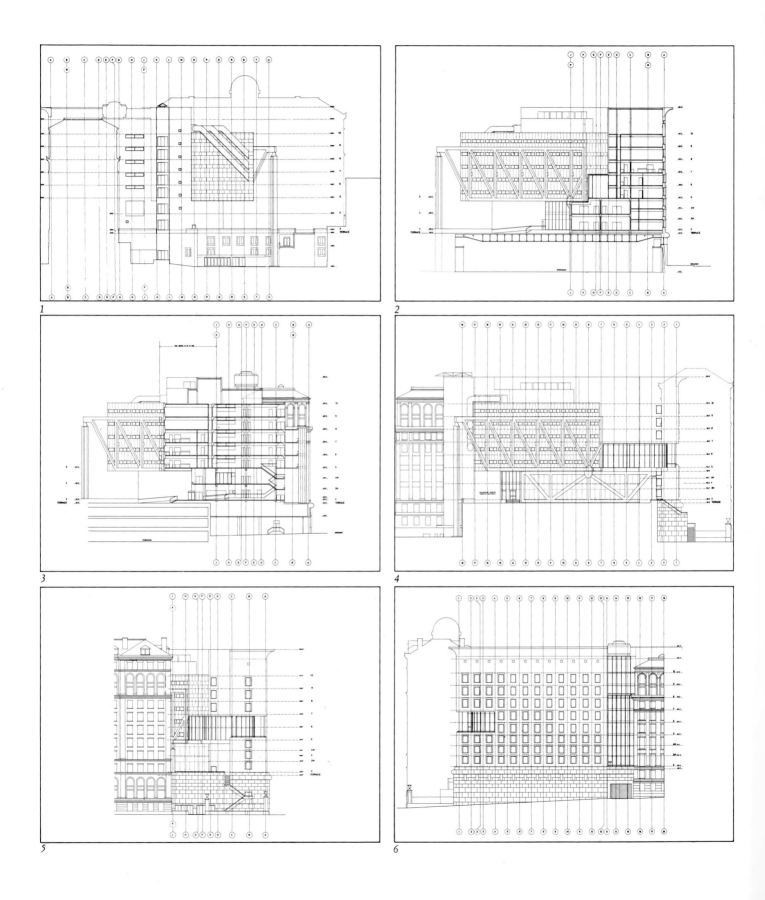

1

2

3

4

5

6

1. *Service yard elevation.*
2. *Cross section over gymnasium.*
3. *Section through gymnasium and new building.*
4. *Elevation to campus.*
5. *120th Street elevation.*
6. *Broadway elevation.*
7. *Perspective: view from Broadway and 120th Street.*

7

Chemistry Department, Columbia University, 1980

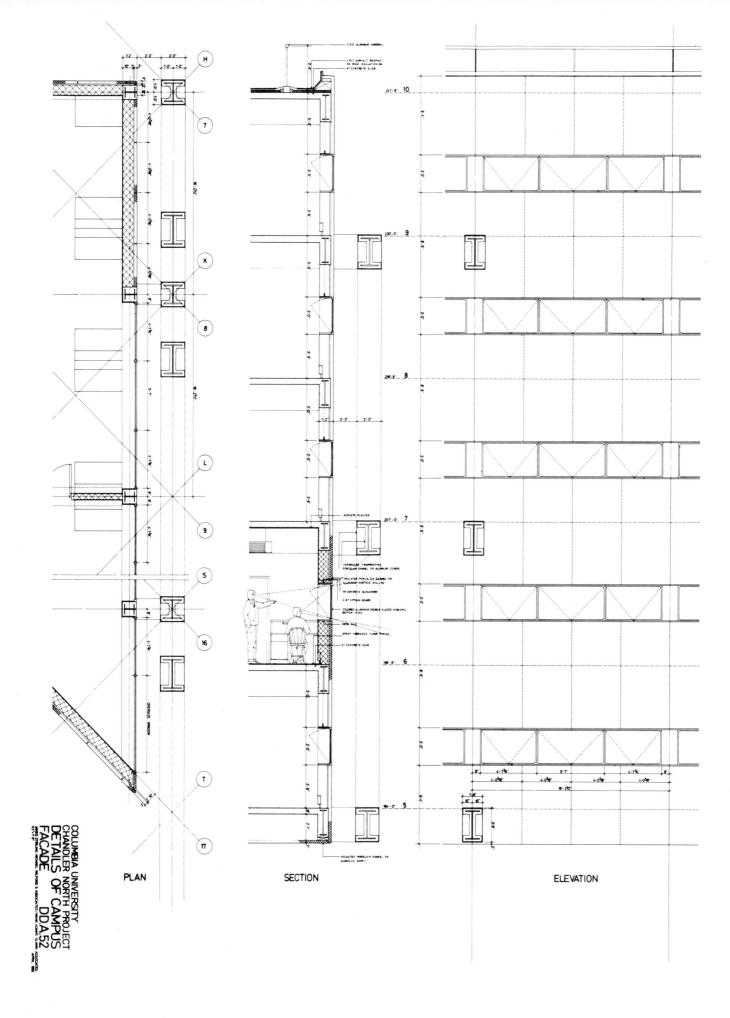

PLAN

SECTION

ELEVATION

Chemistry Department, Columbia University, 1980

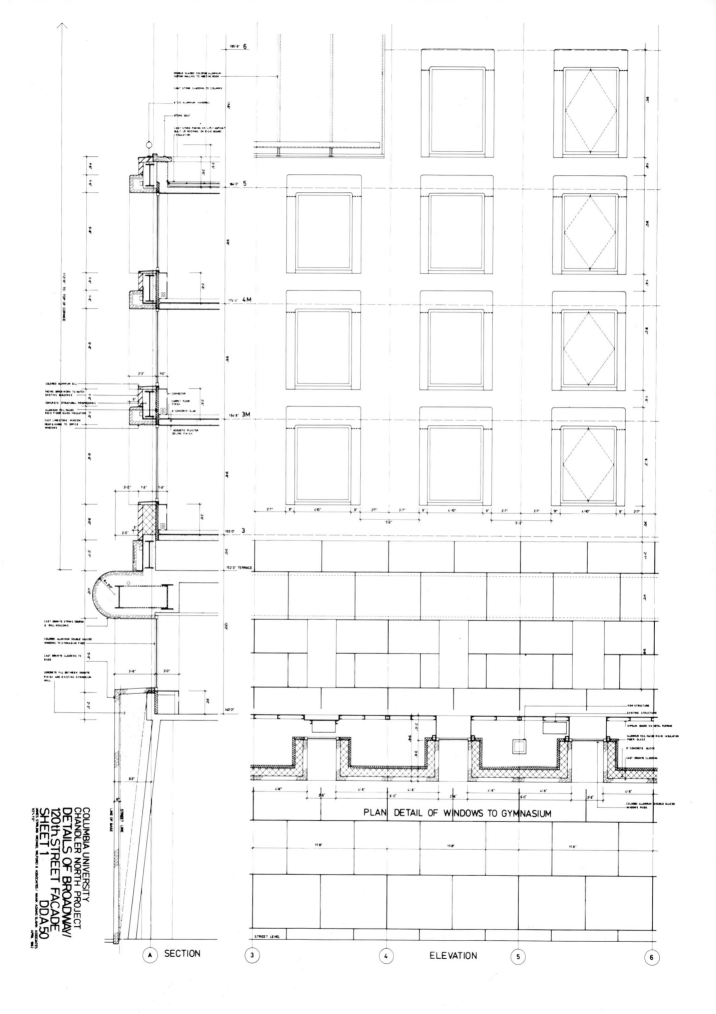

PLAN DETAIL OF WINDOWS TO GYMNASIUM

SECTION

ELEVATION

COLUMBIA UNIVERSITY
CHANDLER NORTH PROJECT
DETAILS OF BROADWAY/
120th STREET FACADE
SHEET 1
DDA.50

Chemistry Department, Columbia University, 1980

321

'In Memoriam'

James Stirling and Michael Wilford
Robert Kahn, Ulrike Wilke
Walter Naegeli
in association with
Wank, Adams and Slavin (New York)

The Performing Arts Centre for the teaching of theatre arts, is also a performance centre for the University, City and region. It is prominently sited on College Avenue, close to the bridge over Cascadilla Gorge, reinforcing this entrance to the campus and the link between the University and Collegetown communities. The design comprises a group of buildings connected by a loggia appropriate to the park-like character of the gorge.

The building is planned to permit two phases of construction. The first phase would establish the building's presence on College Avenue, and includes a plaza, loggia, proscenium theatre, foyer and dance studio. A walled garden could temporarily occupy the site of the second phase building. The second phase would contain additional performance spaces, including a flexible theatre, studios and offices and could be constructed independent of an existing first

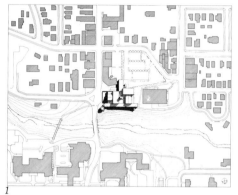

1
phase building.

A pavilion and plaza signal the entrance to the new

complex. The pavilion contains an advance ticket office, a servery for refreshments on the plaza, and provides a shelter for the adjoining bus stop. Two student society rooms are located in its upper level and it is crowned by an illuminated sign announcing current productions.

Entry to the new building is through the loggia, a promenade approach with spectacular views across the gorge. Part of this loggia is glass enclosed to provide an all weather lobby leading to the central foyer. A spiral stair at the west end of the loggia descends to grade allowing access from adjacent footpaths.

1. *Site plan, building with first and second phases.*
2. *Entrance level.*

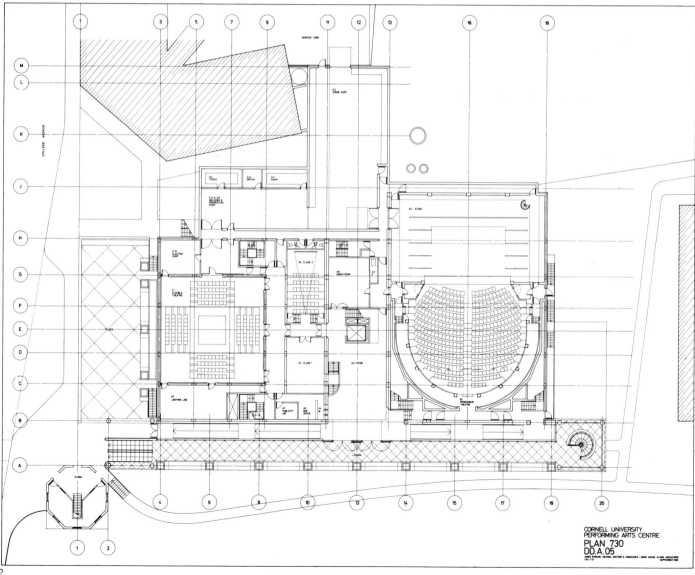

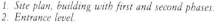

CORNELL UNIVERSITY
PERFORMING ARTS CENTRE
PLAN 730
DD.A.05

2

The foyer, located at the centre of the building, connects all major spaces, encouraging interaction between theatre, dance and film groups and brings guest artists into close contact with students and faculty. This foyer opens to the loggia enabling audiences in the intermissions to stroll in and out to take the view. Foyer and entrance are overlooked by a late sales ticket window.

Proscenium and flexible theatre are entered either side of the foyer. The proscenium theatre seats approximately 500 on a main level and two balconies. Fixed seating has centre and side aisles and the balconies have loose seats. These balconies wrap around the auditorium bringing audience and performers together in a small scale theatre room. An observation gallery (for teaching purposes) is at

the rear of the auditorium. The forestage can adapt to orchestra pit or thrust stage as required. Staircases on both sides connect the balconies with the foyer.

The flexible theatre has multiple entrances to permit arena, thrust, or proscenium configurations. The audience seated on adjustable platforms vary

1

2

Performing Arts Centre, Cornell University, 1982

from 140 to 180 people. Studios and classrooms adjoin the flexible theatre.

On the level below the entrance is the dance performance studio and forum. The dance studio (below the proscenium theatre) accommodates 180 people, with multiple choice of audience and performer relationships. Bleacher seating allows the floor to be cleared for teaching. The forum accommodates 100 people in fixed seating and is suitable for film, lectures and small theatre productions.

Administration and faculty offices are located on mezzanine around the upper part of the flexible theatre with internal access from a balcony

1. Pavilion and Loggia.
2. Walled garden for second-stage building.
3. View across gorge.
4. Pavilion, terrace, garden, loggia.

3

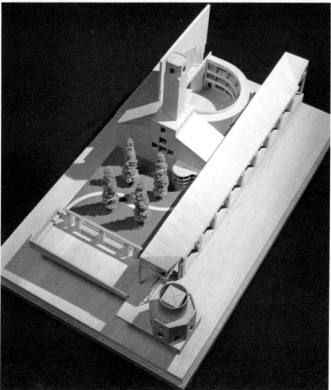

4

overlooking the foyer. An entrance from the footpath around Sheldon Court gives external access to the administration, studios and graduate offices occupying the top floors.

The green room which can be opened to the entrance foyer (for receptions and parties) is at the same level as the proscenium and flexible theatres.

Below the green room are faculty showers and locker rooms which can double as dressing rooms for visiting performers. Above are student dressing rooms, lockers and showers. A back stage stair connects these areas with the performance spaces.

Production support spaces are grouped on the south side of the building with access through soundproof

doors onto the proscenium and flexible theatre stages. A central area in the scene shop has 25' headroom for scenery construction and painting. Truck access at shop floor level allows vehicles to be driven on to the performance stages if required. A costume shop is located below the stage house.

The existing footpath on the old trolley route will

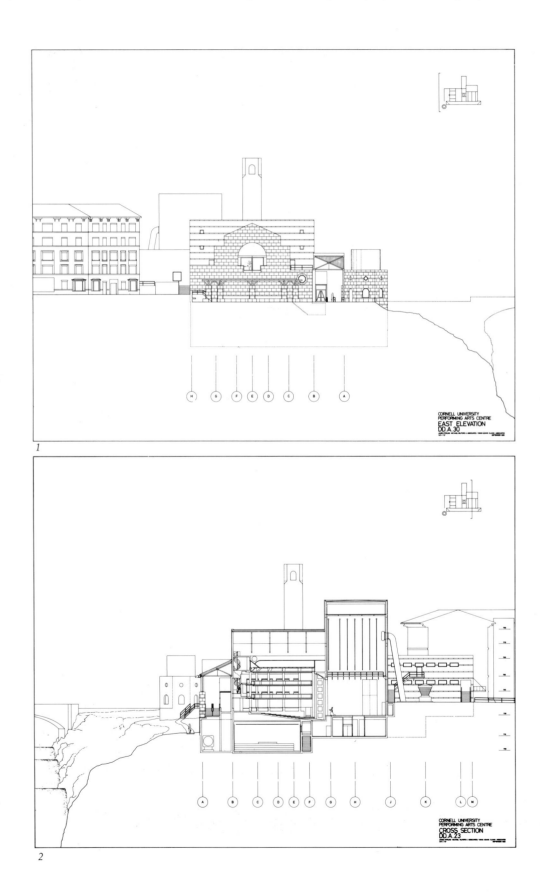

1

2

be diverted towards the gorge through a garden between the new building and Cascadilla Hall. Steps will connect the existing footpath (along the gorge) with the new plaza on College Avenue.

The project can be built independent of further development on the College/Dryden/Cascadilla block. Existing parking lots will be regraded and landscaped, and provision has been made for service access to the Performing Arts building behind Sheldon Court. Access from the parking lot is via a new footpath around Sheldon Court to the plaza on College Avenue. En route, activities in the scene shop can be viewed through windows in the building.

1. Elevation to College Avenue.
2. Section through proscenium theatre.
3. Elevation to gorge.
4. Proscenium theatre.

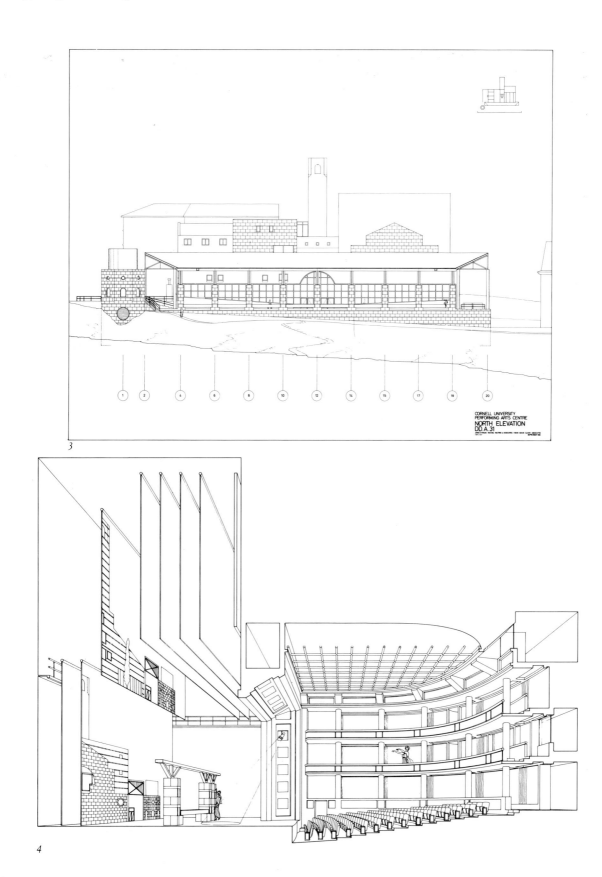

3

4

CORNELL UNIVERSITY
PERFORMING ARTS CENTRE
NORTH ELEVATION
DD.A.31

The building footprint (both phases) is within University boundaries and is back from the edge of the gorge. However, removal of undergrowth, deceased trees and utility poles would allow better views of the gorge, the campus and Lake Cayuga.

External materials have been chosen to relate to adjoining University buildings. The primary facades to College Avenue and the gorge are surfaced in limestone with brick string courses. Other facades are of brickwork with limestone string courses. The loggia has a slate roof and other sloping roofs are clad in metal.

1. Block model.
2. Pavilion, town and loggia.
3. Theatre and garden.
4. View from bridge.

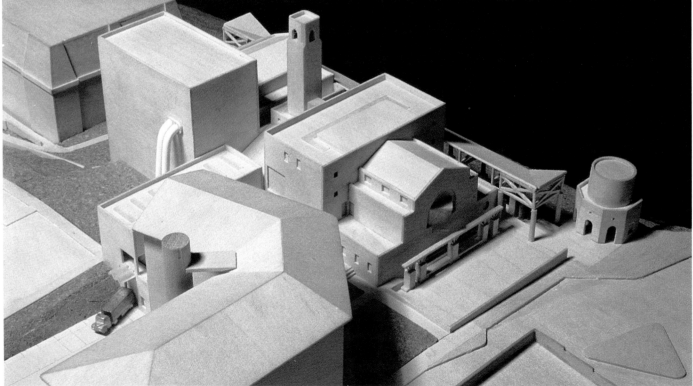

1

2

3

4

Performing Arts Centre, Cornell University, 1982

Performing Arts Centre, Cornell University, 1982

James Stirling

JS 1952

Born: Glasgow (1926) Family moved to Liverpool in 1927

Quarry Bank High School Liverpool, until 1941. Liverpool School of Art 1942

War Service: (D Day Landing)

Liverpool University, School of Architecture, 1945—50 Dipl. Arch (dist) (student exchange to New York 1949)

School of Town Planning and Regional Research, London 1950–52

Senior Assistant with Lyons, Israel and Ellis, 1953–56

Private Practice from 1956 (Partners: James Gowan until 1963, Michael Wilford from 1971.)

Visiting teacher at Architectural Association 1957, also Regent Street Polytechnic 1958–60, Cambridge University 1961

Visiting Critic at Yale University 1960 and 62.

RIBA external examiner for architectural education at The Bartlett (London University) from 1968 to 71. Also at Regent Street Polytechnic from 1965 to 75, and Architectural Association from 1979

Charles Davenport Professor—Yale University from 1967

Banister Fletcher Professor, London University, 1977

Professor, Düsseldorf Kunstakademie, from 1977

Architect in Residence, American Academy in Rome, 1982 *

Honorary Member, Akademie der Künste, Berlin 1969

Honorary Fellow, American Institute of Architects 1976

Brunner Award, The National Institute of Arts and Letters USA, 1976

Alvar Aalto Award 1978

Honorary Member, Florence Academy of Arts 1979

Honorary Doctorate, Royal College of Art, London University 1979

Fellow of the Royal Society of Arts, London 1979

Honorary Member of the Accademia Nazionale San Luca, Italy, 1979

Royal Institute of British Architects, Gold Medal 1980

Pritzker Prize, USA 1981.

Honorary Member, Bund Deutscher Architeckten, 1983

---

*Architectural Awards Presentation, Vicenza, 4 December 1982

Our architectural rambles on this trip have taught us a lot about the history of art and taste. We have learned that G. R. had B. T., that S. M. had B. O., and that A. P. occasionally had E. T. As part of our valedictory ceremony, we would like to present three awards to those members of the group whose architectonic presence has most greatly enhanced our understanding.

The awards take their name from a famous utterance of Frank Lloyd Wright, who was once quoted as saying that "Modern architecture socks." And so we are pleased to present three pairs of Modern Architecture Socks.

This morning in the Villa Rotonda we have seen the importance of decoration in the architectural context. The first award goes to the

architectural person whose design and elegance far surpasses that of the other two recipients. In recognition of her glamor and decorative taste, we present Mary Stirling with a pair of silver-glitter Modern Architectural Socks.

In recent years much ink, blood, and saliva has been shed over the crucial question, "Are P. S. really G. T.?" A survey of modern architects seems to indicate that they are, and we think that we must recognize today a fledgling who may soon drive Daddy Bird from his distinguished nest. We are pleased to present Bob Kahn with a pair of purple Modern Architectural Socks.

We come now to the final award, which goes to the most august personage of the tour. It is with the greatest flatulence and affliction that I raise the tormenting question that has troubled the slumbers of many a modern architect: "Aren't P. S. really O. H.?"

Perhaps no one will ever find a clear answer to this question, but we would like to make a gesture of post-modern elegance to J. S. by affirming publicly that "Y. S. are indeed G. T." I am therefore both mortified and ecstatic to present James Stirling with a pair of yellow Modern Architecture Socks.

We would like to thank all the other contestants who sent their postcard entries, and we are happy to announce that the first 400 runners-up will soon be receiving their Tootsie-Roll rustic columns in the mail, which we hope they will use in harmony with classical proportions and the most rigorous canons of G. T.

Thank you.
David Marsh

Michael Wilford

MW 1982

Born: Surbiton, Surrey (1938)

Kingston Technical School, until 1955

Northern Polytechnic School of Architecture, London 1955–62. Honours Dipl. (dist. in thesis)

Regent Street Polytechnic Planning School, London 1967

Senior Assistant with James Stirling and James Gowan 1960–63

Senior Assistant with James Stirling 1963–65

Associate with James Stirling 1965–71

Partner with James Stirling from 1971

Tutor at the Architectural Association, 1969–73

Visiting Critic at Yale University 1968 and 1975, Sheffield University 1974–79, Toronto University, 1974–83, and Rice University, Houston 1978–79

External Examiner, Royal College of Art, London University, 1978–79. Also of Northern Polytechnic from 1983, and Leeds Polytechnic from 1983

Member of RIBA Education and Professional Development Committee, 1979–81

Professor at Rice University, Houston, from 1980

Graham Willis Visiting Professor, Sheffield University from 1980

Note: country of origin is specified in the first reference
to a magazine or publication; in subsequent references
country of origin is not shown.

1954 Woolton House   *Architectural Design,* July 1956 (UK)

1955 Village Project   *Architects Journal,* September 1957 (UK)

1955 Ham Common Flats   *Architects Journal,* 17 April 1958
The Guardian, 26 July 1958 (UK)
New Statesman, 19 and 26 July 1958, R Banham (UK)
Architectural Review, October 1958 (UK)
Architectural Design, November 1958
Bouw, September 1959 (Holland)
Architecture d'Aujourd'Hui, December 1959 (France)
Domus, July 1960 (Italy)
Bauen & Wohnen, March 1962 (Germany)
Architektur & Wohnform, February 1967 (Germany)
The Buildings of England—N Pevsner (UK)

1956 Isle of Wight House   *Architectural Review,* April 1958
Architects Journal, 24 and 31 July, 28 August and 4 September 1958, J M Richards
Architectural Design, September 1958
House and Garden, November 1958 (UK)

1957 House conversion, Kensington   *Daily Telegraph,* 19 January 1960, A Hope (UK)
Architectural Review, March 1960
Architect and Building News, 20 July 1960 (UK)

1957 Expandable house   *House and Garden,* April 1957

1957 Preston infill housing   *Architects Journal,* June 1961
Architectural Design, July 1961
Architectural Design, December 1961
Casabella Continuitá, February 1962 (Italy)
New Statesman, 9 February 1962, R Banham
Architect and Building News, March 1962
Architectural Forum, March 1962 (USA)
Architecture d'Aujourd'Hui, November 1962
Architecture Canada, April 1968

1958 Churchill College, Cambridge   *Cambridge Review,* 31 October 1959, C Rowe (UK)

**1958 School Assembly Hall,
Camberwell**   *Architects Journal,* September 1962
Architectural Design, March 1963
Architect and Building News, 18 March 1964
Domus, June 1964
Arquitectura 67, July 1964 (Spain)
Bauwelt 43, October 1964 (Germany)
L'Architettura 116, June 1965, R Pedio (Italy)
Werk, September 1966 (Switzerland)
Architecture Canada, April 1968

1959 Selwyn College, Cambridge   *Architectural Review,* January 1961
Bauwelt, February 1963

**1959 Leicester University
Engineering Building**

Architectural Design, October 1962
Sunday Times Colour Supplement, 27 September 1963, R Maxwell (UK)
Architectural Association Journal, December 1963 (UK)
Architects Journal, 15 January 1964
Architectural Design, February 1964, K Frampton
New Statesman, 14 February 1964, R Banham
Architectural Review, April 1964, J Jacobus
Evening Standard, 10 June 1964, J Hillman (UK)
Domus, June 1964, J Rykwert
Arquitectura 67, July 1964
Architectural Forum, August 1964
Glass, August 1964 (UK)
Fortune Magazine, October 1964 (USA)
Architektur Heute, October 1964 (Germany)
Deutsche Bauzeitung 10, 1964 (Germany)
Bauwelt 43, October 1964
British Buildings 1960–64, D Stephens, K Frampton and M Carapetian, 1965,
    Adam & Charles Black Ltd.
Kokusai Kentiku, January 1965 (Japan)
Architecture d'Aujourd'Hui, July 1965
The Buildings of England—Leicestershire, N Pevsner
Bouw, April 1965
Arkitekten 18, 1966, G B Bryant (Finland)
The Brick Bulletin, January 1966 (UK)
Architecture Canada, April 1968
Baumeister, December 1968, P Peters (Germany)
Global Architecture, ADA Edita, 1971 (Japan)
Forum, April 1972, I Brown (USA)
Oppositions 4, 1974, P Eisenman (USA)
De la Ciudad 1, February 1975 (Spain)

1960 Old Peoples Home, Greenwich

New Statesman, 23 April 1965, R Banham
Architectural Review, May 1965
L'Architettura, June 1965, R Pedio
Deutsche Bauzeitung, August 1966
Arkitekten 18, 1966, G B Bryant
Werk, March 1967, R Pedio

1960 Childrens Home, Frogmore

Architectural Design, September 1965
L'Architettura, January 1966
Deutsche Bauzeitung, August 1966
Werk, March 1967
Arkitekten 18, 1966, G B Bryant

**1964 Cambridge University
History Faculty Building**

Architectural Design, May 1964
Architectural Review, June 1964
Bauwelt, October 1964
Arquitectura 7, 1964
Kokusai Kentiku, January 1965
Architectural Review, January 1965
Architectural Design, January 1965
Architecture D'Aujourd'Hui, July 1965
Arkitekten 18, 1966, G B Bryant
Bauen & Wohnen, December 1967

Architecture Canada, April 1968
New Society 313, September 1968, R Banham
Architectural Design, October 1968, A Boyarski
Architectural Forum, November 1968, K Frampton
Architectural Review, November 1968, R Banham
Daily Telegraph Magazine, November 1968, M Duckett
Deutsche Bauzeitung, February 1969
Domus 18, February 1969, J Rykwert
New Statesman, 18 April 1969, N Silver
Glass Age, May 1969 (UK)
Zodiac 18, 1969 (Italy)
Queen Magazine, June 1969, J Vaughan (UK)
The Buildings of England—Cambridgeshire, N Pevsner
Global Architecture, ADA Edita, 1971
De la Ciudad 1, February 1975
Cambridge Review, 30 January 1976 and *Building Design,* 19 March 1976, G Stamp
    (UK), also letters in *Building Design* (i.e. 9 April 1976, C Jencks)
Signs, Symbols and Architecture, 1980, C Jencks (UK)

1964 Residential expansion,
     St Andrews University

Architectural Design, July 1966
Architektur & Wohnform, October 1966
Bauwelt, October 1966
Architectural Design, December 1966, J Donat
L'Architettura 135, 1967, C Assunti
Bauen & Wohnen, December 1967
Architecture Canada, April 1968
Zodiac 19, 1969
Observer Colour Supplement, UK, 31 May 1969, J Hillman
Architectural Design, September 1970, K Frampton
Architectural Forum, September 1970, C Jencks
Domus, November 1970, J Rykwert
Architecture Association Quarterly, Vol. 4, Summer 1972
Editions Techniques, March 1974 (France)
Glasforum 3, Germany May/June 1974

1965 Dorman Long headquarters

Architectural Design, July 1966
Bauwelt, August 1966
Arkitekten 18, 1966
Architektur & Wohnform, January 1967
L'Architettura 135, 1967, C Assunti
Architecture Canada, April 1968

1966 Queens College, Oxford

Sunday Times, 21 July 1968, N Taylor
Architectural Design, October 1968
The Listener, 30 September 1971, S Gardiner (UK)
Space Design 11, November 1971 (Japan)
Building Design, 23 June 1972, S Campbell
Architecture and Urbanism, November 1972 (Japan)
Domus, November 1972, J Rykwert
Architectural Review, November 1972, M Girouard
Architecture Plus, February 1973, R Maxwell (USA)
Isis, 1 June 1973, R Jeffrey (UK)
Bauen & Wohnen, March 1974
De la Ciudad 1, February 1975

Casabella 399, March 1975
Daidalos, 15 September 1982, A Reidmeister (Germany)

1967 Runcorn New Town,
low cost housing

Bauen & Wohnen, December 1967
Domus, November 1972, J Rykwert
Architecture and Urbanism, May 1973
Casabella 399, March 1975
Lotus 10, Autumn 1975 (Italy)
Progressive Architecture 3, 1976 (USA)
Architectural Record, February/March 1976 (USA)
Domus, June 1976
Architecture and Urbanism, July 1976
Architecture d'Aujourd'Hui, October 1976
Oppositions 7, W Seligman
Architectural Review, November 1976
Building Design, 18 August 1981
International Architect No 4, 1981, R Perez de Arce (UK)
Lotus 36, 1982, R Perez de Arce

1968 Redevelopment study
New York

Architectural Design, December 1969
Lotus 6, 1969

1969 Lima, Peru, Housing

Architectural Design, April 1970

1969 Olivetti Training School
Haslemere

Architectural Association Quarterly, September 1970, C Jencks
Domus, November 1972, J Rykwert
Building Design, 22 June 1973
Financial Times, 6 July 1973, H A N Brockman (UK)
Progressive Architecture, August 1973
Architecture Plus, September 1973
Domus, January 1974, J Rykwert
Architectural Review, April 1974, R Banham
Architecture Plus, March/April 1974, C Jencks
Architectural Plastics, May 1974 (UK)
Archithese 11, Summer 1974, C Jencks (Switzerland)
Building Specification, November 1974 (UK)
Architecture and Urbanism, February 1975
Casabella 399, March 1975
The Architects Journal, 22/29 December 1982, R Gradidge

1969 Siemens A.G., Munich

Deutsche Bauzeitung, May 1970, H Hollein
Architectural Design, July 1970
Space Design 10, 10 October 1970
De la Ciudad 1, February 1975

1970 Derby Town Centre

Space Design 11, November 1971
Domus, November 1972, J Rykwert
Architectural Review, November 1972
Milan Triennale XV Catalogue, 1973
De la Ciudad 1, February 1975

1971 Olivetti Headquarters,
Milton Keynes

Architectural Review, April 1974
Architecture and Urbanism, February 1975
Casabella 399, March 1975
Arquitectura, 8 July 1975

**1971 Arts Centre
St Andrews University**

Architecture and Urbanism, February 1975
Casabella 399, March 1975
Architects Journal, 16 July 1975

**1975 Museum for Northrhine
Westphalia, Düsseldorf**

RIBA Journal, March 1976, K Frampton (UK)
Architectural Association Events, 8–12 March 1976 (UK)
Catalog '9 Architects' Exhibition, Dortmunder Architektenausstellung 1976
Architecture and Urbanism, July 1976
Catalog, Venice Biennale, 1976
Architectural Review, November 1976
Architectural Design 9/10, 1977

**1975 Wallraf-Richartz Museum,
Cologne**

Architectural Association Events, 8–12 March 1976
Catalog '9 Architects' Exhibition, Dortmunder Architektenausstellung 1976
Architecture and Urbanism, July 1976
Catalog, Venice Biennale, 1976
Domus, August 1976
Architectural Review, November 1976
Architectural Design, November 1976, G Shane
Lotus 15, 1977
1 Seminario Internacional de Arquitectura, Summer 1977 (Spain)
Architectural Design 9/10, 1977
Skyline, April 1978, T Schumacher (USA)

1976 Meineke Strasse, Berlin

Berliner Morgenpost, 18 January 1977 (Germany)
Architectural Design 9/10, 1977
Lotus 19, 1978
Techniques + Architecture 323, 1979 (France)

1976 Regional Centre, Florence

Casabella, March 1978
Space Design 05, 1978
Domus, April 1978
Parametro 63, 1978 (Italy)
Progetti per l'area Direzionale di Firenze, 1978

**1977 Revisions to the Nolli Plan,
Rome**

Modo, October, 1978 (Italy)
Catalog, Roma Interrotta (Officina Edizioni) 1978
Architectural Design 3/4, 1979, M Graves

1977 Dresdner Bank, Marburg

Architectural Design, 9/10, 1977
Lotus No 18, 1978

**1977 Staatsgalerie New Building
and Workshop Theatre,
Stuttgart**

Architectural Design 9/10, 1977
Wettbewerbe Aktuell, December 1977 (Germany)
(Numerous articles appearing in Bauwelt, Stuttgart Allgemeine, Frankfurt
    Allgemeine)
Bauen & Wohnen, February 1978
Architectural Design 8/9, 1979
Deutsche Bauzeitung, August 1980
RIBA Journal, December 1980, S Games
Architectural Design 3/4, 1981
Building Design, 2 April 1982
Architectural Review, December 1982, P Cook
Architects Journal, 22/29 December 1982, J Waldren

Architectural Review, March 1983, P Cook
Building Design, 28 January 1983, R Maxwell Jr.

1978 Bayer A.G. PF Zentrum, Monheim

Architects Journal, 9, 16 and 30th January 1980
Casabella, February 1980, R Airoldi
Architects Journal, 6 February 1980
Architectural Design 5/6, 1980
Architectural Design 7/8, 1980

1978 11 Townhouses, New York

New York Times, 16 June 1980, P Goldberger (USA)
International Architect 5, 1981, D Chipperfield

1979 Extension of the School of Architecture, Rice University, Houston

Rice Newsletter Vol 1, Spring 1980
Monograph 29 by S Fox, D Turner 1980 (USA)
Architectural Design 5/6 1980
Architectural Design 7/8 1980
Progressive Architecture, October 1980, P Papademetriou
Houston Chronicle, 10 May 1981, A Holmes (USA)
The Houston Post, 27 September 1981, M Crossley (USA)
New York Times, 3 December 1981, P Goldberger
Progressive Architecture, December 1981, D Gebhard
Arts & Architecture, Winter 1981, M Sorkin (USA)
Architectural Review, February 1982, P Papademetriou
Texas Architects, February 1982, L P Fuller (USA)
Casabella 474/475, 1982
Baumeister, April 1982
Global Architecture 5, 1982, P Papademetriou

1979 Wissenschaftszentrum, Berlin

Architects Journal, 27 February 1980
Building Design, 29 February 1980
Architects Journal, 19 March 1980
Bauwelt, April 1980, G Neumann
Architectural Review, April 1980
International Architect 3, 1980
Deutsche Bauzeitung, May 1980
Architectural Design 5/6, 1980
Architectural Design 7/8, 1980
Newsweek, 29 June 1981 (USA)
Casabella, July/August 1981
Architektur & Wohnen, 3 September 1981

1979 Fogg Museum New building, Harvard University

Progressive Architecture 6, 1979
Numerous articles in *Harvard Crimson* (USA) from 15 April 1981–
Architectural Review, May 1981, P Buchanan
Boston Globe, 31 May 1981, R Campbell (USA)
New York Times, 31 May 1981, A L Huxtable
Architecture and Urbanism, July 1981
New Boston Review, October 1981, G Wolf (USA)
New York Times, 27 December 1981, A L Huxtable
Boston Globe, 20 January 1982
New York Times, 21 January 1982, F Butterfield
Boston Globe, 5 February 1982, R Taylor
New York Times, 5 February 1982, M W Miller
New York Times, 9 February 1982

New York Times, 12 February 1982, G Glueck
Boston Globe, 16 February 1982, R Lenzner
New York Times, 20 February 1982, G Glueck
Boston Globe, 21 February 1982, R Levey
New York Times, 22 February 1982
Time Magazine, 29 March 1982, R Hughes (USA)
Art in America, April 1982, S McFadden (USA)
Skyline March/April, 1982, E Constantine
Casabella, May 1982, M Scolari
Lotus 35, 1982
Express, Winter 1982, K M Hays (USA)
Architectural Review, March 1983, J Coolidge

1980 Clore Gallery (Turner Museum)
Tate Gallery, London

Evening Standard, 22 January 1980
The Times, 22 January 1980, K Gosling (UK)
The Times, 7 May 1980, K Gosling
Building Design, 9 May 1980, D Searle
The Times, 25 June 1981
The Guardian, 10 July 1981, S Games
Financial Times, 13 July 1981, C Amery
Architects Journal, 15 July 1981, J Summerson
Building Design, 17 July 1981, D Searle
Sunday Times Magazine, 10 January 1982
Architectural Design, January/February 1982, C Jencks
Sunday Telegraph Magazine, March 1982, P Purser
Lotus 15, 1982
The Times, 19 April 1983, D Sudjic

Exhibitions

"James Stirling—Three Buildings," Museum of Modern Art, New York, 1969.

BC/Arts Council Film: "James Stirling's Architecture," 1973.

"James Stirling—drawings," RIBA Drawings Collection Gallery, 1974 (catalog—2nd edition).

"19 Projects—Travelling Exhibition," (initiated by Naples University and British Council 1975). Exhibited Naples, Rome, Paris, Brussels, Zurich, Lausanne, Trieste, Tehran, Salonika, Athens, Helsinki (catalog).

Venice Biennale, 1976 (catalog).

"9 Architects," Dortmund University, 1976 (catalog).

"Rally Exhibition," Art Net, London, 1976

"James Stirling—Four Projects," Walker Arts Centre, Minneapolis, 1977.

"Architecture 1," Leo Castelli Gallery, New York, 1977.

"Roma Interrotta," Rome, 1978 (catalog).

"Museum Projects," Dortmund University, 1979 (catalog).

"Manhattan Townhouses," The Lobby Gallery, New York, 1980.

"Three German Projects," RIBA, London, 1980.

"New Extension Drawings," Fogg Museum, Cambridge, USA, 1981.

"Ten New Buildings," ICA Gallery, London, 1983 (catalog).

"The Architects Drawings" (Turner Museum) Tate Gallery, London, 1983.

"From Garches to Jaoul." *Architectural Review*, September 1955.

"Ronchamp and the crisis of rationalism." *Architectural Review*, March 1956.

"This is tomorrow." *Exhibition Catalogue*, 1956.

"Regionalism and modern architecture." *Architects Year Book No. 8*, 1957.

"A personal view of the present situation." *Architectural Design*, June 1958.

"Packaged deal and prefabrication." *Design Magazine*, March 1959.

"Afterthoughts on Ham Common." *Architect & Building*, May 1959.

"The functional tradition and expression." *Perspecta No 6*, 1959.

"Architects approach to architecture." *RIBA Journal*, May 1965, also *Zodiac No 16*. 1967.

"Conversations with students." *Perspecta No 12*, 1967.

"Anti-Structure." *Zodiac No 18*, 1969.

"JS in Tokyo." (Interview with A Isozaki) *Architecture and Urbanism*, August 1971.

"Stirling Connexions." *Architecture and Urbanism*, February 1975, also *Casabella*, March 1975 and *Architectural Review*, May 1975.

"Asian Games." *Architectural Design*, January 1975.

"Entretien Avec James Stirling." *Architecture Mouvement Continuité*, December 1975.

"Articles by James Stirling." *School of Architecture, Zurich University*, 1976.

"Letter from London." *Oppositions 5*, Rizzoli, 1976.

"RIBA Gold Medal acceptance." *Architectural Design 7/8*, 1980, *Architectural Design Profile*, Academy Editions/St Martins Press, 1982.

"Pritzker Prize acceptance." *Architectural Design Profile*, Academy Editions/St Martins Press, 1982.

"Richtfest, Topping-Out Ceremony, Stuttgart" *Architectural Design Profile*, *Academy Editions/St Martins Press*, 1982.

"JS Lecture 81." *Collected essays edited by D Lasdun*. Heinemann, 1984.

James Stirling—Buildings and Projects 1950–1974, introduction J Jacobus.

Verlag Gerd Hatje, Germany, 1975.

Thames and Hudson, UK, 1975.

Oxford University Press, USA, 1975.

Comunitá, Italy 1975.

Editorial Gustavo Gili, Spain 1975.

A.D.A. Edita, Japan, 1975.

Reviews:

M Girouard, *Times Literary Supplement,* 29 August 1975.

E Jones, *Built Environment Quarterly,* September 1975.

M Filler, *Architectural Record,* October 1975.

R MacCormac, *Architects Journal,* 26 November 1975.

N Ray, *Architectural Review,* December 1975.

J McKean, *The Architect,* February 1976.

Santomasso, *Progressive Architecture,* October 1977. *Oppositions 7.*

James Stirling—drawings RIBA 1974, (2nd edition) introduction R Banham.

Reviews:

N Jones, "An extra dimension." *RIBA Journal,* April 1974.

"Isometric Stirling." *Design Magazine,* May 1974.

Attenbury, "Heinz Gallery Review." *The Connoisseur,* July 1974.

James Stirling. *Architectural Design Profile 1982.* Academy Editions/St. Martins Press. Introduction R. Maxwell.

General Articles

A Korn, "The work of Stirling and Gowan." *Architect and Building News,* January 1959.

Hara and Futagawa. "Two works by James Stirling, A Portrait." Kokusai Kentiku, January 1965.

"More than Shelter." *House and Garden,* March 1965.

R Banham. "New Brutalism." Architectural Press, 1966.

N Pevsner. "The anti pioneers." *The Listener,* 29 December 1966 and 5 January 1967.

L Biscogli. "L'Opera di James Stirling (1950–1967)." *Casabella 315,* June 1967.

T Stevens. "Observations on New British Architecture." *Bauen & Wohnen,* December 1967.

C Jencks. "Pop non Pop." *Architectural Association Journal,* Winter 1968.

"James Stirling buildings and prospects (1950–1967)." *Kentiku Architecture,* January 1968.

C Dardi. "Lettura di James Stirling." *Lotus 6,* 1969.

C Jencks. "Architecture 2000." Studio Vista, 1971.

P Drew. "The third generation." *Verlag Gerd Hatje,* 1972.

R Maxwell. "New British Architecture." *Verlag Gerd Hatje,* 1972.

B Zevi. "Un Manierista Vinto Dai Rimorsi." *L'Espresso,* 1972.

"Lucky Jim." *Building Design,* 25 May 1973.

"James Stirling—5 Projects." *Genghia Architecture.* Taiwan, June 1973.

C Jencks. *"Modern movements in architecture."* Penguin, London, 1973.

M Girouard. "A modern neoclassicist." *Country Life,* May 1974.

C Jencks. "A detonation in glass and brick." *Times Literary Supplement,* 21 June 1974.

M Tafuri. "L'architecture dans le boudoir." *Oppositions 3,* 1974.

"Architects of the Glass Age: 5, James Stirling." *Glass Age.* August 1974.

K Frampton. "Transformations in Style." *Architecture and Urbanism,* February 1975.

"Racionalismo & Tecnologia."*De la Ciudad 1,* February 1975.

G Koenig. "Jim the Great." *Casabella 399,* March 1975.

C Jencks. "The Language of Architecture." *Sunday Times Magazine,* 10 August 1975.

"Anglo Scottish Architect with Anglo-International Reputation." *House and Garden,* October 1975.

D Stewart. "Demythification and eclecticism." *Architecture and Urbanism,* 1975.

A Izzo and C Gubitosi. "James Stirling Travelling Exhibition." (catalogue) Officina Edizioni, Rome 1976.

"Inside James Stirling." *Design Quarterly 100.* USA, April 1976.

J McKean. "Stirling Quality." *Building Design,* 7 and 14 September 1979.

D Sudjic. "Journey into Ambiguous space." *Guardian,* 17 October 1979.

"RIBA Gold Medal 1980."
Sunday Observer, 9 March 1980
RIBA Journal, March 1980 and January 1981
C Amery. *Financial Times,* 30 June 1980.
Architects Journal, 2 July 1980
RIBA Journal, September 1980

"James Stirling." *Gold Medal Issue. Architectural Design 7/8,* 1980.

C Jencks. "Post Modern Classicism." *Architectural Design 5/6,* 1980.

"The Art of Building—Half a Century annulled." *Der Spiegel,* 7 July 1980.

C Jencks. "Britain's Bad Boy Architect." *Portfolio,* January/February 1981.

"Pritzker Prize 1981."
Express (USA) 3, April 1981
Harvard Post, 16 April 1981
Boston Globe, 17 April 1981
International Herald Tribune, 17 April 1981
Washington Post, May 1981
AIA Journal, May 1981

M Filler. "Architect for a Pluralist Age." *Art in America,* April 1981.

D Davis. "Master of Inconsistency." *Newsweek,* 29 June 1981.

"Interview by L S Zelenko." *American Artist,* July 1981.

"Learning from the past." *Architektur & Wohnen,* 3 September 1981.

A Vidler. "Architecture of James Stirling." *Skyline,* November 1981.

P Jodidio. "The Dynamic Dissonance of James Stirling." *Connaissance des arts 357,* November 1981.

N Polak. "Covjek i Prostor," January 1982.

P Purser. "Stirling Style." *Sunday Telegraph Magazine,* 28 March 1982.

"Sunday Times Magazine," 30 May 1982.

"Stirling—Ever Scornful of the Vogue." *Glass Age,* June 1982.

J Summerson. "Vitruvius Ludens." *Architectural Review,* March 1983.

J Davidson. "Monumental Man of European Architecture." *Glasgow Herald,* 28 March 1983

K Broner. " Arkkitehtuurin liiketila" *Finnish Architectural Review,* 4, 1983

Photo Credits